Creating the Nazi Marketplace

When the Nazis came to power in 1933, they promised to build a vibrant consumer society. But they faced a dilemma. They recognized that consolidating support for the regime required providing Germans with the products they desired. At the same time, the Nazis worried about the degrading cultural effects of mass consumption and its association with "Jewish" interests. This book examines how both the state and private companies sought to overcome this predicament. Drawing on a wide range of sources – advertisements, exhibition programs, films, consumer research, and marketing publications – the book traces the ways National Socialists attempted to create their own world of buying and selling. At the same time, it shows how corporate leaders and everyday Germans navigated what S. Jonathan Wiesen calls "the Nazi marketplace." A groundbreaking work that combines cultural, intellectual, and business history, *Creating the Nazi Marketplace* offers an innovative interpretation of commerce and ideology in the Third Reich.

S. Jonathan Wiesen is Associate Professor of History at Southern Illinois University Carbondale. He is the author of *West German Industry and the Challenge of the Nazi Past, 1945–1955* (2001) – cowinner of the 2002 book prize from the Hagley Museum and Library and the Business History Conference – and the coeditor of *Selling Modernity: Advertising in Twentieth Century Germany* (2007). His work has appeared in a number of scholarly journals, including *Central European History*, *Holocaust and Genocide Studies*, and the *Journal of Contemporary History*.

Creating the Nazi Marketplace

Commerce and Consumption
in the Third Reich

S. JONATHAN WIESEN

Southern Illinois University

CAMBRIDGE UNIVERSITY PRESS
Cambridge, New York, Melbourne, Madrid, Cape Town, Singapore,
São Paulo, Delhi, Dubai, Tokyo, Mexico City

Cambridge University Press
32 Avenue of the Americas, New York, NY 10013-2473, USA

www.cambridge.org
Information on this title: www.cambridge.org/9780521746366

First published 2011

Printed in the United States of America

A catalog record for this publication is available from the British Library.

Library of Congress Cataloging in Publication data
Wiesen, S. Jonathan.
Creating the Nazi marketplace : commerce and consumption in the
Third Reich / S. Jonathan Wiesen.
p.   cm.
Includes bibliographical references.
ISBN 978-0-521-76253-3 – ISBN 978-0-521-74636-6 (pbk.)
1. Consumption (Economics) – Germany – History – 20th century.   2. Consumer
behavior – Germany – History – 20th century.   3. Marketing – Germany –
History – 20th century.   4. Germany – Economic conditions – 1918–1945.
5. National socialism.   I. Title
HC290.5.C6W53   2010
339.4'7094309043–dc22   2010035664

ISBN 978-0-521-76253-3 Hardback
ISBN 978-0-521-74636-6 Paperback

For Natasha

Contents

Figures

Acknowledgments

In the course of writing this book, I have incurred numerous debts to individuals and organizations in the United States and Germany. Without their moral and financial support, this book would not have been possible. First, I would like to thank the Alexander von Humboldt Foundation and the Gerda Henkel Foundation, whose generous research fellowships allowed me two productive and enjoyable years in Berlin. Thanks as well to the German Academic Exchange, which funded a summer of research in the Rhineland, and to Southern Illinois University Carbondale (SIUC), whose research fellowships, sabbatical support, and flexible leave policies allowed me to relocate to Germany several times with my family. Finally, I benefited from a J. Walter Thompson Research Fellowship, which enabled me to work with the fine collections at the John W. Hartman Center for Sales, Advertising & Marketing History at Duke University.

While researching this book, I had the good fortune of meeting many kind archivists, who supported my work with documents, films, photographs, and expert advice. I am particularly grateful to Rüdiger Borstel and his colleagues at the Bayer archive, Wolfgang Bügel at the Henkel archive, Bärbel Kern at the Kraft Foods Deutschland archive, and the staff of the Krupp archive. I also thank the Böttcherstrasse archive, the German Federal Archives and the Film Archive in Berlin, the Prussian Secret State Archives, the Nuremberg–Erlangen University library, and the state archives of Berlin and North Rhine–Westphalia. I am most indebted to the Society for Consumer Research, which made its rich collection of consumer reports available to me, and to Rotary Germany, which granted access to its Nazi-era papers. These two collections have offered treasured insights into German attitudes during the Nazi years. I offer my thanks as well to SIUC's Morris Library, which handled hundreds of interlibrary loan requests, some of them for massive German periodicals.

During my stays in Germany, I benefited greatly from the support and collegiality of several academic institutions. The Berlin School for the Comparative History of Europe at the Free University of Berlin provided a comfortable workplace for me, and its directors, Arnd Bauerkämper and Jürgen Kocka, offered much intellectual encouragement. I also savored the opportunity to present my work at the Institute of Economic and Social History at the University of Göttingen, the Social Science Research Center in Berlin, and the Center for Research on Contemporary History at the University of Potsdam. All three institutions provided me with stimulating forums for my work.

Over the past decade many colleagues have shared their time, friendship, and expertise in German history with me, and I am thankful to be surrounded by such a generous group of people. Ralf Ahrens, Shelley Baranowski, Hartmut Berghoff, Alon Confino, Victoria de Grazia, Christopher Ely, Gerald Feldman, Peter Fritzsche, Peter Hayes, Claudia Koonz, Corey Ross, Pamela Swett, and Jonathan Zatlin all nourished my thinking and encouraged me from this project's inception. I am particularly grateful to Frank Biess and Jan Palmowski, who read through the manuscript on short notice and offered incisive criticism and feedback. I also thank the anonymous readers for Cambridge University Press, whose exacting analysis of my work was most impressive, and my editors, Frank Smith and Eric Crahan, for their support and availability. I am likewise grateful to my colleagues in the History Department at SIUC, who gave me the opportunity to workshop my ideas while they were still gestating, and to Ruth Pincoe for preparing the index. Last but not least, I thank my sons, Daniel and Julian, for their joyful smiles, and my wife, Natasha, who edited my writing countless times and kept me focused on the big questions. I could not have finished this book without her brilliant mind and loving support.

Glossary and Abbreviations

Advertising Council	Werberat der deutschen Wirtschaft (Advertising Council of the German Economy)
BA	Böttcherstrasse archive, Bremen
BAB	Bundesarchiv, Berlin (federal archives of Germany)
BAL	Bayer archive, Leverkusen
DAF	Deutsche Arbeitsfront (German Labor Front)
DDV	*Die Deutsche Volkswirtschaft*
DF	Deutsches Frauenwerk (German Women's Bureau)
Erlangen	University archive, Friedrich-Alexander-Universität Erlangen-Nürnberg
GfK	Gesellschaft für Konsumforschung (Society for Consumer Research)
GfKA	Gesellschaft für Konsumforschung archive, Nuremberg
GStAPK	Geheimes Staatsarchiv Preußischer Kulturbesitz (Prussian secret state archives), Berlin
HA	Henkel archive, Düsseldorf
IfW	Institut für Wirtschaftsbeobachtung der Deutschen Fertigware (Institute for Economic Surveillance of German Products)
KaDeWe	Kaufhaus des Westens

Kampfbund	Kampfbund für den gewerblichen Mittelstand (Nazi Combat League for the Commercial Middle Class)
KdF	Kraft durch Freude (Strength Through Joy)
KFA	Company archive, Kraft Foods Deutschland GmbH, Bremen
Leistung	"Achievement" or "performance"
Leistungsgemeinschaft	"Achievement community"
MR	Motivational research
NS-Hago	Nationalsozialistische Handels- und Gewerbetreibende Organisation (National Socialist Trade and Commerce Organization)
RC	Rotary Club
RI	Rotary International
RMVP	Reichsministerium für Volksaufklärung und Propaganda (Nazi Propaganda Ministry)
RVA	Reichsausschuss für Volkswirtschaftliche Aufklärung Gmbh (National Committee for Economic Enlightenment)
SA	Sturmabteilung – Nazi Storm Troopers
SOEG	Südosteuropa-Gesellschaft (Southeastern Europe Society)
Vertrauen	"Trust"
Volksgemeinschaft	Alternatively "national community," "people's community," or "racial community"
WB	*Westdeutscher Beobachter*
Wirtschaftsgruppen	Reich Economic Groups

Introduction

In the United States and most other industrial countries, we take our roles as consumers very seriously. We speak regularly of "consumer choice," "consumer protection," "consumer rights," and "consumer advocacy." The consumer price index is a key measure of economic health, and the provision of goods and services is a multibillion-dollar industry and, arguably, the foundation of any market economy. We recognize that support for political systems can wax and wane on the basis of consumer satisfaction and that even the health of the planet depends on the monitoring of our consumption habits. In short, "consumption" and "consumer" are important keywords in the modern lexicon.[1]

If the economic, social, and political importance of consumption is obvious to most people today, it was not so during much of the twentieth century, when elites throughout the West were trying to make sense of the democratization of the economy and the rise of mass society. At the center of this society was a new figure: the modern consumer. How important was he or she to the economic well-being and political stability

[1] For critical introductions to the terms "consumption," "consumerism," and "consumer society," see Frank Trentmann, "Beyond Consumerism: New Historical Perspectives on Consumption," *Journal of Contemporary History* 39, no. 3 (July 2004): 373–401; and Trentmann, "Knowing Consumers – Histories, Identities, Practices: An Introduction," in *The Making of the Consumer: Knowledge, Power and Identity in the Modern World*, ed. Frank Trentmann (Oxford: Berg, 2006): 1–27. For introductions to consumption in Europe, see Wolfgang König, *Geschichte der Konsumgesellschaft* (Stuttgart: Steiner, 2000); Hannes Siegrist, Hartmut Kaelble, and Jürgen Kocka, eds., *Europäische Konsumgeschichte: Zur Gesellschafts- und Kulturgeschichte des Konsums (18. bis 20. Jahrhundert)* (Frankfurt am Main: Campus, 1997); Martin Daunton and Matthew Hilton, eds., *The Politics of Consumption: Material Culture and Citizenship in Europe and America* (Oxford: Berg, 2001).

of the nation-state and the global economy? Did everyone need to have access to the same goods and services for economies and political systems to function effectively? These questions were common in Europe and the United States during the twentieth century, but they took on a particular resonance in Germany, which witnessed the end of an empire, two democratic republics, and two dictatorships in the course of seventy years. The political upheavals of modern Germany challenged politicians and economists to provide both necessities and luxuries to their citizens during times of rapid transformation, while also binding them to their visions of a correct economic and political order.[2] The twelve years of National Socialism stand out in this regard, wedged between the Great Depression and the democratic and socialist settings of West and East Germany. For the Nazis, the rejection of liberalism and Marxist socialism, combined with a racist, imperialist mission, demanded a rethinking of the basic relationship between people and the economy. The consumer played a decisive role in the Nazi economic vision. From 1933 to 1945 politicians, company leaders, and marketers devoted intense energy to learning how consumers gained material gratification and to determining the political and social implications of consumption. This book explores these elite investigations into consumers and their world of goods. What role did "getting and spending" play in National Socialist ideology and in the work of business and economic elites?[3]

In a period defined by persecution, war, and genocide, a focus on the consumer economy might at first glance seem trivial. This book argues, however, that to understand the dynamics of Nazi Germany – its racial ideology and its visions of a thriving economic order – we must place consumption and commerce squarely in our analysis. Examining what companies manufactured, what consumers bought, and what people said about their purchasing habits sheds light on the economic priorities of the Nazi state, the relationship of the economy to political violence, and the everyday lives of Germans under a dictatorship.

---

[2] On consumption in Germany, see Hartmut Berghoff, ed., *Konsumpolitik: Die Regulierung des privaten Verbrauchs im 20. Jahrhundert* (Göttingen: Vandenhoeck & Ruprecht, 1999); Heinz-Gerhard Haupt and Claudius Torps, eds., *Die Konsumgesellschaft in Deutschland, 1890–1990: Ein Handbuch* (Frankfurt am Main: Campus, 2009); and Alon Confino and Rudy Koshar, "Régimes of Consumer Culture: New Narratives in Twentieth-Century German History," *German History* 19, no. 2 (May 2001), 135–61.

[3] Susan Strasser, Charles McGovern, and Matthias Judt, eds., *Getting and Spending: European and American Consumer Societies in the Twentieth Century* (Washington, DC: German Historical Institute/Cambridge University Press, 1998).

This is not the first study to consider consumption, commercial culture, and fascism together. Since the 1980s scholars have explored modern states' use of mass media, leisure, and shopping opportunities to both appease and regulate their populations.[4] Historians of Nazi Germany have looked at the regime's creation of travel programs for working and middle-class Germans, as well as its promotion of consumer products that would allow the public a measure of comfort and an appreciation of its racial mission.[5] We are also gaining a clearer picture of how the Nazi years were shrouded in a surface normality. If one was not a racial, political, or religious enemy, one could go about one's daily business more or less unmolested by the state. Germans, argued one historian, lived with a "split consciousness," experiencing both the allures of American-style consumerism in a "state-free sphere" and the radical prescriptions of Nazi racial ideology.[6] Rather than providing a site of political resistance, this world of consumption helped bolster Hitler's regime and facilitate its crimes.[7]

This book builds on these insights, but it differs from recent studies about consumption in the Third Reich in two ways. First, it looks at non-state and non-party actors. While it takes as its starting point Nazi economic policies, its central concern is how business elites and market professionals approached buying and selling under a dictatorship. Although historians have devoted attention to the consumer, there has been little concentrated focus on the set of actors who had perhaps the greatest stake in commerce, namely company owners, marketers, and salespeople. More specifically, while we do have insight into the purveyors of mass

[4] See, e.g., Victoria de Grazia, *The Culture of Consent: Mass Organization of Leisure in Fascist Italy* (Cambridge: Cambridge University Press, 1981); and Corey Ross, *Media and the Making of Modern Germany: Mass Communications, Society, and Politics in Germany from the Empire to the Third Reich* (Oxford: Oxford University Press, 2008).

[5] See Shelley Baranowski, *Strength through Joy: Consumerism and Mass Tourism in the Third Reich* (Cambridge: Cambridge University Press, 2004); Kristin Semmens, *Seeing Hitler's Germany: Tourism in the Third Reich* (Houndmills: Palgrave, 2005); Wolfgang König, *Volkswagen, Volksempfänger, Volksgemeinschaft: "Volksprodukte" im Dritten Reich: Vom Scheitern einer nationalsozialistischen Konsumgesellschaft* (Paderborn: Schöningh, 2004); Irene Guenther, *Nazi Chic? Fashioning Women in the Third Reich* (Oxford: Berg, 2004); Hartmut Berghoff, "Enticement and Deprivation: The Regulation of Consumption in Pre-War Nazi Germany," in *Politics of Consumption*, ed. Daunton and Hilton, 165–84.

[6] Hans Dieter Schäfer, *Das Gespaltene Bewußtsein: Über deutsche Kultur und Lebenswirklichkeit, 1933–1945* (Berlin: Ullstein, 1984), 114.

[7] Baranowski, *Strength through Joy*, 38–39; Semmens, *Seeing Hitler's Germany*, 11–15.

culture in the interwar years, notably newspaper editors and filmmakers,[8] we have yet to explore the individuals who participated in one of the key aspects of commercial culture – the selling of manufactured products, foodstuffs, and luxury goods. This dearth of studies about commerce and consumption is due partly to historians' legitimate interest in the more obviously damning examples of corporate behavior in the Third Reich, namely the Aryanization of Jewish businesses and the use of forced and slave labor.[9] A wealth of research in the past two decades has revealed how much Hitler's crimes depended on the active help of Germany's companies, many of which are still functioning today.[10] This book does not overlook the theme of corporate complicity, but it does proceed from the premise that even as companies supported the regime's racist and genocidal aims, they also engaged in the everyday acts of manufacturing and selling to a targeted customer base. This engagement provoked a number of questions: What was the meaning of mass consumption in an economy famous for high-quality products? What was the relationship between consumption and the Nazis' racial priorities? How could investigations into consumer preferences help elites and politicians understand the meaning of individuality and social responsibility under a dictatorship? How could companies reach consumers during a period of economic regulation and total war? These are a few of the questions that German

[8] See, e.g., Bernhard Fulda, *Press and Politics in the Weimar Republic* (Oxford: Oxford University Press, 2009); and Klaus Kreimeier, *The Ufa Story: A History of Germany's Greatest Film Company, 1918–1945* (New York: Hill and Wang, 1996).

[9] See Frank Bajohr, *"Aryanization" in Hamburg: The Economic Exclusion of Jews and the Confiscation of Their Property in Nazi Germany* (New York: Berghahn Books, 2002); and Ulrich Herbert, *Hitler's Foreign Workers: Enforced Foreign Labor in Germany under the Third Reich* (Cambridge: Cambridge University Press, 1997).

[10] Among the many studies see Paul Erker, *Industrie-Eliten in der NS Zeit: Anpassungsbereitschaft und Eigeninteresse von Unternehemern in der Rüstung- und Kriegswirtschaft, 1936–1945* (Passau: Rothe, 1994); Peter Hayes, *Industry and Ideology: IG Farben in the Nazi Era* (Cambridge: Cambridge University Press, 1987); Hayes, *From Cooperation to Complicity: Degussa in the Third Reich* (Cambridge: Cambridge University Press, 2004); Hans Mommsen and Manfred Grieger, *Das Volkswagenwerk und seine Arbeiter im Dritten Reich* (Düsseldorf: Econ, 1996); Neil Gregor, *Daimler-Benz in the Third Reich* (New Haven, CN: Yale University Press, 1998); Gerald Feldman, *Allianz and the German Insurance Business, 1933–1945* (Cambridge: Cambridge University Press, 2001); Harold James, *The Deutsche Bank and the Nazi Economic War Against the Jews* (Cambridge: Cambridge University Press, 2001); Johannes Bähr, Axel Drecoll, Bernahrd Gott, Kim C. Priemel, and Harald Wixforth, eds., *Der Flick-Konzern im Dritten Reich* (Munich: Oldenbourg, 2008); and Norbert Frei, Ralf Ahrens, Jörg Osterloh, and Tim Schanetzky, eds., *Flick: Der Konzern, die Familie, die Macht* (Munich: Karl Blessing, 2009).

economic leaders asked themselves in the 1930s and 1940s and that this book, in turn, takes up.

Second, this book situates business leaders' interest in consumer society within larger discussions about the economy in the Third Reich. Much has been written about the structure and function of the Nazi economy during peacetime and wartime.[11] Scholars have found that despite the party's early pronouncements against capitalism, many companies and their managers fared well financially during the Third Reich.[12] A lot depended on whether one was a small entrepreneur or a large industrial manufacturer; the latter found richer economic opportunities with the rearmament and expansion of Germany.[13] This book, however, is less concerned with either the issue of corporate profitability or the relationship of big business to the crimes of National Socialism. Rather, it focuses on party theorists' and business leaders' attempts to imbue a violent economy with cultural meaning. We have long associated the Nazi economy with the recovery of Germany from the Great Depression, the exploitation of Jewish businesses, and the drive toward total war. But the economy's symbolic value to both the regime and to ordinary citizens demands further exploration. While historians have debated the relative importance of politics and economics in the Third Reich, the reality is that these realms blended into each other. To speak of the "primacy of politics" over economics or vice versa is to underestimate how much Nazi ideology and practice was premised on a broad definition of the economy as a site of social, political, and cultural virtue.[14] As I will argue, the market stood at the center of this vision: companies were asked to sell goods with as much a mind to national well-being as to profits, and the self-sacrificing consumer was supposed to consider the needs of the state and the racial community when deciding what goods to purchase or do without.

---

[11] For an overview, see Adam Tooze, *The Wages of Destruction: The Making and Breaking of the Nazi Economy* (New York: Viking, 2006).

[12] On profits in the Third Reich, see Mark Spoerer, *Von Scheingewinnen zum Rüstungsboom: Die Eigenkapitalrentabilität der deutschen Industrieaktiengesellschaften, 1925–1941* (Stuttgart: Steiner, 1996). On the questionable profitability of slave labor, see Spoerer, "Profitierten Unternehmen von KZ-Arbeit? Eine Kritische Analyse der Literatur," *Historische Zeitschrift* 268, no. 1 (February 1999): 61–95.

[13] See John Gillingham, *Industry and Politics in the Third Reich* (London: Methuen, 1985); and Tooze, *Wages of Destruction*, 337–47.

[14] On the primacy of politics over economics, see Timothy Mason, "Der Primat der Politik: Politik und Wirtschaft in Nationalsozialismus," *Das Argument* 41, no. 8 (December 1966): 473–94; and Ian Kershaw, *The Nazi Dictatorship: Problems & Perspectives of Interpretation* [4th ed.], (London: Arnold, 2000), 47–68.

This book looks at a "National Socialist" understanding of market relations,[15] but its approach rests on understanding the international context of these ideas. The Nazis' commercial ideal was a response not just to political and economic events in Germany, but also to a global development: the rise of consumer capitalism. The 1920s and 1930s witnessed the emergence of Fordist economies increasingly driven by mass production and mass consumption. This model presented National Socialism with a dilemma. On the one hand, the Nazis' economic vision was predicated on distancing Germany from the seemingly decadent features of consumer society – competitiveness, rampant materialism, and cultural hybridity. In opposition to an "American," "Weimar," or "Jewish" model, National Socialism combined long-standing tropes of German culture, such as a celebration of high-quality, customized goods, with something new: a racialist orientation that sought to purge Jews from the economy, the society, and eventually the world. On the other hand, the Nazis recognized that their political appeal rested on promising Germans the prosperity associated with mass consumption. They could not reject consumer society wholesale, nor did they want to. After the devastation of World War I and the Great Depression, Germans were seeking economic stability and the consumption opportunities enjoyed in the United States.

In response to this dilemma, the Nazis sought to create their own consumer marketplace. The Nazi marketplace, this book argues, maintained certain "bourgeois" norms, like a celebration of competition, high performance, and entrepreneurship. But the regime invested these concepts with ideological meaning: private initiative, manufacturing, and selling, the Nazis argued in their publications, all had to serve the aim of engineering a materially abundant, racially pure society. In short, National Socialism relied on developments in consumer capitalism, such as the emerging field of mass marketing, while simultaneously advancing its specific aims, namely biological purity and the conquering of "living space."

This book explores the Nazi marketplace as a nexus where economic actors sought to work out their relationship to the Hitler regime. It uncovers new insights into the experiences of German consumers, but it sheds a special light on producers – those companies that sought to survive and even thrive in a radically new political setting. What private industry and

[15] On the Nazis' economic principles, see Avraham Barkai, *Nazi Economics: Ideology, Theory, and Policy* (New Haven, CN: Yale University Press, 1990); and Hauke Janssen, *Nationalökonomie und Nationalsozialismus: Die deutsche Volkswirtschaftslehre in den dreissiger Jahren* (Marburg: Metropolis, 1998).

the government made available for purchase, and how these goods were provided, reflected the broad priorities of the state vis-à-vis its people. Companies, economists, and Nazi officials discussed not only the importance of consumption, but also acceptable forms of selling. They explored the suitable ways of moving a product and promoting a company name. How, this book asks, did companies communicate with consumers in the tightly regulated and ideologically driven economy of the Third Reich?

In exploring this question, this volume plays off recent debates about material conditions in Nazi Germany. A basic point of contention is whether Hitler provided sufficient comforts to Germans or whether his drive toward war came at the expense of the public's well-being; did the Nazi regime provide guns or butter?[16] At various times, scholars have shown, National Socialism delivered both. Even though the state ultimately favored arms and heavy industry over the civilian economy, especially during World War II, it still cast specific consumer products as ideologically valuable goods that the population should have steady access to. Moreover, the regime took care to ensure that Germans did not experience the deprivations that had led to so much discontent on the home front during World War I. But did the Nazis succeed in providing the necessities and comforts for its population, especially compared with the governments that proceeded and followed the Third Reich? Some historians have tried to answer the question by addressing whether the Nazis actually created a consumer society, or indeed a modern society more generally, in the 1930s and 1940s.[17] If Weimar Germany witnessed a flourishing of mass leisure and consumer opportunities, what happened when this was interrupted by depression and dictatorship? Was it as the Nazis depicted it and many Germans remembered it after

---

[16] See Werner Abelshauser, "Guns, Butter and Economic Miracles," in *The Economics of World War II*, ed. Mark Harrison (Cambridge: Cambridge University Press, 1998), 122–76; and Fritz Blaich, "Wirtschaft und Rüstung in Deutschland, 1933–1939," in *Nationalsozialistische Diktatur, 1933–1945: Eine Bilanz*, ed. Karl Dietrich Bracher, Manfred Funke, and Hans Adolf Jacobsen (Düsseldorf: Droste, 1983), 285–316.

[17] There is a growing literature on the Third Reich's relationship to "modernity." For good overviews see Riccardo Bavaj, *Die Ambivalenz der Moderne im Nationalsozialismus: Eine Bilanz der Forschung* (Munich: Oldenbourg, 2003); Paul Betts, "The New Fascination with Fascism: The Case of Nazi Modernism," *Journal of Contemporary History* 37, no. 4 (October 2002): 541–58; Mark Roseman, "National Socialism and Modernisation," in *Fascist Italy and Nazi Germany: Comparisons and Contrasts*, ed. Richard Bessel (Cambridge: Cambridge University Press, 1996), 197–229; Norbert Frei, "Wie modern war der Nationalsozialismus?" *Geschichte und Gesellschaft* 19, no. 3 (July–September 1993): 367–87; and Michael Prinz and Rainer Zitelmann, *Nationalsozialismus und Modernisierung* (Darmstadt: Wissenschaftliche Buchgesellschaft, 1991).

World War II: images of empty shops and long breadlines giving way to
restocked shelves, happy travelers on the Autobahn, and a country pulled
out of the doldrums of the Great Depression?[18]

Two broad approaches to these questions animate the literature on the
National Socialist economy. The first posits the view that the population
of prewar Nazi Germany had access to a comfortable consumer marketplace and that the Third Reich laid the groundwork for the West German
consumer society of the 1950s.[19] "[The] social contract of an acquisi-
tive society," writes Michael Geyer, "was formed in the consuming passions of the 1930s and 1940s, rather than in the postwar years."[20] With
reference to the Strength Through Joy (KdF) leisure programs and the
omnipresence of products like Coca-Cola, Dagmar Herzog complements
this view, referring to the "modernization of consumer culture" during
the Third Reich.[21] In other words, rather than experiencing a backward
interregnum in the otherwise progressive unfolding of a consumer society,
Germans in the Nazi years created a commercially advanced society and
accustomed themselves to economic comforts after the scourges of World
War I, inflation, and depression.

Historian Götz Aly has offered a provocative variation on this theme
of material comfort, focusing less on the consumer economy than on
broader Nazi policies he sees as having been enormously favorable to
middle- and lower-income Germans.[22] Progressive tax codes, an expansive welfare state, and the influx of wartime booty gave Germans a high
standard of living and ultimately led to their overwhelming support for

[18] Germans during the mid-1930s spoke of the country's economic comeback as mirac-
ulous. For a critical view see Hans E. Priester, *Das deutsche Wirtschaftswunder*
(Amsterdam: Querido, 1936). On the contested role of the Autobahn in the German
economic recovery, see R. J. Overy, "Cars, Roads and Economic Recovery, 1932–1938,"
Economic History Review 28, no. 3 (August 1975): 466–83; and the ensuing exchange
between G. F. R. Spenceley and Overy in *Economic History Review* 32, no. 1 (February
1979): 100–13.
[19] Hans-Ulrich Wehler portrays the West German combination of planning and market
economics as the logical result of 1930s policies. See Stefan Schwarzkopf, "Kontrolle
statt Rausch? Marktforschung, Produktwerbung und Verbraucherlenkung im
Nationalsozialismus zwischen Phantasien von Masse, Angst und Macht," in *Rausch und
Diktatur: Inszenierung, Mobilisierung und Kontrolle in totalitären Systemen*, ed. Árpad
von Klimó and Malte Rolf (Frankfurt am Main: Campus, 2007), 193–209.
[20] Michael Geyer, "The Stigma of Violence, Nationalism, and War in Twentieth-Century
Germany," *German Studies Review* 15, special issue (Winter 1992): 75–110.
[21] Dagmar Herzog, *Sex after Fascism: Memory and Morality in Twentieth-Century Germany*
(Princeton, NJ: Princeton University Press, 2005), 16.
[22] Götz Aly, *Hitler's Beneficiaries: Plunder, Racial War, and the Nazi Welfare State*
(New York: Metropolitan, 2007).

Hitler's dictatorship. Far from dismissing Nazi Germany as an economic aspirant, Aly sees the material benefits as voluminous and, indeed, as much more decisive a factor than ideology and racism in explaining popular support for National Socialism. In effect, Aly places Nazi Germany on a forward path toward the social market economy and mass consumer society of West Germany.

An alternative approach sees the Third Reich as anything but dynamic and consumer friendly. Adam Tooze, in his definitive study of the Nazi economy, paints a picture of a society beset by shortages and disappointed consumers.[23] As he and others have shown, the Nazis hoped to replicate American prosperity; Hitler declared that Germans "resemble the Americans in that we have wants and desires."[24] But the reality of economic upheaval, ersatz products, and declining quality in the run-up to war undermined this aim. The removal of Jews from business life, the enactment of price controls, and limits on competition revealed the foundations of the economic recovery in the 1930s to be, in Peter Hayes's words, "autarky and armaments."[25] Per capita consumption barely reached Weimar levels, and during the war, shortages in consumer goods challenged Germans' dreams of an economically abundant new order. The Third Reich was, according to Wolfgang König, a "failed consumer society."[26]

This historical question about material conditions in the Third Reich is partly an empirical one, and thus we await more nuanced studies of how Nazi policies affected consumers in different regions and from varied social backgrounds. Certainly, class divisions remained in Nazi Germany, and material comforts from 1933 to 1945 differed according to occupation and family wealth. As German researchers themselves noted in the 1930s, consumer opportunities were not distributed evenly under Hitler. But the two broad approaches sketched in the preceding paragraphs can also be tied to different interpretive questions emerging from social and cultural history. Where one historian might be curious about the relationship of the consumer sector to the military sector, or of the German economy to the global economy, the historian of everyday

[23] Tooze, *Wages of Destruction*, 145–65.
[24] Alon Confino, Introduction to "Histories and Memories of Twentieth Century Germany," *History and Memory* 17, nos. 1–2 (Autumn 2005): 4–11.
[25] Peter Hayes, "Industry under the Swastika," in *Enterprise in the Period of Fascism*, ed. Harold James and Jakob Tanner (Aldershot: Ashgate, 2002), 26–36.
[26] König, *Volkswagen, Volksempfänger, Volksgemeinschaft: Vom Scheitern einer nationalsozialistischen Konsumgesellschaft*.

life might be eager to see what people bought even during a period of shortages, what meanings they attached to these goods, and how they remembered the Nazi years after 1945. This book adheres more to the latter approach by focusing on cultural perceptions of the economy. For even if Germans never enjoyed the living standards of the United States, they still took advantage of a modern economy that provided material comforts. During the Nazi years goods and services were less voluminous than in richer, less regulated economies, but this did not stop Germans from enjoying what they had and trying to attain more. Despite the strictures of the Nazi economy (e.g., price controls and the priority of war production), business leaders sought to create a consumer society, albeit one that both catered to the material needs of the masses and preserved the treasured ethos of high-quality production. They engaged in advertising, public relations, and market research, and they discussed the meanings of mass culture and society. In short, economic elites believed in and strove for a "German" consumer society.

Thus while Götz Aly's view of the Nazis' social and economic largesse, his reductive materialism, and his downplaying of ideology have rightfully been critiqued, his focus on the popular resonance of the economy remains essential. The empirical reality of shortages and the ideological demands of the state did not stop German companies from promoting new products or consumers from exulting in them. In short, the problems that the Nazi economy faced in the prewar years did not dispel popular visions of a thriving consumer marketplace. To be sure, as war revealed itself to be a defining feature of National Socialism, expectations of a prosperous society were deferred to an amorphous "postwar" period. But Germans engaged in the "virtual consumption" (to use Hartmut Berghoff's term) of goods not on the shelf,[27] and promises of delayed gratification sustained most people as they experienced imminent military victory in 1940 and 1941 and eventual defeat.

THE NAZI ECONOMIC RECOVERY: A BRIEF OVERVIEW

While this book foregrounds culture in its analysis of the Nazi marketplace, the specific details of the economic recovery in the 1930s are crucial to this story. What did the economy look like to the men who were devising

[27] Hartmut Berghoff, "'Times Change and We Change with Them': The German Advertising Industry in the Third Reich – Between Professional Self-Interest and Political Repression," *Business History* 45, no. 1 (January 2003): 128–47.

corporate selling strategies? This is not an easy question to answer. First, because Germany's economic well-being was so central to the National Socialist project, decoupling facts from Hitler's propagandistic exploitation of them can be difficult. Germany enjoyed a real economic recovery in the 1930s, but the Nazis applied objective economic data to a violently subjective politics. Second, categorizing the economy of the Third Reich has confronted scholars with a series of thorny questions: What kind of economy could enable both a rapid economic recovery and a genocidal war? Was it a capitalist or a command economy? A "fascist" or "partially fascist" one? Was it a combination of many different systems?[28]

The question of how to characterize the Nazi economy has proved contentious, for until the 1990s the ideological stakes involved in this exploration were paramount. Communist historians, particularly East Germans, insisted that Nazism was the expression of monopoly capitalism, and Western Marxists saw big business conspiring with the state to make war.[29] In turn, other scholars responded defensively, offering their own exaggerated claims about the "innocence" of capitalism in the rise and consolidation of National Socialism.[30] The political climate of the cold war lent these scholarly debates a polarizing dimension. Twenty years after the collapse of communism, however, the political stakes have faded, and there is an emerging consensus that the Nazis relied on a system of "managed" or "organized" capitalism.[31] In the Third Reich, the basics of market economics persisted. But the economy was increasingly directed from above, by a state that steered production and consumption toward brutal ends.

It is important to note that there was considerable continuity between the pre-Nazi and Nazi economies. State intervention, especially in the energy, credit, and transportation sectors, had a long history that had peaked in the 1920s, and the network of cartels that would prove decisive

[28] For a good introduction to these questions, see Kershaw, *Nazi Dictatorship*, 47–68; Michael von Prollius, *Das Wirtschaftssystem der Nationalsozialisten, 1933–1939: Steuerung durch emergent Organisation und politische Prozesse* (Paderborn: Schöningh, 2003): 327–59; Ludolf Herbst, "Die nationalsozialistische Wirtschaftspolitik im internationalen Vergleich," in *Der Nationalsozialismus: Studien zur Ideologie und Herrschaft*, ed. Wolfgang Benz, Hans Buchheim, and Hans Mommsen (Frankfurt am Main: Fischer, 1993), 153–76; and Janssen, *Nationalökonomie*, 13–25.
[29] See Peter Hayes's introduction to Franz Neumann, *Behemoth: The Structure and Practice of National Socialism, 1933–1944* [1942] (Chicago: Ivan R. Dee, 2009), vii–viii.
[30] See S. Jonathan Wiesen, *West German Industry and the Challenge of the Nazi Past, 1945–1955* (Chapel Hill: University of North Carolina Press, 2001), 1–16.
[31] Barkai, *Nazi Economics*, 248.

to Nazi military production emerged from the consolidations of the Weimar years.[32] This top-heavy system was itself a product of a longer statist tendency in Germany that has envisioned more room for an activist government than an "Anglo-Saxon" model.[33] What was new after 1933 was the linking of the marketplace to the project of racial purification. The Nazis hoped to create a German-dominated European economic union that would allow them to exploit natural resources, land, and labor for the benefit of a biologically pure populace. Thus while basic economic structures did not change under Hitler, their political significance certainly did. The Nazis, writes Werner Plumpe, altered the parameters of economic discussions so that "business activities were made in service of the regime's larger goals."[34]

The continuity between the pre-1933 and post-1933 economy should not obscure a simple but crucial point: Hitler's aims could never have been realized without a broad and sustained economic recovery. In other words, if some features of the economy remained consistent, the health of the economy changed dramatically. The Nazis took over a country racked by low productivity, declining exports and imports, and a withered gross national product, and they presided over a profound reversal of fortunes. From 1932 to 1938 national income increased 82 percent and industrial production more than doubled.[35] Germany's total gross domestic product also more than doubled between 1932 and 1944.[36] In the late 1930s Nazi magazines contrasted the decimated economy that Hitler had inherited with a bright new reality: the country was richer, industrial production was up, and factories were churning out everything from soap to windowpanes to alarm clocks.[37] While the Depression had

---

[32] On the Weimar economy see Gerold Ambrosius, *Staat und Wirtschaft im 20. Jahrhundert* (Munich: Oldenbourg, 1990), 75–88.

[33] Volker R. Berghahn, "Das 'Deutsche Kapitalismus-Modell' in Geschichte und Geschichtswissenschaft," in *Gibt es einen deutschen Kapitalismus? Tradition und globale Perspektiven der sozialen Marktwirtschaft*, ed. Volker Berghahn and Sigurt Vitols (Frankfurt am Main: Campus, 2006), 24–42.

[34] Werner Plumpe, "Die Unternehmen im Nationalsozialismus – Eine Zwischenbilanz," in *Wirtschaftsordnung, Staat und Unternehmen. Neuere Forschungen zur Wirtschaftsgeschichte des Nationalsozialismus: Festschrift für Dietmar Petzina zu seinem 65. Geburtstag*, ed. Werner Abelshauser, Jan-Otmar Hesse, and Werner Plumpe (Essen: Klartext, 2003), 243–66.

[35] R. J. Overy, *The Nazi Economic Recovery: 1932–1938* (London: Macmillan, 1982), 29.

[36] Abelshauser, "Guns, Butter and Economic Miracles," 124.

[37] See, e.g., the statistics and drawings in *Mitteilungen der Kommission für Wirtschaftpolitik der NSDAP* 2, no. 13 (July 1937): 25.

already reached its nadir in 1932 and Hitler benefited from a cyclical upswing, he did not hesitate to take credit for these improvements.[38]

Most striking was the rapid reemployment of Germany's population. In January 1933, the month that Hitler came to power, unemployment had peaked at just over 6 million; in the fall of 1938 it hovered around 150,000, or less than 1 percent.[39] The Nazis took Weimar era forms of labor conscription, such as agricultural workforces, and supplemented them with new, often compulsory initiatives.[40] Infrastructural repairs and civil engineering projects, notably the construction of the Autobahn system, were the most celebrated sources of employment.[41] But the mining, iron and steel, and chemical sectors, which serviced the regime's armaments drive, also relied on massive reemployment. And despite the push to reinstate traditional gender divisions, the number of women increased in all sectors of the economy.[42] In actuality, the Nazis' commitment to public works projects was more short lived and tepid than was once assumed.[43] But it mattered little to contemporary observers, who considered Hitler's employment policies ingenious. By 1938 the economy was even suffering from labor shortages, necessitating a turn to foreign workers to staff farms, factories, and households.[44] The government's "battle for work" had led to jobs for the throngs of young men and women who had been shut out of the economy earlier in the decade.[45]

The return to full employment was an obvious boon to the Nazi regime, which could boast in 1937 that the U.S. unemployment rate was still 20 percent, and Britain's was more than 10 percent.[46] Soaring employment

[38] On whether this was primarily a cyclical recovery, see Harold James, "Innovation and Conservatism in Economic Recovery: The Alleged 'Nazi Recovery' of the 1930s," in *Reevaluating the Third Reich: New Controversies, New Interpretations*, ed. Thomas Childers and Jane Caplan (London: Holmes & Meier, 1993), 114–38; Christoph Buchheim, "Das NS-Regime und die Überwindung der Weltwirtschaftskrise in Deutschland," *Vierteljahrshefte für Zeitgeschichte* 56, no. 3 (July 2008): 381–414; and Dan P. Silverman, *Hitler's Economy: Nazi Work Creation Programs, 1933–1936* (Cambridge, MA: Harvard University Press, 1998), 238–41.
[39] Silverman, *Hitler's Economy*, 252–53.
[40] R. J. Overy, "Unemployment in the Third Reich," *Business History* 29, no. 3 (July 1987): 253–81.
[41] Overy, "Cars, Roads and Economic Recovery."
[42] Tim Kirk, *The Longman Companion to Nazi Germany* (New York: Longman, 1995), 81.
[43] Silverman, *Hitler's Economy*, 245; and Buchheim, "Das NS-Regime."
[44] Herbert, *Hitler's Foreign Workers*, 48.
[45] Richard J. Evans, *The Third Reich in Power* (New York: Penguin, 2006), 322–36.
[46] Abelshauser, "Guns, Butter and Economic Miracles," 125.

also offered a major psychological boost to the German public and the business community, and Hitler benefited from the desperately low expectations that had greeted him in 1933. The German recovery attracted admiration from American observers, who inevitably drew comparisons to the policies of their own Depression era leader.[47] More than any other public figure, President Franklin Roosevelt (who came into office a month after Hitler) has been associated with government spending and job creation as a means of economic recovery. But the Nazis did this earlier and more intensely than the Americans. "The Nazi 'economic miracle,'" writes Werner Abelshauser, "preceded the 'Keynesian Revolution.'"[48]

Scholars have debated whether Hitler's policies were themselves Keynesian in their reliance on public expenditures.[49] If so, they were of a particular type – a "military Keynesianism" that depended on the enormous expansion of armaments production as opposed to increasing consumer spending.[50] In the three years after Hitler came to power, the German military accounted for 42 percent of the country's GDP growth,[51] and in 1938 public expenditures on the military were almost triple the amount devoted to infrastructure.[52] Newly employed Germans poured into factories, which churned out tanks, guns, ammunition, and military vehicles. They entered mines in search of the iron ore and oil that would propel the Nazis' future military adventures, and they harvested the grain that would feed the mobilized soldiers. In short, from its inception the economy of the Third Reich was oriented toward war.[53]

This military-driven economic recovery was infused with a sense of racial mission. Full employment, for example, was not just cast in economically positive and socially inclusive terms. It was also about exclusion: Jews and other minorities were denied jobs and civil rights while Aryans enjoyed them.[54] To be sure, Jews were a small enough minority that Nazi economic successes did not depend on their exploitation. But anti-Jewish financial measures played a highly visible symbolic role.

---

[47] For an early American analysis of Nazi unemployment policies, see Friedrich Baerwald, "How Germany Reduced Unemployment," *American Economic Review* 24, no. 4 (December 1934): 617–30.
[48] Abelshauser, "Guns, Butter and Economic Miracles," 131.
[49] Overy, *Nazi Economic Recovery*, 52–53; Evans, *Third Reich in Power*, 336.
[50] Abelshauser, "Guns, Butter and Economic Miracles," 169.
[51] Tooze, *Wages of Destruction*, 63.
[52] Abelshauser, "Guns, Butter and Economic Miracles," 138.
[53] Tooze, *Wages of Destruction*, 659.
[54] See Avraham Barkai, *From Boycott to Annihilation: The Economic Struggle of German Jews, 1933–1943* (Hanover, NH: University Press of New England, 1989).

They helped mollify those Germans who felt that the country's economic collapse had been due to Jewish financial control. Boycotting Jewish businesses could lead to increased foot traffic in Aryan stores. The expropriation of Jewish companies could mean more managerial opportunities for non-Jews and more corporate profits for "Aryan companies." And restricting the amount of money Jewish émigrés could transfer to their new countries meant that cash and property would remain in Germany for non-Jewish beneficiaries.[55] The regime's increasingly exploitative financial measures, such as a "punitive" community tax on Jews after the Reich pogrom of 1938 and "export taxes" on personal goods sent abroad, were eventually supplanted by much more brutal methods during World War II. Pillaged property from the war zone and gold fillings from murdered Jews made their way to the households of Germans and to the vaults of Germany's biggest banks.[56]

Who benefited from this economic and racial reordering? Were the rewards spread evenly in the 1930s? Again, these are difficult questions. On the one hand, the Nazis' economic policies benefited large producers and financial institutions. Corporate profits soared in the 1930s,[57] some companies (like automobile firms) received tax breaks, and the regime's promotion of Aryanization led to additional assets for large manufacturers. On the other hand, the population reveled in the return to full employment and expanding opportunities for shopping and leisure. Yet the regime was keenly aware of the potentially negative effects massive military outlays might have on the civilian economy. The Nazis faced a dilemma: they could limit consumer goods to free up resources for armaments while printing money to prime the economy. But this would inevitably lead to inflation, of which Germans had terrible memories: the 1923 inflation had led to the decimation of personal savings and the obliteration of the German currency.[58] The regime therefore devised a system in which prices and wages were carefully regulated, imports and exports were strictly controlled, and production priorities were dictated from above, all with the aim of keeping labor costs down, channeling resources toward the military, and keeping workers happy.[59]

[55] Martin Dean, *Robbing the Jews: The Confiscation of Jewish Property in the Holocaust, 1933–1945* (Cambridge: Cambridge University Press, 2008), 61–62.
[56] Ibid., 359–61; and Hayes, *From Cooperation to Complicity*, 148–94.
[57] Tooze, *Wages of Destruction*, 109.
[58] Gerald D. Feldman, *The Great Disorder: Politics, Economics, and Society in the German Inflation, 1914–1924* (Oxford: Oxford University Press, 1997), 3–28.
[59] André Steiner, "Umrisse einer Geschichte der Verbraucherpolitik unter dem Nationalsozialismus der Vorkriegszeit," in *Wirtschaftsordnung, Staat und Unternehmen,*

This formula met with only marginal success. The specter of inflation always hung over the German economy, such that by 1935 Carl
Goerdeler, the Reich price commissioner, presided over, in Adam Tooze's
words, "a comprehensive system of state-supervised price setting."[60] Even
with this top-heavy system (and despite Nazi claims), consumer prices,
especially those of foodstuffs, rose markedly in the years following the
Nazi takeover of power. For example, from the summer of 1934 to the
summer of 1935, the cost of fresh fruits in one Berlin district went up
300 percent, with legumes and leafy greens increasing up to 100 percent
and eggs and dairy products up to 40 percent.[61] Indeed, throughout the
1930s, the retail price of most basic foods – beef, poultry, eggs, milk –
rose steadily, with only fish becoming more affordable.[62] In response to
these trends, the Nazi leadership implemented a price freeze in the fall of
1936, followed by the rationing of butter and fats on January 1, 1937.[63]
With import limitations, however, the availability and quality of food,
clothes, and other products plummeted, effectively rendering the price
stop of 1936 meaningless.

Consumers, in short, paid the price for a military-driven recovery.
Longer hours and stagnant wages, combined with a rise in the cost of
necessities, led to diminished rates of private consumption.[64] Moreover,
the crushing of the labor movement (collective bargaining and the right
to strike were abolished in 1933) meant that workers lost the ability to
negotiate better pay packages. And far from being smug over Germany's
"awakening," consumers grumbled about shortages and lower product quality in the 1930s.[65] In the last years of the decade, the Four Year
Plan for war readiness, which was announced in 1936 with great fanfare, did allow for a measure of economic self-sufficiency. Its goal was to
free Germany from its dependence on foreign natural resources. But this
was not to the benefit of the consumer, who dealt with fewer goods and

ed. Abelshauser et al., 279–303. On wages see Overy, "Unemployment in the Third
Reich," 269; and Tooze, *Wages of Destruction*, 141–43.
[60] Tooze, *Wages of Destruction*, 108.
[61] Robert A. Brady, *The Spirit and Structure of German Fascism* (London: Victor Gollancz,
1937), 240.
[62] Kirk, *Longman Companion*, 99; and Abelshauser, "Guns, Butter and Economic
Miracles," 147.
[63] Fritz Blaich, *Wirtschaft und Rüstung im "Dritten Reich"* (Düsseldorf: Schwann, 1987),
21–26; and Evans, *Third Reich in Power*, 347.
[64] André Steiner, "Zur Neuschätzung des Lebenshaltungskostindex für die Vorkriegszeit des
Nationalsozialismus," *Jahrbuch für Wirtschaftsgeschichte*, 2005, no. 2 (2005): 129–52.
[65] Tim Kirk, *Nazi Germany* (Houndsmill: Palgrave, 2007), 65–66.

higher costs. While demand for basic foodstuffs like meat and bread was met domestically, the regime still depended on the import of fats, oils, and eggs. In the run-up to war, the state acknowledged that it could not meet the demand for certain seemingly nonessential foodstuffs, like coffee and fruit, which began to be rationed in the spring of 1939.[66] The Four Year Plan, writes Abelshauser, was predicated on the idea of "as much butter as necessary, as many guns as possible."[67] Yet often the population and the regime had different conceptions of what was necessary. As we explore the consumer economy, therefore, we are reminded that the Nazi "economic miracle" of the 1930s was marked by a combination of shortages and high costs that left much to be desired for the average German.[68]

This dissatisfaction must be put in proper perspective, however. When the Nazis trumpeted the comeback of the German economy, their words resonated with a population that was now overwhelmingly employed. And as Ian Kershaw has pointed out, the popular gratitude toward Hitler was widespread;[69] indeed in 1951, five years after the regime's collapse, almost half of West Germans still found job opportunities and living standards to have been the best aspects of National Socialism.[70] Finally, while the cost of living rose throughout the 1930s, Germans always contrasted their fortunes with what they had experienced at the beginning of the decade, when they were mired in a punishing depression. The standard of living in Germany was never as high as that in the United States, but it was still a comfortable one for many people.

ORGANIZING CONCEPTS AND CHAPTER OVERVIEWS

Against the backdrop of this economic recovery, the Nazi state took an active role in promoting "proper" forms of commerce. In turn, Nazi leaders worked with those most closely invested in the flow of goods and

---

[66] Evans, *Third Reich in Power*, 349.

[67] Abelshauser, "Guns, Butter and Economic Miracles," 131.

[68] Mark Spoerer, "Demontage eines Mythos? Zu der Kontroverse über das nationalsozialistische 'Wirtschaftswunder,'" *Geschichte und Gesellschaft* 31, no. 3 (July–September 2005): 415–38.

[69] Ian Kershaw, *The "Hitler Myth"*: Image and Reality in the Third Reich (Oxford: Oxford University Press, 1987), 61–62.

[70] Richard L. Merritt, *Democracy Imposed: U.S. Occupation Policy and the German Public, 1945–1949* (New Haven, CN: Yale University Press, 1995), 100. On positive memories of the Third Reich, see also Ulrich Herbert, "Good Times, Bad Times: Memories of the Third Reich," in *Life in the Third Reich* [2d ed.], ed. Richard Bessel (Oxford: Oxford University Press, 2001), 97–111.

services – advertisers, designers, economists, and business leaders – whom
Lisa Tiersten has referred to as "market professionals."[71] This book draws
on internal company records, letters, journals, published writings, and
consumer reports to paint a picture of these economic leaders, who were
guided not only by Nazi ideals and diktats, but also by business norms
that transcended the time and national space of Nazi Germany. While the
word "marketing" did not enter the German language until after World
War II, business leaders took advantage of a number of practices that
anticipated modern marketing tools.[72] They looked back to Weimar and
across the Atlantic to devise effective means of communicating with the
consumer. Some of these were given a unique cast to conform to Nazi
rules about proper selling practices. Others pushed against and often
beyond the prescribed rules of play. This tension between "normal" corporate self-promotion and practices that were aligned with the regime's
directives meant that market professionals were kept guessing about what
the state would tolerate or prohibit. As we will see throughout this book,
company leaders often butted heads with Nazi officials as they tried to
conduct business as usual.

In highlighting tensions between the Nazi marketplace, on the one
hand, and a "conventional" marketplace, on the other, this book reveals
three dynamics: continuity, compatibility, and autonomy. The first, continuity, calls into question the decisiveness of the historical rupture of
1933. While this year saw the accession of a brutal dictatorship, economic leaders continued to rely on business practices they had learned
during the first three decades of the twentieth century. They drew on
sales and retailing practices, as well as on a large body of literature on
mass psychology, in an attempt to move their merchandise. As the Nazi
state attempted to reconcile consumer capitalism with its political aims,
market professionals proceeded with their own project: studying international trends in advertising, debating the nature of consumer desire, and
creating images to accompany the country's economic recovery.

The second dynamic concerns the compatibility of corporate and governmental goals. This did not have to do only with business and Nazi aims
regarding the exploitation of Jewish assets and the appropriation of Jewish
businesses. When it came to the consumer economy, companies' desires to

[71] Lisa Tiersten, *Marianne in the Market: Envisioning Consumer Society in Fin-de-Siècle France* (Berkeley: University of California Press, 2001), 8.
[72] Hartmut Berghoff, ed., *Marketing-Geschichte: Die Genese einer modernen Sozialtechnik* (Frankfurt am Main: Campus, 2007), 29.

reach their customers and Nazi demands for socially and culturally German forms of marketing were often compatible. Maximizing profits and functioning in a "sanitized" marketplace need not work at cross-purposes. Despite attempts to retool the economy along less crassly competitive lines, the Third Reich made room for consumers to assert their wishes and corporations to respond. In short, a racist utopia and a commercial utopia went hand in hand. But as we will see, the willingness of business elites to adhere to the Nazis' marketing norms also had its limits.

These limitations are indicative of a third dynamic, namely autonomy. Despite the regime's attempts to keep companies and their directors on a tight leash, business leaders and market professionals maintained room to maneuver in devising and implementing corporate communications strategies. While the Nazis issued regulations about correct business practices, companies still had many marketing tools at their disposal. Through ads, trade fairs, sales pitches, and films, they found ample opportunity to promote their products. The Nazis obliterated a public sphere based on political pluralism, rational discourse, and individual empowerment. But business elites still behaved as if they were speaking to citizen consumers whose wants, needs, and idiosyncrasies could find expression in the economy. In this way, both companies and consumers saw the marketplace as a locus of personal meaning.

The six chapters of this book reveal the dynamics of continuity, compatibility, and autonomy at play. Chapter 1 explores Nazi Party and economic leaders' views of commerce. In particular, it looks at the state's regulations and practices with respect to consumption and marketing. While eviscerating German Jews' status as producers and consumers, the regime also aimed to regulate "Aryan" purchasing habits and manufacturers' sales practices. It hoped to both defend "healthy" forms of competition and guide them along ideological lines, two goals that eventually proved difficult to implement simultaneously.

Chapter 2 highlights the on-the-ground application of these ideas about proper forms of marketing. In crafting advertisements, creating pavilions at exhibitions, commissioning industrial films, and setting up window displays, companies encountered a dilemma: How could they promote their reputations at home and abroad while also adhering to the collectivist and nationalist demands of the state? This chapter focuses, in particular, on three prominent firms in the chemical, pharmaceutical, and foodstuffs sectors (Henkel, Bayer, and Kaffee HAG) that developed sophisticated forms of marketing and that therefore tackled this question directly. All these companies, moreover, had a special relationship to

Nazi ideology: Bayer produced medicines, Henkel cleaning supplies, and Kaffee HAG decaffeinated coffee that was supposed to calm the nerves and lead to high performance. These three companies found great advantages in marketing goods that were seen as contributing to the health of the *Volk*. But they also encountered difficulties when they tried to take advantage of *völkisch* motifs for overtly commercial purposes.

Chapter 3 focuses on Germany's Rotary Clubs, the first of two institutional settings this book highlights where business leaders confronted consumer society. Until the clubs' dissolution in 1937, industrialists and other businessmen met over weekly lunches to discuss the social and intellectual issues of the day. For over four years, Rotarians tried to merge their self-understanding as bourgeois elites with the precepts of the Nazi racial state. Part of this process of intellectual accommodation entailed discussing the meaning of buying and selling in the new Germany, in the United States (the "home" of mass consumption), and in mass society more generally. They lectured on the importance of leisure, discussed the increasing demand for goods and services in a traditionally producerist economy, and examined the seeming decline of German culture with the rise of new technologies. For Rotarians and other interwar elites, understanding consumers and consumption was not only a business undertaking, but also an intellectual and cultural one. Moreover, it was a project that resembled and gave nourishment to the Nazis' own attempts to understand mass consumption.

Chapter 4 offers a focused study of one form of marketing: consumer research. It looks at Nuremberg's Society for Consumer Research (GfK), an institute where, as in the Rotary Clubs, elite views of the masses merged with practical business needs. The institute was the brainchild of market researcher Wilhelm Vershofen and Wilhelm Mann, a director of the IG Farben chemical conglomerate. Its advisory board included executives and owners from a variety of German companies, who commissioned dozens of reports on consumer attitudes and habits. From 1935 until the end of the war, members of the GfK met to talk not only about their research – which revealed a vivid picture of consumers' daily lives – but also about the larger cultural and economic implications of mass consumption. They defended brand names against cheap imitation products, probed the nature of individual desire, and explored the merits of applied psychology in their research.

Chapter 5 focuses on commerce and consumption during World War II. It shows that despite shortages in the economy and mobilization on behalf of total war, economic leaders continued to devise ways of reaching the consumer. Discussions about consumption and the practice of selling proceeded apace, as Germans readied themselves for a post-victory consumerist utopia. But this intellectual work came at a price: the autonomy of economic elites was increasingly challenged, and business leaders and market experts could not escape being drawn into the violent aims of the regime, eventually assisting in its plans for exploiting newly occupied territories in Southeastern Europe. Moreover, as the dream of wartime victory gave way to the expectation of defeat, the Nazi regime had to rethink its plans for a German-led consumer society in a "new Europe." Its commercial vision was ultimately too conflict ridden, and it collapsed under the weight of its own contradictions; the Nazis could not at once support mass consumption and prepare the country for war.

Finally, the book's conclusion addresses the relationship of consumption to popular and elite attitudes during the Third Reich. Did consumption practices help legitimate the existing order? Did business leaders, in creating the semblance of consumer normality, lend stability to the Nazi regime? This final chapter also explores briefly marketing practices and discourses on consumption in West Germany after 1945. In the 1950s the social market economy emerged with its own set of claims about virtuous commercial behavior. To what extent did this replicate ideas advocated during the Nazi years and before, both in Germany and abroad?

Throughout this book, I never lose sight of the fact that the Nazi economy was violent at its core. Hitler and his coterie called upon mainstream monetary policies, but for them money was tainted with Jewish influence. They presided over a stunning economic recovery but put it in the service of conquest and persecution. They wanted consumer goods to satisfy the population's needs, but they demanded loyalty, conformity, and the exclusion of unwanted minorities from this utopian vision. In short, racial ideology stood at the center of the Third Reich, and any study of commerce and consumption must keep this central point in mind. By focusing on buying and selling, therefore, one can determine how ideology worked its way into the most mundane corners of everyday life, providing dreams of abundance and social status. Whether these fantasies of a consumer-friendly marketplace translated into popular support for the regime remains open to debate. But the juxtaposition of consumerist visions and marketing practices, the moral claims of the state, and the murderous reality of National Socialism reveals the brutal contradictions that defined German society in the 1930s and early 1940s.

I

National Socialism and the Market

In September 1936 the National Socialist newspaper *Westdeutscher Beobachter* (*WB*) advertised itself in a business journal with the provocative question "Man or Market?" Flanked by the sculpted imagery of a stalwart mother and her sword-bearing son, the ad copy implied that people, in all their heroic guises, were more important than the impersonal workings of the economy. Specifically, the advertisement drew attention to the role of the human being (*Mensch*) in Germany's economic recovery. The "new Reich's" rebirth was not the result of desk workers pouring over dusty files and market reports. Rather it was due to "the mobilization of all human values and existential claims." With more than 200,000 subscribers, the *WB* hoped to contribute to this activist spirit by offering advertising space to Germany's companies. Advertising was more than a "thing in itself," the *WB* proclaimed. It was an expression of the "new communal will," and by highlighting the fruits of economic recovery through ads and in turn exploiting the purchasing power of Germans, the *WB* hoped to serve as "an essential medium between production and consumption."[1]

With its vague references to "community" and "will," its celebration of Germany's rebirth, and its promotion of a product, this advertisement was familiar fare in the 1930s. It tapped into a sense of economic optimism and offered familiar nationalist tropes to its audience of business professionals used to creating such ads themselves. For the historian, the advertisement sheds light on commercial relations in the Third Reich. First,

[1] "Mensch oder Markt?"Advertisement for *Westdeutscher Beobachter*, opposite inside cover of *Seidels Reklame* 20, no. 9 (September 1936).

22

it demonstrates how both private and state-run businesses, in this case a party newspaper, appealed to Nazi ideals without explicitly using the regime's racist terminology; sacrifice, mobilization, and national recovery were stock populist concepts, and marketers knew how to employ them to maximum effect. Second, it reveals the importance of "consumption" as a word that had immediate resonance for business leaders in the 1930s. No longer was it assumed that producers were the engine of the economy; goods also had to be consumed by the masses, and a company's success depended on understanding the relationship between what they produced and what the public wanted. Finally, by positing an inherent opposition between human beings and markets, the advertisement revealed the Nazi Party's uneasiness with modern forms of commerce. National Socialist economists felt that, in and of themselves, buying and selling were soulless, even inhuman, exercises. But by sanitizing commercial relations and binding them to the fate of the Aryan race, the Nazis hoped to dissociate consumption and marketing from crude materialism. As we will see, the Nazis defended the right of biologically acceptable individuals to buy and sell freely and to exercise their creativity in the marketplace, but they also demanded that production and consumption speak to the higher goals of the community, the nation, and the Volk.

This chapter takes the *WB* advertisement as a starting point for exploring the Nazi regime's broader ideas about commerce and consumption. How did the Nazis conceive of the market? How did they navigate the twin goals of aligning commerce with National Socialist ideology and maintaining high levels of production and consumption? How did they attempt to impose their ideas of correct market behavior on business leaders and consumers? In addressing these questions, this chapter will explore the Nazis' ambivalence about consumer capitalism. On the one hand, Nazi leaders associated mass consumption and commerce with insidious elements – liberalism, materialism, Americanism, and Jewish financial interests. Wrote a Nazi periodical, "The Americans, whose main representatives are the Jews, think commercially in everything, whether in art, scholarship, or social and family life."[2] On the other hand, the Nazis committed themselves to pulling their country out of the Depression and to creating a racially pure Germany that enjoyed a high standard of living;[3] they thus depended on the very tools of mass

---

[2] "Nachkrieg als Geschäft," *Nationalsozialistische Wirtschaftspolitik*, nos. 3–4 (May 1944): 108. The name of the journal was changed to *Wirtschaftspolitische Parole* in 1937.

[3] Josef Wagner, "Preisbildung und Lebensstandard," *Vierjahresplan* 2, no. 3 (March 1938): 131–33.

consumption that they decried. Nazi thinkers addressed this dilemma by
creating a vision of the market that was an amalgam of "bourgeois" and
völkisch ideas. In party newspapers and official declarations, they drew
on existing ideas about consumer capitalism and suffused them with a
racial sensibility. Their market ideal attempted to address the practical
demands of economic recovery, the consumer's desire for material gratification, and the goal of a racial and ideological reordering. This chapter
will begin by exploring these multiple strands of the Nazi marketplace
and the contradictions inherent in them. It will then look at the specific role consumption played in the Nazi economic vision. Finally, it will
examine the regime's attempts to promote this commercial ideal and to
enforce proper forms of buying, selling, and consuming. By sanitizing
consumer capitalism and laying out guidelines for the practice of marketing, the regime hoped to engage producers and consumers in the building
of a wealthy *Volksgemeinschaft*.

THE NAZI MARKETPLACE

Characterizing the role of the market in National Socialist ideology is
a difficult task. In the Third Reich, practical needs often overrode principle, political expediency frequently trumped economic considerations,
and Nazi ideologues worked side by side with pre-1933 economists who
never belonged to the party faithful. But in a setting where most policies
were enacted to serve the Volk, Nazi economic programs – marked by
the rejection of liberalism, state interventionism, autarky, the search for
full employment, and the desire to expand living space – were saturated
with ideology.[4]

In a sense, the market stood at the core of the Nazi utopian ideal.
Economists conceived of a German-dominated Europe, stretching from
the West to far into the Soviet Union, as one large marketplace, where
the exchange of goods and services would be regulated to the benefit
of the German Volk. Manufacturing, marketing, retailing, shopping, and
consuming would all take place in a vast realm where the economies of
individual nation-states would serve Germans in their goal of racial expansion. Within this European "large space economy" (*Grossraumwirtschaft*)
there were to be clear hierarchies. The racially superior country Germany
and those of Northwestern Europe would serve as the manufacturing

---

[4] Avraham Barkai, *Nazi Economics: Ideology, Theory, and Policy* (New Haven, CT: Yale
University Press, 1990), 243–49.

base, while the lesser peoples of Eastern Europe and the Soviet Union would provide foodstuffs and raw materials.[5]

Despite this racist and imperialist vision, which would propel Germany toward World War II, most prewar discussions of the market were, on their surface, more modest and more familiar. Nazi visions of market behavior were an amalgam of existing ideas and new priorities, and in crafting a commercial ideal, party leaders drew on long-standing philosophical and economic preoccupations. Voltaire had seen the market as a site of virtue, where the stultifying search for religious salvation (and its potential to lead to strife) was supplanted by the more pacific quest for wealth.[6] Adam Smith had seen self-interestedness in the marketplace as leading ultimately to the greater communal good, a point that Marx and Engels explicitly rejected.[7] In the more immediate German context, sociologist Max Weber had dismissed the classical liberal position that sought to maximize the happiness of individuals, arguing, in Jerry Z. Muller's words, that "the proper goal of the economy was the good of the German people (*Volk*), the pursuit of which would at times conflict with the interests of particular groups within society."[8]

Among Max Weber's contemporaries, the tension between the individual and the community found expression in Ferdinand Tönnies's famous distinction between "society" and "community" (*Gesellschaft* vs. *Gemeinschaft*).[9] The idea that modern capitalist society, with its hyperindividualist focus on monetary relations, had effaced the more affective ties of family and neighborhood resonated in Weimar Germany; conservative economists brought this tension to the fore in their critiques of both free-market capitalism and Marxism. For many of these writers, conceiving of the market – and the economy more broadly – as an expression of higher values offered a way beyond the economic self-interestedness of liberalism. Othmar Spann, who exercised great influence on Nazi economic theory, conceded that capitalism was the most productive system, but he bemoaned its "spiritual and moral" deficiencies.[10] As an alternative to purely materialist conceptions, Spann conceived of "the economy

[5] Alan S. Milward, *War, Economy, and Society, 1939–1945* (Berkeley: University of California Press, 1977), 8–14.
[6] Jerry Z. Muller, *The Mind and the Market: Capitalism in Modern European Thought* (New York: Knopf, 2002), 34–35.
[7] Ibid., 60–67, 181.
[8] Ibid., 233.
[9] Ferdinand Tönnies, *Gemeinschaft und Gesellschaft* (1887) [8th ed.] (Leipzig: Buske, 1935).
[10] Hauke Janssen, *Nationalökonomie und Nationalsozialismus: Die deutsche Volkswirtschaftslehre in den dreissiger Jahren* (Marburg: Metropolis, 1998), 107.

as a part of life" and "trade as an expression of the *Geist* (spirit)." His main intellectual goal was to determine how the economy was a key part of "human society."[11] Spann built upon the idea of the corporate state (*Ständestaat*), which considered economic actors not in their capacity as individuals but as members of a specific profession. In his ideas about the human dimensions of the economy, Spann echoed his fellow conservative economist Werner Sombart, who appealed to a "German socialism" that prioritized the nation's spiritual and economic health over the individual's.[12]

In drawing together a philosophy of the market, Hitler and his cohort called on this corporatism and antiliberal organicism but also soundly rejected the command economics of the Soviet Union. They tried to craft a third way that maintained the advantages of capitalism, such as the basic principles of supply and demand, but that jettisoned its negative manifestations, such as "Jewish" or "Marxist" materialism and bourgeois selfishness. With respect to commerce, we can locate three concepts that Nazi thinkers tried to recast and align with their racial ideology: competition, performance, and consumption. There are other, narrower themes one might consider when discussing commerce, such as pricing, wholesaling, retailing, distribution, consumer credit, and packaging. But in economic handbooks and periodicals, Nazi writers devoted an exceptional amount of space to these three words. The first of these, competition, was a source of much debate among modern economists, some of whom depicted it as a hallmark of liberalism that undermined social harmony. Thinkers on both the Left and Right condemned the cutthroat nature of capitalist competition and imagined more collectivist means of producing and distributing goods. Despite the omnipresence of their slogan "common good before self-interest" (*Gemeinnutz vor Eigennutz*) in the 1920s and 1930s, however, the Nazis conceived of private initiative, and by extension competition, as natural urges and as essential to Germany's economic recovery.[13] Railing against egoism in the marketplace did not mean denying people their competitive urges. Just as races and nations struggled for supremacy, so did individuals in all walks of life. This was certainly the case for businessmen and inventors, for whom the desire to innovate and to outperform a competitor led to newer products and,

[11] Ibid., 83.

[12] Ibid., 68–74; Werner Sombart, *Deutscher Sozialismus* (Charlottenburg: Buchholz & Weisswange, 1934).

[13] Karl Erich Kohlen, "Unternehmerinitiative als wirtschaftspolitische Forderung," *Wirtschaftspolitische Parole* 3, no. 14 (July 1938): 423–26; and Janssen, *Nationalökonomie*, 92.

ultimately, economic progress. According to Hans Peter Danielcik, a Nazi lawyer and head of the Hanseatic Federation of Commerce, Trade, and Industry (Hansabund für Gewerbe, Handel und Industrie), "[C]ompetition is essential to the National Socialist economy."[14] So too, argued other Nazi leaders, were private property and the quest for profit, which the Nazis defended both in theory and in practice.[15] This was by no means an endorsement of laissez-fairism, which Danielcik denounced as "the unlimited free play of forces"; competition instead had to be "orderly" and "fair" (*lauter*) and "not take on damaging forms."[16] Despite these provisos, the state was in no way abandoning market economics. Indeed, it forcefully acknowledged that private business interests and, at least in theory, supply and demand were essential to the economic and spiritual well-being of Germany.

This defense of economic competition was highly contentious, of course, for it touched on the party's wider views about the capitalist system and the role of large companies within it. In the 1920s and early 1930s, the National Socialist Party was internally divided over its stance toward capitalism, with the workers (represented by the Nazi Storm Troopers – SA) and so-called left-wing Nazis taking a harsher stance against big business than the more pragmatic leaders of the party.[17] While the party's 25 Points from 1920 had an anticapitalist thrust, Hitler came to understand that political success depended on not alienating the country's economic elite, which found the Left's attacks on private property and the language of class war deeply threatening. According to a Nazi economic newspaper from 1936, nobody would gain by "causing the businessman ... problems."[18] Rather than simply asserting an inclination toward big business, however, the Nazis were careful to portray competition as conducive to all forms of production. The competitive urge united

---

[14] Hans Peter Danielcik, "Neues Wettbewerbsrecht," *Die Deutsche Volkswirtschaft* [hereafter *DDV*] 4, no. 12 (April 1935)]: 385–87. On competition in the Nazi lexicon, see also Jan-Otmar Hesse, "Zur Semantik von Wirtschaftsordnung und Wettbewerb in nationalökonomischen Lehrbüchern der Zeit des Nationalsozialismus," in *Wirtschaftssteuerung durch Recht im Nationalsozialismus: Studien zur Entwicklung des Wirtschaftsrechts im Interventionsstaat des "Dritten Reichs,"* ed. Johannes Bähr and Ralf Banken (Frankfurt am Main: Vittorio Klostermann, 2006), 473–508.

[15] Christoph Buchheim and Jonas Scherner, "The Role of Private Property in the Nazi Economy: The Case of Industry," *Journal of Economic History,* 66, no. 2 (June 2006): 390–416.

[16] Danielcik, "Neues Wettbewerbsrecht," 386.

[17] See Peter D. Stachura, *Gregor Strasser and the Rise of Hitler* (London: Allen & Unwin, 1983).

[18] "Die Lage: Leistungsentfaltung," *DDV* 5, no. 15 (May 1936): 451–58.

big and small companies, which worked together as essential components of the völkisch economy.

Had they stopped here, the Nazis could have been criticized for adhering to essentially "bourgeois" economic ideas. After all, laws about honest competition had existed since the prior century, designed not to undermine but to prop up the existing economic order. The Nazis, therefore, wedded their idea of legitimate competition to a second, more ideologically rich concept, namely *Leistung* – "achievement" or "performance."[19] Here, again, the Nazis took a word from the liberal vocabulary and reworked it to serve their own purposes. The word "Leistung" was a common, if much debated, term among economists, referring to profit, to the total monetary value of a company's output, and to other measures of productivity.[20] It was also a stock phrase in commercial advertising, at once speaking to the individual desire to achieve at work and play and to Germans' long-standing understanding of their country's products as high performing.[21] In the 1930s and 1940s the Nazis kept these associations in tact, but they invested "Leistung" with ideological meaning. They acknowledged the natural urge to attain wealth and status through hard work and success – key tenets of the liberal order. But individual accomplishment had to be linked to the well-being of the nation and the race. "The existence of our Volk and our position in the world," wrote a leading Nazi economic periodical, "depends upon the blossoming of Leistung." In turn, "the restless exhaustion of the German Volk's talents and of all the energies of the German space" would produce a *Leistungsgemeinschaft*, or "achievement community." In contrast to the bourgeois *Leistungsgesellschaft*, or "achievement-oriented *society*," this community recognized the organic relationship between the various factions vying for success, whether they were employers and employees or manufacturers competing for a market share.[22] The achievement community, according to Nazi theorists,

[19] See "Persönlichkeit und Leistung," *Der Deutsche Unternehmer* 33, no. 1 (7 January 1934) [unpaginated]; and Carl Fluhme, "Leistungsgedanke und Leistungsfreude," *Mitteilungen der Kommission für Wirtschaftspolitik der NSDAP* 2, no. 14 (July 1937): 12–15.

[20] Theodore Beste, "Was ist Leistung in der Betriebswirtschaftslehre?" *Zeitschrift für Handelswissenschaftliche Forschung* 38, no. 1 (1944): 1–18.

[21] See chapter titled "Der Kampf um die beste Leistung" in Werner Sombart, *Der moderne Kapitalismus: Historisch–systematische Darstellung des gesamteuropäischen Wirtschaftslebens von seinen Anfängen bis zur Gegenwart* [1916] (Munich: DTV, 1987), 432–49. In this case Sombart is talking mostly about product performance.

[22] Hans Peter Danielcik, "Leistungsgemeinschaft als Rechtsprinzip," *DDV* 4, no. 22 (August 1935): 704–5. See also Georg Seebauer, "Leistungssteigerung als Kampfmittel," *Vierjahresplan* 3, no. 18 (September 1939): 1064–67.

recognized – indeed embraced – individual initiative and the will to power. But what ultimately mattered was a "communal sense that classes and professions are with and for each other."[23]

It is important to note the intellectual progeny of these ideas. In many ways they were in keeping with long-standing German views about the individual's relationship to the state. In particular, Hegel recognized the ethical dimensions of the economy, and he granted the state the power not only to regulate the flow of goods and services, but also to make possible and protect individual freedom. He saw an organic relationship between human autonomy and national authority, and he defended private property, economic efficiency, and governmental welfare as morally indispensable.[24] Derivations of this "Hegelian" economic philosophy could be found across the German political spectrum; it endowed not only conservatism, but also liberalism, with a larger communitarian and statist component than was present in the Anglo-American world.[25]

Ideas about Leistung, therefore, resonated with large sections of the German intellectual elite. But Nazi thinkers felt compelled to explain it in especially clear terms to businessmen, who were accustomed to defending private initiative in less soaring language. According to Nazi economist Heinrich Hunke, the industrialist had an essential role in the "conquering of new performance territory" (*Leistungsraum*), in which all Germans would exercise their right to work according to their natural abilities. In this struggle, industrialists, wrote Hunke, would serve as inventors, discoverers, organizers, and teachers. As "pioneers of new markets," they would invest all of their personality and "creative initiative" in the defense of the commonweal.[26] In keeping with this ideal, the German Labor Front (Deutsche Arbeitsfront – DAF) declared a "performance struggle for German companies" in 1936 and henceforth awarded the title of National Socialist Model Factory to those companies demonstrating the performance principle and a commitment to Nazi ideals. Clean and well-lighted premises, a well-ordered company hierarchy, happy employees, and high-quality products could warrant this commendation, which the regime bestowed on scores of Germany's small and large firms, from

---

[23] "Die Lage: Leistungsentfaltung," 457–58.

[24] Wilfried Ver Eecke, *Ethical Dimensions of the Economy: Making Use of Hegel and the Concepts of Public and Merit Goods* (Berlin: Springer, 2008), 3, 13–25.

[25] On liberalism, the state, and the economy, see James J. Sheehan, *German Liberalism in the Nineteenth Century* (Chicago: University of Chicago Press, 1978), 86–88.

[26] Heinrich Hunke, "Aufgabe, Weg und Zukunft des deutschen Unternehmertums," *DDV* 6, no. 5 (February 1937): 167–69.

Dr. Oetker food products, Berliner Kindl beer, and Siemens electronics to the BMW, Daimler-Benz, and Bosch automotive companies.[27]

It is important to realize that race underpinned all of this language about competition and achievement, and one cannot understand the Nazis' conceptions of the marketplace without recognizing the regime's attempts to root out biological undesirables. The Nazi leadership justified its eugenics policies, forced sterilizations, and persecution of "asocials" and "community aliens" in part by referencing their seeming inability to play a constructive role in society – to compete and achieve in social Darwinian terms. Moreover, when the Nazis proclaimed their support of "performance competition" but not "speculative competition,"[28] they were tapping into a common association of exploitative behaviors with Jewry. The public would have no trouble conjuring images of money lending, usury, and other "Jewish" misdeeds. According to Avraham Barkai, the Nazi Party, under the sway of economist Gottfried Feder, relied on a basic gimmick: "equate finance capital with international Jewish capital, and the social unrest simmering in large sections of the public would naturally turn to anti-Semitism."[29] More than simply a strategy, however, the Nazis' persistent equation of economic misbehavior with Jewish financial power was directly linked to a basic racial understanding of the Volksgemeinschaft. The economy of the Third Reich would be purged not only of Jewish behaviors, whether "speculative," "individualist," "bourgeois," "liberal," or "egotistical." It was to be purged of Jews.

It is worth noting that these ideas of achievement and competition are not just incidental motifs culled from disparate National Socialist thinkers. Rather, they saturated speeches, proclamations, and professional and party publications in the Third Reich. Legal journals parsed Nazi dictates about proper competition; trade publications discussed how to apply Nazi rules about Leistung to a particular branch of industry; and the journals *Der Deutsche Volkswirt* (The German economist) and

---

[27] On the granting of this honor, see correspondences and declarations in NS 22/778, Bundesarchiv Berlin (hereafter BAB), e.g., "Auszeichnung 'Nationalsozialistischer Musterbetrieb,'" 26 August 1936. See also Matthias Frese, "Vom 'NS-Musterbetrieb' zum 'Kriegsmusterbetrieb': Zum Verhältnis von Deutscher Arbeitsfront und Grossindustrie, 1936–1944," in *Der Zweite Weltkrieg: Analysen, Grundzüge, Forschungsbilanz*, ed. Wolfgang Michalka (Munich: Piper, 1989), 382–401. For the example of one firm, see Rüdiger Jungbluth, *Die Oetkers: Geschäfte und Geheimnisse der bekanntesten Wirtschaftsdynastie Deutschlands* (Frankfurt am Main: Campus, 2004), 153.
[28] "Leistungswettbewerb," DDV 4, no. 18 (June 1935): 562.
[29] Barkai, *Nazi Economics*, 23.

FIGURE 1. "There's no place here for the Jewish method!" declared a Nazi magazine, as it touted the successful building of "the first truly German economy." "We're rid of him!" (the Jew). (*Wirtschaftspolitische Parole* 4, no. 1 [January 1939]: back cover.)

the more wide-ranging *Deutsche Zukunft* (The German future) became forums for economists to espouse the regime's ideas about performance.[30] The Nazis' Institute for Economic Propaganda (Institut für Deutsche Wirtschaftspropaganda) took the regime's ideas to trade fairs and exhibitions,[31] district economic leaders received a newsletter updating them on the regime's prescriptions,[32] and Nazi Party members subscribed to the bimonthly publication *Wirtschaftspolitische Parole* (Economic-political watchwords), which promoted a crudely racial understanding of the economy. Published by Bernhard Köhler, head of the Nazi Party Commission for Economic Policy, the latter journal interspersed pictures and charts illustrating the Nazis' economic achievements with articles about consumption, performance, the need for "living space" in Europe and overseas, and diatribes against Jews and "Jewish" forms of economic activity. The cover of each issue carried an inspiring quote from Hitler about the productive capacities of the German people and the promise of a glorious economic future. And dozens of illustrations contrasted the Depression era economy, run by grotesque Jewish capitalists, to the growing material comfort of Aryans under Hitler.[33]

Perhaps the most important vehicle for the promotion of the regime's commercial vision was the semiofficial Nazi business journal *Die Deutsche Volkswirtschaft* (The German economy – *DDV*). Founded in 1932, *DDV*'s primary purpose, according to Nazi economist and parliamentarian Carl Lüer, was to "decisively influence economic-political discussions according to National Socialist principles."[34] The editor of the paper was Heinrich Hunke, who by the late 1930s had, according to Harold James, become "the most influential of National Socialist economic theorists."[35] Hunke was a former Nazi Reichstag deputy, adviser to

---

[30] See, e.g., Hans Culemann, "Die Bedeutung der Imperativform in der Werbung und ihre Unterscheidung von der Tatsachenbehauptung," *Deutsche Juristen-Zeitung* 40, no. 21 (1935): 1280–82; Culemann, "Wie darf ich werben?" *Licht und Lampe* 1 (1935): 53–54; Karl Guth, "Marktordnungsgrundsätze der Reichsgruppe Industrie," *Deutsche Volkswirt* 9, no. 38 (21 June 1935): 1763–65; and "Wirtschaft unter neuer Führung: Das 'Gesetz zur organischen Wirtschaftsordnung'," *Deutsche Zukunft* 2, no. 11 (18 March 1934): 111.

[31] See propaganda ministry report on the institute, written to the Berlin police, 12 May 1936, R55/354, BAB.

[32] *Der Gauwirtschaftsberater.*

[33] See, e.g., Bernhard Köhler, "Jüdische Wirtschaft," *Mitteilungen der Kommission für Wirtschaftspolitik der NSDAP* 1, no. 6 (August 1936): 2–8; and Carl Fluhme, "Die Jüdische Methode," *Wirtschaftspolitische Parole* 2, no. 20 (October 1937): 10–16.

[34] "5 Jahre 'Die Deutsche Volkswirtschaft,'" *DDV* 6, no. 1 (January 1937): 17–19.

[35] Harold James, *The Deutsche Bank and the Nazi Economic War Against the Jews* (Cambridge: Cambridge University Press, 2001), 30–31.

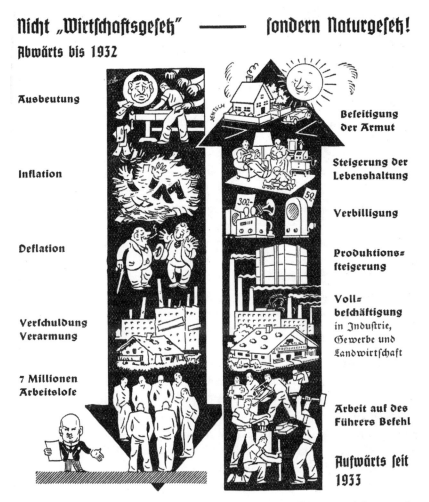

FIGURE 2. "Downward until 1933 – upward since 1933." Image celebrating the changes in Germany in the five years since Hitler had come to power. "Jewish-capitalist" exploitation, poverty, and joblessness had given way to a rising standard of living, increased production, cheaper goods, and full employment "on order of the Führer." (*Wirtschaftspolitische Parole* 2, no. 22 [November 1937]: 7.)

the district economic chamber in Berlin, honorary professor at the Berlin Technical College, and the Nazi Party's future point man on the Deutsche Bank board of managing directors from 1943 to 1945.[36] He was also the future deputy director and president of the Nazis' Advertising Council,

[36] Janssen, *Nationalökonomie*, 576.

which, as will see, indicates the importance of marketing within the Nazi economic vision.[37]

From its beginning in 1932 to its demise in 1945, *DDV* served as, in the words of Hjalmar Schacht, economics minister and Reichsbank president, a "comrade-in-arms" in Germany's struggle for its "social existence." The journal hammered home the regime's understanding of the economy as the site of material and spiritual renewal. Blanketing its pages were disquisitions on the "struggle for achievement" (*Leistungskampf*), the "triumph of achievement" (*Triumph der Leistung*), and the relationship between personal happiness and the "will to achieve" (*Leistungswille*).[38] Editor Hunke's and other economic leaders' meditations on the meaning of the Nazi revolution were juxtaposed with reflections on the American economy under Franklin Roosevelt, the search for living space, progress reports on the economic campaign against Jews, and more sober-minded analyses of business trends. Finally, the newspaper devoted much space to the third feature of the Nazis' commercial vision – consumption.

VISIONS OF CONSUMPTION

In the Nazis' racist and nationalist economic discourse, consumption played a key role. With the rise of mass society, the provision of goods and services to an ever-larger public became of the utmost social and political importance. Widespread discussions about "the masses" and their political and economic power greatly influenced party leaders, who recognized that a dictatorship forged in the depths of the Great Depression could maintain legitimacy only if it provided for the population's material needs. To the regime, consumption had both practical and nonmaterial merits. In a speech to the National Socialist Factory Cell Organization (Nationalsozialistische Betriebszellenorganisation) in March 1933, Hitler spoke of consumption in sanguinary terms. "It is not enough to give a fresh start to production," Hitler declared. "But one must develop consumption power. Just as for a time too much blood was pumped into German economic life from abroad, so much blood has been

---

[37] On Hunke's career and work with the Advertising Council, see Pamela E. Swett, "Preparing for Victory: Heinrich Hunke, the Nazi Werberat, and West German Prosperity," *Central European History* 42, no. 4 (December 2009): 675–707.

[38] For the terms "Leistungskampf" and "Leistungswille," see "Die Lage: Lebensfreude und Leistungswille," *DDV* 6, no. 32 (November 1937): 1071–72; for the latter term see also "Triumph der Leistung," *DDV* 6, no. 14 (May 1937): 455.

FIGURE 3. Window-shopping on Tauentzienstrasse, Berlin, 1938. (172 412;. courtesy of Landesarchiv Berlin.)

drawn off that the circulation has been stopped."[39] Not only did domestic consumption fuel Germany's economy; Germans' "joy in life" depended on their access to material goods. According to Nazi economist Bruno Kiesewetter, people had a "right to consume" just as they had a "right to work." Consumption was about staking a "claim to the enjoyment of all goods produced in the economy."[40]

If the Nazis asserted people's right to consume all goods produced, they did so with some trepidation. Sociologist Thorstein Veblen had famously bemoaned conspicuous consumption in 1899, and the Nazis shared a fear of overindulgence.[41] In the 1920s they adopted essentially

[39] Speech to the National Socialist Factory Cell Organization, 1 March 1933, excerpted in Norman H. Baynes, ed., *The Speeches of Adolf Hitler* [vol. 2: April 1922–August 1939] (Oxford: Oxford University Press, 1942), 829–30.

[40] Bruno Kiesewetter, "Kartell, Marktordnung, Recht auf Verbrauch," *DDV* 6, no. 17 (June 1936): 536–38.

[41] Thorstein Veblen, *The Theory of the Leisure Class* (New York: Macmillan, 1912), 66–101.

an anticonsumption stance, seeing it as fostering cosmopolitan distractions from higher commitments to the state and the leader. This hostility was greatly tempered by 1933, especially when the regime realized that high levels of consumption might bolster Germany's economic recovery, but the party still warned against treating consumption as "an end in itself." Nor should consumption take the form of "wasteful spending."[42] Rather, it was to serve a higher purpose, namely the enrichment of the Volk during its struggle for global and racial dominance. In this respect, goods and services had a national, even moral, rationale. Party leaders did not deny the dangers inherent in the homogenization of tastes or in the "creation of needs" fostered by modern marketing. But they recognized that they presided over an advanced economy whose economic strength required a vibrant sphere of consumer activity. While Veblen had, in historian Lisa Tiersten's words, tied "the advent of the modern market to moral decline," the Nazis sought to link the market to moral rehabilitation.[43]

National Socialism was hardly the only political movement to explore the implications of consumption. By virtue of their critical stance toward capitalism, interwar socialists and communists also saw consumption as potentially diverting workers from their historical mission.[44] Many bourgeois commentators also shared the concern that consumption was distracting and spiritually damaging. During the Third Republic, French commentators saw a hyperindividualist consumer marketplace as harmful to republican virtues and civic life. But they also considered commerce a source of wealth and prestige.[45] In the United States, Progressive Era reformers likewise worried about the effects of mass merchandising on product quality, and local business interests feared the power of large retailers. Both, however, appreciated the advantages of easy access to goods and services.[46] Finally, in the 1930s Roosevelt's reliance on Keynesian pump priming was a formal acknowledgment that consumer demand represented the American economy's salvation.[47]

---

[42] Kiesewetter, "Kartell, Marktordnung, Recht auf Verbrauch," 538.

[43] Lisa Tiersten, *Marianne in the Market: Envisioning Consumer Society in Fin-de-Siècle France* (Berkeley: University of California Press, 2001), 9.

[44] Peter N. Stearns, *Consumerism in World History: The Global Transformation of Desire* (London: Routledge, 2001), 64.

[45] Tiersten, *Marianne in the Market*, 6.

[46] Susan Strasser, "Customer to Consumer: The New Consumption in the Progressive Era," *OAH Magazine of History* 13, no. 3 (Spring 1999): 10–14.

[47] Lizabeth Cohen, "The New Deal State and the Making of Citizen Consumers," in *Getting and Spending: European and American Consumer Societies in the Twentieth Century*,

Whatever concerns about its corrosive effects, National Socialism thus shared with other movements and ideologies a recognition of mass consumption's appeal and its potential dangers. Gemany's devastating military loss in 1918, the violence of the postwar years, and the particularly harsh privations of the Depression gave consumption a symbolic and practical urgency in the Third Reich. The regime therefore trumpeted its ability to provide for the populace and reminded Germans of the hardships they had suffered on the home front in the Great War, especially during the "hunger winter" of 1916–17. During World War I, the German state had forcefully addressed the demands of the unhappy citizenry, but its responses were piecemeal and disorganized, and by 1918 the government could no longer stave off revolution and military collapse.[48] Before and during World War II, the Nazis worked to avoid a repeat of the food crises that had led to long lines and discontent during the naval blockade of Germany. In his electoral campaigns in the early 1930s, Hitler built his vision for Germany not just on an industry-driven economic recovery, but also on the promise to better Germans' lives after the shocks of war, inflation, and depression.[49]

In the minds of Nazi Party leaders, consumption would lead not only to the fulfillment of basic needs but to the flowering of a material-rich society. "The only purpose of technical and economic progress," wrote Gustav Plum, who analyzed *DDV*'s balance sheets, "is optimizing the lives of the people."[50] A key measure of Leistung, therefore, was the regime's ability to raise Germans' standard of living, despite the country's relative dearth of raw materials, and eventually catch up to and surpass that of Americans.[51] The propaganda ministry, the economics ministry, and publications like *DDV* kept constant watch on consumer prices and levels of consumption in Germany compared with those in other advanced countries.[52] They also acknowledged the emergence of a new political and economic force – "the consumer."

ed. Susan Strasser, Charles McGovern, and Matthias Judt (Washington, DC: German Historical Institute/Cambridge University Press, 1998), 111–26.

[48] Belinda J. Davis, *Home Fires Burning: Food, Politics, and Everyday Life in World War I Berlin* (Chapel Hill: University of North Carolina Press, 2000), 2.

[49] On Hitler's appeal during the 1930 and 1932 elections, see Ian Kershaw, *The "Hitler Myth": Image and Reality in the Third Reich* (Oxford: Oxford University Press, 1987), 13–48.

[50] Gustav Plum, "'Kraft durch Freude': Wirtschaftspolitisch gesehen," *DDV* 4, no. 13 (May 1935): 404–7.

[51] See "Triumph der Leistung"; and Adam Tooze, *Wages of Destruction: The Making and Breaking of the Nazi Economy* (New York: Viking, 2006), 138–47.

[52] See, e.g., Alfred Jacobs, "Preisgefüge und Verbrauch," *DDV* 6, no. 32 (November 1937) 1081–82.

It was not a given that the consumer would play a central role in Nazi economic visions. Historians have emphasized the producerist basis of the German economy and Germans' "Old World" suspicion of American consumer capitalism, which supposedly broke down hierarchies of taste as it fed the public shoddy, mass-produced goods.[53] But despite European elites' ambivalence about mass consumption, in the 1920s the consumer became a political force in his or her own right, as demands for products and services dictated economic policies that no longer spoke to a narrow middle class with superior means.[54] By the 1930s, therefore, Nazi economists took it for granted that consumers had both obligations and privileges in the marketplace. Unlike in the United States, however, these "citizen consumers" were defined more by their duties than their rights.[55] As members of the biological whole, consumers had to behave with a mind to their neighbors and fellow citizens, for damage to a single organ could cause harm to the entire racial body. As the Nazis put Germany on a war footing in the late 1930s, "doing without" – without favorite brands, without a bounty of choices – became an expression of patriotism. Hoarding was a violation, greed was frowned upon, and patience in an economy of scarcity was celebrated. As we will see, the regime could not reconcile the dream of creating a Nazi consumer economy with the push toward war. Any positive obligations associated with consumption, such as sharing individual wealth with needier members of the Volk, were eventually trumped by a negative responsibility to temper consumption habits altogether.

Consumers had fundamental responsibilities to the Volksgemeinschaft, but this did not obviate their claim to certain rights vis-à-vis the state. For one, "the protection of the consumer," wrote *DDV*, demanded a "socially

[53] Victoria de Grazia, *Irresistible Empire: America's Advance through Twentieth Century Europe* (Cambridge. MA: Harvard University Press, 2005), 4.

[54] On the political importance of the consumer in 1920s Germany, see Claudius Torp, "Das Janusgesicht der Weimarer Konsumpolitik," in *Die Konsumgesellschaft in Deutschland, 1890–1990: Ein Handbuch*, ed. Heinz-Gerhard Haupt and Claudius Torp (Frankfurt am Main: Campus, 2009), 250–67.

[55] On the concept of citizen consumers see Lizabeth Cohen, *A Consumers' Republic: The Politics of Mass Consumption in Postwar America* (New York: Knopf, 2003), 18–19; and Frank Trentmann, "Bread, Milk and Democracy: Consumption and Citizenship in Twentieth-Century Britain," in *The Politics of Consumption: Material Culture and Citizenship in Europe and America*, ed. Martin Daunton and Matthew Hilton (Oxford: Berg, 2001), 129–63. On citizenship and consumption see also Martin Daunton and Matthew Hilton, "Material Politics: An Introduction," in Daunton and Hilton, *Politics of Consumption*, 1–32.

just distribution of products in limited supply," which only a managed economy could provide.[56] In particular, the Nazis saw as their responsibility the provision of foodstuffs and other basic necessities and the regulation of their prices.[57] The regime was not only responsible for maintaining a basic standard of living; it was also obliged to shield consumers from a host of threats: faulty merchandise, wasteful products, manipulative ad campaigns, and harmful behaviors like smoking.[58] If one were to identify the real danger lurking in the consumer economy, however, it was the Jewish businessman. The Nazis saw the removal of Jews from face-to-face commercial transactions as one of its highest obligations, and the 1 April 1933 boycott of Jewish businesses was premised in part on this desire to mark and punish a corrosive force that existed on the ground level of society. Aryanization too was not only about an abstract removal of "Jewish" economic power, but about the actual transfer of capital to the racially worthy. In the Third Reich, the very acts of buying and selling, owning and consuming had an explicitly racial component. Nazi consumption policy was not only geared toward providing wealth and happiness to the Volk; it also was about declaring who had the right to function in the economy at all. Once Jews were gone, "the marketplace," to borrow Lisa Tiersten's words with reference to France, "could metamorphose from a destabilizing social force into one for the social good."[59]

On a superficial level, consumption represented an uncomplicated feature of the Nazi ideology; the goal was to increase the purchasing power of Aryans and take away that of non-Aryans. However, this vision was always tempered by social and economic reality. In the Third Reich the politics of consumption were marked by, in Hartmut Berghoff's words, "the constant juxtaposition of enticement and deprivation."[60] On the one hand, certain sectors seen as politically vital – such as radios and movies, housing and furniture, and telephones – saw increased sales; the state's support of mass entertainment and its pro-family schemes allowed these

[56] Dr. Völz, "Vebrauchsregelung durch Marktordnung," *DDV* 7, no. 8 (March 1938): 277–79.
[57] On food politics in the Third Reich, see Uwe Spiekermann, "Vollkorn für die Führer: Zur Geschichte der Vollkornbrotpolitik im Dritten Reich," *1999: Zeitschrift für Sozialgeschichte des 20. und 21. Jahrhunderts* 16, no. 1 (March 2001): 91–128.
[58] Consumers also had to be protected from dangerous ad inserts, such as ones that contained play ammunition that children could shoot at each other: "Gefährliche Werbeartikel," *Wirtschaftswerbung* 2, no. 10 (May–June 1934): 68–69.
[59] Tiersten, *Marianne in the Market*, 9.
[60] Hartmut Berghoff, "Enticement and Deprivation: The Regulation of Consumption in Pre-War Nazi Germany," in Daunton and Hilton, *Politics of Consumption*, 165–84.

industries to flourish. On the other hand, in other sectors the promise of plentiful goods was never met by reality.[61] The latter case is exemplified by the Volkswagen project, which dangled the hope of mass motorization over the population but never produced a civilian vehicle until after 1945. Consumption suffered under the reality that Nazi economic policy was overstretched; providing jobs, building loyalty, safeguarding precious raw materials, and preparing for German hegemony in Europe took precedence over providing bountiful consumer opportunities. Managed consumption in the service of war, rather than ever-expanding access to the joys of material goods, was the reality for most Germans in the Third Reich.[62]

Given these contradictions, the Nazi regime could not simply pretend that heightened military production had no effect on the civilian economy. Therefore, it was intent on preparing the public for sacrifice. While price freezes were initiated to protect against inflation, the Nazi government asked companies, advertisers, and consumers to do their part in regulating themselves within an economy of scarcity. They drew upon the language of household rationalization, which had been common in the 1920s, and applied it to the regime's immediate political aims.[63] In 1936 the National Committee for Economic Enlightenment (Reichsausschuss für Volkswirtschaftliche Aufklärung – RVA) led Germans in a "Fight Against Waste" (*Kampf dem Verderb*), whereby housewives would learn to correctly store fruits, vegetables, and other perishables during the winter.[64] Other state-run campaigns throughout the late 1930s provided colorful brochures, flyers, and films designed to regulate private behavior. Saving soap, battling garden and household pests, and washing laundry correctly all became the business of the government in its attempt to

[61] Hartmut Berghoff, "Methoden der Verbrauchslenkung im Nationalsozialismus: Konsumpolitische Normensetzung zwischen totalitärem Anspruch und widerspenstiger Praxis," in *Wirtschaftskontrolle und Recht in der nationalsozialisten Dikatur*, ed. Dieter Gosewinkel (Frankfurt: Vittorio Kostermann, 2005), 281–316.

[62] On managed consumption in the Third Reich, see Dirk Reinhardt, *Von der Reklame zum Marketing: Geschichte der Wirtschaftswerbung in Deutschland* (Berlin: Akademie, 1993), 446; and Uwe Westphal, *Werbung im Dritten Reich* (Berlin: Transit, 1989), 137.

[63] See Mary Nolan, *Visions of Modernity: American Business and the Modernization of Germany* (Oxford: Oxford University Press, 1994), 217–26.

[64] On this and other measures see Wolfgang König, *Volkswagen, Volksempfänger, Volksgemeinschaft: "Volksprodukte" im Dritten Reich – Vom Scheitern einer nationalsozialistischen Konsumgesellschaft* (Paderborn: Schöningh: 2004), 137–50; Jill Stephenson, *Hitler's Home Front: Württemberg under the Nazis* (London: Hambledon Continuum, 2006), 166; and Nancy Reagin, *Sweeping the German Nation: Domesticity and National Identity in Germany, 1870–1945* (Cambridge: Cambridge University Press, 2007), 152.

save precious resources.[65] The latter campaign consumed the energies of private companies, Reich business groups, the German Women's Bureau (Deutsches Frauenwerk – DF), and advertisers, who calculated to the exact reichsmark how much clothes damaged by poor laundering habits cost the national economy.[66]

After 1936, when the Four Year Plan became the face of the German economy, inculcating a correct consumption sensibility into the German population became a major propaganda undertaking, one that involved economists, publicists, and large sections of the government and the party. Messages of frugality and self-sufficiency were taken to schools, exhibitions, and "educational shows" throughout the country.[67] The official Four Year Plan magazine complemented *DDV* as a major purveyor of Nazi economic ideals, and in this literature business leaders and consumers became coequals in the struggle for autarky.[68] The language of sacrifice and deferred gratification saturated both public and private space. Admonishments against profligacy arrived in the mail, were displayed in shops, and adorned kitchen walls. And the quest for new sources of fat, oil, and raw materials became a national fixation. German ships embarked with great fanfare to the Arctic and Antarctic in search of whale oil.[69] Large restaurants were ordered to gather and dry used coffee grounds, after which fat, wax, resin, and cellulose could be extracted and reused in industrial production.[70] And Germans adjusted their diets to include healthier and less resource intensive foods, like whole-grain bread.[71] In short, the Four Year Plan was a massive PR effort on behalf of proper consumption. While the regime always envisioned a future of affluence, in the short term righteousness would be found in struggle, not enrichment.

---

[65] Westphal, *Werbung im Dritten Reich*, 142–45.

[66] Aufklärungs-Aktion des Waschmittel-Einzelhandels über das Thema "Wasche Wäsche Weiss". Vortragsmanuskript für die Amtsträger der Fachgruppen, 18 July 1939, R5002/26, BAB.

[67] A. Hetzel, "Austellungswesen im Dienste des Vierjahresplanes," *Vierjahresplan* 4 (1940): 946.

[68] See, e.g., "Nationalsozialistische Verbrauchslenkung," *Vierjahresplan* 1, no. 3 (March 1937): 159–60.

[69] See, e.g., Wilhelm Schultze, "Strukturwandel des Walfangs," *Deutsche Volkswirt* 13, no. 15 (1938–39): 718–22; and Nicolaus Peters, ed., *Der neue deutsche Walfang: Ein praktisches Handbuch seiner geschichtlichen, rechtlichen, naturwissenschaftlichen und technischen Grundlagen* (Hamburg: "Hansa" Deutsche Nautische Zeitschrift Carl Schroedter, 1938).

[70] "Kaffeesatz und Vierjahresplan," *HAG-Post* 9 (4 December 1937): 4–5, box 1937 (0096 4370), Kaffee HAG archive, Kraft Foods Deutschland archive, Bremen [hereafter KFA].

[71] Spiekermann, "Vollkorn für die Führer."

LEGISLATING COMMERCIAL MORALITY

The Nazis' policies toward consumption were marked by a basic tension. On the one hand, the regime saw the accumulation of material goods as a way of solidifying the Volksgemeinschaft and enabling German power to spread. On the other hand, preparing for war meant that this goal was constantly undermined; the regime had to preach self-denial even as it promised indulgence. Despite disadvantaging the consumer sector, however, the government in prewar Germany counseled against economic asceticism, realizing that the country's recovery depended on healthy commercial exchange. The regime still saw the market as a vibrant place where consumers and producers – inspired by the language of performance competition – interacted and bettered their personal lives and the public weal. But it was intent on regulating potential abuses within the marketplace.

This section focuses on the state's attempts to regulate commercial behavior, particularly marketing, and it highlights the challenges the regime encountered as it tried to implement the Nazi commercial vision. Imposing rules about market behavior proved difficult because Nazi authorities could not plan for every contingency in the world of commerce. Nor were they themselves clear about which marketing practices were ideologically proper. Juggling the interests of small and big business, determining whether a product was "German" or "foreign," and regulating the use of race in marketing proved to be tricky undertakings.

As much as the Nazis understood the importance of commerce, they also understood that it could be a source of great danger. These were not just symbolic perils, centered on "Jewish" forms of capitalism. They were also manifested in the damage commercial culture wrought on cities and the countryside. The Weimar years had witnessed dizzying displays of commerce: bright advertisements bathed streets with light; hawkers and peddlers accosted pedestrians with sales pitches; consumers jostled each other to purchase sale items before they were gone; and billboards spread into rural settings.[72] The rapid developments of consumer capitalism produced a nervousness and disorientation that cultural critics on the Left and Right bemoaned.[73] Weimar's urban authorities were intent

---

[72] Molly J. Loberg, "Berlin Streets: Politics, Commerce and Crowds, 1918–1938" (Ph.D. diss., Princeton University, 2006), 70–117.

[73] See Anton Kaes, Martin Jay, and Edward Dimendberg, eds., *The Weimar Republic Sourcebook* (Berkeley: University of California Press, 1994), esp. 655–72.

on rooting out decadent forms of commercial exchange, and upon taking power the Nazis continued this drive to clean up the streets. They concerned themselves not only with advertisements, storefronts, and fairs (the subjects of the next chapter), however, but also with less visual forms of commerce. With respect to producing, marketing, and selling, the regime tried to uphold practices that would support fair competition among producers and allow a transparency for consumers.

The Nazis did not need to invent new categories of commercial morality. Many existing ideas about business ethics fit in well with their desire to tame egregious forms of capitalism and root out abuses. The regime was guided by a general rule that commercial behaviors could not violate the sensibilities of the public. Nazi law drew upon the existing concept of "common decency" or "public morality" (*gute Sitten*), which was inherited from Roman law and found expression in paragraph 826, among others, of the 1900 German Civil Code. It mandated that "whoever causes damage to another on account of behavior that violates public morality is responsible for compensation."[74] What constituted public morality, however, was open to debate and remains so: Is it a legal morality, a Christian morality, or an absolutist human morality?[75] Is a violation of common decency necessarily a violation of the law, or vice versa? In 1901 a German court tried to offer guidance by defining public morality as "the sense of decency of all proper and right-thinking people."[76] This clarification, however, was barely more precise than the original wording, and its vagueness allowed ample room for interpretation under National Socialism. Indeed, after 1933 decency was no longer informed by bourgeois norms or German customs but by race.

When it came to commercial activity, the concept of public morality was given more specificity in the 1909 law against unfair competition (*Gesetz gegen den unlauteren Wettbewerb*), which defined the numerous ways that a company or employer could violate common decency, such as producing comparative advertisements that misrepresented

---

[74] See par. 826, Bürgerliches Gesetzbuch vom. 18 August 1896. http://lexetius.com/BGB/826 (accessed 24 June 2009).

[75] On the history and meaning of "gute Sitten," see Konstantin Smitis, *Gute Sitten und Ordre Public: Ein kritischer Beitrag zur Anwendung des par. 138 Abs. BGB* (Marburg: Elwert, 1960), 3–9; and Alfons Kraft, *Interessenabwägung und gute Sitten im Wettbewerbsrecht* (Munich: Beck, 1963), 134–38.

[76] Rudolf Callmann, *Der Unlautere Wettbewerb: Kommentar zum Gesetz gegen den unlauteren Wettbewerb mit Notverordnung vom 9. März 1932 und zu dem materiellerechtlichen Vorschriften des Gesetzes zum Schutze der Warenbezeichnungen* (Mannheim: J. Bensheimer, 1932), 47.

a competitor's goods, betraying trade secrets, and making false claims about a product.[77] The law was amended in 1932, and the Nazis kept it in operation. They even revisited it in 1935 and added new emendations and ordinances. They closed loopholes, limited retailers' giveaway of free gifts, and curtailed the use of product rebates. They inveighed against product dumping, selling below cost, and various forms of predatory pricing, and they put an end to white sales and other special events when products were deeply discounted.[78]

What was the motivation behind these changes? A number of Nazi actions were justified on the grounds that they prevented unfair competition and protected public morals. But they were also enacted to force commerce along ideological lines. When the Nazis shut down local newspapers that did not support the regime, they did so on the grounds that they were eliminating "unhealthy competition."[79] In 1933 the government introduced licensing agreements and corporatist arrangements to the recording industry ostensibly to protect it against unhealthy competition, but the new regulations were really about controlling all forms of aural media.[80] Ironically state interference in the economy – shuttering businesses, regulating prices, establishing cartels and monopolies – was justified in the name of *facilitating* competition. The Nazis used old language about clean forms of marketing and retailing, which had been designed to broaden competition, to shut out economic forces that it deemed politically dangerous.

Even the assault on Jewish businesses was justified in part by the belief that Jews were practitioners of unfair competition. Jews' tendencies toward profiteering and deceitfulness, and their leaching off of "productive labor," could manifest themselves in the larger system of exploitative capitalism and in everyday violations of business norms. If Jews advertised their businesses using a professional title, like "attorney," that had been stripped from them in 1933, they were accused of practicing

---

[77] For the latest version of the law from December 2008, see http://bundesrecht.juris.de/ uwg_2004/BJNR141400004.html#BJNR141400004BJNG000100000 (accessed 24 June 2009).

[78] Matthias Rücker, *Wirtschaftswerbung unter Nationalsozialismus: Rechtliche Ausgestaltung der Werbung und Tätigkeit des Werberats der deutschen Wirtschaft* (Frankfurt am Main: Peter Lang, 2000), 72; and Danielcik, "Neues Wettbewerbsrecht." For protests against these decisions see, e.g., R3101/13827 and surrounding files, BAB.

[79] Corey Ross, *Media and the Making of Modern Germany: Mass Communications, Society, and Politics from the Empire to the Third Reich* (Oxford: Oxford University Press, 2008), 299.

[80] Ibid., 286.

unfair competition.[81] When a Jewish company produced a badly worded advertisement, it was threatened with prosecution for violating the statute against unfair competition.[82] Phrases like "unfair competition" and "unhealthy business methods" were used interchangeably or in conjunction with "racial defilement," "treachery," or "damaging the health of the Volk."[83] By drawing on standard commercial language to attack Jews, the regime was adding a legal veneer to its extralegal actions.

Preventing unfair competition was a major component of the state's larger attempt to sanitize commerce in the Third Reich. It dovetailed with the Nazis' desire to limit rapacious forms of big capital and level the playing field for shopkeepers and small and medium-sized producers; this had been a key goal of the National Socialist Party since its inception. The May 1933 Law for the Protection of the Retail Trade, therefore, banned the new establishment of chain stores and single-price shops, and it prohibited existing businesses from adding new lines of merchandise.[84] In particular, the law targeted the department store – the ultimate symbol of exploitative Jewish capital.[85] Beginning with its 1920 platform, the Nazis had railed against department stores as the embodiment of "big capitalism" and exploitative commerce. Emporiums like Tietz, Karstadt, Wertheim, and Berlin's Kaufhaus des Westens (KaDeWe) were owned and managed primarily by Jews and thus were coded as dangerous.[86] As part of solving the "department store problem" and in keeping with the party program, the state also prohibited the existence of independent shops within department stores and closed their cafeterias and bars. By removing nonessential, "foreign bodies" from the department stores, the regime hoped to divert customers to independently run restaurants.[87] The Nazis also attacked food cooperatives, which they saw as unfair conglomerations of power at the expense of the shopkeeper.[88]

---

[81] Dirk van Laak, "'Arisierung' und Judenpolitik im 'Dritten Reich': Zur wirtschaftlichen Ausschaltung der jüdischen Bevölkerung in der rheinisch–westfälischen Industrieregion," 7, http://www.geschichtskultur-ruhr.de/links/dvlaak.pdf (accessed 10 June 2009).

[82] Frank Bajohr, *"Aryanisation" in Hamburg: The Economic Exclusion of Jews and the Confiscation of their Property in Nazi Germany* (New York: Berghahn Books, 2002), 110.

[83] Van Laak, "Arisierung," 29, n. 119.

[84] Adelheid von Saldern, *Mittelstand im "Dritten Reich": Handwerker – Einzelhändler – Bauern* (Frankfurt am Main: Campus, 1979), 61–63.

[85] See Detlef Briesen, *Warenhaus, Massenkonsum, und Sozialmoral: Zur Geschichte der Konsumkritik im 20. Jahrhundert* (Frankfurt: Campus: 2001), 178–85.

[86] David Schoenbaum, *Hitler's Social Revolution: Class and Status in Nazi Germany, 1933–1939* (Garden City, NY: Doubleday, 1966), 133–34.

[87] "Schutz des Einzelhandels," *DDV* 4, no. 5 (February 1935): 141.

[88] "Konsumgenossenschaft nach der Gleichschaltung," *Deutsche Zukunft* 1, no. 7 (26 November 1933): 12; and Karl Ditt, "Die Konsumgenossenschaften im Dritten

Protecting small business was a key motivation behind the Nazis'
marketplace regulations, but the initial burst against large economic
institutions soon gave way to pragmatism. Much to the disappoint-
ment of the party's commercial base, represented by the Nazi Combat
League for the Commercial Middle Class (Kampfbund für den gewer-
blichen Mittelstand) and the National Socialist Trade and Commerce
Organization (Nationalsozialistische Handels- und Gewerbetreibende
Organisation – NS-Hago), most department stores and some co-ops were
kept open to prevent job losses and to provision the populace. Moreover,
the limitations on sales and rebates favored larger manufacturers with
massive inventory and put smaller producers, as well as chain stores, at
a disadvantage.[89]

The state's symbolic gestures against big business were part of its
attempt to appease its base, but as the regime came to rely on large
manufacturers and retailers, commercial legislation was less about attack-
ing capitalism than about taming and reshaping it according to National
Socialist precepts. This project demanded the cooperation of trade and
professional organizations, civil courts, and the regime, and the Nazis
set up a number of offices devoted to the everyday work of regulating
business activity. One was called the Reich Office for Economic Morality
(Reichsstelle für Wirtschaftsmoral), which was headed by Nazi industrialist and Reich economic chamber leader Albert Pietzsche. In conjunction
with the economics ministry and local business organizations, it investigated complaints about price gouging, favoritism, and other forms of
"economic criminality," and it weighed in on issues like fire safety in
business establishments and parking structures.[90] A more important body,
however, was the Nazi Advertising Council of the German Economy
(Werberat der deutschen Wirtschaft). Founded in October 1933, the
Advertising Council was placed under the auspices of the propaganda
ministry and given the task of regulating private and public advertising,
as well as trade fairs, exhibitions, and other forms of display that served
"economic purposes."[91] Principally the creation of *DDV* editor Heinrich

Reich," *Internationale wissenschaftliche Korrespondenz zur Geschichte der deutschen Arbeiterbewegung* 23, no. 1 (1987), 82–111.
[89] Heinrich Uhlig, *Die Warenhäuser im Dritten Reich* (Cologne: Westdeutscher, 1956), 183–88.
[90] See letters to office in R3101/13800, BAB; and Jürgen Hasse, *Übersehene Räume: Zur Kulturgeschichte und Heteropologie des Parkhauses* (Bielefeld: Transcript, 2007), 108–9.
[91] On the Advertising Council, see Rücker, *Wirtschaftswerbung*, 103–74. On specific regu- lations, see Hartmut Berghoff, "'Times Change and We Change with Them': The German

Hunke,[92] the Advertising Council was responsible for issuing licenses to publish print advertisements or display goods, and it used warnings and the power of the propaganda ministry to enforce "commercial morality." It did not have the legal authority to punish violators; that was left to civil courts. However, it could rely on moral suasion and the threat of police intervention or punishment through other state agencies to keep the marketplace free of negative influences.[93]

The Advertising Council issued a stream of regulations dealing with marketing and advertising. These will be examined in closer detail in the next chapter, but what is notable here is how improvised and confusing the council's rules could be. Because marketing and retailing saw rapid developments, economic leaders before 1933 had always struggled to keep laws about commercial behavior current. How, they asked, could rules about honest salesmanship devised in the nineteenth century be updated to reflect the onset of mass marketing? The Nazis faced this same challenge, but it was exacerbated by their own conflicted understanding of consumer capitalism and by the sometimes competing demands of ideology and pragmatism. For example, in 1936 a court in Saalfeld sentenced a store owner to five days in jail for directing a customer who had asked for Maggi soup spices toward a competing brand. The seller had violated the rule that if a customer asked for specific brand, one was forbidden to provide a rival product. More precisely, one could do so, but only in the process of displaying one's expertise and not, say, because one got a rebate for selling a certain product.[94] With this judgment, the court was reminding shopkeepers that purely pecuniary interests should not guide commerce. Consumers should expect an honest relationship with a salesperson, guided by knowledge of a product's benefits and not by money. This judgment against the shopkeeper revealed the Nazi court's static understanding of market relations. Despite the reality that in the age of mass consumption salespeople were rarely "experts," the ruling drew upon a dying figure of the shopkeeper as authority, who presided over a wealth of knowledge about competing products. It reflected an uneasiness with consumer capitalism by glossing over the fact that

Advertising Industry in the Third Reich – Between Professional Self-Interest and Political Repression," *Business History*, 45, no. 1 (January 2003): 128–34.

[92] Hunke was deputy director until 1939 and then its president from 1939 to 1945; Reinhardt, *Von der Reklame zum Marketing*, 42.

[93] Rücker, *Wirtschaftswerbung*, 154–74.

[94] "Unlauterer Wettbewerb durch Hingabe anderen Ware," *HAG-Post* (special edition from 16 November 1936), p. 5, box 1936 (0096 4167), KFA.

commerce was becoming increasingly impersonal. The romantic image of neighborly capitalism, which the court invoked, was being supplanted by the reality of uninformed salespeople and unfamiliar customers.[95]

This ruling revealed a court struggling with modern forms of commerce. In the name of business morality, it punished a shopkeeper for breaking down the already thin lines of communication between buyer and seller. But this does not mean that the Nazis always deferred to a puritanical view of market relations. When the stakes were higher for the regime, such as when they involved the potential for major revenues, the Nazis could strike a balance between völkisch morality and good economic sense. An example concerns the practice of gambling, which in most societies is a lightning rod for discussions about public decency. Different forms of gambling had been under attack in the Weimar years, and when Hitler came to power, he faced a quandary: how could the state take advantage of the profits that gambling generated while also regulating a behavior most people deemed a vice? In 1933 he answered this question by lifting a decades-old ban on casinos, which he recognized as important sources of tax revenues and tourist expenditures. Yet the regime limited the opening of new casinos to just one, in Baden-Baden, and regulated the days all of them could be open.[96] Nazi officials also worried that the sale of national and state lottery tickets violated public morality by encouraging gambling. Here again, the potential for revenues, especially when earmarked for Nazi charities like the Winter Help, overrode moral qualms. Instead of banning lotteries, the government took control of them away from the states, established a national lottery in 1938, and regulated the distribution of tickets. In effect, it shifted the locus of corruption from the action – gambling – to its method of promotion. The Advertising Council condemned the mailing of unsolicited lottery tickets to consumers, arguing that this practice deceived the public into thinking a ticket automatically had value when in fact it was activated only when a payment was sent to the lottery office. In contrast, the Reich economics ministry argued that the success of the lottery depended on the mass distribution of unsolicited tickets. An accommodation was reached in January 1939. Direct solicitation through the mail was deemed

[95] Uwe Spiekermann, "From Neighbour to Consumer: The Transformation of Retailer–Consumer Relationships in Twentieth Century Germany, in *The Making of the Consumer: Knowledge, Power and Identity in the Modern World*, ed. Frank Trentmann (Oxford, Berg, 2006), 147–74.

[96] Meredith Rucker Hunter, "Gambling," in *A Comparative Perspective on Major Social Problems*, ed. Rita J. Simon (Lanham, MD: Lexington Books, 2001), 131–52.

acceptable, but no pressure tactics could be used. The customer must be reminded that a ticket was valueless until forwarded with payment and that no one was under obligation to send it back. A return envelope had to be provided to the customer to simplify the process. The lottery could send a customer a follow-up notice to return the ticket, as long as it was in a sealed envelope (not on a postcard) and did not bear the word *Mahnung* (reminder), which usually suggested a forthcoming late fee.[97]

As this example suggests, the tension between public morality and good business practices could be resolved to the regime's satisfaction. The state could collect proceeds from lottery ticket sales while presumably protecting the public from deceptive forms of marketing. But this nod to economic reality had its limits, and this was revealed in the regime's decision on 1 August 1939 to forbid the sale of lottery tickets to Jews.[98] Here the Nazis' overriding obsession with race undermined market logic; for if financial exigency warranted submitting the public to morally suspect practices like gambling, it would seem sensible that Jews, a "decadent" people often tapped for their money, be *invited* to participate. Yet as the 1930s wore on, removing dangerous elements from the world of commerce overrode the desire to exploit these same elements financially. The lottery, if it was to maintain any integrity, could not be open to Jews. Moreover, the state would be in a bind should a Jew actually possess a winning ticket, as it had no desire to pay out prize money to non-Aryans. It was not the vice itself, which could be exploited and managed, but its distance from degenerate forces – racial and commercial – that became a test case in public morality.

When it came to regulating commerce, the presence of Jews in the economy clearly presented the regime with a quandary: should it exploit Jews financially or should it remove them entirely from the economy (and from the country)? The transfer of Jewish businesses to "Aryan" owners and the Reich Flight Tax, which mandated that Jews fleeing Germany cede a large percentage of their net worth to the state, are two examples of how the Nazis addressed the "Jewish problem" before settling on genocide.[99] So too was the removal of Jews from department stores'

---

[97] On these debates and resolutions, see, e.g., Vermerk of 28 Mai 1936, prepared by the Advertising Council, and the surrounding correspondences in R55/344, BAB.

[98] See "Examples of Anti-Semitic Legislation," United States Holocaust Memorial Museum, http://www.ushmm.org/wlc/article.php?lang=en&ModuleId=10007459 (accessed 25 June 2009).

[99] Martin Dean, *Robbing the Jews: The Confiscation of Jewish Property in the Holocaust, 1933–1945* (Cambridge: Cambridge University Press, 2008), 17–53.

managements, which allowed the regime to maintain this vital expression of consumer capitalism while claiming to have purged it of impurities. But even after they were pushed out of the German economy, Jews' lingering symbolic relationship to commerce presented the Advertising Council with unexpected challenges. For example, in the late 1930s Aryanized businesses continued the practice of acknowledging important company anniversaries, whether the twenty-fifth, fiftieth, or hundredth. Indeed, Aryanization gave business leaders the opportunity to highlight the longevity and reliability of their newly acquired company and also to rejoice in the ridding of its Jewish influence. But the regime considered any references to an Aryanized business's origins as risky, as it might cast the Jewish phase of a company's history in a positive light. The Advertising Council thus declared that in celebrating a company anniversary or preparing marketing materials, an Aryanized company could not (with some exceptions) count the "Jewish years" in the total age of the firm. Instead, it had to measure its age from the year it became "Jew free."[100] One might then assume, conversely, that the regime would encourage businesses that had never been Jewish to tout this fact. But this was not the case either. Phrases like "Aryan since its founding" (*Arisch seit Gründung*) or "for a hundred years owned by an Aryan family" (*Seit 100 Jahren in arischem Familienbesitz*) were also forbidden (in 1938), on the grounds that they put Aryanized firms at a commercial disadvantage, as such firms could not claim the same thing.[101] In short, you could not use the "Jewishness" of your firm to your advantage, and a competitor could not use it to your disadvantage.

At the heart of these decisions was an uncertainty about the symbolic power of Jews. While referencing a Jewish past might resonate positively with the public, *denying* the Jewishness of a company could also lend unfair commercial advantage. To cover its tracks, the regime concluded that it was better not to reference the racial history of a company at all. Or more accurately, one could presumably advertise the fact that a company was "Aryan" so long as a negative comparison to other companies' pasts was not implicit in the ad. With these prohibitions, the dual nature of Nazi commercial morality is brought into relief. On the one hand, the regime was engaging in the long-standing effort to protect businesses from comparative ads; the Advertising Council's job was to even the commercial

---

[100] "Keine Jüdische Denkmäler," *DDV* 7, no. 31 (1. Novemberheft 1938): 1134.
[101] "'Arisch seit Gründung,'" *Wirtschaftswerbung* 5, no. 8 (August 1938): 64–65; "'Arisch seit Gründung,'" *DDV* 7, no. 25 (September 1938): 920.

FIGURE 4. The windows of the Jewish-owned store Hemdenmatz, a men's clothier, covered with graffiti and rhyming anti-Semitic verse, Berlin, 1 April 1933. (78589A, United States Holocaust Memorial Museum, Washington, DC; courtesy of Raphael Aronson.)

playing field. On the other hand, the regulations about mentioning race were part of a larger attempt to extricate a minority from the German economy. Rules about not mentioning Jews, therefore, did not represent a squeamishness about the Jewish question as much as an attempt to make sense of racial persecution for the purposes of marketing. Indeed, the Nazis had no problem with assaulting businesses that they deemed truly Jewish or that had not yet been secured from their Jewish owners. Vandalizing a Jewish business or scrawling *"Jude"* on a storefront was not subject to the rules of commercial morality. In short, Nazi commercial policies were defined by a brutal duality: the establishment of strict rules about fair competition for Aryans and their contravention when it came to Jews.[102]

Jews were not the only targets in these attempts to purify commercial relations. The Nazis wanted to remove from the Third Reich all institutions that had a "foreign character" – to, in effect, Germanize the economy. In an age of global capitalism, this proved extremely difficult, as

[102] See "Jüdische Auffassung von 'Sittenwidrigem' Wettbewerb," *Mitteilungen der Kommission für Wirtschaftpolitik der NSDAP* 2, no. 6 (March 1937): 17.

many multinational firms had subsidiaries in Germany. Already in 1932 regional courts had dealt with a case where a competitor branded the Sunlicht laundry detergent company foreign because it was a subsidiary of the English Lever company. The court ruled that since Sunlicht was incorporated in Germany, employed almost exclusively Germans, and limited its market to Germany, it was in fact a German company. It did not matter that it was reliant on foreign capital. The civil courts of the Third Reich initially upheld this interpretation, but they added a racial component. After 1933 a company could designate itself as German if it was headquartered in Germany and its owner was not a foreigner or a non-Aryan. The Advertising Council set an even higher standard in 1935 by including the racial makeup of the employees and a firm's reliance on foreign capital in determining whether it was German.[103] In all of these deliberations, the courts and the Advertising Council never prohibited branding a competitor foreign. Rather, what was at stake was finding a precise definition that could bolster the state's nationalist and racist aims. Once a company was determined to be foreign, it in effect lost the protection of laws against unfair advertising. Like the case of company anniversaries, what mattered was defending a business's right to compete *if* the company was "Aryan" and "German." If a company did not fall into these categories, a competitor was free to use negative advertising against it.

Debates over the meanings of "German" and "foreign" were not limited to a company's capital and personnel. They extended to its name, the location of its factories, and the source of its raw materials and lines of credit.[104] Most important, they concerned a company's merchandise. The regime grappled with questions that had long preoccupied market professionals: How could the positive spirit of a company, or the country in which it functioned, be transmitted through a product itself? How could a product embody, in the words of a Nazi expert on advertising, a "German essence."[105] Since the late nineteenth century "made in Germany" – as a marketing phrase and an actual stamp on a product – provided an answer to this question. While originally a term of opprobrium in late Victorian England, the phrase had by 1900 become a badge of pride, worn by German industrialists and politicians, who reveled in the international

---

[103] For all these points, see Erich Naue, "'Deutsches Geschäft' in Rechtsprechung und Schrifttum," *DDV* 4, no. 27 (September 1935): 863–65.

[104] Ibid.

[105] Erich Naue, "Was ist ein 'Deutsches Geschäft'?" *DDV* 4, no. 28 (October 1935): 889–90.

respect for German goods, whether cannons, toys, porcelain, or clocks.[106] It conveyed craftsmanship and commanded confidence.

In the Third Reich, the "made in Germany" moniker persisted, but it provoked concerns that foreign business interests could exploit the word "German" on their packaging, in advertising, or on the goods themselves. Nazi economists therefore tried to determine how much of the labor, ownership, and raw materials had to be physically derived from Germany for a firm to declare its goods German. Courts had addressed this question during World War I, and they took it up again in the 1930s. But their rulings on the meaning of "German" could not settle the issue, nor could the Advertising Council's vague pronouncement in 1935 that "German products" were made by German workers and from German materials "to the extent that the German raw materials situation allowed it";[107] for after 1933 the definition of "German" underwent a more abstract shift, one that could not be measured. Did the company reflect the "Führer leadership principle," whereby everyone knew his or her organic position in the workplace hierarchy? Did the owners have a heroic and pioneering spirit? Did they put community before self-interest? Such questions revealed the impossibility of devising and imposing a coherent commercial ethic. A single company could embody National Socialist values but also use methods deemed improper. A firm could make highly valued goods but not embrace Nazi labor principles. A producer could have "foreign" elements in its management and workforce but also be committed to Nazi aims. In short, the vagaries of the business world hampered attempts to legislate commercial behavior according to abstract principles.

BRAND NAMES AND THE QUALITY ETHOS

Thus far, we have seen how the Nazis' approach to commerce was riddled with contradictions: consumer capitalism was a source of both decadence and mass wealth; Jews and Jewish institutions had to be exploited financially and removed altogether; small business was ideologically vital but big business was economically necessary; vices like gambling offended public decency but were a source of revenue; Germany was obligated to make good commercial use of its well-made products but only if they were truly "German." In some ways, all of these attempts to Germanize market

---

[106] On the history of the term "made in Germany," see David Head, *"Made in Germany": The Corporate Identity of a Nation* (London: Hodder & Stoughton, 1992).

[107] Erich Naue, "'Deutsches Erzeugnis' in Rechstsprechung und Schrifttum," *DDV* 4, no. 32 (November 1935): 1026–8.

activity bespoke the difficulty of reconciling a nationalist vision with a globalizing economy; for while the Nazis wanted to remove foreign elements from the marketplace, they also wanted to protect Germany's vital export market.[108] This meant acknowledging the porous and multinational nature of capitalism: foreign products flowed across borders, and foreign actors sat on company boards. The Nazis were playing a dangerous game in this respect. A policy of autarky meant cutting ties to global markets and threatening much needed imports. And British and Americans Jews' boycott of German goods in the 1930s was a response to the regime's determination to persecute Jews, even at the expense of foreign business relations.[109] In reality, the leadership wanted to have its cake and eat it – to "sanitize" the domestic market while remaining an active player globally. One means of achieving this was to confront a specific innovation of consumer capitalism, namely brand names, which carried messages of reliability and performance to far-flung markets. The party's reaction to branding is indicative of its conflict-ridden approach to marketing, the difficulty of navigating practical and ideological aims, and the troublesome goal of combining conventional and National Socialist business ethics.

In the first decades of the twentieth century, German companies – like many firms throughout the world – turned to branding to secure loyal domestic and international customer bases. They saw brands as connoting trustworthiness and disseminating a corporate identity more effectively than any other form of marketing.[110] Through brand recognition, consumers could avoid deliberating over a product's advantages and instead rely on familiarity and reputation. In the process, they might pay a high price for a good that was manufactured relatively cheaply. According to a German market research study in 1936, 74 percent of those asked saw a trademarked brand name as a mark of quality.[111]

Branding found wide support among German consumers and large manufacturers in the Third Reich. The former welcomed the post-Depression ability to buy their favorite goods, and the latter saw brands

---

[108] Tooze, *Wages of Destruction*, 91–95.

[109] See Sharon Gewirtz, "Anglo-Jewish Responses to Nazi Germany, 1933–1939: The Anti-Nazi Boycott and the Board of Deputies of British Jews," *Journal of Contemporary History* 26, no. 2 (April 1991): 255–76; and Tooze, *Wages of Destruction*, 273.

[110] Nicolai Oliver Herbrand and Stefan Röhrig, eds., *Die Bedeutung der Tradition für die Markenkommunikation: Konzepte und Instrumente zur ganzheitlichen Ausschöpfung des Erfolgspotenzials Markenhistorie* (Stuttgart: Neues Fachwissen: 2006), preface, 1.

[111] "Untersuchung über die Bedeutung des Warenzeichen in den Augen der Verbraucher unter besonderer Berücksichtigung des Pfeilring-Zeichens," January 1936, S 1900 012, p. 4, Gesellschaft für Konsumforschung Archive, Nuremberg (hereafter GfKA).

as increasing domestic and foreign sales. Despite the expansion of the practice, economists debated the utility, cost, and cultural significance of branding. Brands represented the larger shift in the global market away from small producers toward large manufacturers who had the means to mass-market goods at home and abroad. Shopkeepers who sold unpackaged and bulk goods saw brands as expressions of corporate power, which foisted marketing costs on the public through high, fixed prices.[112] Brands therefore put the Nazi regime in the position of having to pay lip service to small manufacturers while not hurting the interests of big business or the wider economy.

Brands had been on the defensive before the onset of National Socialism. In the first years of the Great Depression, generic products and cheaper "no-name" brands flooded the market to satisfy the public's need for affordable products. Chancellor Heinrich Brüning's deflationary policies led to less money in consumers' hands and the death of small brand-name companies that could not compete with firms with a higher turnover. In 1934 advertising innovator Hanns Brose foretold "the apocalypse of the brand-name good," as older, established names were lost in the wash of new, cheap brands.[113] He longed for the days when Pelikan pens, Rosenthal porcelain, and Waldorf-Astoria cigarettes did not have to compete with shoddy alternatives. After the Nazis came to power promising to protect small businesses, branding remained a source of contention.

As with other areas of the economy, the Nazis erred on the side of big business when devising a response to the debate over brands. They acknowledged that Germany's eight hundred or so brand-name companies served a number of important economic functions. First, they provided employment to the graphic designers and artists who produced ad copy and packaging, to the workers who manufactured the products, and to the people who sold them. They also put to work chemists and food scientists whom wealthy companies supported in the search for high-quality products and foodstuffs. Second, brands reflected the Nazi regime's aim of stabilizing prices; the retail cost of name goods tended to fluctuate less widely than that of unbranded goods, and the regime saw this stability as

---

[112] De Grazia, *Irresistible Empire*, 220–21.

[113] Hanns W. Brose, *Götterdämmerung des Markenartikels? Neue Wege zu neuen Käufern* (Gärtner: Schwarzenberg, 1934), 7–8. See also de Grazia, *Irresistible Empire*, 220–21. On Brose's career, see Dirk Schindelbeck, "'Asbach Uralt' und 'Soziale Marktwirtschaft': Zur Kulturgeschichte der Werbeagentur am Beispiel von Hanns W. Brose, 1899–1971," *Zeitschrift für Unternehmensgeschichte* 40, no. 4 (1995): 235–52.

a positive development. Third, brands were a key source of exports: from Krupp steel to Bayer aspirin, German products found their way into factories and households throughout the world.[114] Fourth, brands protected the health of the Volk. The propagation of popular wash powders, toiletries, and household chemicals helped sustain a message of cleanliness and self-care among Germans. With reference to Odol toothpaste, Hanns Brose proclaimed that "brand names taught people how to brush their teeth."[115] Finally, plenty of small shops sold trademarked goods; it was not just the big department stores, which often created their own brands. In short, brands were inextricably tied to a global consumer economy and to Germany's economic and biological health.

Brands also, according to some Nazi economists, had a cultural component, expressing at once the greatness of Germany and "high culture and the broad masses' distinct sense of quality."[116] Each brand had its own personality, which in the "achievement community" of the Third Reich embodied the National Socialist performance spirit. Hans Domizlaff, known as the father of German branding, tied the common idea of "brand personality" to Nazi biologism. He suggested that brands, like organisms, evolved spontaneously, spread like viruses, and could live and die according to the laws of nature.[117] This was a martial, Darwinian struggle, and it was up to the "brand technician" to hone the proper weapons. "Branding," wrote Domizlaff in his 1939 classic textbook, "is the art of creating mental weapons in the struggle for truthful performances and for new ideas for winning public trust."[118]

The attitude of small producers and sellers toward brands was decidedly less enthusiastic than Domizlaff's. Where some saw brands as culturally uplifting and an important source of exports, others, such as members of the Retail Trade Economic Group (Wirtschaftsgruppe Einzelhandel), which represented small shopkeepers, saw the "homogenization and

---

[114] Rot. Dr. Heinz Goldhammer, "Der Markenartikel als Qualitäts- und Kulturfaktor: Gütezeichen für Markenartikel?", 19 February 1935, Hauptabteilung 1, rep. 228 (Rotary International), Rotary Club Halle, file 618, Geheimes Staatsarchiv Preußischer Kulturbesitz, Berlin [hereafter GStA PK, I. HA rep. 228, file 618.]

[115] Brose, *Götterdämmerung*, 19.

[116] Goldhammer, "Der Markenartikel als Qualitäts- und Kulturfaktor."

[117] Holm Friebe, "Branding Germany: Hans Domizlaff's *Markentechnik* and Its Ideological Impact," in *Selling Modernity: Advertising in Twentieth Century Germany*, ed. Pamela Swett, S. Jonathan Wiesen, and Jonathan R. Zatlin (Durham, NC: Duke University Press, 2007), 78–99.

[118] Hans Domizlaff, *Die Gewinnung des öffentlichen Vertrauens* [1939] [7th ed.] (Hamburg: Gesellschaft für angewandtes Marketing, 2005); quoted in ibid., 89.

leveling of consumer taste" through exaggerated brand marketing.[119] In general, they deemed brands threatening to their very livelihoods – "to the most basic tasks of the individual shopkeeper, namely advising the consumer."[120] Brands, argued the group in its 1937–38 work report, led to the proliferation of salespeople who knew little of the product.[121] Here the fear of big retailers was extended to the big manufacturers as well; producers, distributers, and department and chain stores were all conspiring to drive out the independent business owner. In 1934 the Nazi newspaper *Völkischer Beobachter* denounced branded goods for their inelasticity. Because brand prices remained high even during economic downturns, single-price shops and "peddlers" rushed to put cheap "pseudo-brands" on to the market, leading to the proliferation of trademarks and the further lowering of quality, all to the detriment of the small owner whose livelihood depended on the sale of unbranded products and bulk goods.[122] Brands, argued some, actually violated the spirit of National Socialism. As the flashy creations of large companies, they were expressions of corporate self-interest and served the ego of an owner rather than the community.[123]

The regime's pragmatic concessions to big business meant that these arguments never carried the day and that branded goods were never really in danger. To the consternation of branding's critics, Nazi courts upheld the practice of resale price maintenance, or fair trade (*Preisbindung der zweiten Hand*), by which a manufacturer set a minimum price at which a retailer must sell its branded product. In the United States such agreements were judged illegal until 1937, as they were seen as violating antitrust law.[124] From the start, however, Nazi economists felt that challenging such arrangements would hurt manufacturers and would be harmful to the recovering civilian economy. In fact, small retailers, like

---

[119] "Einzelhandel und Markenartikel," *DDV* 7, no. 30 (October 1938): 1097. On the history of the tensions between shopkeepers and large companies in Germany, see Uwe Spiekermann, *Basis der Konsumgesellschaft: Geschichte des modernen Kleinhandels in Deutschland 1850–1914* (Munich: Beck, 1999): 134–217; on Nazi policies toward small business, see von Saldern, *Mittelstand*, 16–92.

[120] "Einzelhandel und Markenartikel."

[121] Ibid.

[122] "Schluss mit misbräuchlicher Preisstellung!" *Völkischer Beobachter* 321 (17 November 1934), 11 (cited in "Markenartikel mit Gütezeichen?" *DDV* 4, no. 2 [January 1935], 43–44).

[123] "Diskussion um die Markenartikel," *DDV* 4, no. 4 (February 1936): 107–8.

[124] Jonathan Bean, *Beyond the Broker State: Federal Policies toward Small Business, 1936–1961* (Chapel Hill: University of North Carolina Press, 1996), 67–88.

druggists, also saw resale price maintenance as advantageous because it prevented large chain stores from selling products too cheaply. But small and middle-sized manufacturers that produced generic goods, local chambers of industry and commerce, and some consumers abhorred this practice of jacking up prices, and it became one of the main points in the case against brands.[125]

To appease these smaller manufacturers, Nazi spokespeople in 1935 proposed regulating branded goods not by removing them from shelves but by submitting them to National Socialist "performance thinking." The idea was that the regime would issue a government seal for worthy products and withhold it from those deemed inferior. Companies could introduce new brands, but their right to retail price maintenance would be contingent on a brand's having received this "stamp of quality" (*Gütesiegel* or *Gütezeichen*), which could reflect such factors as high craftsmanship and whether the brand was produced by a labor force that demonstrated "teamwork." This system, it was hoped, would naturally lead to fewer brands, more elastic prices, greater education of the consumer, and a more even playing field for smaller producers and retailers. It would, according to *DDV*, "protect the mass of consumers, who have to make do with their incomes, from the unruliness of branded goods."[126]

Brand-name companies lobbied hard against this idea of a national seal through their trade organization, the Association of Brand Name Manufacturers (Verband der Fabrikanten von Markenartikeln-Markenschutzverband), which represented two hundred manufacturers of some of the most famous clothing, food, and body care products. They rejected the premise that prices of branded goods went beyond what their quality warranted. Because these goods were produced in mass quantities, they argued, the prices were *held down*, not artificially raised.[127] Inherent in these defenses was a critique of Hitler's intervention in the market. According to Heinz Goldhammer, editor of the *Neckar-Zeitung*, it should be up to the consumer and the mechanisms of supply and demand – not the state – to determine what products should stay on the shelf. The government's granting of quality seals would only lead to the elevation of potentially inferior products into the same category as well-made goods. Moreover, added Goldhammer, there would be multiple difficulties in

---

[125] "Markenartikel mit Gütezeichen?"
[126] "Schutz der Marke," *DDV* 7, no. 30 (October 1938): 1096.
[127] Goldhammer, "Der Markenartikel als Qualitäts- und Kulturfaktor."

implementing the proposed system of quality control. What would be the basis for granting the right, and who would decide it? How could you remove the biases from the process? (After all, most people who would be involved in the decision-making process would have their own businesses and thus a personal stake.) How would you judge pharmaceutical goods, which depended on the testimony of doctors and patients?[128]

A government-mandated stamp never came to be. Instead, the issuing of quality seals fell under the purview of specific branches of industry, which could decide whether a bar of soap, a sofa, or a piece of cardboard was produced according to industry standards.[129] This was a triumph for brand-name companies and for those who felt product quality control should be left to private industry. But it was a hollow victory, given the state's intervention in almost all areas of the economy. As the decade wore on and the preparation for war led to shortages and fears of inflation, the quality issue became less urgent. It gave way to general pressure on companies to reduce their prices, especially after the state-mandated prize freeze in the fall of 1936, from which many firms had been exempted. Even though higher taxes and raw materials costs cut into their profit margins, large brand-name companies responded to state pressure by lowering their prices by 5 to 10 percent in the fall of 1937. The office of the Reich price commissioner congratulated them on this selfless act and predicted a smooth Christmas shopping season.[130] They thus avoided the formal control and restructuring of the branded-goods industry, which had taken place in the Soviet Union when the state eliminated brands altogether after the Russian Revolution.[131] Throughout the 1930s Nazi economists and marketers continued to praise brands as cultural goods; they acknowledged their importance to the establishment of new markets abroad and to purveying the German quality ethos at

---

[128] Ibid.

[129] On the textile industry's quality mark, see the pamphlet "Schutz der Qualität vom Rohstoff bis zur Fertigware: Ein Program" (1939), R3101/13801, BAB; and "'Gütezeichen,'" *Wirtschaftswerbung* 4, no. 11 (November 1937): 85–86. The idea of a national quality mark, however, continued to be floated througout the Third Reich. See Werner Suhr, "Zur Idee einer Nationalmarke," *Wirtschaftswerbung* 10, no. 3 (May 1943): 57–61.

[130] Wilhelm Rentrop, "Die Preissenkung für Markenartikel," *DDV* 6, no. 31 (November 1937): 1049–51. On Christmas in the Third Reich, see Joe Perry, "Nazifying Christmas: Political and Popular Celebration in the Third Reich," *Central European History* 38, no. 4 (December 2005): 572–605.

[131] Marshall I. Goldman, "Product Differentiation and Advertising: Some Lessons from the Soviet Experience," *Journal of Political Economy* 68, no. 4 (August 1960): 346–57.

home and internationally. But the heyday of brand names was over. As we will see, the shift to a war economy – and not per se the flood of "pseudo-brands" – led to the disappearance of beloved names from the shelves.

Branding was one of many themes that preoccupied the state and market professionals in Nazi Germany. It did not carry the weight of more pressing economic and ideological issues like autarky, war preparation, and racial engineering. But in a small way it exemplified the challenges of legislating a new market sensibility in the Third Reich; for determining what kind of commercial behavior was proper and then establishing coherent guidelines were always complicated by attempts to reconcile ideology and economic reality. Consequently, the Nazis adjusted their rationales and actual polices according to the immediate political and economic needs of the regime. While they celebrated the purity of small business, they also acknowledged the importance of big business for the provisioning of mass goods to a large populace and to war making. While they hoped to eliminate foreign elements from the German economy, they did not want to lose their niche in foreign markets. If brands were seen as carriers of quality, the more important demands of war meant that quality had to suffer. In short, the Nazis could not reconcile all the inconsistencies that arose in a modern industrial society recovering from a depression, led by a dictator, and bent on war.

 Nazi Germany was an industrialized autocracy, but it was also a nascent consumer society, and this fact provided the biggest challenge to the state as it tried to regulate market behavior. According to some Nazi ideologues, consumer capitalism bore all the hallmarks of decadence. Multinational firms that catered to a large consumer base were breeding grounds for racial mixing; department stores were "Jewish" enterprises that fostered self-indulgent and materialist fantasies; consumer credit and installment buying were byproducts of a corrupt and overly indulgent Weimar capitalism, and big business was an exploitative force that leeched off the productive capacities of true working folk. On the other hand, the Nazis' utopian visions could be realized only by sustaining these institutions of consumer capitalism. Multinationals, department stores that allowed for credit financing, and large firms with branded goods remained active and healthy throughout the Third Reich.[132] Indeed, they were called upon to translate the vision of a Nazi consumer society into reality.

---

[132] Little has been written on consumer credit in the National Socialist period. See, however, Jan Logemann, "The American Influences? Consumer Credit in Germany from

Despite the incoherence of National Socialist ideals and the ad hoc nature of Hitler's economic policies, the regime was consistent in its desire to align commercial morality and völkisch morality. The Nazis hoped to tame the excesses of consumer capitalism by legislating a market sensibility that spoke both to older norms of public decency and to the new demands of the racial state. Rules about fair competition, high performance, and virtuous consumption were designed to do many things – support a vibrant marketplace, regulate commercial behavior, pave the way for war, and guide Germans toward an awareness of biology as the basis of national greatness. A cruel duality thus marked commerce in Nazi Germany. Egregious violations of Jewish interests existed alongside, and were often packaged as, mundane attempts to regulate abuses in the marketplace.

We cannot overstate the challenges the Nazis faced in enacting their commercial vision. The problems they encountered in this area reflected the larger difficulty of reconciling political aims with socioeconomic realities. As historians have pointed out, Hitler's reactionary ideas about domesticity were undermined by the military necessity of female labor; the lofty rhetoric about a "struggle for performance" in the workplace translated into longer hours, more factory accidents, and sicker employees;[133] what was a necessity for the wealthy was a luxury for poorer Germans; Jews were both a source of economic exploitation and a force to be eliminated. In short, Germans experienced the actual economy along axes of gender, class, and race, and abstract notions of righteous behavior could go only so far in shaping reality.

As we will see, the contradictions inherent in the Nazi commercial vision would eventually prove irreconcilable, especially as war revealed itself to be the Nazis' raison d'être. But until World War II the Nazis could argue with some justification that they had created a workable commercial vision that successfully addressed the state's practical and ideological aims. Even if the regime did not admit as much, the Nazi marketplace proved a plausible alternative to the "bourgeois" marketplace precisely because it sustained many features of the latter: competition, individual success, hard work, and entrepreneurial initiative. Even the main category

---

a Transnational and Comparative Perspective, 1860s–1960s" (paper delivered at the conference "Consommer à crédit en Europe au XXe siècle," Université de Paris Ouest Nanterre – La Défense, Paris, 21 January 2010). I thank the author for a copy of this paper.

[133] Matthias Frese, *Betriebspolitik im "Dritten Reich": Deutsche Arbeitsfront, Unternehmer und Saatsbürokratie in der westdeutschen Grossindustrie, 1933–1939* (Paderborn: Schöningh, 1991), 1.

of bourgeois commercial morality – honest competition – could be used to forge a new, völkisch commercial morality that supposedly transcended the era in which it developed. In short, at a moment when the liberal order was on the defensive – associated as it was with financial specu- lation, greed, and the horrors of the global economic crisis – the Nazis revived its key features and gave them a racial imprimatur. In a short span of time, Hitler pulled the country out of the Depression, shredded the Treaty of Versailles, and created numerous opportunities for Germans' social advancement, and Nazi theorists credited these successes in part to a flexible political and commercial vision that made room for practical and ideological imperatives.

The regime also took pride in having created an expansive economic vision that included the consumer. Even with a lagging civilian sector, Germans acknowledged their own good fortunes in the revived economy of prewar Nazi Germany; until World War II, the unfilled promises of consumption that historians have recently located were trumped by the subjective experience of well-being, both material and spiritual, that the Nazis engendered. Finally, by 1939 the regime could boast that it had removed from society not just political and racial opponents but also economic undesirables. The presence of concentration camps, and later ghettos and death camps, meant that the Nazi marketplace would not be sullied by the presence of Jews, Marxists, trade unionists, and other criminals. Thus when the *WB* declared in 1936 its desire to humanize commerce – to place "man" at the center of the market – it was clear that it had only certain humans in mind.[134]

[134] "Im Mittelpunkt: Der Mensch," *DDV* 10, nos. 1 and 2 (January 1941): 26–27.

2

Commerce for the Community

Advertising, Marketing, and Public Relations in Hitler's Germany

The Nazi marketplace was an amalgam of pre-1933 ideas about proper commercial behavior and the new state's racial priorities. The regime took familiar features of consumer capitalism, reshaped them along ideological lines, and applied them to the practical challenges of pulling the country out of the Depression and preparing for war. From the state's perspective, Germany could have everything the United States had and more: thriving consumer opportunities, a high standard of living, an economy that protected the "humanity" of Germans, and eventually a European empire that would last a thousand years. Moreover, it could avoid the negative features of the American model: crude commercialism, cutthroat competition, and racial mixing. If the tensions inherent in this vision were substantial, the regime did not concede as much.

It was one thing for the state to project ideas about the market, but how did those with a great investment in commerce – business leaders, company and shop owners, manufacturers – react to the regime's imperatives? This chapter addresses this question by focusing on three business practices that became essential with the rise of consumer capitalism: advertising, public relations, and marketing. As we will see, even as the Nazi state exerted greater control over the economy, companies maintained wide latitude to market their goods to a broad consumer base. Like the regime, market professionals drew upon pre-Nazi ideas about buying and selling and applied them to their business models in the 1930s. But they always

Portions of this chapter are drawn from S. Jonathan Wiesen, "Creating the Nazi Marketplace: Public Relations and Consumer Citizenship in the Third Reich," in Geoff Eley and Jan Palmowski, eds., *Citizenship and National Identity in Twentieth-Century Germany* (Stanford, CA: Stanford University Press, 2008), 146–63. Reprinted with permission.

faced the risk of crossing a blurry line of correctness when crafting publicity materials. How could companies promote themselves aggressively without violating the regime's dictates about correct market behavior? To what extent could they maneuver through the ideological strictures imposed by the state? By focusing on different forms of corporate self-promotion, this chapter shows how manufacturers bought into and took advantage of Nazi ideology for their own purposes. Simultaneously, they encountered the reality that the state put its own, often-inconsistent priorities above a company's desire for profit. Marketing in the Third Reich was defined by the regime's and private industry's mutual exploitation, but also by companies' real frustrations about how to assert their own interests while adhering to Nazi dictates.

ADVERTISING AS BUSINESS PRACTICE
AND IDEOLOGICAL SHOWPIECE

In the preceding chapter we saw how the Nazi regime legislated a commercial morality. Through its Advertising Council, it sought to regulate the most ubiquitous and potentially the most dangerous expressions of consumer culture: retailing, advertising, and branding. But how did advertising actually function in Nazi Germany beyond the symbolic level? This section takes a closer look at developments within this medium during the Third Reich. Beyond simply focusing on print advertising and its creators, it argues that more innovative forms of company publicity from the pre-Nazi years found wide support after 1933, as market professionals mobilized a variety of modern media in order to communicate with a public still reeling from the economic depression. In widening their stock of marketing tools, companies encountered both a confusing bureaucracy and multiple ideological contradictions. Before looking at specific corporate publicity initiatives, however, it is useful to analyze the relationship of advertisers to the regime, which attempted to promote the ad industry in service of economic revival. There were three areas where the Nazi state involved itself in advertising during the prewar years. The first had to do with promoting a specifically "German" form of advertising, in part by regulating distinctions between national and international advertising norms. The second concerned the professionalization of advertising under the aegis of the state and the party. And the third area dealt with the use of advertising for nationalist purposes.

When the Nazis came to power, they faced the challenge of negotiating their relationship to a practice that had long been criticized as a dangerous

emodiment of "massification." Since the late nineteenth and early twentieth centuries, the growing presence of advertising had sparked concerns
about its cultural, psychological, and moral effects.[1] Werner Sombart had
seen advertising as reflecting the "imbecility of the great mass,"[2] while
businessmen themselves often felt that ads pandered to a vulgar clientele
to which their high-quality products were ill-suited. The labeling of advertising as seductive, crass, and socially disruptive was hardly exclusive to
Germany. But such concerns had greater resonance in a country where
the upheavals of war, revolution, and the shift from monarchy to democracy exacerbated fears about social dislocation. From Imperial Germany
through the Weimar years, advertisements and their producers were common scapegoats for what elites saw as the morally and socially debilitat-
ing effects of mass culture.[3] Despite such criticisms, by the early 1930s
companies and critics alike had more or less accepted the reality that
advertising was indispensable to the selling of goods. Meanwhile, politicians began to take full advantage of visual media in their campaigning.
In 1929 the World Advertising Congress (*Welt-Reklame-Kongress*) was
held in Berlin, an acknowledgment that the German capital had become
a global center for commercial media; political dignitaries and economic
leaders welcomed and took an active part in the event.[4]

Despite the growing influence of advertising in Germany, Adolf Hitler
came to power at a time when the country's ad industry was still seeking
public legitimation. The Depression had hurt the industry through the
decline in purchasing power, and more than ever, critics dismissed ads as
wasteful and immoral.[5] The Nazi regime did not put an end to negative
assessments of this medium but instead channeled them into the work of
the Advertising Council, which sought to counter potential abuses in commercial imagery. The Advertising Council tried to create a new form of
"German advertising" (*Deutsche Werbung*) that would be stripped of the
supposedly decadent features of international advertising and would promote the racially pure Volksgemeinschaft.[6] "Advertising must be German"

---

[1] See essays in Peter Borscheid and Clemens Wischermann, eds., *Bilderwelt des Alltags:
Werbung in der Konsumgesellschaft des 19. und 20. Jahrhunderts* (Stuttgart: Steiner, 1995).

[2] Uwe Westphal, *Werbung im Dritten Reich* (Berlin: Transit, 1989), 8.

[3] Warren G. Breckman, "Disciplining Consumption: The Debate about Luxury in Wilhelmine
Germany, 1890–1914," *Journal of Social History* 24, no. 3 (Spring 1991): 485–505.

[4] Victoria de Grazia, "Preface," in *Selling Modernity: Advertising in Twentieth-Century
Germany*, ed. Pamela E. Swett, S. Jonathan Wiesen, and Jonathan R. Zatlin (Durham,
NC: Duke University Press, 2007), xiii–xviii.

[5] See Introduction to ibid., 8–9.

[6] Westphal, *Werbung im Dritten Reich*, 50–57.

(*Werbung muss Deutsch sein*), proclaimed the Advertising Council, but as we saw in the preceding chapter, what counted as German was difficult to determine.[7] For example, in the desire to foment a national consciousness, the Advertising Council proscribed the use of foreign words in ads. But it inevitably encountered dilemmas. What did one do when it came to terms like "whiskey," which did not have a German equivalent, or "pyjamas" (pajamas), which was becoming as common in everyday language as the German word *Schlafanzug* (sleeping suit)?[8] Expunging non-German words from ads did not mean they could be removed from people's vocabularies.

Where the Advertising Council saw greater success was in demarcating political propaganda from commercial advertising. Here, they targeted ads that they believed offended the sensibilities of the Volk, took commercial advantage of Nazi ideology, or tarnished the landscape. Starting in January 1936, the Advertising Council banned advertising on the radio, which the regime saw as a precious propaganda tool not to be mixed with commerce. Pictures of swastikas or SS men, as well as portraits of the Führer and Nazi phrases, were also prohibited from appearing in ads or being displayed on storefronts, and the Advertising Council eventually mandated the end of roadside billboards, product plugs in editorials, and the unauthorized use of celebrities and politicians in advertisements.[9] Many companies pleaded to the Advertising Council and the economics ministry to overturn these rulings, which they considered damaging to business.[10] But these appeals were usually of no avail. The regime felt that the purification of advertising would keep commerce honest and the population focused on the ideological tasks at hand, particularly the push for economic self-sufficiency.

While the Nazi regime attempted to ensure that advertising was in accord with its own aims, the ad industry of the 1930s was not immune to developments beyond Germany's borders. Despite the Nazis' proclaimed aversion to foreign influences, advertisements after 1933 began to resemble those produced in the United States. A number of factors,

[7] Ibid., 50.

[8] Ibid., 51–52.

[9] Dirk Reinhardt, *Von der Reklame zum Marketing: Geschichte der Wirtschaftswerbung in Deutschland* (Berlin: Akademie, 1993), 429–41, 447; and Hartmut Berghoff, "'Times Change and We Change with Them': The German Advertising Industry in the Third Reich – Between Professional Self-Interest and Political Repression," *Business History* 45, no. 1 (January 2003): 128–47.

[10] See, e.g., Ingenieure Gies & Messerklinger Elektro-Akustic to Economics Ministry, 27 February 1935, R 3101/13791, BAB.

including expanding markets, the need to entice a socially diverse customer base, Germans' experiences working for U.S. ad agencies before 1933, and, ironically, the Nazis' own propagandistic innovations, led to an "Americanization" of German advertising in the "expanding use of text, of consumer-centered argumentation, of color printing and photography."[11] The European "punch in the eye" or "yelling" posters of the 1920s, in which a product stood boldly in the foreground accompanied by sparse text, gave way to ads that often had lengthy copy addressing the target audience by describing the merits of a product.[12] The importance of text did not, however, diminish the centrality of the image, and German ads in the 1930s were noted for their craftlike artistry, which often played a larger role in an ad's conception than did pure commercial interests.[13]

Thus advertising in Nazi Germany moved in opposing directions at once – toward a greater "Americanization" and toward an effort to create a pure German form. This tension makes it difficult, therefore, to generalize about the ideological content of advertisements in Nazi Germany. Much depended on the nature of a product, the audience, and the medium in which it was presented. While one might suspect that ads bore the hallmarks of Nazi racial ideology – blond subjects, anti-Semitic language, and conservative gender roles – the reality is that ad motifs varied widely and often did not reflect anything uniquely "German" or "National Socialist." The contradictions abounded. Fashion magazines highlighted the new woman in ways that were indistinguishable from American advertising (sometimes she even had a cigarette in her hand).[14] Ads in forestry journals, however, reminded readers that trees, like people, showed signs of degeneration and that German forestry should not countenance the presence of biologically lesser species.[15] Racist ads caricaturing Jews, Africans, and Black Americans were to be found, but even here they often resembled those in the United States or Britain, or images from

---

[11] Corey Ross, "Visions of Prosperity: The Americanization of Advertising in Interwar Germany" in *Selling Modernity*, ed. Swett et al., 52–77; also Alexander Schug, "Wegbereiter der modernen Absatzwerbung in Deutschland: Advertising Agencies und die Amerikanisierung der deutschen Werbebranche in der Zwischenkriegszeit," *WerkstattGeschichte* 34, no. 2 (2003): 29–52.

[12] Victoria de Grazia, *Irresistible Empire: America's Advance through Twentieth Century Europe* (Cambridge, MA: Harvard University Press, 2005), 257.

[13] Ross, "Visions of Prosperity," 58.

[14] Westphal, *Werbung im Dritten Reich*, 56.

[15] Michael Imort, "'Planting a Forest Tall and Straight like the German *Volk*': Visualizing the *Volksgemeinschaft* through Advertising in German Forestry Journals, 1933–1945," in *Selling Modernity*, ed. Swett et al., 102–26.

colonialist advertising.[16] Ads for Coca-Cola, to some an unsightly "foreign" or "Jewish" corporate presence, were so common that some people assumed that it was a German product.[17] Clearly, despite attempts to Germanize advertising, the Nazi regime recognized the economic value of "non-German" brands and motifs. It used a rhetoric of purity and invested the Advertising Council with the power to strip offensive advertisers of their right to work. But it tolerated certain forms of "foreignness," provided they did not violate the Nazis' prescribed norms of taste.

The regime showed a calculated flexibility with respect to the form and content of ads, but this was not the case with the ad industry's structure and personnel. Indeed, in the 1930s advertising in Germany was successfully "brought into line." Foreign agencies like J. Walter Thompson, which had arrived in 1928, either closed shop or were Aryanized, and they would not return to (West) Germany until after the war.[18] Jews were removed from their work with ad agencies and companies, making way for upstarts who showed loyalty to the regime. Here we encounter the Nazis' second major intervention in advertising: their attempt to professionalize the industry. Since World War I German artists and designers, like their counterparts in other countries, had sought professional recognition. In Imperial and Weimar Germany, there were several organizations for advertisers, but practitioners bemoaned the lack of respect accorded to them (in distinction, they pointed out, to their American counterparts).[19] After 1933, however, the Nazis gave professionalization a boost with the formation of new organizations, notably the National Socialist Federation of German Advertisers (NS-Reichsfachschaft Deutscher Werbefachleute), which was a compulsory state-run association representing anybody active in business, freelance, or public advertising work.[20] The Nazis resolved a Weimar era "lack of orientation"[21] in the field by establishing other related

[16] See Anne McClintock, *Imperial Leather: Race, Gender and Sexuality in the Colonial Contest* (New York: Routledge, 1995), 207–31. On racism in German colonial advertising, see David Ciarlo, *Advertising Empire: Race and Visual Culture in Imperial Germany* (Cambridge, MA: Harvard University Press, 2010).

[17] Jeff Schutts, "'Die erfrischende Pause': Marketing Coca-Cola in Hitler's Germany," in *Selling Modernity*, ed. Swett et al., 151–81.

[18] See S. Jonathan Wiesen, "Miracles for Sale: Consumer Displays and Advertising in Postwar West Germany," in *Consuming Germany in the Cold War: Consumption and National Identity in East and West Germany, 1949–1989*, ed. David F. Crew (Oxford: Berg, 2003), 151–78.

[19] Westphal, *Werbung im Dritten Reich*, 7.

[20] Berghoff, "'Times Change,'" 131.

[21] Reinhardt, *Von der Reklame zum Marketing*, 445.

organizations in their first two years in power: the Reich Federation of Advertisers (Reichsverband der Werbungtreibenden), the German Advertising Federation (Deutscher Reklame-Verband), the Advertising Protection Federation (Reklameschutzverband), the Federation of German Commercial Artists (Bund Deutscher Gebrauchsgraphiker), and the Federation of German Advertising Agencies (Verband Deutscher Annoncen-Expeditionen).[22] Such associations gave designers and admen a number of professional homes and with them opportunities to publish in journals, most notably *Seidels Reklame*, which had been on the shelves since 1913; *Gebrauchsgraphik*, on sale since 1924; and *Wirtschaftswerbung*, the official organ of the Advertising Council.[23]

Why did the regime push for the professionalization of advertising? The desire to streamline and control the industry notwithstanding, the Nazi leadership was trying to delineate the boundaries between Nazi ideology and commerce. While advertising was supposed to bear the hallmarks of a "German" sensibility, it was not supposed to *exploit* Germanness or National Socialist motifs for the purposes of profit. Not surprisingly, advertisers and artists found this directive distressingly vague. For example, in 1938 Fritz Sage, a Berlin painter who produced images of factories, machinery, farms, and landscapes (*Heimatbildschauen*), was taken to task for making valuable nationalist motifs available to firms for commercial purposes. Sage was expelled from the Reich Association of Visual Artists, and his company, German Rural and Cultural Images Advertising Propaganda (Deutsche Landes- und Kulturbilder-Werbepropaganda), was condemned for giving the misleading impression that its owner had the official sanction of the state in the production of "homeland" imagery. Sage, in turn, complained of being smeared by the Gestapo and for being insufficiently rewarded for his contribution to national propaganda though his images of Germans at work. Such complaints only brought more grief to the artist, who lost his permission to use *Heimat* images to advertise his own business. The regional (*Gau*) leadership in Berlin gathered evidence that his marriage did not conform to National Socialist principles and that he had called his wife a "cow" in earshot of his neighbors. His claims that he had been a Nazi since 1928 and that he refused to do business with Jews fell

[22] Ibid., 445–46.
[23] On attempts to turn advertising into a scholarly enterprise, see Claudia Regnery, *Die Deutsche Werbeforschung, 1900 bis 1945* (Münster: Monsenstein und Vannerdat, 2003), 41–43, 131–36.

on deaf ears. After three years of appeals, Sage lost the right to depict himself as a propagandist or artist.[24]

As Sage's case illustrates, advertisers' attempts to assert their own identities and use nationalist motifs for profit could come at a high price under a dictatorship. But even if they frowned on the seemingly arbitrary proclamations by the Advertising Council, most market professionals were pleased to be gaining public recognition. Indeed, in the mid-1930s, advertising saw a rebound from the Depression years in the number of ads produced, a strengthening of advertising departments within companies, a renewed interest in commercial psychology, and a resurgence of attention to innovations from the 1920s.[25] Advertising also came into its own as a distinct area of study. The Nazis encouraged the recognition of the medium through the opening in 1936 of the Reich Advertising Academy (Höhere Reichswerbeschule) in Berlin, which, writes Pamela Swett, "offered a multi-disciplinary education from the newest innovations in marketing techniques to art and design."[26] The goal, according to one of the school's professors, was to promote "men with practical organizational experience, propagandists of a rational practice of economics, and pioneers of methodical sales through masterful advertising!"[27]

This desire to create a new breed of "economic propagandist" speaks to the third aspect of the state's involvement, namely the mobilization of advertising for nationalist purposes. The regime had misgivings about exaggerated and socially disruptive advertisements, and companies were forbidden to profit from protected German or Nazi symbols in their ads, but this never translated into a wholesale dismissal of the medium. Quite the contrary, the regime went so far as to depend on advertising to promote its grandiose visions of national renewal. Indeed, Hitler's visions of a technologically modern Germany, connected by superhighways, relied upon the work of advertisers and graphic designers. Even though the mass production of Volkswagens never came to be under Hitler, the widespread depictions of "strength through joy cars" moving along sleek new Autobahns helped spark a widespread anticipation.[28]

[24] See, e.g., Reichard (President of Werberat) to Sage, 11 July 1938, and accompanying letters in R55/344, BAB.
[25] See Reinhardt, *Von der Reklame zum Marketing*, 447.
[26] Introduction to *Selling Modernity*, ed. Swett et al., 10; see also K. Th. Senger, "Zur Eröffnung der Reichswerbeschule," *Seidels Reklame* 20, no. 7 (July 1936): 234–35; and Westphal, *Werbung im Dritten Reich*, 90–96.
[27] Senger, "Zur Eröffnung der Reichswerbeschule."
[28] Wolfgang König, *Volkswagen, Volksempfänger, Volksgemeinschaft: "Volksprodukte" im Dritten Reich: Vom Scheitern einer nationalsozialistischen Konsumgesellschaft* (Paderborn: Schöningh: 2004), 151–91.

Not only did the regime recognize the indispensability of advertisements; it also asserted that advertising itself could be an expression of national greatness. Nowhere was this view more obvious than in an exhibition devoted to advertising in the new state: the Reich Exhibition of German Advertising (*Reichsausstellung Deutsche Werbung*), held in Essen in September and October 1936. The exhibit boasted seven large showrooms highlighting the work of advertising, film, radio, and the press as vital media for political propaganda. It spotlighted public service ads for the Nazi Winter Relief charity and for more mundane exercises in public safety, namely the purchasing of accident insurance for mishaps at home and in public places. It had special exhibits celebrating the national railway and postal services, as well as the state-owned airline Lufthansa. The event brought together industrialists, small entrepreneurs, retailers, salespeople, handworkers, and artists to celebrate advertising as a central part of the "economic reconstruction of the German Reich."[29]

At the same time, the exhibition highlighted the importance of the advertising medium for the private sector. Graphic designers, photographers, and printers demonstrated their crafts, a reading room filled with periodicals and books about advertising was open to visitors, displays of posters, placards, catalogues, advertising letters, and business cards lined the halls, and a life-size model of a company's advertising department was re-created. There were exhibitions on window displays, and visitors could watch advertising films, highlighting the bounty of popular products on the store shelves of Germany. The show also offered a sample of the new Reich Advertising Academy's lesson plans. A special exhibit called *100 Years of Germans Ads* (*100 Jahre deutsche Anzeige*) was created to give visitors a sense of pride in the long tradition of artful ads; for contrast, a tongue-in-cheek chamber of horrors of German advertising (*Schreckenskammer deutscher Werbung*) highlighted ghoulish advertising kitsch. Finally, the host city, Essen, treated the advertising exhibition as a major event in the Ruhr, with local newspapers holding competitions for the best ads and regional companies showcasing themselves with factory tours.

The national exhibition was successful in several respects. It boosted the reputation of advertisers and recognized them as useful members of the national community rather than as manipulative outcasts. It demonstrated that the public maintained a keen interest in the visual dimensions of the German economy and the ad industry more specifically; for every

[29] "Aufbau und Bedeutung der Reichsausstellung 'Die Deutsche Werbung,' *Seidels Reklame* 20, no. 9 (September 1936): 309–12.

person who dismissed advertising as an invasive and crude medium, there were many more who delighted in a firsthand look at commercial artistry. Finally, the event highlighted a theme that the regime would propagate throughout the 1930s: corporate imagery played a crucial role in Germany's economic reconstruction and, in turn, Nazi ideology. A writer for *Seidels Reklame* put it clearly when he indicated what was truly on display in Essen: "the political propaganda of National Socialism."[30]

Thus far, we have looked at advertising as part of the Nazis' ideological and bureaucratic reordering after 1933. But the state's promotion of advertising was always tied to its long-term goal, especially after 1936, of privileging production, achieving economic autarky, and steering consumer behavior along National Socialist lines. In pursuit of these aims, Joseph Goebbels created the Advertising Council as an arm of the propaganda ministry, and used advertising and propaganda to promote proper consumer behaviors. This work came under the purview of the National Committee for Economic Enlightenment (RVA), a limited liability company that was in reality a not-for-profit subdivision of the Advertising Council. As we will see, the RVA would play a major role in steering consumption during World War II, but it was also responsible during the 1930s for so-called community advertising or common-cause advertising (*Gemeinschaftswerbung*). In the 1890s companies began the practice of uniting with their competitors to produce ads advocating the specific branch of industry to which the firms belonged.[31] Through the 1920s one ad might promote several competing companies, while another touted the advantages of, for example, high-quality umbrellas and the independent businessmen who sold them. Community advertisements also promoted in a single visual image products that were often associated in consumers' minds, like cigarettes and armchairs, or cameras and cigarette lighters (presumably the sort of sophisticated people who bought cameras were also smokers).[32]

After 1933 community advertising became less about the joint promotion of a branch of industry for commercial purposes than about creating a portrait of consumer prosperity. In the late 1930s the RVA produced community advertising for porcelain, toys, hats, vinegar, German jewelry, and the hairdressing business, and it even put out annual "steering

[30] Ibid.
[31] Reinhardt, *Von der Reklame zum Marketing*, 148–68.
[32] Ibid., 149.

of consumption" (*Verbrauchslenkung*) calendars.[33] While such ads promoted a diversity of product sectors, their broader aim was to convince
consumers that Germany was still rich in shopping opportunities, despite
increasing austerity measures, and that the government would educate
the populace in correct forms of consumption. There was thus a thin line
between advertising and propaganda in the RVA's work. This was clear
in the organization's "laundry action" (*Waschaktion*), which Hermann
Göring ordered the RVA to conduct in 1936 in conjunction with the
Four Year Plan as a means of weaning Germans from expensive, energy-
inefficient methods of cleaning clothes.[34] According to Hanns Brose, who
lent his talents to the campaign with the slogan "Wash laundry white"
(*Wasche Wäsche Weiss*), 100 million marks worth of textiles were damaged every year as a result of bad washing techniques. One might consider laundry a private matter, argued Brose in 1939, but as long as the
state had decreed price and wage freezes, it was up to the government
to teach the Volk how to save money and resources.[35] Private companies played a key role in this campaign, at once promoting their own
products and proving their allegiance to the state. For example, Henkel,
the manufacturer of Germany's most popular laundry detergent, Persil,
worked with the RVA before and during the war, encouraging the use of
its water-softening agent, Henko, which enabled women to clean clothes
effectively and save soap.[36] (Soap was made with precious fats that were
increasingly rare due to the lack of imports.)

Because of the propagandistic value of advertising, the industry
retained its valued status over the course of the 1930s, in part because
it was promoted by a state that had every interest in keeping businesses
profitable and consumers happy. The public was also intrigued by the
industry, as evidenced by the success of the Essen exhibition. But despite
these inroads, professional admen still faced two suspicions: first, that
they manipulated the public into buying goods and, second, that the
costs of advertising increased the final price of merchandise. Ad executive

---

[33] See letters from the President of the Advertising Council to the RVA, 1938–1940,
R5002/7, BAB.
[34] On the participation of housewives and women's organizations in this propaganda, see
Nancy Reagin, "*Marktordnung* and Autarkic Housekeeping: Housewives and Private
Consumption under the Four Year Plan, 1936–1939," *German History* 19, no. 2 (June
2001): 162–83.
[35] Hanns Brose, speech manuscript on "Wasche Wäsche Weiss," 18 July 1939, R5002/26,
BAB.
[36] See Chapter 5.

Harry Damrow, who produced ads for Aschinger foods and hotels and
for the 1936 Olympic games, insisted in his 1981 autobiography, "I was
not a hidden persuader" (*Ich war kein geheimer Verführer*). Damrow
was referring not only to his postwar career, when fears of "totalitarian"
mass manipulation dominated cold war discourses about advertising, but
also to the concern that he trafficked in lies and exaggeration during the
Nazi years. To the contrary, insisted Damrow, "while in politics National
Socialism worked with lies and half-truths, advertising saw the reestab-
lishment of clarity, truth, and fair rules of engagement for all parties."[37]
Even with the increased respect for advertisers in the Nazi state, the
profession still had to make a public case for its virtues, and its leaders
pushed practitioners not simply to advertise products, but also to produce
"advertisements on behalf of advertising" (*Werbung für die Werbung*, an
updated version of the older slogan *Reklame für die Reklame*).[38] The goal
of self-promotion, argued an article in *Seidels Reklame*, was to correct a
false view that advertising served self-interested rather than "national-
economic" ends.[39] In the 1930s advertisers had to simultaneously affirm
their nationalism while fighting for the same resources available to their
American counterparts. Establishing the Reich Advertising Academy was
a good start, but some advertisers wanted more support for the profession. In 1938 the Advertising Council looked into the establishment of
an academic research center for economic advertising, which would be a
small step toward emulating Britain and the United States, where there
were "countless professorships and research centers for advertising."[40]
This goal was realized in part in the form of an archive in Austria. After
the *Anschluss* in the spring of 1938, Austrian advertiser Theodor Lach
established the Advertising Science Archive (Werbewissenschaftliches
Archiv) in Graz. It contained more than 200,000 objects for teaching
and exhibition and included a specific department devoted to advertising law and an information center containing examples of every type
of advertising the world over.[41] Director Lach excitedly summed up the

[37] Harry Damrow, *Ich war kein geheimer Verführer: Aus dem Leben eines Werbeleiters*
(Rheinzabern: Dieter Gitzel, 1981), 47.
[38] Advertising Council President Ernst Reichard to RVA re. campaign "Werbung für die
Werbung," 24 August 1938, R5002/7, BAB.
[39] S. A. Ehrler, "Werbung für die Werbung," *Seidels Reklame* 20, no. 10 (October
1936): 343–46.
[40] Denkschrift über die Gründung einer Wissenschaftlichen Forschungsstelle für
Wirtschaftswerbung. Sent by Reichard to Karl Hanke of Advertising Council board,
February 1938, R55/345, BAB.
[41] Theodor Lach, "Ideen und praktische Verwirklichungsvorschläge zur Gründung des
Deutschen Werbe-Archives," 14 April 1938, R55/345, BAB.

aims of the archive in terms that his colleagues and the propaganda ministry would surely have approved of: "Advertising is more than a field of research; it is an expression of a political and economic era."[42] For Lach, this era was defined by both the international norms of product promotion and the specific ideological aims of the Nazi state.

BEYOND THE AD: MARKETING, PUBLIC RELATIONS, AND THE PRAGMATICS OF SELLING

"One can safely say that in the field of advertising, there has been no noticeable progress in the past twenty-five years. It has been at a standstill. This is due to the disappearance of the economic means during the long crisis years."[43] So wrote Theodor Lach shortly before he unveiled his new archive in Graz. But was Lach right? From the outbreak of World War I in 1914 up through Weimar and the first five years of the Nazi state, had there really been no advances in this area? Lach was correct that most innovations in advertising – from displays in store windows to ads on billboards or the sides of railcars – had their modern origins in the nineteenth and early twentieth centuries.[44] But while these forms of company publicity could be found in an earlier era, they gained in popularity during the interwar years. Only gradually did companies accept the necessity of marketing aggressively not only their products but also their names.

The preceding section of this chapter focused on the ideological and professional imperatives that lay behind the revival of the ad industry in Nazi Germany. Despite the push to create a distinct form of German advertising, the regime, having based its own success on visual agitation, countenanced the use of international advertising norms in the name of Germany's economic revival, provided they did not cross barriers of taste or violate national interests. But on an everyday level, how did companies take advantage of these opportunities and negotiate the state's mandates? What tools did they use in order to sell products and services? In particular, how did Bayer and Henkel, two companies that sold medicines and cleaning products and thus could claim a special relationship to völkisch

[42] Ibid.
[43] Ibid.
[44] Reinhardt, *Von Reklame zum Marketing*, 169–329; and Uwe Spiekermann, "Window-Display Advertising in German Cities during the 19th Century: A Story of an Enduring Success," in *Advertising in the European City: Historical Perspectives*, ed. Clemens Wischermann and Elliott Shore (London: Ashgate, 2000), 139–71.

health, take advantage of the Nazis' devotion to racial purity? Answering this question requires looking not only at advertising but also at companies' broader promotional activities in the 1930s. Business leaders in the Third Reich experimented with a diversity of marketing and public relations methods that had predated the Nazi years and that were employed in multiple countries. In turn they faced the often arbitrary reactions of the state toward attempts to sell merchandise and services solely for their companies' financial benefit.

Distinguishing between advertising and other forms of corporate communications is not easy, as many publicity practices are subsumed under the broad category of "advertising." But even before the English word "marketing" entered the German lexicon, economic leaders understood that selling depended on a much wider collection of practices than simply the visual ad spot. This wider understanding was reflected in a linguistic development. *Reklame*, from the French word for "advertising" (*réclame*), had been in wide use since the nineteenth century and remains so today, but during the 1930s professionals and the public increasingly employed the German word *Werbung*.[45] "Reklame" bore negative associations with crude hucksterism, and it was also seen as limited in application. When denouncing advertising, critics would refer to "Reklame" more often than to "Werbung."[46] Although the latter term technically also meant "advertising," it came in the interwar years to embody a wider variety of approaches to product communication, more akin to our contemporary understanding of "marketing." A *Werbeabeilung* (literally "advertising department") became responsible over the course of the twentieth century for most matters of company publicity, not just visual representations of the goods on sale.

Reflecting this interest in a diversified medium, *Seidels Reklame* in the 1930s bore all the features of a modern journal devoted to the international practices of company publicity. A single issue from 1936 excerpted articles from the American ad journal *Printers' Ink* on the importance of humor in advertising, offered features on advertising in Estonia and Britain, surveyed the effectiveness of advertisements for beauty products, debated the use of arguments in ads, and discussed the merits of placing ads in address books and calendars. But it also went beyond the print

[45] On *Reklame* and its critics see Christiane Lamberty, *Reklame in Deutschland, 1890–1914: Wahrnehmung, Professionalisierung und Kritik der Wirtschaftswerbung* (Berlin: Duncker & Humblot, 2000), 54–58.
[46] There were plenty of critics of *Werbung* too.

advertisement as such, offering tips about the use of lighting in window displays and documenting the growing sophistication of company films.[47] The latter medium, in particular, flourished during the Weimar years and especially during the Third Reich. Product films (*Produktenfilme*), three- to five-minute-long advertising films (*Wertwerbungsfilme*), scientific films (*wissenschaftliche Filme*), and a variety of cinematic company profiles known as "cultural films" (*Kulturfilme*) were screened at exhibitions, at schools, during company tours, at special showings for professionals and party members, and in movie theaters before a main feature.[48] UFA and other major movie studios often produced them, and they starred pop- ular actors and made use of innovations in sound, lighting, and anima- tion. The Nazi years saw a steep rise in the number of these movies, which Henkel's advertising director, Paul Mundhenke, praised for offer- ing "new methods of mass influence."[49] A highlight was the February 1937 profile of the steel company Mannesmann, which opened at the UFA Palace cinema at the Berlin Zoo. A forty-piece orchestra conducted by film composer Wolfgang Zeller provided the accompanying music and debuted the especially composed "Mannesmann Overture." Later that year the film was acknowledged for its "aesthetically valuable" qualities at annual film festivals in Venice and Paris.[50]

A burst of creative energy in company publicity coincided with the economic recovery of the 1930s. But simultaneously, the reorientation of the economy according to the Four Year Plan for austerity created a quandary for companies as they exploited new marketing tools. These firms, increasingly beholden to governmental production priorities, should have had little incentive to concern themselves with the demands and wishes of their customers. The top-down approach to the economy would presumably have mandated a reorientation of marketing methods,

[47] For these articles see *Seidels Reklame* 20, no. 3 (March 1936): 77–138.
[48] For an introduction to advertising and industrial films in Germany, see Manfred Rasch, Karl-Peter Ellerbrock, Renate Köhne-Lindenlaub, and Horst A. Wessel, eds., *Industriefilm – Medium und Quelle: Beispiele aus der Eisen- und Stahlindustrie* (Essen: Klartext, 1997); also Reinhardt, *Von der Reklame zum Marketing*, 330. See also "Chronologische Darstellung der Entwicklung der Bayer-Filmstelle von Dr. Weintraud," 1.6.6.31, undated, Bayer Achive, Leverkusen [hereafter BAL].
[49] Paul Mundhenke, "Werbefilm-Erfahrung und Werbefilm-Erfolg," H430 (Filme – 1927–1939), Henkel Archive, Düsseldorf [hereafter HA].
[50] Horst A. Wessel, *Filmschätzen auf der Spur: Verzeichnis historischer Filmbestände in Nordrhein-Westfalen* (Düsseldorf: Staatliche Archive des Landes Nordrhein-Westfalen, 1994), 143–69; and Wessel, *Kontinuität im Wandel: 100 Jahre Mannesmann, 1890–1990* (Gütersloh: Mohndruck, 1990), 22.

not just production aims. Yet even if the Nazi economy was based on "dictatorial state interventionism,"[51] profit motives remained, and advertisers and economists freely explored the latest methods and rationales for selling their products. If they felt constrained by the new push to propagandize for the state, this did not stop the production of purely commercial images. Indeed, the dictates of the state allowed for a measured utilization of patriotic motifs for sales purposes. Here the idea of public relations becomes key: it stood for strategies of selling during the Third Reich that relied on a more expansive view of corporate communications and social responsibility. The company was not just a profit-maker but a corporate citizen as well.

In order to analyze corporate public relations under National Socialism, it is important to provide a cursory history of the concept. While the 1910s and 1920s saw an explosion of PR agencies in the United States, the self-conscious use of the English phrase "public relations" did not become commonplace in Germany until the founding of the Federal Republic in 1949.[52] Yet historians of modern Germany have located the *practice* of public relations in the latter half of the nineteenth century. More than simply product advertising, public relations revolved around the dissemination of a positive image of the corporation and the national economy writ large. For example, in 1851 the Krupp concern displayed its massive cannons and won a number of prizes for high-quality production at London's Great Exhibition of the Works of Industry of All Nations (Crystal Palace Exhibition).[53] Its "publicity work" soon entailed

---

[51] Avraham Barkai, *Nazi Economics: Ideology, Theory, and Policy* (New Haven, CT: Yale University Press, 1990), quoted in Pierre Aycoberry, *The Social History of the Third Reich, 1933–1945* (New York: New Press, 1999), 115.

[52] On the origins of public relations in the Federal Republic, see S. Jonathan Wiesen, *West German Industry and the Challenge of the Nazi Past, 1945–1955* (Chapel Hill: University of North Carolina Press, 2001), 101–13; Elisabeth Binder, *Die Entstehung unternehmerischer Public Relations in der Bundesrepublik Deutschland* (Münster: Lit, 1983); and Christian Kleinschmidt, *Der Produktive Blick: Wahrnehmung amerikanischer und japanischer Management- und Produktionsmethoden durch deutsche Unternehmer, 1950–1985* (Berlin: Akademie, 2002), 204–21.

[53] Barbara Wolbring, *Krupp und die Öffentlichkeit im 19. Jahrhundert: Selbstdarstellung, öffentliche Wahrnehmung und gesellschaftliche Kommunikation* (Munich: Beck, 2000), 95–100. On the development of public relations during this period, see also Astrid Zipfel, *Public Relations in der Elektroindustrie: Die Firmen Siemens und AEG, 1847 bis 1939* (Cologne: Böhlau, 1997); and Reinhardt, *Von der Reklame zum Marketing*, 429–41; on the Weimar and Nazi period, see Marius Lange, *Zwischen Demokratie und Diktatur: Unternehmerische Öffentlichkeitsarbeit in Deutschland, 1929–1936* (Frankfurt am Main: Peter Lang, 2010), 23–28.

the advocacy of business-friendly government policies, close links to the news media, product advertising, and careful exercises in damage control when members of the much-followed Krupp family misbehaved. In the late nineteenth century, Krupp and other large companies founded their own news and press offices, as well as in-house advertising and cultural branches.[54] Company literary bureaus and historical archives were created to build links to industry's new discovery – "the public."[55]

But what, exactly, was the nature of this relationship between the company and the public? Today, many PR experts see their work as a mutual dialogue with rational consumers, who maintain considerable power to accept or reject the offerings of a given firm.[56] But this idea of public relations as a "two way street,"[57] grounded in the open exchange of ideas, did not represent the views of early corporate publicity experts. In the 1920s American PR counsel Edward Bernays (Sigmund Freud's nephew) portrayed public relations not as an exercise in democratic discourse but rather as company-driven "propaganda."[58] As the number of PR firms and advertising agencies mushroomed in the United States and abroad, their chief spokesmen, eager to craft a scientific rationale for publicity, drew upon concepts culled from modern psychology, including "herd instinct," "suggestion," and "mass persuasion."[59] These works anticipated an understanding of the public that would inform modern public relations. Publicity experts also turned to earlier studies of "the masses,"

[54] Michael Kunczik, *Geschichte der Öffentlichkeitsarbeit in Deutschland* (Cologne: Böhlau, 1997), 193–95.

[55] On the utility of this concept for historians, see Axel Schildt, "Das Jahrhundert des Massenmedien: Ansichten zu einer künftigen Geschichte der Öffentlichkeit," *Geschichte und Gesellschaft* 27, no. 2 (April–June 2001): 177–206. For a media studies perspective, see Peter Szyszka, ed., *Öffentlichkeit: Diskurs zu einem Schlüsselbegriff der Organisationskommunikation* (Opladen: Westdeutscher, 1999).

[56] On the history of PR from the perspective of mass communications, see Heinz D. Fischer and Ulrike G. Wahl, eds., *Public Relations/Öffentlichkeitsarbeit: Geschichte – Grundlagen – Grenzziehungen* (Frankfurt am Main: Peter Lang, 1993). For a good volume that brings together the insights of media studies and history, see Clemens Wischermann, Peter Borscheid, and Karl-Peter Ellerbrock, eds., *Unternehmenskommunikation im 19. und 20. Jahrhundert: Neue Wege der Unternehmensgeschichte* (Dortmund: Gesellschaft für Westfälische Wirtschaftsgeschichte, 2000).

[57] Stuart Ewen, *PR! A Social History of Spin* (New York: Basic Books, 1996), 186.

[58] Edward Bernays, *Propaganda* (New York: Liveright, 1928).

[59] On Sigmund Freud's influence on advertising and PR, see Eli Zaretsky, *Secrets of the Soul: A Social and Cultural History of Psychoanalysis* (New York: Knopf, 2004), 144, 237. On advertising, public relations, and the shift from Freudian to behaviorist understandings of consumer behavior, see Olivier Zunz, *Why the American Century?* (Chicago: University of Chicago Press, 1998), 57–61.

notably the fin-de-siècle works of French sociologist Gustave Le Bon. Whereas Le Bon saw Europe as entering an "era of crowds," defined by a collective and dangerous irrationality,[60] other social psychologists like Gabriel Tarde charted the transformation of these "masses" into a more rational "public." "The crowd" could be gathered in a discrete physical space, while the "public" was a metaphysical entity, composed of widely dispersed individuals venturing into the market with shared values and demands for personal fulfillment.[61]

Le Bon and Tarde provided two different models – one negative and one affirmative – for understanding group psychology, and in the early twentieth-century companies reflected both in their publicity strategies. Responding to the latent needs of the "masses" while satisfying the more rational demands of the "public" became a fundamental challenge, which companies met through advertising, marketing, and the projection of corporate integrity.[62] With the acceleration of mass consumption in the 1920s, company publicists studied and debated Fordist ideas of production and consumption, and pursued the practices of "psychotechnics" and "human relations" in order to chart both factory workers' and the broader public's shifting desires.[63] While the United States was the undisputed forerunner in PR practices, Weimar Germany saw similar, if also more ambivalent attempts to understand citizens as consumers who could exercise power though making choices in the marketplace.[64]

---

[60] Gustave Le Bon, *The Crowd: A Study of the Popular Mind* [1895] (Atlanta: Cherokee Publishing, 1982), xv.

[61] See Gabriel Tarde, "The Public and the Crowd," in Tarde, *On Communication and Social Influence: Selected Papers*, ed. Terry N. Clark (Chicago: University of Chicago Press, 1969), 277–96. On the relationship between Le Bon's and Tarde's ideas, see Ewen, *PR!* 64–70; Dominik Schrage, "Integration durch Attraktion: Konsumismus als massenkulturelles Weltverhältnis," *Mittelweg 36* 12, no. 6 (2003): 57–86; Clark McPhail, *The Myth of the Madding Crowd* (New York: Aldine de Gruyter, 1991), 2–9; and Rosalind H. Williams, *Dreamworlds: Mass Consumption in Late-Nineteenth-Century France* (Berkeley: University of California Press, 1982), 322–84.

[62] On the idea of the "virtuous" company having a "soul," see Roland Marchand, *Creating the Corporate Soul: The Rise of Public Relations and Corporate Imagery in American Big Business* (Berkeley: University of California Press, 2001), 7–26.

[63] See Mary Nolan, *Visions of Modernity: American Business and the Modernization of Germany* (Oxford: Oxford University Press, 1994), 84–98. On advertising psychology, see Reinhardt, *Von der Reklame zum Marketing*, 49–99.

[64] On the links between personal gratification, political empowerment, and economic choice for Weimar women, see Julia Sneeringer, "The Shopper as Voter: Women, Advertising, and Politics in Post-inflation Germany," *German Studies Review* 27, no. 3 (October 2004): 476–502.

Public relations entailed a new understanding of the modern citizen, but it also called for the recognition that the fates of big business and the nation were entwined. This link between the company and the nation endowed publicists with a sense of mission: businesses would have to instill trust in the institutions of government and industry at times of political and economic upheaval. Thus corporate publicists and professional advertisers were concerned not only with the promotion of specific products, but also with the potential power of a company name to induce feelings of national pride or tap into consumers' unspoken desires for comfort and safety. What made people choose one product or one company over another? Were consumers more receptive to subliminal enticements or to more transparent accounts of a product's advantages? How could the health of a company be tied to national vitality? By the 1930s these were the defining questions for PR advisers in Europe and the United States.

One can trace the introduction of the concept of public relations in Germany to an article by Carl Hundhausen in 1937. In the 1920s Hundhausen studied economics and worked as a financial consultant to the Krupp concern. He spent the years 1927–31 in New York as an assistant treasurer of a bank on Wall Street, returning again to the United States in 1937 as marketing director of Dr. Hillers AG (a manufacturer of peppermint drops), where he studied the latest methods of corporate publicity. Hundhausen believed that modern "American" public relations could be imported to a National Socialist setting.[65] He argued that while Germans had always engaged in public relations, companies would be wise to follow the lead of American firms in promoting "goodwill." More than simply advertising, public relations sought to circulate a "truthful" interpretation of a company, so that its reputation would match its inner character. Hundhausen did not ignore the differences between Nazi Germany and the United States, "the land of so-called *civil liberty*," where economic individualism and a "Jewification" of society undermined communal thinking. But he detected in his country the same "desires for security," and he called upon companies to attend to "the sociological aspect of human relations" in their attempts to earn public confidence.[66] The notion of "winning public trust," as articulated by both

[65] Carl Hundhausen, "Public Relations," *Zeitschrift für Betriebswirtschaft* 15, no. 1 (1938): 48–61. On Hundhausen's career see Eva-Maria Lehming, *Carl Hundhausen: Sein Leben, sein Werk, sein Lebenswerk – Public Relations in Deutschland* (Wiesbaden: Deutscher Universitäts-Verlag, 1997).
[66] Hundhausen, "Public Relations," 49.

Hundhausen and Hans Domizlaff, the father of German branding, would become central to PR theories in West Germany.[67] But already by the late 1930s, it resonated with Nazi ideology, which celebrated the concept of trust (*Vertrauen*) in the name of racial and national unity.[68] (In a 1940 speech, Hitler used the word "Vertrauen" ten times.)[69] The Nazi marketplace thus depended on public relations to engender a sense of national vitality. It made room for companies to promote themselves, as long as this self-endorsement shed light on Germany's economic greatness.

It is, again, important to note that the boundaries between advertising, marketing, publicity, and public relations were always vague, and this goal of projecting goodwill could be accomplished through a variety of means that defy easy categorization. The key point is that companies and the state began to amass a bigger variety of tools for promotion in the 1930s. A list of the holdings in the Advertising Council library around 1937 reveals the breadth of interests in the many facets of corporate communications. The library was broken down into categories that included reference works, the legal aspects of the ad industry, socialism and the economy, and economic conditions in foreign countries. Prominent on its bookshelves were works on consumer psychology and "economic propaganda" written by prominent admen like Domizlaff, who designed logos for Siemens and Reemstma with the goal of penetrating the "mass brain."[70] Advertising Council employees also had access in the library to Hitler's *Mein Kampf* and numerous books on anti-Semitism and Jews in the economy, such as Werner Sombart's *The Jews and Economic Life*. The Nazis may have purged public libraries and burned books by Jewish authors, but the Advertising Council was keen to access the insights of Jews who had published on marketing. In its library one could find

[67] See Carl Hundhausen, *Werbung um öffentliches Vertrauen: "Public Relations"* (Essen: W. Girardet, 1951); and Hans Domizlaff, *Die Gewinnung des öffentlichen Vertrauens* [1939] [7th ed.] (Hamburg: Gesellschaft für angewandtes Marketing, 2005).

[68] For the importance of trust to National Socialism, see Eugen Diesel, "Die Welt ohne Vertrauen," *Deutsche Rundschau* 64 (1937): 81–85; and Bruno Bauch, "Das Vertrauen als ethisches Problem," *Die Tatwelt* 14 (1938): 67–74. For recent literature on Vertrauen, see Ute Frevert, "Vertrauen: Historische Annäherungen an eine Gefühlshaltung," in *Emotionalität: Zur Geschichte der Gefühle*, ed. Claudia Benthien, Anne Fleig, and Ingrid Kasten (Cologne: Böhlau, 2000), 179–97.

[69] "Adolf Hitler Rede am 30. Januar 1940 im Sportpalast Berlin," http://www.worldfuture-fund.org/wffmaster/Reading/Hitler%20Speeches/Hitler%20Rede%201940.01.30.htm (accessed 5 September 2007).

[70] Rainer Gries, Volker Ilgen, and Dirk Schindelbeck, eds., *"Ins Gehirn der Masse kriechen!" Werbung und Mentalitätsgeschichte* (Darmstadt: Wissenschaftliche Buchgesellschaft, 1995), 45–73.

four books on economics by murdered Jewish businessman and former German foreign minister Walter Rathenau, advertising pioneer and publisher Rudolf Mosse's and his family's newspaper catalogues, and countless books by Americans and Britons, some of them Jews, who were leaders in the fields of advertising and marketing. The library contained Edward Bernays's *Propaganda* (1920), the German translation of Henry Ford's *Moving Forward* (1930), and department store founder and frequent European traveler Edward Filene's *The Way Out: A Businessman Looks at the World* (1925).[71]

The Advertising Council's exhaustive and racially undiscriminating literature on advertising, sales, marketing, and distribution mirrored the multiple forms of marketing methods of which companies availed themselves in the Nazi years. Even with the constraints imposed by the regime and the attempts to Germanize ads, corporate publicity in the 1930s proceeded from the idea that international practices could ultimately be reconciled with National Socialist goals of inspiring confidence in the Volksgemeinschaft. Ironically, the more companies were forced to follow the dictates of a "nonegotistical" advertising, the more they relied on PR conventions that transcended national boundaries and that are still familiar today.[72] Hot air balloons and airplanes bore corporate logos and advertising slogans; companies christened ships bearing their names; and business leaders led Nazi politicians, visiting foreign dignitaries, and Olympic athletes on factory tours.[73] During the peak year of 1938, Henkel led eighty thousand guests on such visits, where they could watch workers at their stations and view high-budget promotional films that they may have missed in their local theaters.[74] All of these gestures at once reinforced confidence in a company name and contributed to the visual spectacle that accompanied economic renewal in the 1930s.

The Henkel chemical company was particularly skilled at adapting its public image to the new political setting, and it offers a window into the common workings of public relations and marketing in the Third Reich and into companies' attempts to navigate the Nazi marketplace. Already

[71] Advertising Council library holdings in "Bücherei des Ad Counciles der deutschen Wirtschaft," R2301/6991, BAB. On Filene, see de Grazia, *Irresistible Empire*, 137–40.

[72] For a discussion of the different publicity means available to companies, see Paul Mundhenke, "Wirkungsgrenzen der Markenartikel – Insertion und deren Beurteilung durch den Vertreter," *Blätter vom Hause* 18, no. 1 (1938): 7–13, HA.

[73] See "Olympiade – '*Bayer*' Tag: Programm für die Fabrikbesichtigung," 168/2.29, BAL.

[74] Wilfried Feldenkirchen and Susanne Hilger, *Menschen und Marken: 125 Jahre Henkel, 1876–2001* (Düsseldorf: Henkel, 2001), 257.

famous for its advertisements, particularly its 1922 "White Lady" (*Weiße-Dame*) – the stylish "new woman" clad in a flowing white dress and hat and holding a box of Persil detergent – Henkel saw numerous opportunities for publicity under National Socialism.[75] Like most firms, the company aligned itself with Nazi aims and reported on Hitler's public events and proclamations with great fanfare. But Henkel also promoted the virtues of its own products and its ethos of customer service in an increasingly global marketplace. Throughout the 1930s the company set up "Persil instructional institutes" and "mother schools" in Germany and abroad.[76] There, housewives learned how to "soften the water" with the help of Henkel's lime removers and produce the cleanest laundry possible with Persil detergent. Along with these hands-on promotional efforts, Henkel hoped to reach "in-house" consumers and company salespeople through employee magazines, which made creative use of its Persil trademark. In a regular feature column, readers followed the travels of the wide-eyed protagonist, "Persil," who regularly wrote a letter to his *Lieber Reiseonkel* (dear globetrotter) to report the company's many exciting public events, like the unveiling of the Henkel pavilion at the 1937 World's Fair in Paris. "Persil knights" saved the housewife from backbreaking labor, and "Persil pioneers" forged new paths in research and production. At trade fairs and in their accompanying literature, poets and songwriters paid homage to Henkel products, while managers asked company employees to use the slogan "cared for by Persil" (*Persil-gepflegt*) whenever possible in conversation.[77] The overwhelming presence of Persil can be compared to product saturation today, carrying in the 1930s a comforting message of familiarity and reliability: in the face of rapid change, to invoke the famous slogan, *Persil bleibt Persil* (Persil is still Persil).[78]

Another company from the chemical sector that was attuned to broader forms of corporate promotion was Bayer. Here too we witness the aggressive steps businesses took to promote themselves. The company, part of the IG Farben combine, had its own "internal propaganda

[75] See Elisabeth Schmidt, *Musterbetriebe Deutscher Wirtschaft: Henkel & Cie A.G. Chemische Produkte Düsseldorf* (Leipzig: Übersee-Post, 1934), 65.
[76] "Zur Eröffnung des Persil-Instituts in Zürich," *Blätter vom Hause* 19, no. 3 (1939): 131, HA; and "Mütterschulungskursus," *Henkel-Bote* 7, no. 4 (1938): 189, HA. On state-sponsored household training for women, see Reagin "*Marktordnung*," 162–83.
[77] Paul Mundhenke, "Der Begriff 'persil-gepflegt' als Bestandteil des hausfraulichen Sprachschatzes," *Blätter vom Hause* 17, no. 7 (1937): 274–75, HA.
[78] This slogan was ubiquitous; see, e.g., "Brief aus Düsseldorf," *Blätter vom Hause* 15, no. 11 (1935): 423, HA. On Henkel's and other companies' marketing slogans during the Nazi period, see O. F. Döbbelin, ed. *Tausend und ein Slogan* (Berlin: Kurt Elsner, 1937).

office," which issued reports describing the applications and advantages of every Bayer product. These were disseminated to company employees, especially its sales personnel, who would be well versed in products as diverse as cameras, insect repellent, waterproofing chemicals, and toothbrushes. Employees were even supposed to be aware of seasonal fashion trends: the propaganda office reminded them that the color of the summer of 1939 was fuchsia.[79] In addition, Bayer employees were supposed to talk up the company's products whenever possible, but not to overuse the Bayer cross logo when producing visual material; this risked saturating the public with too much Bayer imagery. Public relations was about more than selling products, and therefore the company's education division also coordinated public and employee concerts and a number of leisure events in conjunction with KdF and the propaganda ministry.[80] In keeping with a key lesson of modern public relations, Bayer (with help from the Nazi Party) hoped to spread goodwill and company loyalty both inside and beyond the walls of the firm.

One more part of Bayer's massive publicity apparatus is worth mentioning. The company in Leverkusen maintained a "central propaganda" branch, which had its own film division and published a newspaper that kept its finger on the pulse of corporate communications abroad.[81] For example, it regularly excerpted the work of Herbert Newton Casson, a prolific British expert on sales, marketing, management consulting, and financial self-help, who had written seventy books and pamphlets by the early 1930s.[82] Before moving to Britain, Casson had worked in the United States, where he helped found the powerful ad agency H. K. McCann in 1912. McCann, whose most prominent client was Standard Oil, embraced the concept of "total marketing," which included motivational research, the use of in-house libraries, sales promotion and production surveys, and the building of goodwill for the firm by selling "your company as well as your goods."[83] In Germany dozens of Casson's

[79] Rundschreiben no. 12/1939, Werksmäßige Aufklärungs–Propaganda für I.G.–Produkte des tägl. Bedarfs, 3 July 1939," 237/3.4.13, BAL.

[80] See files in 237/2, BAL.

[81] "Filmarbeit der Zepro-Zweigstelle," *Zepro-Nachrichten* 1 (1938): 9–10, 167/9.1–167/9.4.1, BAL.

[82] On Casson and management consulting, see Michael Ferguson, *The Rise of Management Consulting in Britain* (Burlington, VT: Ashgate, 2002), 32–33.

[83] Herbert N. Casson, *Tips for the Traveling Salesman* (New York: B. C. Forbes, 1927), 75. On McCann and "total marketing," see http://adage.com/century/people061.html (accessed 10 November 2009). McCann established a branch in Berlin in 1927.

translated books found their way onto the shelves of company publicity divisions like Bayer's and the Advertising Council's library.

The interest in Casson's work reflected the fact that most large German companies still had to think not only about international trends but also about an international clientele. Multinational firms like Bayer depended on sales throughout the world, and they were compelled to devise ways of appealing to foreign consumers, foreign visitors, and a domestic population that valued the company's international stature. One medium that Bayer used to consolidate its link to the world was the window display, a subject about which Casson had written.[84] According to a 1937 company booklet, window displays were only then coming into their own as a form of company promotion, and Bayer hoped to be on the cutting edge of this medium. The fact that window displays had been used for many decades did not stop the Bayer writer from making this claim.[85] There was a time not long ago, the pamphlet argued, when the druggist took little interest in decorating his or her store window. "Today, however, the pharmacist knows the propagandistic values of the window display."[86] The idea was to catch people's attention while they were passing by a shop, thereby enticing them to enter. In this area, Bayer claimed to be doing "pioneering work" by creating decorative displays and educating pharmacies in Germany and abroad about the importance of the store window. Because Bayer had markets all over the world, the window display was a key form of so-called prestige advertising (*Prestigewerbung*), which would highlight the superiority of the company to foreign and domestic customers.[87]

Bayer's window displays reflected a combination of motifs that would both appeal to an international audience and convey the unique attributes of the company to its domestic customer base. Highlighting the attractiveness of other cultures was one way of appealing to Germans' sense of adventure and wanderlust. In 1937 Bayer drafted a series of pharmacy window displays that celebrated the company's fiftieth anniversary. The aim was to showcase visually the overwhelming presence of the firm in

[84] Herbert N. Casson, *Twelve Tips on Window Display* (London: Efficiency Magazine, 1931).

[85] On window displays in Wilhelmine Germany, see Lamberty, *Reklame in Deutschland*, 54–58, and Gudrun M. König, *Konsumkultur: Inszenierte Warenwelt um 1900* (Cologne: Böhlau, 2009), 126–41.

[86] "Bayer" *überall in der Welt: Zepro Schaufenster-Vorschläge zum "Bayer-Jubilaüm"*, in Sonder-Ausgabe der *Zepro-Nachrichten* (December 1937), 167/9.1, BAL.

[87] Ibid.

FIGURE 5. Mock-up of Bayer window display: the Rainbow Bridge in Utah, 1937. (*"Bayer" überall in der Welt: Zepro Schaufenster-Vorschläge zum "Bayer"-Jubilaüm*, in Sonder-Ausgabe der *Zepro- Nachrichten*, December 1937, 167/9.1; courtesy of Bayer Archive, Leverkusen.)

the global marketplace by offering an "exotic moment" for German and foreign passersby. Designers placed images of Bayer products against colorful East Asian backgrounds with text headings like "The Strange World of the Far East" (with the subtext "Strange world in the Far East, strange values, strange culture, but even there one takes aspirin for headaches, rheumatism, and the flu").[88] In these mock-ups, Bayer pain relievers also stood in front of the Rainbow Bridge National Monument in Utah, which evoked the rugged and enchanting American West. They were similarly juxtaposed with images of the Mexican desert landscape, with cactuses and sombrero-wearing natives. Declared one ad: "The Mexican takes ... aspirin and Pyramidon with the same confidence and as eagerly as the European."[89] Other suggested displays showed local celebrations and peoples in their native dress in India, China, Indonesia, and Morocco.

These dazzling images of the "Wild West" and the Orient suggested a visual world far removed from the ideological setting of the

[88] Ibid.
[89] Ibid.

FIGURE 6. Mock-up of Bayer window display: images of the Far East, 1937. (*"Bayer" überall in der Welt: Zepro Schaufenster-Vorschläge zum "Bayer"-Jubilaüm,* in Sonder-Ausgabe der *Zepro- Nachrichten,* December 1937, 167/9.1; courtesy of Bayer Archive, Leverkusen.)

Volksgemeinschaft. On their face, they worked to distance Bayer from the Nazi regime and associate it instead with global diversity. But they actually mirrored values promoted by the National Socialist leadership: a crude nationalism, the exporting of German "civilization," and scientific benevolence. It is likely that Bayer's images spoke, in particular, to a public still mourning the loss of Germany's overseas possessions after World War I. While the Nazis were careful in their first three years not to force the issue of the former colonies, by 1937 Hitler was declaring that they were "our lost property and the world will be obliged to return them."[90] Bayer's orientalist images thus combined jingoism with older motifs of the "civilizing mission" that Germany and its companies carried over from the colonial era into the interwar years. "Bayer Drugs for the

---

[90] Mary E. Townsend, "The German Colonies and the Third Reich," *Political Science Quarterly* 53, no. 2 (June 1938): 186–206. On colonialism in the Third Reich, see Sabine Hake, "Mapping the Native Body: On Africa and the Colonial Film in the Third Reich," in *The Imperialist Imagination: German Colonialism and Its Legacy,* ed. Sara Friedrichsmayer, Sara Lennox, and Susanne Zantop (Ann Arbor: University of Michigan Press, 1998), 163–88.

Colonies?" queried one wartime ad. Bayer products, the text concluded, "are indispensable for the protection of health in the colonies."[91] Other ads dealt less with German territorial claims than with the delivery of German ingenuity to underdeveloped areas of the globe. An ad bearing the words "Adventure in the Andes" (*Abenteuer in den Anden*) featured a picture of a mule perched on the side of a cliff and carrying Bayer products. According to the ad, the mule rider is greeted with joy in the smallest village, for he brings the "advances of medical science deep into the wilderness."[92] Bayer, and by extension German know-how, had penetrated even the most backward areas. This notion of a company as an embodiment of the nation – engaged in civilizing global backwaters and freeing them from disease – was not unique to Germany. Britain's Pears Soap ads from the nineteenth century are perhaps the best known example of an imperialist commercialism that called on tropes of cleanliness.[93] Bayer's PR work fell in this vein, expressing the delicate balance between commerce, nationalism, health, and racism. It revealed both "Nazi" values (or, more accurately, long-standing values that the Nazis tried to make their own) and the tropes of international publicity. It also revealed the difficulty of determining from ad content alone whether a company was breaking with or bolstering the regime. The reality was that the Nazi marketplace was flexible enough to accommodate publicity norms that were not, as such, "German" and that could be effective beyond the borders of the Reich.

Another aspect of Bayer's and other companies' public relations reveals this tension between conventional and ideologically laden public relations: namely, the idea of building bonds of trust with the public. The concept of trust, or Vertrauen, was the cornerstone of Bayer publicity and appeared often in its ad copy and its promotional materials.[94] As we have seen, the word also took on a National Socialist cast, with trust being a necessary component of the relationship between Volk and the Führer. In ads and on product packaging, the Bayer cross was often accompanied by the phrase "the mark of trust" (*Das Zeichen des Vertrauens*). This moniker implied trust not just in a given product, but also in the scientists and workers who stood behind them. Building confidence in merchandise and services merged with the aims of building trust in professionals, the

---

[91] Ad in *Kölnische Illustrierte Zeitung* (1944), 167/8, BAL.
[92] Ibid.
[93] McClintock, *Imperial Leather*, 207–31.
[94] See "Kundendienst hilft verkaufen," *Zepro-Nachrichten* 1 (1938): 14–15, 167/9.1–167 /9.4.1, BAL.

state, its leaders, and Germany's seemingly humanitarian mission. Bayer ads thus harked back to the genius of creation by invoking images of scientists, doctors, and pharmacists of old, whose discoveries were German gifts to humankind. One ad mourned the loss of "one of the great creative men of Germany, Albrecht Dürer," who died of malaria in an era when Bayer antimalarial drugs did not exist.[95] "Trust is the first step in healing," proclaimed another ad.[96] Company-sponsored consumer reports in the 1930s also attested to the power of trust. A 1939 survey of Bayer's so-called goodwill or trust advertising (*Vertrauenswerbung*) documented how medical practitioners, pharmacists, and laypeople responded to the company's public service spots and products.[97] Such advertising included exhortations that people see their doctors before a disease progressed, and the survey found this and other forms of early prevention advocacy to be effective with the public. It also revealed that "Vertrauen" had many meanings, including trust in doctors and trust in the truthfulness of Bayer's ads. Interviewees praised both the message of the ads and their formal merits, from their artistic qualities to their use of "great men, like politicians, poets, and researchers."[98]

In these examples of marketing and public relations, Bayer did not reference National Socialism directly; indeed, in most respects it was forbidden to do so. But these marketing undertakings did not need to mention Nazism, for the company understood that its product lines occupied a valuable place in a society devoted to health and racial purity, and the regime, in turn, lavished its praise. Bayer made it clear, for example, that its many films – which addressed the diverse themes of sleep, jaw surgery, blood, and the wonders of the microscope – were "in service of the Volk's health."[99] The Nazis were particularly excited about a 1938 Bayer film directed by Walter Ruttmann, famous for his studies of film and rhythm and his 1927 classic, *Berlin: Die Sinfonie der Grossstadt* (Berlin: Symphony of a great city). Like most other industrial films of the period, Ruttmann's *Im Zeichen des Vertrauens* (literally "In the Sign of Trust," liberally translated by the company as "In Service of Humanity")

95 Ad in *Atlantis* (1938), 167/8, BAL.
96 Ad in *Kölnische Illustrierte Zeitung* (1943), 167/8, BAL.
97 "Die 'Bayer'-Vertrauenswerbung im Urteil der Ärzte," August 1939, S 1939/10/1, BAL; and "Die 'Bayer'-Vertrauenswerbung im Urteil des Laien," 1939, S 1939.10/2, GfKA. See also "Die 'Bayer'-Wertwerbung 1941 im Urteil des Lesers," Summer 1941, S 1941/7, GfKA.
98 "Die 'Bayer'-Vertrauenswerbung im Urteil des Laien," 94.
99 "Bayer-Filme, Aufstellung Jahreswende 1935/36," Werksfilme, 92/1 (unpaginated), BAL.

had no Nazi images, as it was made to promote Bayer abroad. (It focused on the mission of Bayer in the global fight against syphilis, influenza, typhus, and other tropical diseases.) But the film did not have to display Nazi imagery for its domestic audience either. By its very message, according to the Nazi newspaper *Völkischer Beobachter*, the movie advanced a distinct ideology, not just for the company, but for Germany.[100] In short, both the company and the state were keen to promote German ingenuity as part of the state's "peaceful" approach to international relations. With its products and films, Bayer was proving itself a model corporation, attuned to the demands of maximizing company profits and protecting the national community.

Again, it would be facile to characterize such standard forms of corporate public relations, especially for a pharmaceutical company, as uniquely fascist. These examples of marketing and advertising were common methods of product placement and self-promotion. Publicity practices, notably advertising, from the Weimar years could not simply be abandoned overnight with the Nazi takeover of power.[101] But German companies faced the challenge of reconciling their images as international firms (which depended on marketing strategies that transcended domestic concerns) with the reality that they now operated in a radically new, hypernationalist political setting within Germany. Even as companies celebrated international solidarity in their advertisements or through their participation in world fairs, corporate public relations served the racist and paternalistic aims of the Nazi state. In a Leistungsgemeinschaft, the regime joined with companies to project images of strength and quality production. This ideological goal rested on the "education" of the public through organizations like the RVA and in KdF events. A Persil teaching institute could at once serve the needs of a company and the state by cultivating brand loyalty and instructing the public in the virtues of sacrifice and hard work.

Moreover, the regime saw itself as educating the population in the values of biological purity. Thus despite German companies' employment of common publicity methods of the 1930s, one must not underestimate the uniquely racist setting in which they were produced. In employee magazines, articles about marketing were routinely juxtaposed with others that honored the Nazi leadership and the company's contribution to the

---

[100] See reviews excerpted in brochure for *Im Zeichen des Vetrauens*. Provided by BAL achivist, 29 April 2005.
[101] Berghoff, "'Times Change,'" 144–45.

building of a Volksgemeinschaft. Firms like Henkel and Bayer manufactured health-care and cleaning products that supported the Nazi vision of a healthy Volk. During the war Henkel's employee publication, like other companies', occasionally called up images of unsavory, hook-nosed Jews delighting in their financially driven war against Germany.[102] Henkel also mobilized not only vague colonialist stereotypes about scientific beneficence, but also cruder images of African savages cleansing themselves of their blackness by bathing in or drinking Henkel detergents.[103] Bayer's wartime film *Abenteuer im Urwald* (Adventure in the jungle) also showed stereotypical cartoon images of clownish Africans stung by mosquitoes while dancing. Resochin, the company's antimalarial drug, would soon cure them.[104]

Given the relative infrequency of racist ads compared with less offensive fare, one may wonder what commercial advantage such imagery had for companies. This is not easy to determine. Most likely, company advertisers were not making strategic decisions to include racist images, as much as merely expressing prejudices that consumers shared. In the Third Reich, Germans were confronted on a daily basis with both mundane commercial imagery and more crudely racist propaganda. The fact that the two existed side by side in company publicity should not be surprising, as a firm hoped to reach a broad customer base by tapping into both wishes and fears, many of them racialized. Moreover, this was a key feature of the Nazi marketplace, namely the juxtaposition of conventional forms of commercialism – which had themselves drawn on racist themes since the nineteenth century – with more virulent forms of Nazi racism.

Of course, despite the continuities in advertising, companies did feel pressured to provide their National Socialist bona fides, and in this regard we cannot separate marketing decisions from the context of a punishing dictatorship. A company had the advantage of being directly in touch with consumers, which meant that it could serve as a conduit for repressive messages coming from above. In Henkel's advice to traveling salespeople,

---

[102] See the cartoons in Dr. Meyersahm, "Englische Gewaltpolitik: Der Raub der dänischen Flotte im Jahre 1807," *Blätter vom Hause* 20, no. 14 (1940): 341, HA.

[103] P. Maywald, "Mohrenwäsche: Eine Betrachtung über Reinlichkeit der Neger in den afrikanischen Kolonien Deutschlands," *Blätter vom Hause* 19, no. 5 (1939): 188–92. See cartoon of a colonial explorer presenting Persil to a scantily clad African carrying a tray of tropical fruit on his head. The caption reads, "Armer Mensch, so schwarz! Probieren Sie's doch mal damit! [Poor man. So dark! Give this a try!]," in Mundhenke, "Wirkungsgrenzen," HA.

[104] *Abenteuer im Urwald* (1941/42), BAL.

for example, the company indicated that if a customer complained that the quality of soap had declined (something that would become increasingly true under the Four Year Plan),[105] one should respond with a flat-out denial. First, however, the salesperson should remind the customer of how "dangerous" it was to "spread unsubstantiated rumors about the products of German industry."[106] While it was unlikely that Henkel found any commercial advantage in threatening its customers, it clearly felt that it had to protect itself by reprimanding those who did not watch what they said. Functioning in a repressive environment, however, could more directly advantage a firm. When a biography was too critical of a company, as was the case with Bernhard Menne's 1937 history of the Krupp firm, the book was referred to the Gestapo and censored.[107] When assessing public relations and marketing in the Third Reich, then, one cannot forget the larger picture of racism, repression, and intimidation. A dialectic between opportunism and anxiety defined most companies' and their customers' relationship to the Nazi marketplace.

PRIVATE SATISFACTION, PUBLIC GOOD, AND PROFIT: OPPORTUNITIES AND TENSIONS IN THE RACIAL STATE

Thus far I have demonstrated how multiple forms of corporate publicity, emerging from transatlantic practices before 1933, dovetailed with – and took advantage of – the aims of the Nazi state. By linking shopping and national renewal, companies applied prevailing methods of marketing and public relations to a fascist setting and turned average Germans into patriotic consumers who served the public good by supporting the economy. Despite increasing regulations on advertising and economic activity, the visual manifestations of this public good remained decidedly commercial throughout the prewar years. In advertisements, in storefronts, and on packaging, national well-being was on full display. There were two other sites where the same dynamics were at work: trade fairs and exhibitions. On the fairgrounds visitors bore witness to business efforts to align their fates with that of the nation. Unlike other forms of marketing, which

---

[105] On the use of cheaper materials and ingredients in consumer goods and foods, see Reagin, *Marktordnung*, 183.

[106] "Ein aktuelles Zwiegespräch zwischen Hausfrau und Werbedame," *Blätter vom Hause* 15, no. 4 (1935): 169, HA.

[107] Bernhard Menne, *Krupp: Deutschlands Kanonenkönige* (Zurich: Europa, 1937). On Krupp's reaction to the Menne book, see files in WA 56/164, Krupp Archive, Essen. Menne was writing from abroad and remained untouched by the Gestapo.

depended on the consumer stumbling upon motifs of economic renewal in a product ad or at the point of sale, the fair represented an orchestrated expression of patriotic commercialism, which the public willingly participated in. The marketing efforts of private firms, the ideological value of consumption, and messages of national greatness all came together in the many exhibitions held throughout the Nazi years.

The regime was actually ambivalent about fairs and exhibitions, worrying that too many public spectacles that were not specifically devoted to Nazi ideals led to overcompetition and materialism. In response to complaints about the skyrocketing number of fairs, the Advertising Council put a stop to the proliferation of exhibitions, leading to a steep decline in their occurrence. Yet there remained more than two thousand such events in prewar Nazi Germany, reflecting the power of profit and visual display to project national strength in the Third Reich.[108] Bayer, Henkel, and numerous other companies showcased their contributions to völkisch health in annual exhibits like the annual Brown Trade Fair (*Braune Messe*), the Reich Garden Show (*Reichsgartenschau*), "Nature and Volk" (*Natur und Volk*), and 1935's "The Wonder of Life" (*Das Wunder des Lebens*), which highlighted new developments in racial hygiene.[109] These exhibitions culminated in the summer of 1937 with the World's Fair in Paris and the simultaneous Düsseldorf exhibition *Schaffendes Volk* (translated sometimes as "A People at Work," but more meaningfully as "A Nation of Creators").[110] The latter, billed as the first Reich exhibition to celebrate the rebirth of the economy, was a showpiece of the Nazis' Four Year Plan for economic self-sufficiency, and with the eager patronage of Hermann Göring, it highlighted the role of the country's companies in providing jobs, promoting technical ingenuity, and fostering innovative energy- and food-saving techniques on the personal and national level. On the exhibit fairgrounds, Germany's largest companies displayed their wares and production techniques. Seven million visitors enjoyed themselves by walking though a reconstructed Coca-Cola bottling plant and drinking the popular soft drink for 25 pfennig.[111] Companies arranged special day

[108] Westphal, *Werbung im Dritten Reich*, 77; and Berghoff, "'Times Change,'" 135.

[109] *HAG-Post* no. 6 (7 July 1936), KFA. On this last exhibit, see Arie Hartog, "Eine bloße Fortsetzung der Politik mit anderen Mitteln? Zur Ideengeschichte der Böttcherstrasse bis 1945," in *Projekt Böttcherstrasse*, ed. Hans Tallasch (Delmenhorst: Aschenbeck & Holstein, 2002), 341–60.

[110] See "Schaffendes Volk," *Vierjahresplan* 1, no. 5 (May 1937): 283; and E. W. Maiwald, *Reichsausstellung Schaffendes Volk–Düsseldorf 1937: Ein Bericht* (Düsseldorf: A. Bagel, 1939).

[111] Schutts, "Die erfrischende Pause," in *Selling Modernity*, ed. Swett et al., 168.

FIGURE 7. Deputy Führer Rudolf Hess looking at a handicrafts display at Schaffendes Volk exhibition, Düsseldorf, 1937. (RWB 1284/17; photograph: Pressebilderdienst C.A. Stachelscheid Düsseldorf; courtesy of Landesarchiv Nordrhein–Westfalen.)

trips for their employees, who would combine a visit to Schaffendes Volk with a trip down the Rhine River.[112] By visiting the exhibition, ordinary Germans could witness, according to one observer, "how the generation of economic value and the multifarious ramifications of technical progress provide the Volk with what is needed to live, while also uniting with the Volk's cultural achievements to form a harmonious whole."[113]

One of the most popular sites at Schaffendes Volk, the Henkel exhibition, brings into relief the Nazis' goal of regulating private consumption for the national good. The Düsseldorf chemical company built a pavilion that contained a model home filled with its products and sanitized with its cleansers. Sparkling kitchens gave way to dining rooms and living rooms decorated with furniture made from synthetic materials. Walls were adorned with placards explaining Henkel's products in detail.

[112] "Programm für den Werksausflug der Kammerich-Werke AG, Brackwede-Süd, zur Reichsausstellung 'Schaffendes Volk,'" RWK 703, Nordrhein-Westfälisches Hauptstaatsarchiv, Düsseldorf.

[113] Ernst Poensgen, "'Schaffendes Volk,'" *Stahl und Eisen* 17, no. 18 (6 May 1937): 466. Quote from Schutts, "Die erfrischende Pause," 168.

FIGURE 8. Henkel pavilion at Schaffendes Volk. (RWB 3289/1; courtesy of Landesarchiv Nordrhein–Westfalen.)

A child's bedroom was spruced up with Henkel paint, its furniture was sealed with Henkel glue, and a bathtub was made of Henkel plastic. Visitors, including Adolf Hitler, could browse through a photo exhibit highlighting the life and achievements of company founder Fritz Henkel, watch a demonstration of Henkel's scientific laundering methods, or view a film about the firm's contributions to national productivity.[114] In an internal memo about the exhibition, the Henkel management asked its employees to promote these displays in the spirit of both a "propagandist and skilled worker."[115] They should take care to emphasize that Henkel products were the result of individual craftsmanship, not impersonal assembly-line manufacturing, and they should employ whenever possible the company slogan "Choose Henkel – choose quality" (*Wer Henkel wählt – wählt Qualität*).[116]

The exhibition's appeal to the domestic realm suggests a tension at the heart of many companies' marketing undertakings in the 1930s. In its

[114] On this exhibit see file H480/229 (Ausstellungen – "Schaffendes Volk"), HA.

[115] Hubert Werthenbach to "Meine lieben Arbeitskameraden!" undated, H480/229, HA.

[116] Ibid. For a study of Schaffendes Volk from a design historian's perspective, see Stefanie Schäfers, *Vom Werkbund zum Vierjahresplan: Die Ausstellung "Schaffendes Volk," Düsseldorf 1937* (Düsseldorf: Droste, 2001).

FIGURE 9. Adolf Hitler visiting the Henkel pavilion. (RWB 3845/2; courtesy of Landesarchiv Nordrhein–Westfalen.)

model house filled with time-saving devices and stylish furniture, Henkel put the private sphere and the possibilities of personal satisfaction within it on dramatic display. Even though it was billed as evidence of collective endeavor, Schaffendes Volk relied upon notions of individual gratification within the private realm. By consciously selecting Henkel products, men and women could enhance their leisure activities and fill their homes with objects of their desire. In the process they would support the nation's economic, hygienic, and racial revitalization, and public sacrifice would be rewarded with personal satisfaction. As Nancy Reagin has shown in her study of the Four Year Plan, even though the consumer sector was curtailed during the late 1930s, the state continued to portray shoppers, particularly women, as politically vital. By sustaining the private sphere of the home through their thrifty purchasing decisions, women were contributing to the autarkic aims of the state in their capacities as "housewife-consumers." While women's choices were ultimately limited by the poor selection of consumer goods, the identification of domestic self-sufficiency with the public good accorded women a measure of social power, however limited.[117] The symbolic connection between the public good and private consumption was not exceptional to National

[117] Reagin, *Marktordnung*, 184.

Socialism. Indeed, the United States in the 1930s saw similar rhetorical links between consumer empowerment and the revitalized health of the economy. But this connection took on a unique cast in a setting where the boundaries between the private and the public were continually and often violently breached. Corporate public relations appealed to a domestic, private sphere as a locus of personal gratification at a moment when this sphere was highly permeable and vulnerable to the state.

In addition to foregrounding privacy, such marketing also appealed to notions of difference and heterogeneity. Here, too, there was a tension between corporate communications and Nazi ideology. This could be seen in the training tips that Henkel gave to its traveling salespeople. Despite the regime's official promotion of social conformity, Henkel advised representatives to personalize the sales experience by addressing their customers' sense of individuality and their human need for respect.[118] "We must not forget," wrote Henkel's advertising director Mundhenke, "that people are all different – different in character, in disposition, in temperament. They are different in manners of thinking and logic, and different in age, sex, and origin."[119] This respect for diversity, according to Mundhenke, ought to inform not only the company's promotional efforts, but also its intimate contacts with clients. Let the customer "mother" the salesperson in her own home, give her a sense of control over the conversation, let her show off her knowledge of a product, and be sure to impress her with small details about her personal life on subsequent visits.[120] This advice about personalizing the sales experience was echoed in the work of other companies. Herbert Casson's 1927 book, *Tips for the Traveling Salesman*, caught the attention of Bayer. Ten years after its publication, the company published excerpts in its employee magazine, including such advice to salespeople as "Don't take 'no' for a final answer," and "Keep mentally and physically fit."[121] In its in-house publications, Bayer encouraged its representatives to heed the "voice of the public" in ways that honored individual differences.[122]

---

[118] Norbert Stern, "Über den persönlichen und geschäftlichen Takt," *Blätter vom Hause* 16, no. 9 (1936): 331–32, HA.

[119] Mundhenke, "Wirkungsgrenzen," HA.

[120] "Frontmensch Vertreter," *Blätter vom Hause* 18, no. 9 (1938): 330–55, HA.

[121] Casson, *Tips for the Traveling Salesman*; see individual chapter titles for these tips. Translated as "12 Winke für den reisenden Kaufmann," *Zepro-Nachrichten* 1 (1937): 2–3, in 167/9.1, BAL.

[122] See feature called "Die Stimme des Publikums," *Zepro-Nachrichten* 3 (1938): 11–14, BAL.

The use of standard marketing and sales strategies suggests that company publicists were trying to navigate a number of tensions within Nazi Germany: between the national and the global, between the private and the public, and between manipulation and consent. While in some respects Hitler wanted to see Germans as a racially pure mass – a single entity that would respond in unison to visual and rhetorical cues – private companies had a stake in appealing to people as individuals with idiosyncrasies. By proclaiming the consumer's right to choose from a variety of products or to be treated as special, companies played to people's sense of personal entitlement and uniqueness. At the same time, publicity experts understood that modern marketing required homogeneity: by buying a particular car or detergent, the customer satisfied personal desires while also making the same choices as millions of others. This interplay between individuality and conformity is a key component of modern marketing, but, again, it was uniquely pronounced in the Third Reich, where political and racial conformity were mandated by the state. If "the masses" were vulnerable to manipulation through a few rote slogans and more subtle persuasion, "the public" was much savvier, holding greater power to disrupt the ideological status quo through expressions of consumer dissatisfaction. The challenge for company publicity experts in the 1930s, therefore, was to determine when exactly people acted as rational consumers and when they relinquished their individuality and became part of the crowd.[123]

A final tension that shaped the operation of marketing under National Socialism concerned the relationship between Nazi ideology and company self-promotion. As we have seen, while the regime welcomed expressions of National Socialist ideals in commercial publicity, any attempt to *exploit* Nazi ideology for business purposes would be confronted head-on. This in turn caused confusion among company leaders about what the safe boundaries for marketing were. There are numerous cases of firms stepping over this undemarcated line of "proper" commerce. For example, in April 1934 the Continental rubber company erected a brightly lit tire advertisement in a Berlin plaza that had been renamed Adolf Hitler Square the preceding year (today Ernst Reuter Platz). After receiving complaints about the plaza's "crude and

---

[123] On the relationship between personal agency, individuality, and mass thinking, see, e.g., G. A. Pfarrius, "Persönlichkeit," *Blätter vom Hause* 16, no. 10 (1936): 360–61, HA; see also Kurt Stern, *Masse-Persönlichkeit und Gemeinschaft: Ein Beitrag zur Frage der Auflösung der Masse* (Stuttgart: Verlag für Wirtschaft und Verkehr, 1938).

disfigured" appearance, the government forced the company to remove its sign because it caused aesthetic damage to a public space dedicated to the Führer.[124] The Nazi state also began to appropriate language that it felt should no longer belong to the corporate world. Notably, the word "propaganda" was banned from commercial use in 1937; the Advertising Council ruled that it could no longer be used as a substitute for "advertising" but only for political purposes.[125]

Another word removed from companies' marketing arsenals was *Rundfunk*, or "radio," which Goebbels declared to be the property of the propaganda ministry, given how important this medium was for the dissemination of National Socialist ideals. Companies that had tapped into the mass appeal of radios – from the Hamburg firm Walter Messmer, with its "radio coffee" (*Rundfunkkaffee*), to the Berlin furniture company Möbel-Hübner, with its "radio kitchen" (*Rundfunk-Küche*, a kitchen counter cabinet with a radio built in) – now had to eliminate the treasured word from their domestic advertising by specified dates.[126] The affected businesses registered their frustration with this rule. Messmer protested to the Advertising Council that its radio coffee brand had been a staple of its public relations for five years – appearing in films, in fashion shows and theater works, and on street signs and postcards – and that it would be financially damaging to give it up; the company had already poured 600,000 reichsmarks into this cornerstone of its corporate identity.[127] The propaganda ministry was not persuaded, however, and stuck to its decision. Möber-Hübner, however, met with greater success. After it lodged a protest, the Advertising Council, the propaganda ministry, and the Reich Chamber of Radio decided the company could contintue to call its product "the radio kitchen," given that "there is a direct connection between the piece of furniture and the radio apparatus." Ultimately, ten other companies were banned from using the word "radio" to sell products. "Radio magic tobacco" (*Rundfunkzauber*), "radio razor blades" (*Runkfunkklingen*), and a variety of other products took on new names. Moreover, on order of the propaganda ministry, there was to be no such

---

[124] Staatskommission der Hauptstadt Berlin to Reichswirtschaftsministerium, 29 November 1935, R3101/13793, BAB.

[125] *HAG-Post*, no. 5 (29 June 1937), box R2 94/7, file 0096 4370, KFA.

[126] Advertising Council to Goebbels, 22 June 1938, R55/344, BAB; and President of Advertising Council to Propaganda Ministry (RMVP), 21 November 1938, R55/344, BAB.

[127] Abschrift, Rechtsanwälte E. A. Utescher et al. to the President of the Advertising Council, 6 April 1938, R55/344, BAB.

thing as a "radio begonia," a popular type of flower known to botanists, as of January 1941.[128]

Another example of a company running into trouble with the authorities involved higher stakes and a greater presence. It concerned one of Henkel's most elaborate PR undertakings, namely the production and screening of the 1938 UFA film *Henkel – ein deutsches Werk in seiner Arbeit* (Henkel: A German company and its work). Like the Bayer film mentioned earlier, this was directed by Walter Ruttmann, who used typical KdF images of clean factories and joyful workers to highlight the company's products and its contribution to the greater social good; its aim was to create a "monument to the name and concept 'Henkel.'"[129] Scenes showed Henkel employees checking out books from the company library, engaging in group calisthenics, relaxing on park benches, and taking walks on the company grounds.[130] In early 1939 the Henkel management was particularly excited about its plans for screenings in one hundred cinemas around Germany, including the UFA Palace in Berlin.[131]

At first glance the film did not appear to be controversial. At the end of 1938 the censors in the propaganda ministry approved the film, but it ran into trouble with the Advertising Council. The council accused the film of exploiting National Socialist ideals to promote Henkel's own reputation. In particular, Henkel was showcasing for marketing purposes the social benefits and leisure opportunities that every company should be providing to its workforce. The company was directed to remove all images relating to employee welfare; otherwise it would have to cancel its nationwide screenings and show the film only to its workers.[132]

The Henkel management was dumbfounded. After spending many years conforming to the regime's ideological standards for workplace camaraderie, cleanliness, and leisure, the company argued, it was now

---

[128] President of Advertising Council to RMVP, 13 August 1949, R55/344, BAB.

[129] "Wir fangen an. Wieder: Henkel-Film-Matineen!" *Blätter vom Hause* 20, no. 1 (1940): 21, HA.

[130] For images from the film see E. Endress, "Henkel – Geist im Henkel Film: Ein UFA Mitarbeiter berichtet über seine Eindrücke vom Henkel-Werk," *Blätter vom Hause* 19, no. 3 (1939): 120–25, HA. On the technical and aesthetic aspects of this film, see Jeanpaul Goergen, *Walter Ruttmann: Eine Dokumentation* (Berlin: Freunde der Deutschen Kinemathek, 1988), 154–55.

[131] Werbeabteilung (Advertising Branch) Henkel to Firma Universum Film A.G. (UFA) in Berlin, 25 January 1939, Zug – no. 438 (Press Office files), file 4 (Censoring of the film "Henkel – ein deutsches Werk in seiner Arbeit" 1938–39), HA.

[132] Ibid.

FIGURE 10. Scene from *Henkel – ein deutsches Werk in seiner Arbeit*, 1937. Henkel employees engage in group calisthenics. (Courtesy of Bundesarchiv-Filmarchiv, Berlin.)

asked to remove any visual depictions of its successes.[133] Nor was it easy to excise this major portion of the film without destroying the work's integrity and coherence. In its written protests to the Advertising Council, the company was careful to celebrate the Nazi factory community. But the management could not avoid airing its frustration about the regime's prohibitions against economic "opportunism." Wrote Paul Mundhenke, "What's the point of even making a company film if it can't be used for advertising purposes?" If the company had just shown people in their work clothes at their stations, the management insisted, Henkel would have been accused of *failing* to portray National Socialist principles. Henkel also posed to the Advertising Council a series of questions that exposed the shakiness of Nazi policies regarding marketing and public relations. Should the company sports teams carry flags with the swastika,

[133] On the Nazis' Beauty of Labor program, see Alf Lüdtke, "The 'Honor of Labor': Industrial Workers and the Power of Symbols under National Socialism," in *Nazism and German Society, 1933–1945*, ed. David F. Crew (London: Routledge, 1994), 67–109.

the company logo, or both, or carry no flags at all? If it was acceptable to tout the company's ideological contributions in anniversary volumes, firm histories, and brochures, why could it not do so in ads or in films?[134]

The Advertising Council did not have immediate answers, but it did demand further alterations to the film. In keeping with its laws against competitive advertising, the Advertising Council found other problems with the film. Henkel had to remove the statement "Persil is in every case superior," unless it could document that this was true. Henkel could not present its antibacterial soap as essential to fighting infant mortality, given that there were other methods necessary for lowering the death rate among children. Finally, in showing crosses to depict death, Henkel was coming too close to promoting Christianity.[135]

In response to these complaints, the company scoured back-issues of the Advertising Council's journal, looking in vain for indications that these scenes from the film violated Nazi policy. It compiled worldwide statistics and presented bacteriological studies on mortality to defend its claims about soap and infant deaths, and it besought the Advertising Council to consider the *Henkel* movie more as a "filmed rendition of a factory tour" than a publicity work.[136] In the end, faced with Henkel's exhaustive defense of the film, the Advertising Council appears to have backed down;[137] in the course of 1939, the movie was shown to thirty-seven thousand viewers in fifty-one cities. While the war interrupted the screening, it resumed in the winter of 1940 to much critical praise.[138]

The eventual resolution in favor of the company reveals a flexibility within the regime's censorship apparatus. But the controversy also exposes the challenges of marketing in Nazi Germany. Henkel, which had built a reputation as a producer of high-quality goods and images, hoped after 1933 to continue promoting its name. Yet with increasing demands for ideological conformity, the company found itself frustrated in its attempts to speak to the public without violating the state's anticompetitive dictates. In effect, the firm was expected to promote itself in an entirely selfless manner, which, to its management, was oxymoronic. The

---

[134] Loose page "2a," excerpted from a draft letter from Henkel Werbeabteilung to UFA, 31 December 1938, Zug – no. 438, file 4, HA.

[135] President of Advertising Council to Henkel, 16 January 1939, in ibid.

[136] Werbeleitung Henkel to UFA, 19 January 1939, in ibid.

[137] The correspondences in the Henkel archive end before a final decision about whether to keep the film intact has been rendered. However, the existing film itself contains all of the controversial claims and images, with the apparent exception of crucifixes. Film available at the Bundesarchiv–Filmarchiv, Berlin.

[138] "Wir fangen an. Wieder," HA.

conflict between Henkel as a capitalist firm and Henkel as a standard-bearer of Nazi ideology comes into relief. Despite calls for a moderniza-tion of commercial publicity in the Third Reich, companies confronted several challenges by the late 1930s: How did one market goods and induce brand loyalty in a regulated economy? More important, was there a *need* to maintain aggressive publicity efforts in a society marked by limited economic choices, price controls, and censorship? While Henkel reconciled itself to, and even benefited from, National Socialist mandates, the company made it clear in 1939 that it wanted not only to sell the ideals of the Volksgemeinschaft, but to actually sell itself.

A CASE STUDY IN IDEOLOGICAL MARKETING: LUDWIG ROSELIUS AND KAFFEE HAG

Within the larger context of coercion, National Socialism opened up new professional possibilities for the ad industry, protected preexisting public-ity practices, and encouraged innovations in the realms of marketing and public relations. The regime's combination of pragmatism and ideology benefited multinational companies like Bayer and Henkel that offered healthy products for the Volk and that could also use their market posi-tions abroad to shed light on German ingenuity. Despite the frustrations market professionals faced, commercial imagery, profit, and nationalism worked hand in hand in Nazi Germany, and this is exemplified by the firm Kaffee HAG and its director, Ludwig Roselius. HAG represented the convergence of artistry, marketing, and social thought that stood behind the corporate communications of the 1930s, and it is therefore useful to focus on this company as an embodiment of the Nazi marketplace, with all of its opportunities and limitations.

Much of the discussion in the 1930s about advertising, marketing, and public relations was conducted by specialists who did freelance work for companies and who were known primarily in professional and busi-ness circles. They were hardly household names. There were, however, more prominent figures who became proponents of new approaches to marketing, particularly during a period of transformation from democ-racy to dictatorship. Among these was Ludwig Roselius, the inventor of decaffeinated coffee and the director of the Bremen company Kaffee HAG. Roselius stood at the crossroads of ideology and marketing over the course of three decades. He came to embody the engaged business leader who saw National Socialism as an expression of both racial and commercial morality. As advertiser, company executive, philanthropist,

German nationalist, and fitness guru, Roselius reveals how compatible corporate self-promotion and Nazi ideology could be.[139]

A former apprentice in a coffee-roasting house, Roselius became part owner of his father's import and wholesale coffee company in 1897. In 1905 he patented the procedure for the decaffeination of coffee and the following year founded the Kaffee Handels-Aktiengesellschaft (Kaffee HAG), which began showcasing its decaffeination techniques at culinary exhibitions, inventors' conferences, and gatherings of drug researchers and manufacturers. HAG soon established markets and subsidiaries abroad, including in the United States in 1914. During this pre–World War I period, the company focused on alluring packaging and advertising, which Roselius, a wealthy patron of the arts, felt depended on high aesthetic standards.[140] With the help of its advertising advisers, Runge & Scotland, the company created arresting ads and posters, exquisitely decorated coffee cans, and a line of HAG tableware on Tettau and Rosenthal porcelain. HAG also offered incentives to purchase its products in the form of collectibles. From 1913 to 1937, consumers found in HAG coffee packets stickers bearing images of castles, knights, and coats of arms. The foremost authority on German heraldry, Professor Otto Hupp, produced drawings of hundreds of villages and towns and their corresponding heraldic symbol. Collectors could place the sticker in a special HAG album.[141] HAG also committed itself to diversified branding, introducing a variety of products outside Germany, including Sanka (in France the "H" in HAG was too difficult to pronounce – thus "Sanka," from *sans caffeine*). In the United States the Sanka Coffee Corporation was founded in 1924, replacing the name of HAG in the American market; this subsidiary became part of the General Foods group, with Roselius retaining some control over the product. Another brand was Kaba, a hot cocoa drink, introduced in 1929 and promoted as "Kaba, the plantation

[139] For an introduction to Roselius see Herbert Schwarzwälder, "Ludwig Roselius (1874–1943): Ein Mann ohne Schatten?" in *Berühmte Bremer*, ed. Herbert Schwarzwälder (Munich: Paul List, 1972), 118–51; and Bernd Ulrich Hucker, "'Die Kaffeebohne und die Kunst' – Ludwig Roselius (1874–1943): Ein Unternehmer, die geistigen Wurzeln seiner Welt und die Bremer 'Böttcherstrassenkultur'," in *Persönlichkeit und Zeitgeschehen: Beiträge zur Geschichte des 17. bis 20. Jahrhunderts*, ed. Alwin Hanschmidt and Bernd Ulrich Hucker (Vechta: Eiswasser, 2001), 161–81.

[140] Svenja Kunze, "'Kaffee HAG schont Ihr Herz': Zur Entstehung und Entwicklung eines klassischen Markenartikels in der deutschen Kaffeebranche, 1906–1939," *Hamburger Wirtschafts-Chronik* 4 (2004): 85–120.

[141] See "Deutsche Ortswappen," no. 2 (1925), 850236 CAB 213, KFA.

FIGURE 11. Ludwig Roselius, 1930s. (Courtesy of Kraft Foods Deutschland Services GmbH & Co. KG, Bremen.)

drink" (*Kaba, der Plantagentrank*), and HAG-Cola, a decaffeinated soda introduced in 1937.

During the 1910s and 1920s, Ludwig Roselius recognized the great marketing possibilities available to him by selling a product that could be perceived as healthy, and HAG duly promoted its decaffeinated coffee as contributing to both individual and public health. Chemists and doctors advised the company on the medicinal effects of caffeine-free coffee, and Roselius linked his product to a broader interest in mind and body cultivation. HAG participated in Dresden's international Hygiene Exhibition in 1911, which was devoted to the promotion of sports, and in 1922 Roselius helped sponsor the nationalist fitness event North German Week (*Norddeutsche Woche*), later known as the Bremen Sport and Homeland Week (*Bremer Sport und Heimatwoche*). In 1931 the company experimented with producing nicotine-free tobacco, and later that year, Roselius

FIGURE 12. Roselius's Institute for Health and Performance, 1930s. (Courtesy of Kraft Foods Deutschland Services GmbH & Co. KG, Bremen.)

and HAG founded the Institute for Health and Performance (Institut für Gesundheit und Leistung). More than thirty thousand people visited the institute in 1932, indulging in massages and using its boxing ring, exercise bicycles, and gymnastics equipment.[142] After the Nazis came to power, the Reich sports führer Hans von Tschammer und Osten became the patron of the institute, which was rededicated in September 1933, with fawning speeches about its importance to the health of the Volk, the cultural mission of the Führer, and the regeneration of the German body and soul.[143] As we saw with Bayer and Henkel, health products and fitness regimens merged well with the Nazis' own vision of racial purity, as is evinced by the regime's embrace of Roselius's new institute.

---

[142] "Der Roselius-Bau in Bremen: Ein Institut für Gesundheit und Leistung," *Deutsche Allgemeine Zeitung* (date cut off, sometime in 1933), Böttcherstrasse Archive, Bremen [hereafter BA]. See also Lilian Mrusek, "Das Haus Atlantis," in Tallasch, ed., *Projekt Böttcherstrasse*, 169–95.

[143] "Weihe des Instituts für Gesundheit u. Leistung," *Weser Zeitung* (25 September 1933), BA.

Well before the Nazi years, HAG had taken advantage of the Weimar era fitness craze in its marketing and public relations. In 1920 the company unveiled coffee ads showing a fashionably dressed, young male tennis player, cradling a racket under his arm and holding a cup of HAG coffee.[144] The clear message was that decaf coffee was part of a healthy and active lifestyle. In 1925 and 1926 HAG introduced a red heart on its posters and packaging with the slogan "Kaffee HAG protects your heart" (*Kaffee HAG schont Ihr Herz*).[145] The company called upon pharmacologists and psychologists to explore the effects of caffeine-free coffee and its chocolate drink on the body and mind.[146] Other advertising slogans spoke to the theme of mental and physical health and, implicitly, to the once common diagnosis of neurasthenia. "Nervous?" asked one ad. "Then Kaffee HAG."[147] Other ads featured clients with their doctors and modern women relaxing in the sun with a cup of HAG, which promised beneficial effects for the nerves, heart, and digestion.

While the theme of völkisch health predated the rise of Nazism, it dovetailed with key features of National Socialist ideology. Indeed, in 1922 Roselius met Hitler, who wanted the coffee magnate's assistance in building the Nazi Party. The two shared reflections on the Nordic race and their admiration for the anti-Semite and racial theorist Houston Stewart Chamberlain. Roselius at first demurred from joining the party, arguing that he had to be above politics to help Germany.[148] But he eventually joined in 1925, remaining an on-again, off-again member until he rejoined for good in 1933. What did Hitler see in Roselius? For one thing, their shared interest in völkisch culture manifested itself in Roselius's sponsoring of events like the first and second Nordic Parliament (*Nordisches Thing*) in 1933 and 1934. These were scholarly gatherings and artistic displays devoted to the study and promotion of German history, Germanic customs and dress, and the "production of heroes [as] the ultimate purpose of

[144] See Susan Henderson, "Böttcherstrasse: The Corporatist Vision of Ludwig Roselius and Bernhard Hoetger," *Journal of Decorative and Propaganda Arts* 20 (1994): 164–81.

[145] Kunze, "'Kaffee HAG schont Ihr Herz.'"

[146] Niederschrift der Wissenschaftlichen Gespräche mit Generalkonsul Dr. h.c. Ludwig Roselius, von Dr. Ing. Wilhelm Roselius, 2 June 1974, 00576642, KFA. See also "Kaba. Der Plantagentrank: Urteile von Ärzten, Groß-Verbrauchern und Verbrauchern" (1935), box R2 94/7, file 0096 3556 (folder 2), KFA.

[147] Ad in *HAG-Post*, no. 7 (1 June 1927), KFA. Note that for issues before 1932, the *HAG-Post* records do not have file numbers; they are in a box labeled "HAG-Post (1927)".

[148] See preface to Ludwig Roselius, *Briefe und Schriften zu Deutschlands Erneuerung* (Oldenburg: Gerhard Stalling: 1933), 5–6. This volume, dedicated to Chamberlain, was composed of essays originally written in 1918.

Nordic life." For Roselius, the Nordic spirit of adventure was exemplified by flying ace Charles Lindbergh, for whom he erected plaques and whose image appeared in his coffee ads.[149]

Perhaps more significant than this common interest in Nordic culture was Hitler's and Roselius's mutual devotion to propaganda as a means of swaying the masses. Like many other cultural and business elites, Roselius studied literature about the rise of the "mass man" that publishers were churning out in the interwar period. He even invited Spanish philosopher José Ortega y Gasset, author of the best-selling study *The Revolt of the Masses* (1930), to give the first lecture at 1934's Nordic Parliament (Ortega canceled due to illness).[150] For Roselius and other conservatives, Germany had lost World War I because it did not take advantage of propaganda the way the Americans had.[151] Even before the war, Roselius had addressed the importance of both commercial and state propaganda. While a government could use coercion against a population, advertising demanded more pacific means. "The easiest way to manage the masses is by force," he wrote. But when an organization lacked the ability to use physical power, propaganda was the next means.[152] Whether in business or politics, propaganda must conform to high ethical standards. He argued that one should "never lie" in advertisements and that consumers should never feel forced to buy a product; rather, they should be *persuaded* of its superior features. Propaganda experts, as the Advertising Council would later argue, must demonstrate high "moral qualities."[153]

During World War I Roselius had offered his skills as a propagandist to the German foreign office, which he felt needed to exercise aggressive agitation abroad, based on promoting the military and economic power of Germany. He established a Help Committee for National Propaganda (Hilfskomité für nationale Propaganda), which included the heads of leading German exporters like Bahlsen cookies, Henkel chemicals, Odol personal hygiene products, Maggi foodstuffs, and Roselius's own company. These firms and their leaders, according to Roselius, would stand

[149] See Hartog, "Eine bloße Fortsetzung"; and "Nordic Cult Honors Its Heroes in Bremen," *New York Times* (18 May 1934), 25. See also "Heldisches im nordischen Menschen," *Hamburger Tageblatt* (19 May 1934), and related articles in newspaper clipping binder, BA.

[150] "Das zweite Nordische Thing in Bremen," *Altonaer Nachrichten* (19 May 1934), BA.

[151] On this theme see Corey Ross, "Mass Politics and the Techniques of Leadership: The Promise and Perils of Propaganda in Weimar Germany," *German History* 24, no. 2 (April 2006): 184–211.

[152] Christian Wilckins, "Pioniere der Werbung," *Annoncen Expedition* (30 June 1933), BA.

[153] Schwarzwälder, "Ludwig Roselius," 124.

as models of German commercial might.[154] After World War I Roselius tried to diagnose what had gone wrong with the war. German propagandists, he contended, had failed to give the citizens a true picture of the military effort, and now the public was feeling the pain of defeat particularly acutely. Moreover, the Reich government would have been well served by following HAG's example. Declared Roselius, "If only the German Reich had been led the way Kaffee HAG was, then Germany would not have lost."[155]

This interest in propaganda and the failures of Germany's efforts were shared by other economic and intellectual leaders, including the founder of American Studies in Germany, Friedrich Schönemann, who wrote about the superiority of American propaganda and marketing, and sociologist Johann Plenge, who was a proponent of a "conservative" or "German" socialim.[156] Roselius shared the latter's hostility to democracy, his anticommunism, and his dreams of a "third Reich,"[157] and in 1920 the two inaugurated a political science institute at the University of Münster, which was to educate students in Plenge's vision of an "organized" economy. Roselius supported the institute financially and also used it to promote his own interest in social psychology. He established a chair for propaganda at the institute and called for an understanding of the "psyche of the masses," based on the findings of economic propaganda and the use of radio. Although the institute existed for only three years, during that time Roselius consolidated his reputation as a patron of and contributor to nationalist scholarship. He came to embody the elite businessman who challenged the perceived boundaries between economics and culture.

Roselius shared with conservative elites a distrust of the masses and a belief that they could be moved through imagery, whether economic or political. He also demonstrated a mix of commercial and intellectual endeavor in a variety of publications by Kaffee HAG's house press. In 1911 Roselius took over *Die Güldenkammer* (Golden chamber), a journal of fiction and scholarship that boasted contributions by Georg Simmel, Arnold Zweig, and Aleksei Tolstoi. Articles on art, philosophy, nature, racial hygiene, classical music, vitalism, and the United States appeared

---

[154] Ibid., 125.
[155] Ibid., 127.
[156] Axel Schildt, "Ein Konservativer Prophet moderner nationaler Integration: Biographische Skizze der streitbaren Soziologen Johann Plenge (1874–1963)," *Vierteljahrshefte für Zeitgeschichte* 35, no. 4 (October 1987): 523–70.
[157] Hartog, "Eine bloße Fortsetzung."

alongside more business-minded pieces and profiles of "men of success" like Andrew Carnegie.[158] The Verlag Kaffee HAG also published the journal *Die Böttcherstrasse*, named after the old Bremen street that Roselius renovated into a city attraction over the course of the 1920s. The alley, still one of the city's biggest tourist sites today, was lined with buildings designed with a craftsman ethos and inspired by Nordic themes. It contained shops, steel and mortar structures, the HAG House restaurant, Roselius's health institute, and a museum devoted to expressionist artist Paula Becker-Modersohn.[159] Its namesake journal was inaugurated in May 1928 with a special issue on "the press." German Chancellor Wilhelm Marx, Foreign Minister Gustav Stresemann, and Cologne Mayor Konrad Adenauer offered welcoming words about the press's importance to politics and foreign relations. And sociologist Ferdinand Tönnies penned an article on public opinion as a "modern phenomenon," derived from his famous survey of the media as a potentially liberating but also dangerous force.[160]

These multiple activities suggest that Roselius was a renaissance man of a national conservative ilk. But how did his long-standing interest in the visual and commercial arts, Nordic philosophy, and the psychology of the masses affect his views of Nazism? Very positively, as it turned out. When Hitler came to power in 1933, Roselius placed his full support behind the Führer and his "struggle for the German soul," despite the latter's rejection of overtly religious forms of spirituality.[161] He even declared that Hitler had been "sent by God to the German people."[162] This support for the new regime required that Roselius turn his back on the modern art that he had once patronized so generously, and he now lent his support to conferences about cultural decay and regeneration (with participants touring the Böttcherstrasse and the fitness center).[163] Despite his rhapsodic support of the Nazi revolution, Roselius nonetheless suffered from some of his choices during the Weimar years. His supposed change of

[158] H. Prehn-von Dewitz, "Männer des Erfolges," *Die Güldenkammer* 4, no. 3 (December 1913): 162–68.

[159] For an American's perspective on the Böttcherstrasse in the 1930s, see Floyd D. Rogers, Jr., "Now Stands a Street in Bremen ...," *American German Review* (September 1936), BA.

[160] Ferdinand Tönnies, "Die Öffentliche Meinung Deutschlands in ihren jüngsten Phasen," *Internationale Zeitschrift "Die Böttcherstrasse"* 1, no. 1 (May 1928): 36–42. For quotes by the these writers, see pp. 2–5.

[161] Roselius, *Briefe und Schriften*, 270.

[162] Hartog, "Eine bloße Fortsetzung," 349.

[163] "Gegen den Kulturverfall der Form," *Bremer Nachrichten* (21 February 1934), BA.

heart regarding expressionist art did not stop the SS and Hitler from condemning the modernist and religious motifs of "Böttcher-Strasse Kultur," which the Führer saw as employing empty Nordic language for commercial aims. Moreover, the SS denounced the "influence of decadence and Jewishness" that lay behind the art displayed in the Böttcherstrasse and ordered the Modersohn exhibition closed.[164] KdF tours began skipping the Böttcherstrasse in 1937, much to the frustration of HAG and Bremen tourist officials.[165] The matter was resolved the next year when Hitler declared the street a protected monument, albeit as a negative example of degenerate art and architecture; he allowed tourists to visit as they wished, provided that the tour guide kept to a strict script and all publicity materials were approved by the party.[166] Despite (or perhaps because of) such attacks on the Böttcherstrasse, the street remained a central tourist spot in Bremen, and Roselius maintained healthy relations with the political and financial powers in Berlin until his death in 1943.[167]

The story of Ludwig Roselius begs a question about the relationship between his devotion to "National Socialist" ideals and the marketing work of his company, Kaffee HAG. With respect to advertising, it does not appear that the company was any more nationalist or nazified than other firms during the interwar years; its ads boasted the familiar motifs of active adults, happy kids drinking cocoa, and high-achieving professionals. Roselius was pragmatic enough to realize that to sell a product one need not rely on Nazi motifs; indeed, the regime, as we saw, openly discouraged the commercialization of National Socialist symbols. Surveying the company's PR newsletter in the late 1920s and 1930s, we can observe the broad array of "propaganda measures" of which HAG availed itself.[168] Whether one focuses on the message of völkisch health or on marketing tools themselves, HAG's corporate communications strategies bear a striking continuity before and after Hitler. Well before 1933 the company saturated the public with images of HAG. In Hermann Bahr's stage comedy *Das Prinzip*, a character is pleasantly surprised that decaffeinated coffee tastes so good.[169] HAG officials persuaded the

[164] "Bremer Böttcherstrasse geschlossen," *Hakenkreuzbanner* (24 September 1936), BA.
[165] See, e.g., Heinz Puvogel to KdF, Gau Weser-Ems, 22 September 1937, in binder "Böttcherstrasse und 3. Reich," BA.
[166] Binder "Böttcherstrasse und 3. Reich," BA.
[167] Roselius was a member of the central committee of the Reichsbank and chairman of the supervisory board of Focke Wulf AG. See Hartog, "Eine bloße Fortsetzung," 352.
[168] "Propaganda-Massnahmen im In- und Ausland," *HAG-Post*, no. 1 (1 March 1927), KFA.
[169] *HAG-Post*, no. 2 (15 March 1927), KFA.

theater house in Hamburg to use the company's porcelain during this scene. Reports also flooded in to the Bremen company that parliamentarians were spotted drinking HAG in the Reichstag in Berlin. Meanwhile, doctors were bombarded with brochures about caffeine and poison, and the company set up "health and performance" stands at Dresden's Hygiene exhibition in 1931.[170] In addition, by the summer of 1931, HAG had published ads in almost two thousand newspapers.[171] Finally, the company even reached out to Berlin's Jewish community by announcing that its coffee was "kosher for Passover," brewed under the strictest ritual oversight by Hamburg's chief rabbi, Samuel Spitzer.[172]

After 1933 the company proceeded with these marketing tactics, even as the Advertising Council clamped down on more tasteless forms of publicity and forbade appeals to Jewish consumers. Reports of professionals and white collar workers achieving higher performance rates filled the pages of the company publicity newsletter *HAG-Post*, as did sightings of the product in movies and on stage. Company-sponsored advertising films and poems celebrated the coffee, Kaba-themed games were made for kids, and HAG placed concessionaires at the Berlin Olympics in 1936 to sell coffee and promote the importance of fitness in a Leistungsgemeinschaft. In this vein, famous athletes were closely identified with the product; world heavyweight boxing champion Max Schmeling made regular plugs for the company. A few months after the prizefighter's humiliating loss to the American Joe Louis, HAG boasted that "Max Schmeling still drinks Kaffee HAG as ever."[173]

With paeans to sports heroes and popular adventurers, Kaffee HAG was presumably appealing to a wide consumer base. Yet HAG's marketing actually reflected an ambivalent attitude toward "mass" marketing. Although HAG products were consumed by the broad public, the company directed its products less at the masses than to a specific class: gentlemen and their refined wives who served hot drinks in porcelain. The company offered advice about how HAG could be part of proper socialization and "good composure." Nazi Germany purported to have turned against corrosive bourgeois norms, but this was more rhetoric than reality. The HAG drinker had a distinctly *bürgerlich* bearing: upright, polite, diligent, and punctual.[174] Moreover, the artistic and entrepreneurial spirit

[170] *HAG-Post*, no. 3 (4 June 1931), KFA.
[171] *HAG-Post*, no. 4 (29 July 1931), KFA.
[172] *HAG-Post* no. 2 (15 March 1927), KFA.
[173] *HAG-Post*, no. 12 (8 October 1938), box R2 94/7, file 0096 4891, KFA.
[174] *HAG-Post* no. 14 (14 November 1938), box R2 94/7, file 0096 4891, KFA.

FIGURE 13. Kaffee HAG window display, 1930s. (Courtesy of Kraft Foods Deutschland Services GmbH & Co. KG, Bremen.)

was celebrated throughout HAG's PR literature and company magazines. The message of high performance, creativity, and drive resonated well with Nazi aims. "Leistung" was a common word in Roselius's writings, as each person was to perform to the best of his or her abilities, ultimately benefiting the Volksgemeinschaft.[175] Nutritional experts and experimental psychologists continued working and testifying for HAG in the Third Reich, determining, for example, that after three cups of caffeinated coffee, an employee's performance declined.[176] Moreover, Roselius was hailed as the embodiment of the Nazi elite. He was portrayed as a "pioneer of advertising" and celebrated for his merging of propaganda and völkisch health. An oft-repeated claim that Roselius's father had died of caffeine poisoning bolstered the image of the company founder passionately protecting the creative, nutritional, and racial potential of the Volk.[177] Under

---

[175] See Roselius on Leistung contributing to the greater good in "Ludwig Roselius: Briefe und Schriften zu Deutschlands Erneuerung," *Bremer Nachrichten* (13 August 1933), BA.
[176] *HAG-Post*, no. 3 (17 March 1936), box R2 94/7, file 0096 4891, KFA.
[177] Wilckins, "Pioniere der Werbung."

the Nazi regime, the entrepreneur who provided for the enjoyment and well-being of the consumer was welcomed into the pantheon of model public figures.

To be exalted as an upstanding citizen in the 1930s did not necessarily mean one was a died-in-the wool Nazi. Ludwig Roselius straddled the worlds of the cultural avant-garde, pragmatic business leaders, and völkisch ideologists. One could therefore argue that HAG's relationship to Nazi ideology was merely incidental – that the company went about its business of promoting nutrition and health and that its goals at best overlapped with National Socialist aims. But HAG did align itself directly with official Nazi public events and party activities. For example, the company reported excitedly that Mussolini, whose healthy lifestyle the company lionized, drank Kaffee HAG during his visit to Berlin in November 1937 and that a bus bearing the logo of HAG was spotted in a beautiful nighttime photo of Unter den Linden boulevard during the Duce's visit.[178] At the Schaffendes Volk exhibition, caffeine-avoidant visitors could enjoy Kaffee HAG in fourteen cantinas and restaurants.[179] The DAF had special training courses for its employees, which included lectures on decaffeination and tours of a plant in Bremen.[180] Kaba was part of the official catering plan for the Hitler Youth. The company boasted that at the Nuremberg party rally of 1936, forty-two thousand Hitler Youth members had sipped the chocolate drink while learning its nutritional benefits over a loudspeaker.[181] "It is immoral," declared one HAG ad, "to deny the damage that caffeine causes to the health of the Volk."[182] All of this activity does not in and of itself reflect the nazification of the firm. But it does show that, like most companies, Kaffee HAG made itself fully available to and benefited from the new regime.

Ludwig Roselius built a company that embodied all the elements of the Nazi marketplace. It protected its own business interests, but it also sustained the ideals of the Volksgemeinschaft. It built a visual world of products that nurtured high-functioning social elites and consuming masses and also took advantage of publicity methods that the Nazis themselves could support. In accordance with the führer principle, Roselius was a leader in multiple realms – as inventor, artist, philanthropist, and company boss – and presiding over a socially engaged capitalism. Like

---

[178] *HAG-Post* no. 8 (6 November 1937), box R2 94/7, file 0096 4891, KFA.
[179] *HAG-Post* no. 6 (31 July 1937), box R2 94/7, file 0096 4891, KFA.
[180] *HAG-Post* no. 7 (22 September 1937), box R2 94/7, file 0096 4891, KFA.
[181] Ibid.
[182] *HAG-Post* no. 24 (16 December 1933), box R2 94/7, file 0096 4891, KFA.

HAG, many companies could claim they were contributing to the individual and the common good; scores of firms were honored as National Socialist Model Factories. This merging of profit and the public weal was commonplace before and after 1933 and in numerous national settings. But Roselius's and HAG's attention to health, visual beauty, mass persuasion, and Nordic philosophy, combined with appeals to the public good, resonated especially loudly in a state devoted to economic and, above all, racial purity.

Marketing in the prewar Third Reich was defined by three dynamics: autonomy, continuity, and compatibility. While advertising, public relations, and other corporate communications strategies ostensibly served the regime's interests, companies in fact found that the reach of the state was limited. They therefore drew upon their pre-1933 discourses and practices, which found a home under a regime that proclaimed the importance of mass leisure and mass consumption. Attempts to Germanize advertising – through the increased use of gothic script, the banning of foreign words, and regulations regarding formatting – did not radically change the visual representations of a company or its language of trust, achievement, and performance. Indeed, the very fact that the Advertising Council promoted rather "fuzzy notions"[183] of what was "correct" and "German" meant that companies could engage in marketing efforts with some freedom. Moreover, the demands that companies behave selflessly – not just in their visual work but in the promotion of the common good – enabled them to sell a broader message of patriotism and communal devotion that could translate into a broad customer base and steady profits. In their desire to market goods and ideals, the regime and private industry had a mutual interest.

Despite such compatibilities, as we have seen, companies found some of the Nazis' regulations puzzling and random, and they pushed back when they felt their interests were at stake. They petitioned the propaganda and economics ministries when they found a ruling disadvantageous, and they openly questioned whether profit and altruism could always be aligned. In short, the measured autonomy that market professionals enjoyed allowed them to identify which Nazi policies suited their interests and which undermined them. Of course, the government and the law courts had the final say about commercial practices, and there was no mistaking that the state possessed an extralegal authority to

[183] Berghoff, "'Times Change,'" 141.

deprive professionals of their livelihoods. But on the whole, marketing in Nazi Germany was defined not by coercion, but by the state and private industry's reciprocal exploitation.

It was also defined by a steady modernization. Advances in printing and film technologies meant more stylized depictions of a company, more variety in packaging, and the more targeted use of advertising.[184] And the professionalization of the advertising industry allowed admen to exchange ideas, to exhibit their skills in national venues, and to lobby on behalf of their trade. In short, market professionals in the Third Reich witnessed the flowering of corporate communications strategies that had debuted before 1933 and that would continue to gain importance after 1945. Without state regulation of commercial practices, these innovations might have proceeded faster. Certainly the United States saw the earlier and more aggressive application of marketing methods. But the interventions of the National Socialist regime did not stop companies from promoting themselves and the Nazi "economic miracle" with the most modern tools available.

[184] On some of these innovations in the 1930s, see Hanns W. Brose, *Die Entdeckung des Verbrauchers: Ein Leben für die Werbung* (Düsseldorf: Econ, 1958), 67–70; and Reinhardt, *Von der Reklame zum Marketing*, 447.

3

Rotary Clubs, Consumption, and the Nazis' Achievement Community

As we saw in the two preceding chapters, Nazi economic policy was not only centered on putting people back to work and preparing the country for war. It was also about engineering a proper racial and commercial sensibility. In the Nazi marketplace, the state and private companies communicated with Germans in their capacities as consumers, who held symbolic and actual power. Consumers had the ability to withhold support from the regime if the economy remained weak and to undermine a company by not buying its goods. Marketers and the Nazi Advertising Council therefore relied upon a number of tools to both appease and educate consumers. In the Third Reich companies found multiple opportunities for business, but the disparate aims of private industry and the regime created an uneasy tension. Schooling consumers in patience, frugality, and racial difference could be at odds with the desire to move products. Business leaders, who were encouraged to maintain a semblance of normality, were confused about how to implement a National Socialist agenda while protecting their own interests.

Who exactly were these business leaders? How did they understand the new ideological terrain on which they operated? This chapter takes a closer look at these individuals – managers, company owners, and economists – and their participation in German Rotary Clubs during the Third Reich in order to understand the milieu in which Nazi ideas about commerce and consumption circulated. In a sense, this chapter uses the example of one civic association to understand the broader social and intellectual context of the Nazis' market vision. As we will see, business in the Third Reich was not only about maintaining profits and healthy markets. The ascent of National Socialism also gave economic leaders an opportunity to explore their self-understanding as elites and to ask how their unfolding relationship with the consuming masses might be transformed after the tumultuous Weimar years. Nazism challenged them to forge an understanding of modern consumer society that would serve both their business interests and the Volksgemeinschaft. In their weekly conversations and debates, these bourgeois gentlemen breathed life into the ideas about achievement, trust, and virtuous economic behavior that were the hallmarks of the Nazi marketplace.

The business world is not, of course, monolithic, and depicting attitudes within it risks being a reductive exercise. The interests of retailers differ from those of manufacturers, big industrialists have a different agenda from local merchants, and economists disagree about the best ways to ensure growth. There are, however, places where business-related discussions transcend company size and sector. For example, national business journals speak to a wide range of economic interests, and business schools disseminate a variety of perspectives about the economy.[1] Another setting where business attitudes, broadly speaking, are on display is the elite men's club, where leaders of all stripes mix and mingle. Victoria de Grazia has introduced scholars to German Rotary Clubs, where elites after World War I explored ideas about consumption, international relations, and the cultural power of the United States. Rotary drew businessmen into the company of intellectuals and artists to socialize and discuss the meaning of bourgeois elitism in the age of the masses.[2]

This chapter focuses on Rotary Germany as a case study in elites' understanding of consumer society. It takes inspiration from de Grazia's work, which focuses primarily on the Weimar years, but it differs from it by asking how Rotarians, many of whom were businessmen, responded to events after 1933. During the Nazi years, economic leaders who remained in the organization saw in Rotary an opportunity to merge their inherited notions of bourgeois elitism with the Nazis' devotion to a society based on individual achievement, sacrifice to the community, and selfless economic behavior. Unlike Rotary in the late Weimar period, the organization under National Socialism was less about the attraction to a quintessentially American service club and its subsequent Germanization

---

[1] On business schools in the Nazi period, see Hauke Janssen, *Nationalökonomie und Nationalsozialismus: Die deutsche Volkswirtschaftslehre in den dreißiger Jahren* (Marburg: Metropolis, 1998), 441–63.

[2] Victoria de Grazia, *Irresistible Empire: America's Advance through Twentieth Century Europe* (Cambridge, MA: Harvard University Press, 2005), 15–74.

than about elites finding an opportunity to understand the contours of modern consumer society in a racist ideological setting. Rotary became an impoverished and troubled organization after the dismissal and resignation of its early, illustrious members; it was not, in the end, a success story. But for those who stayed on – and there were still many prominent figures – Rotary remained a social and cultural laboratory, where elites could experiment with different interpretations of the Volksgemeinschaft, at once populated by businessmen, consumers, and "mass men."

ROTARY IN THE THIRD REICH

Linking civic organizations to broader social and cultural trends is not a new exercise. Jennifer Jenkins has shown how business leaders and patrons of the arts in late-nineteenth-century Hamburg tried to inculcate a cultural sensibility into their fellow citizens. A sense of conviviality carried from older lodges and guilds motivated these bourgeois gentlemen to explore their status and power in the semiprivate setting of the voluntary organization.[3] Indeed, most large cities boasted men's organizations, some of which remain to this day. The Club zu Bremen, which was founded in 1783, has represented the merchant and industrial powers of this Hanseatic city for 228 years. In the years between the two world wars, Berlin had three elite organizations, the Herrenclub, the Nationale Club, and the Club von Berlin, where members of the political and economic elite, including some future Nazi leaders like Joachim von Ribbentrop, socialized with other professionals.[4] While in Wilhelmine Germany individuals with a quasi-political agenda had found common cause in national associations like the Navy League and the Pan German League,[5] Berlin's civic clubs, at least in principle, offered more urbane forms of sociability.

[3] Jennifer Jenkins, *Provincial Modernity: Local Culture and Liberal Politics in Fin-de-Siècle Hamburg* (Ithaca, NY: Cornell University Press, 2003), 115–45.

[4] Rüdiger Hachtmann, "Eine Erfolgsgeschichte? Schlaglichter auf die Geschichte der Generalverwaltung der Kaiser-Wilhelm-Gesellschaft im 'Dritten Reich,'" http://www.mpi-wg-berlin.mpg.de/KWG/Ergebnisse/Ergebnisse19.pdf, pp. 28–29 (accessed 27 July 2009); and Marion Welsch and Ariane Knackmuss, eds., *Willkommen in Club? Die Geschichte des Clubs von Berlin und das Schicksal seiner jüdischen Mitglieder im Nationalsozialismus* (Berlin: Edition Andreae, 2007).

[5] On both of these organizations, see Geoff Eley, *Reshaping the German Right: Radical Nationalism and Political Change after Bismarck* (New Haven, CT: Yale University Press, 1980), 48–58, 68–85.

One of the richest sources of information about interwar business attitudes is the Rotary movement, by virtue of both the diversity of professional and industrial interests represented in its clubs and the meticulous recording of minutes, lectures, and discussions that took place at its meetings. Because Rotary functioned in both Weimar and Nazi Germany, the organization provides a particularly clear view of elite attitudes during a time of upheaval. Rotary first came to Germany in 1927. At the time German leaders, notably industrialists, were looking to the United States for models of modern business practices – whether in Fordist assembly-line production, mass consumption, or human relations.[6] It is not surprising that Wilhelm Cuno, general director of the Hamburg–American Steamship lines, was Germany's first Rotarian. The industrialist and former German chancellor brought the American service organization to a city, Hamburg, known for its openness to outside cultural influences, especially from the Anglo-American world. At the time of its German debut, Rotary was the oldest and the largest of what would eventually be the "big three" service organizations: Rotary, Kiwanis, and Lions. It was founded in 1905 in Chicago and spread quickly, with every major American city having a Rotary Club by 1911 and many European countries founding clubs in the 1920s and 1930s.[7] Of the major organizations, Rotary carried the most prestige, celebrated for its merging of business, culture, and social activism. It was based on an ethos of fraternity, philanthropy, and professional networking. To this day, Rotary Clubs around the world attempt to realize, in the words of Jeffrey Charles, "the advancement of international understanding, good will and peace through a world fellowship of business and professional men united in the ideal of service."[8]

These goals were apparent from Rotary's arrival in Germany. Rotary Club (RC) Munich drew the likes of Thomas Mann into the world of male fraternizing.[9] In Club Dresden, free professionals ranging from the lord high mayor of the city, to the chief of police, to bankers and theater directors, met weekly over lunch and at formal celebrations to discuss the social and intellectual issues of the day. Whether at RC Berlin or RC

[6] See Mary Nolan, *Visions of Modernity: American Business and the Modernization of Germany* (Oxford: Oxford University Press, 1994).
[7] Jeffrey A. Charles, *Service Clubs in American Society: Rotary, Kiwanis, and Lions* (Urbana: University of Illinois Press, 1993), 9, 124–40.
[8] Ibid., 128.
[9] De Grazia, *Irresistible Empire*, 19–22.

Cologne, members came together for a dialogue about the meaning and practice of "world citizenship."[10] German Rotarians were "practical idealists," whose commitment to bourgeois humanism entailed a greater turn to philosophy and the arts than their more commerce-minded counterparts in the United States.[11] By 1937, when Rotary Germany dissolved itself under pressure from the Nazi government, there were forty-two clubs with approximately 1,200 members.[12]

Thomas Mann stands out as perhaps the most illustrious Rotarian, but one must not underestimate the appeal that Rotary Germany held for a wide range of elites before 1933. Friedrich Bergius, who shared the Nobel Prize for Chemistry in 1931 with Carl Bosch, was a member of RC Heidelberg. The philosopher Paul Tillich belonged to Club Frankfurt, where he regularly dined with board members from the chemical concern IG Farben. There the great theologian could be found engaging in discussions about the economy and technology with Max Muß, economics professor at the Technical University of Darmstadt; Heinrich Scharp, editor in chief of the *Rhein-Mainischen-Volkszeitung*; and Ernst Kahn, a lecturer on economics at the University of Frankfurt and a director of Hartmann & Braun, a major electronics and instrumentation company.[13] RC Berlin had perhaps the most elite membership, which included the former German chancellor, future Reichsbank director, and ambassador to the United States, Hans Luther, as well as executives of Dresdner Bank, Deutsche Reichsbahn, AEG electronics, and the Berliner Kindl brewery. From the retailing sector came Georg Tietz, co-owner of the Hermann Tietz company, which owned dozens of department stores, most prominently the resplendent KaDaWe emporium in Berlin. His cousin, Alfred Leonhard Tietz, director of the firm's Rhineland branch (which owned the department store Kaufhof), enjoyed the company of his Rotarian friends several hundred miles west in RC Cologne. Also in Berlin was Max Hartmann, the deputy director of the Kaiser Wilhelm Institute for Biology, and Edmund Stinnes, the son of steel magnate Hugo Stinnes and owner of a railway advertising company. Notable from the world of the arts were opera singer Rudolf Bockelmann and pianist Edwin Fischer. Clubs Cologne and Düsseldorf were also noteworthy for the presence of

---

[10] Ibid., 61.
[11] Ibid., 49.
[12] Ibid., 33.
[13] Max Muss, President of RC Darmstadt, "Zur Frage des Technischen Fortschritts in der Wirtschaft," 25 October 1932, GStA PK, I. HA rep. 228, no. 665.

leading industrialists and bankers. In short, for the elite of the day, Rotary had a powerful draw.[14]

Not every club was composed of such nationally important figures. Depending on the region, a club could comprise fewer, less elite professions. For example, the club in Pforzheim, the Black Forest town famous for its jewelry and watchmaking, attracted small and middle-sized company owners. This professional homogeneity caused some concern in the Rotary International (RI) offices. RI had a rule against more than three members of a club belonging to the same major professional classification, such as "medicine" or, in this case, "jewelry and watches." Clubs were supposed to represent a cross section of a city's professional class, but in Pforzheim's case there was not much more than jewelry and watchmaking. The Rotarians improvised, giving classifications like "rolled gold jewelry manufacturing," "automatic chains manufacturing," and "gold and silverware manufacturing" to members' professions and thus circumventing the strict rules.[15]

On the whole, the clubs of District 73, which comprised Germany and Austria, were regionally and professionally diverse, and Rotary was not merely a voice of industry, or even business more generally. In some clubs, businessmen represented perhaps a third of the membership, with attorneys, professors, physicians, and artists constituting the bulk of the roster. Nonetheless, in the view of the general public and indeed many of its members, Rotary remained predominantly a high-society gentlemen's club, where business networking was more important than cultural edification as such. Of course, there were multiple reasons for joining Rotary, and some members testified that they simply wanted a place to meet other professional men in an increasingly atomized society.

To this day, most German Rotarians see 1933 as a turning point. A mere six years after Rotary had established its first German club, it faced a challenge of immense proportions when the Nazis came to power. From the start the relationship between Rotary and National Socialism was fraught. On the one hand, by 1933 many business elites welcomed an aggressive attempt to lift the economy out of the Depression and unite the country.[16] On the other hand, for a movement devoted to international

---

[14] For these members, see membership indexes, GStA PK, I. HA rep. 228; and de Grazia, *Irresistible Empire*, 60.
[15] Rotary Int. Secretariat in Zürich to G. Weekind, secretary of RC Baden-Baden, 15 May 1931, GStA PK, I. HA rep. 228, no. 72.
[16] See Henry A. Turner, *German Big Business and the Rise of Hitler* (Oxford: Oxford University Press, 1985); and Reinhard Neebe, *Grossindustrie, Staat, und NSDAP,*

understanding, Hitler's coming to power represented a potential threat.
A great many members were directors of companies dependent on exports
and on friendly relations with industrialists throughout the world. The
coming of a violently nationalist movement threatened to undermine
this. Likewise, a central component of Rotary was its establishment of
"sister clubs" throughout the world, the regular visiting of Rotarians
in other countries, youth exchanges, and international art and philan-
thropic undertakings. In 1933 National Socialism – defined by a hyper-
nationalism and a backward provincialism – threatened to undermine
this world.[17]

Rotarians' fears of Nazi hostility proved well founded. The new government initially lumped the movement together with Freemasonry,
portraying both as international secret societies that were under Jewish
influence and that challenged the nationalist foundations of Nazi ideology.[18] The party immediately issued decrees banning membership in
Rotary for party members and civil servants. However, after appeals by
Rotary leaders, this decree was reversed in July 1933, with Masons now
remaining the most visible lodge to be outlawed. In the hope of coordi-
nating it along their ideological lines, the Nazis declared that Rotary was
not a secret society and had nothing to do with Freemasonry.[19] Yet even
with this reprieve, many Nazi officials remained suspicious of Rotary's
internationalism.

Despite this temporary resolution, the "Jewish question" weighed
heavily on Germany's Rotary Clubs. Under the dictates of the civil service law of 7 April 1933, non-Aryan state employees (with the exception
of Jewish war veterans) were summarily dismissed from their jobs, and
thus lost the professional status necessary for membership in a Rotary
Club.[20] Among them were many professors and directors of state-funded
institutes. During 1933 Rotary Germany lost 500 of its 1,700 members
through the resignation of Jews and non-Jews who expressed their solidarity with persecuted members or who simply abhorred Nazism.[21]

1930–1933: *Paul Silverberg und der Reichsverband der Deutschen Industrie*
(Göttingen: Vendenhoeck & Ruprecht, 1981).
[17] Manfred Wedemeyer, *Den Menschen verpflichtet: 75 Jahre Rotary in Deutschland,
1927–2002* (Hamburg: Der Rotarier Verlags-GmbH, 2002), 64–72.
[18] Hauptstabsleiter des Reichsorganisationsleiters to Gauleitung Thüringen, 1 September
1932, NS 22/444, BAB.
[19] For this July law and the relief it engendered, see Wedemeyer, *Den Menschen
verpflichtet*, 65.
[20] De Grazia, *Irresistible Empire*, 68.
[21] Wedemeyer, *Den Menschen Verpflichtet*, 64.

Banker Max Warburg of Club Hamburg and author Karl Wolfskehl of Club Munich left Germany after the Reichstag fire in February 1933.[22] Rotarian Adolf Morsbach, director of the Kaiser Wilhelm Society and the German Academic Exchange Service, was arrested and spent two months in jail before losing his membership.[23] Non-Jews Paul Tillich and Thomas Mann also left Rotary and Germany altogether in 1933.

The removal of Jews from Rotary Germany represented a massive blow to the organization. To offer one example, eighteen members of RC Darmstadt were listed in the 1932 membership index. By 1934 there remained only eleven members, with two of these having joined that year. The club lost nine, or exactly one-half, of its members in two years.[24] Despite these losses, enough members threw in their lot with the Nazis to ensure that the clubs survived. Part of this was pragmatic. Rotarians were faced with the reality that they could maintain their clubs only by demonstrating loyalty to the regime. There were also, however, an increasing number of devout Nazis in the clubs. Nonetheless, after 1933 Rotary maintained its original appeal as a "nonpolitical" gathering of elites. The organization attracted new members who saw the professional and social benefits of joining a respected men's lodge. For example, Club Düsseldorf welcomed into its ranks the chief doctor of a hospital and the head of the Düsseldorf branch of the Rhineland-Westphalia stock exchange. Louis Lochner, the American head of the Associated Press Germany, joined RC Berlin in 1934 as a way to maintain contact with men involved in international affairs. Rotary Germany also included a number of figures who would contribute to the persecution and murder of Jews. Club Frankfurt admitted Hermann Schlosser, who would become the chair of the managing board of the Degussa chemical concern during World War II and a business manager of the Degesch company, which produced Zyklon B for death camps in Poland.[25] The respected art dealer Karl Haberstock

[22] On Warburg and Wolfskehl see Ottfried Dascher, "'Nach Taten, nicht nach Worten soll man Freunde wägen,' Vortrag auf der Jubiläumsveranstaltung des Distrikts 1900 in Hattingen," 23 February 2005, p. 3, http://www.rotary1930.org/archiv/2005–2006/ Clubberichte/NACH_TATEN_NICHT_NACH_WORTEN.pdf (accessed 19 October 2007).

[23] See DAAD chronology in http://www.daad.de/portrait/en/1.4.2.html (accessed 19 October 2007).

[24] Membership indexes of 1932 and 1934, GStA PK, I HA rep. 228. Eventually, Rotary returned to its pre-1933 numbers with the addition of new members in 1934. Wedemeyer, *Den Menschen Verpflichtet*, 64.

[25] Peter Hayes, *From Cooperation to Complicity: Degussa in the Third Reich* (Cambridge: Cambridge University Press, 2004), 279.

joined Club Berlin in 1930 and later played a central role in the confiscation of "degenerate art" from museums under the Nazis.[26] While no one,
of course, had foreknowledge of these later developments, the presence
of these figures indicates the broad appeal of Rotary in the 1930s; its
members ranged from big businessmen to cultural figures, and from avid
republicans to enthusiastic Nazis.

Despite Rotary's concessions to National Socialism and the increasing
presence of Nazis in its clubs, the ceasefire between the movement and
the regime proved only temporary. In 1937 the Nazis relaunched their
attack on Rotary, arguing again that this organization with an interna-
tionalist outlook and foreign headquarters was incompatible with the
nationalist aims of Nazism. It was decreed that party members and civil
servants could not be Rotarians and vice versa. After a flurry of meetings
and appeals, Rotarians concluded that they should dissolve their organization. Rotary Germany ceased to exist in October 1937.[27]

ROTARY AND THE NAZI LEISTUNGSGEMEINSCHAFT

The demise of Rotary reflected the wider stifling of independent discourse
in Nazi Germany. Partly out of pressure from the regime and partly out of
enthusiasm for National Socialism, elites abandoned their sites of bourgeois sociability. Organizations that did survive, such as the Club von
Berlin, which merged with the Deutscher Klub in 1937, became rather
unimportant in German public life.[28] During the almost five years that
Rotary existed in the Third Reich, however, the organization was a site
of dialogues about subjects of great interest to business leaders, from
the work of the Nazi Advertising Council to the economic importance
of the Autobahn.[29] Before we look closely at these themes, we must first
consider how economic leaders involved in Rotary understood their relationship to National Socialism. So much activity of interest to them –
manufacturing, retailing, labor relations, price policy – was contingent

---

[26] On Haberstock, "degenerate art," and plunder, see Jonathan Petropoulos, *The Faustian Bargain: The Art World in Nazi Germany* (Oxford: Oxford University Press, 2000), 87–90.
[27] Wedemeyer, *Den Menschen verpflichtet*, 68–72. The Rotary Clubs of Austria were dissolved at the same tame, having belonged to the same district as Germany.
[28] For a history of the club, see http://www.clubvonberlin.de/main/main.html (accessed 24 September 2009).
[29] Hermann Neuerburg (of Haus-Neuerburg cigarettes), RC Cologne, "Der Werberat der deutschen Wirtschaft," 3 May 1937; Fritz Neumeyer, RC Nuremberg, "Autobahnen," 22 August 1933, GStA PK, I. HA rep. 228, in nos. 666 and 945, respectively.

upon the regime's ideological priorities that they spent much time analyzing the Nazis' understanding of the economy. In their capacities as economic leaders and Rotarians, they asked themselves if they had a place at the Nazi table. For some, National Socialist ideas about achievement, trust, and sacrifice provided a way forward for a movement devoted to "service above self" (Rotary's motto).

It is not easy to discern a unified Rotarian response to National Socialism, given that the organization had more than a thousand men with both liberal and conservative political backgrounds. The challenge for some of its members was to proceed in ways that were unthreatening to the regime; given their pragmatic desire for their clubs to stay alive, these Rotarians retreated into "internal emigration" and withheld criticism of the state. Others, however, were ambivalent about National Socialism and waited to see whether they could combine their club activities with a cautious support of the regime. Still others welcomed the Nazi "revolution" and combined an adherence to National Socialism with a devotion to Rotarianism.[30] Regardless of their political leanings, however, many Rotarians were optimistic that the regime's priorities would be compatible with their club and professional activities. In particular, the Nazis' commitment to proper market behavior resonated with Rotary's businessmen, who had already spent much time looking at the philosophical underpinnings of commerce.[31] In a speech given to his club colleagues a few months after Hitler's coming to power, RC Heidelberg's Johann W. Ludowici, the owner of a Ludwigshafen brick factory, praised the Nazis for initiating a moral reordering of the economy. In particular, the new regime understood that "trust is the foundation of every economy" and that the economy must serve the state.[32] As we have seen, "trust" was a popular catchword in the business world; it was used to engender positive relationships among employees, between workers and owners, and between consumers and the products they bought. In the Third Reich Vertrauen became especially potent, utilized to give spiritual content to the interactions between the racialized Volk, professional and community leaders, and the state.

[30] On the range of Rotarian responses to National Socialism, see Friedrich Wilpert, *Rotary in Deutschland: Ein Ausschnitt aus Deutschem Schicksal* (Bonn: Buchhandlung H. Behrendt, 1991), 65–70.
[31] See Max Grassmann, RC Munich, "Philosophie in der Wirtschaft," 28 June 1932, GStA PK, I. HA rep. 228, no. 618.
[32] Ludowici, "Gedanken zum deutschen Aufbau," ca. Spring–Summer 1933, GStA PK, I. HA rep. 228, no. 827.

By invoking trust, Ludowici was not as such offering a Nazi economic
vision. But he paired Vertrauen with another omnipresent concept in the
Nazi lexicon: Leistung. In the new economy, "performance" would serve
as the basis for determining wages and salaries, argued Ludowici. But this
was the least of its functions. More important, Leistung was an expression of the mutual trust between members of the Volk. In other words,
without the desire to benefit your race and nation, performance was a hollow and selfish exercise. Argued Ludowici, "Everyone who works should
serve in accordance with the state's desire to fulfill its cultural, social
and economic tasks," two of which were "settlement and colonization."[33]
With this statement, we see the ultimate point of Ludowici's imprecise
thoughts – the conquering of living space from racial inferiors. In bringing
together trust, achievement, and colonization, Ludowici was expressing
the Nazis' basic conception of the economy: Hard work and selflessness
would bind Germans together in service of a higher calling, namely the
racial and economic reordering of Europe. Trust would grease the wheels
of this system and would allow the creativity of the individual and the
racial community to blossom.

In echoing the regime, Ludowici was not necessarily speaking for his
Rotary colleagues. In fact, he stood out as a partisan Nazi who tried
to shape Club Heidelberg according to Nazi principles.[34] Yet while his
views on the economy were drawn from the regime, Ludowici also drew
on his own instincts as a Rotarian, whose civic-mindedness and service
ethic elevated the creator (whether in art or the economy) above the egoism induced by personal achievement. In other words, the Rotary motto
"service above self" was flexible enough to encompass, for Ludowici
and others, a communitarian urge that included the Nazis' own slogan,
"common good before self-interest," and their commitment to individual performance. In a similar vein, Stuttgart Rotarian Rudolf Ludwig
Mehmke, a civil engineer and economics publicist, declared a direct affin-
ity between Rotary and National Socialism. Speaking to his club in July
1933, Mehmke asserted that both organizations were devoted to the service ideal. "Like the new state, we [Rotary] have left behind the individualist teachings of liberalism. Our service ideal likewise distances itself
from the collectivist class-egoism of Marxism and from a pacifism that
is hostile to the Fatherland."[35] He aligned the first three official goals

---

[33] Ibid.
[34] See Ludowici's correspondence from 1933 in GStA PK, I. HA rep. 228, no. 827.
[35] Mehmke, "Rotary und der neue Staat," 17 July 1933, GStA PK, I. HA rep. 228, no. 657.

of Rotary (which proclaimed the importance of service and the ethical foundations of private, public, and business life) with National Socialism, declaring that both organizations sprang from the same *weltanschaulichen* roots. With reference to blood and soil, nationalism, ethnic unity, and the importance of the family as the basis of the new order, Mehmke insisted that in the new state "we are all equal."[36]

Ludowici and Mehmke were two Rotarians who saw no conflict between their political views and the tenets of their fraternal society. They were convinced that the Nazis would protect individual achievement and that the German economy would be bolstered by the infusion of völkisch ideology. Not all their colleagues, however, were so confident. Many members of Rotary and other men's organizations worried that National Socialism was an anti-elitist movement that would challenge the economic and social position of business leaders with an assault on private property and profits. They also feared that Nazism would be too socially egalitarian. In a 1933 meeting with the Deutscher Klub, Johann Ludowici's friend SS leader Heinrich Himmler tried to dispel such misconceptions. Often misunderstood as an apotheosis of the "small man," National Socialism, conceded Himmler, did provide opportunities for the able and competent to move beyond their social origins. But these opportunities represented something entirely different from the "leveling down" promoted by the "Weimar system." National Socialism was very much about the *inequality* of people – implicitly with respect to both race and merit. You could call this principle aristocratic if you wished, Himmler explained, but whatever the case, the SS leader was convinced that the goals of National Socialism and those of men's associations could be brought into harmony.[37]

Himmler was not incorrect in his claim that fraternal organizations and National Socialism shared superficial similarities. In particular, Rotarians and Nazi theorists both struggled to understand the blessings and dangers of social equality. In both movements, hard work and drive would lead individuals to excel and to attain a social position from which they could engage in community service. Whether in the army or in the business world, self-motivation and self-sacrifice were intertwined, together producing an elite that balanced privilege and responsibility. To be sure, there was nothing implicitly racist in Rotary's communitarian elitism, and older, "enlightened" notions of hierarchy embraced by the

---

[36] Ibid.
[37] No name to Dr. Degener-Grischow, 21 November 1933, GStA PK, I. HA rep. 228, no. 199.

professional class were very much open to interpretation and bastard-
ization by fascism. But Rotarians' responses to speeches like Himmler's
reveal their hope that the regime would not challenge their meritocratic
ideals.

The achievement ethos had practical and ideological implications for
a movement like Rotary that needed to reshape itself according to the
political dictates of the time. As self-defined members of the *Bürgertum*,
Rotarians were encouraged to channel their self-understanding, honed in
a seemingly discredited "bourgeois era," into a new political and racial
awareness.[38] In this endeavor, Rotarians involved in the economy had
help from their colleagues in the academy, who led discussions about
great works of philosophy and literature that could shed light on the
Rotary mission. A Rotarian interest in Nietzsche, for example, reflected
a common literary interest at the time but also the group's fascination
with ethics and inequality.[39] In an era of total war and economic depression, which drove people toward mass political movements, Nietzsche
helped Rotarians to maintain their faith in the importance of an elite.
And the Nazis' own cooptation of Nietzsche as a philosopher of race
made him a natural subject of interest.

Even before Hitler's coming to power, the advent of National Socialism
compelled Rotarians to reflect on the meanings of achievement, equality, and individuality, especially in the economy. In 1932 a liberal Jewish
attorney in RC Mainz, Paul Simon, delivered a speech to his club about
what he called "the future of individualism." He acknowledged that the
age of liberalism, defined by a raw economic egoism, was over. People
were getting drawn to the crowd and searching for a leader. "Indeed it is
Rotary that serves the totality and not just the economy and that stands,
above all else, for the value of the personality; [it must] advocate for the
separation of economic individualism and spiritual, moral, and cultural
individualism."[40] In this speech, Simon articulated the organization's
commitment to personal distinction, but he also acknowledged the rise

[38] On Rotarian ideas about "the bourgeoisie" see, e.g., Rot. Surmann, RC Plauen, on "Kleines
Bürgerlob," 16 July 1932, GStA PK, I. HA rep. 228, no. 635. On National Socialism as an
antibourgeois movement, see Hermann Beck, *The Fateful Alliance: German Conservatives
and Nazis in 1933 – The Machtergreifung in a New Light* (New York: Berghahn Books,
2008), 299–303.

[39] Arthur Mendt (philosopher at the Technical University Chemnitz), RC Chemnitz,
"Friedrich Nietzsche und Wir," no date, but after 1933, and Karl Weidel (philosopher of
religion and Schleyermacher expert), RC Magdeburg, "Nietzsche und das dritte Reich,"
23 May 1934. Both in GStA PK, I. HA rep. 228, no. 685.

[40] Simon, "Die Zukunft des Individualismus," GStA PK, I. HA rep. 228, no. 695.

of mass movements and the desire for strong leadership. He saw Rotary as a synthesis of individualism and selflessness in keeping with a new era, when the economy, now thrown into instability, had to be infused with a spiritual essence.

This attack on economic individualism might seem surprising coming from a self-proclaimed liberal.[41] But we must recall that the search for meaning in the economy and politics had a long intellectual pedigree that transcended party and ideology. While national-conservative economists attempted to build a völkisch economy, German liberals since the nine-teenth century had also attempted to reconcile their individualist notions with a romantic commitment to Volk and nation.[42] Moreover, the success of Marxism lay in its ability to envision a world that transcended the raw egoism of the market. In short, Simon shared with both socialists and Nazis (like fellow Rotarians Mehmke and Ludowici) a view that public life needed to be infused with a nonmaterial, even mystical, character that classical liberalism was incapable of providing.

This critique of liberalism had an even wider resonance than poli-tics, and it dovetailed with interwar intellectuals' search for "authen-ticity." This quest was manifested in both Martin Heidegger's embrace of National Socialism,[43] which the philosopher saw as ushering in an existential transformation of the German people, and in less racialized critiques of the existing political order. In the latter vein, the authoritar-ian conservative Oswald Spengler, whose diagnoses of Western decline resonated with some Rotarians' cultural pessimism,[44] found little appeal in either liberalism or in the crude Germanophilia of National Socialism. The interwar search for existential meaning was also embodied in diverse strains of Catholic and Protestant antiliberalism, some of which rejected and some of which celebrated the Nazi project.[45] The broader point is

[41] On his career and politics, see Paul Simon, *Meine Erinnerungen: Das Leben des jüdis-chen Deutschen Paul Simon, Rechtsanwalt in Mainz* (Mainz: Verein für Sozialgeschichte Mainz, 2003).

[42] James J. Sheehan, *German Liberalism in the Nineteenth Century* (Chicago: University of Chicago Press, 1978), 79–122.

[43] Victor Farias, *Heidegger and Nazism* (Philadelphia: Temple University Press, 1987), 96–112; and the more controversial book by Emmanuel Faye, *Heidegger: The Introduction of Nazism into Philosophy in Light of the Unpublished Seminars of 1933–1935* (New Haven, CT: Yale University Press, 2009).

[44] See, e.g., Rot. Bessel's speech on Spengler, RC Bremen, 29 May 1936, GStA PK, I. HA rep. 228, no. 685.

[45] See Donald J. Dietrich, "Catholic Theology and the Challenge of Nazism," in *Antisemitism, Christian Ambivalence, and the Holocaust*, ed. Kevin P. Spicer (Bloomington: Indiana University Press, 2007), 76–101; and Richard Steigmann-Gall, *The Holy Reich: Nazi*

that the themes taken up by Rotarians were vast and complex, and they spoke to wide scholarly currents that defy easy categorization. Rotarians were products of their time, and their goal was not to promote a political philosophy as such, but to understand the intellectual underpinnings of their achievement PK ethos and to make themselves culturally relevant. When they scoured Aristotle for lessons about "self-recognition," or explored the meaning of "character building," or advocated a politically engaged humanism, they were bolstering their own self-image as practical idealists, who felt comfortable in the market and in the academy.[46]

Of course, these reflections were not only about Rotarians' self-understanding as elites. They served the immediate aim of proving that the organization's bourgeois orientation could be aligned with the precepts of National Socialism. Indeed, because the concept of the "bourgeoisie," or *Bürgertum*, was itself so malleable (referring as it did to class, profession, education, and a cluster of elitist and paternalist values) and because it always had a more communitarian resonance in Germany than in France or the Anglo-American world, Rotarians could claim that the bourgeois era was a natural precursor to the Nazi era.[47]

One must not overstate the intellectual affinities between these movements. While both Rotarians and Nazi thinkers sought to understand the relationship between culture, the economy, and society, their basic orientations were different, and this helps explain the untimely dissolution of Rotary. What is striking, however, is that the same premises of the achievement community that underpinned Nazi commercial ideals also enabled business leaders to carve out a niche in the Third Reich. By entering a milieu of artists, musicians, and philanthropists, Rotarians linked their professional work with cultural elitism; they had demonstrated the Leistung that supported their rarefied social status. This elitism would in turn affect they way they understood their relationship to the consuming masses. This does not mean that every businessman or market professional in Germany saw himself as an elite. A sales director, business owner, or advertising agent might never dine with a powerful banker or

---

Conceptions of Christianity, 1919–1945 (Cambridge: Cambridge University Press, 2003), 13–50.

[46] See Rot. Prof. Ludwig Brecht, "Das Idee der Persönlichkeit bei Aristoteles," RC Karlsruhe, 30 April 1935; and Rot. E. Wilser, "Über Charakterbildung," RC Karlsruhe, 11 February 1936, both in GStA PK, I. HA rep. 228, no. 685.

[47] On the broader history of "bourgeois" thinking, see the essays in Jürgen Kocka, ed., *Bürger und Bürgerlichkeit im 19. Jahrhundert* (Göttingen: Vandenhoeck & Ruprecht 1987).

FIGURE 14. Rotary flag hanging next to the swastika at a Rotary banquet. Rotary Germany District Conference, Wiesbaden, 10–12 May 1935. (I. HA, rep. 228, no. 977; courtesy of Rotary Germany and Geheimes Staatsarchiv Preußischer Kulturbesitz, Berlin.)

university professor. But in the late Weimar and early Nazi years, business leaders were always attuned to larger debates about culture, politics, and society, and this engagement could not help but shape their understanding of their own work.

ROTARIANS, MARKETING, AND MASS CONSUMPTION

These discussions about elitism, individualism, and the masses could be heard at Rotary Club luncheons throughout Germany in the early Nazi years. In many respects they were a continuation of Weimar debates about social and cultural change, now conducted in the context of a self-proclaimed racial state. But what did they have to do with commerce and consumption? Abstract discursions into elites and masses often grounded more practical discussions about how to provide goods and services to the public. How could producers respond to the material and spiritual needs of consumers? What were the responsibilities of economic elites in providing leisure opportunities to the masses? Was mass marketing a positive or negative business development? In addressing these questions,

Rotarians revealed both an attraction to and ambivalence toward mass production and consumption, and this tension mirrored National Socialist attitudes toward the economy. In their own way, Rotarians, like the Nazi leadership, attempted to understand the marketplace in moral terms. They were guided by the ethic of service – to the consumer, the community, and ultimately the Volk.

Discussions about the social, economic, and cultural implications of mass consumption were hardly limited to the private setting of the inter-war men's club. Since the late nineteenth century, German business leaders had pondered the meaning of mass society and the implications of social leveling. Drawing on writers like Le Bon, Ortega y Gasset, and American intellectual Walter Lippmann, they had explored the implications of the masses' increased access to politics, leisure, and consumer opportunities.[48] Rotary sheds light on such preoccupations, for since its arrival in Germany, members had been eager to understand the nature of modern society, defined by rapid social, cultural, and technological change and a breakdown between "high" and "low." Rotarians devoted numerous speeches to the challenge of mass society and, more specifically, mass leisure. They shared news about the latest developments in advertising, the introduction of television, and their curiosity about whether, for example, aviation and motorcycle riding were elite sports or should be available to the masses. They talked about the "Rotarian" way to drive a car, which included making sure that the brakes were working properly to protect women and children passengers. Club members also traded insights into the importance of the camera, radio, gramophone, and cinema for cultural life and political propaganda. They debated whether talking films ruined the beauty of silent movies and corrupted children and whether stage plays, now under assault from moving pictures, were themselves becoming too accessible to the "lazy" mass public.[49] In short, Rotarians in the Third Reich partook of wider, international discussions about mass consumer society.

Rotarians merged these discussions of leisure with reflections on the relationship between mass consumption, economics, and German culture. Specific references to consumption often emerged in debates about

---

[48] On market professionals' views of the masses, see Alexander Schug, "Wegbereiter der modernen Absatzwerbung in Deutschland: Advertising Agencies und die Amerikanisierung der deutschen Werbebranche in der Zwischenkriegszeit," *WerkstattGeschichte* 34, no. 2 (2003): 29–52.

[49] For these discussions see the collection of speeches on radio, cinema, cars, sports, art, and photography in GStA PK, I. HA rep. 228, nos. 636, 639, 668.

department stores. Rotarians' views of the department store reflected broader attitudes about the social implications of consumption, and it is worth considering the arguments. Since the nineteenth century, the department store had been seen as the ultimate symbol of mass leveling, with goods increasingly being made available to the broadening middle and working classes.[50] Movements on the Right, representing the interests of shopkeepers and artisans, saw the department store as a mortal enemy. They believed it promoted moral laxness through its temptation of shoppers and its seductive powers over women, who were prone to bouts of kleptomania.[51] As we have seen, in the early 1930s the Nazi Party stepped up its critique of department stores as Jewish-owned exemplars of big business power over the small man. During the elections of 1930 and 1932, this hostility became a particularly potent weapon in the Nazis' arsenal. The department store represented a cultural and economic threat, as smaller retailers were supposedly getting squeezed, and family-run companies were forced to compete with lower-quality products stocked by the big emporiums.

Before and after the Nazi seizure of power, Rotarians had much to say about this theme. In 1931 the department store mogul Georg Tietz lectured to his club friends in Berlin about the claims being leveled against this form of retailing. Not only did he dispute assertions that department stores peddled poor-quality goods and drove out "the little man"; he also pointed out the hypocrisy of his critics: the very people who were denouncing the department store for political gain were also shopping there. He rejected a common complaint that department stores made more and more money on product advertising, explaining that low costs were determined by the turn to mass production and by taking advantage of a "dead season" in factories. But most important, the department store fulfilled cultural and social functions, providing "the decorations, displays, and buildings through which artists obtain jobs." Department stores offered a substantially lower price "that reflected only a marginal difference in quality, enabling the poor man to become that much richer."[52]

---

[50] See Geoffrey Crossick and Heinz-Gerhard Haupt, eds., *The Petit Bourgeoisie in Europe, 1780–1914* (London: Routledge, 1997), 110, 165.

[51] Paul Lerner, "Consuming Pathologies: Kleptomania, Magazinitis, and the Problem of Female Consumption in Wilhelmine and Weimar Germany," *WerkstattGeschichte* 42 (Summer 2006): 46–56.

[52] Tietz lecture, ca. 18 February 1931, GStA PK, I. HA rep. 228, no. 662. Rotarian Henry Grundmann, a non-Jewish director of the Sternfeld department store in Danzig, reminded

Tietz's sentiments were echoed by another Rotarian, Martin Cohn, director of the Passage department store in Saarbrücken, who lectured to his club friends in late 1932 about the "significance of the department store." Linking the *Warenhaus* to the Rotary service ethic, Cohn argued that more than the earning of profit, "the true function of the department store is the provisioning of the masses in the poorer classes." Cohn asserted that "responsibility created joy in work. Everyone must make a contribution so that the greater totality is served. The department store, indeed our department store, is a totality."[53] Such defenses of the department store were not surprising at a time when the Nazi Party was stepping up its attacks. Indeed, Tietz and Cohn, soon to be removed from their clubs as "non-Aryans," were pleading to the public and fellow Rotarians to divorce the department store from its association with predatory, Jewish economic control. They also cast their words in terms of the larger attempt to raise the "common man," suffering under the weight of the Depression, to loftier heights. Hardly a source of despair for most Germans, the department store held the power to fulfill the dreams of average citizens – to bring to life their fantasies of abundance during a time of privation.

Tietz's and Cohn's reflections remind us that the desire to make consumption socially relevant was not unique to the Nazis. It had been a hallmark of both liberal and conservative thinking since the nineteenth century, and in the late Weimar years, when capitalism was on the defensive, it was endowed with a new urgency. Despite their apologetic overtones, Tietz's and Cohn's thoughts also reveal an excitement about mass consumption that many of their colleagues would continue to share after the two men were gone from Rotary. Rotarians who represented large producers and retailers were particularly eager to promote the benefits of mass consumption. But not everyone shared this enthusiasm. Some Rotarians agreed with the Nazi Kampfbund that mass retailing and marketing were driving out the independent entrepreneur who had the practical expertise that larger retailers lacked. They blamed the department store for introducing generic product brands, which some associated with the loss of Germany's own uniqueness (linked as it was to the ethos

his colleagues that department stores accounted for only 4% of total retail sales and thus did not represent a threat to the small retailer. Rot. Grundmann, "Zwischen Produzent und Konsument – Probleme der modernen Güterverteilung," 1 November 1932, GStA PK, I. HA rep. 228, no. 662.

[53] Cohn, "Die Bedeutung der Warenhäuser," 31 October 1932, Anlage zum Wochenbericht III/19 (99), GStA PK, I. HA rep. 228, no. 622.

of the small businessman).[54] When the owner of a furniture company complained at a RC Baden-Baden lunch about "unsavory elements" that were doing damage to the small-time salesman, he was implying that "big capitalism" (coded "Jewish") was the culprit and that the state would have to intervene.[55]

Anti-Semitism informed debates about department stores and mass consumption more generally. But for Rotary's businessmen, so too did the organization's service ethic. In ways superficially similar to those of the Nazis, Rotarians were trying to understand the nonmaterial dimensions of the economy by appealing to the ideal of service. Who could attend to consumers and the wider community more effectively: large retailers, who provided a multitude of affordable goods, or small merchants, who provided knowledge and guidance in the marketplace? The question was never answered definitively, but it did reveal a desire of club members to prove their relevance in a new state that turned "service" and "sacrifice" into ideological keywords. Rotarians suggested that they had a unique mission under National Socialism to take care of their customers.[56] Whether it was during a visit to an Autobahn construction site (Rotarians considered mass motorization important for facilitating greater sociability through faster interclub visits) or in welcoming foreign colleagues to the 1936 Berlin Olympics, they asserted the necessity for elites to provide the masses with leisure travel, entertainment, and consumer goods. They spoke about the obligations of manufacturers, retailers, and shop owners to treat their clientele with respect and to create a consumer-friendly economy. And they lectured about consumer products as cultural goods that would serve the larger community and, by extension, humanity.[57] The service ethic also extended to foreigners, whom businessmen were to treat hospitably. Günther Beindorff, who would one day head the Pelikan pens company, spoke at his Hanover Rotary Club about the importance of modern office equipment for the smooth functioning of a business and for international goodwill. Meeting with a group of British

---

[54] See the response to this claim in Rot. Dr. Heinz Goldhammer, "Der Markenartikel als Qualitäts- und Kulturfaktor: Gütezeichen für Markenartikel?" RC Heilbronn, 19 February 1935, GStA PK, I. HA rep. 228, no. 618.

[55] Max Rahnefeld, "Die Nöte meines Berufes," 28 October 1935, GStA PK, I. HA rep. 228, no. 622.

[56] M. Schub, "Rotary," RC Munich, 2 February 1937, GStA PK, I. HA rep. 228, no. 618.

[57] On these discussions see GStA PK, I. HA rep. 228, nos. 618 and 622.

Rotarians after a Sunday of golf, tennis, and swimming, he gave his guests a tour of a Pelikan ink factory.[58]

By aligning consumption with service to society, Rotarians demonstrated an excitement and an ambivalence about mass consumption. Like the Nazi regime, they saw consumption as both good for business and potentially damaging to cultural traditions. Whether out of a bad conscience, a commitment to ethical principles, or a political pragmatism, they therefore justified their own work on behalf of consumption as an expression of altruism; provisioning the population with goods and services was a humanitarian gesture that allowed for social uplift and material pleasure. This attempt to package consumption in the language of humanism sometimes mirrored the Nazis' race-inflected language about the Mensch. "Humans, in their capacity as consumers, are the key objects of the economy," declared Rotarian Otto Blum, professor at the Technical University of Hanover. More than objects, however, they were economic and racial subjects: "In all economic creation, the human being, as producer, is the most important 'factor of production.'... [He] must never be considered only economically, but rather as a member of the Volk. Any overexploitation of his body, mind, or spirit is a crime against Volk and Fatherland."[59]

In expressing this view, Blum combined his Rotarian beneficence with a völkisch sensibility. He saw consumers as human beings and as racial actors, whose individual behavior in the marketplace had implications for the larger biological whole. It was not enough to declare that the consumer was the engine of the economy, however; he or she had to be linked to a higher calling, namely protecting the Volk body. Blum not only sanitized consumption by linking it to race, however. He also gave consumption a higher meaning by aligning it with Germany's producerist ethos. Blum argued that consumers were not just objects, who passively received goods that the state and private industry provided. They were also creators, who demonstrated their utility to the community through labor. In packaging consumption in the rhetoric of "creation," Blum echoed ideas about "quality work," "the honor of labor," and "community of the enterprise," which made their way onto the factory floor and reflected at once Nazi communal ideas and less ideological attempts to

---

[58] Beindorff, "Aus der Geschichte und über die Herstellung einiger viel gebrauchter Büroartikel," GStA PK, I. HA rep. 228, no. 622.

[59] Blum, "Die Eingliederung des Verkehrs in die nationale Wirtschaft," *Verkehrstechnische Woche* 28, no. 25 (20 June 1934), reprinted in GStA PK, I. HA rep. 228, no. 666.

understand consumers and producers as one and the same.[60] In short, Blum was eager to acknowledge the importance of consumption, but he had to give it a higher purpose. Consumers were fundamentally workers and members of the Volk community. As such they were indispensable, and elites like Blum were obliged to attend to their material and spiritual needs.

It is tempting to see these views as simply the abstract reflections of a professor and ideologue. But references to production, consumption, hard work, and Leistung penetrated everyday language in the Third Reich and became the guiding themes of fairs and national celebrations. Rotarians attended these events with great enthusiasm and found in them the practical manifestations of their own values. The 1936 Olympics in Berlin and Garmisch-Partenkirchen, for example, gave politicians and members of men's associations the opportunity to reflect on the meaning of individual performance and achievement. During the winter and summer games, Rotarians opened their club doors to guests from abroad, who were regaled with speeches about diligence, international harmony, and the similarity of the Rotarian ideal and the Olympic ideal.[61] At the summer games, Joseph Goebbels delivered a speech about the "resonating power of personal relationships between individuals from country to country." Rotarians in Club Bielefeld remarked with excitement that the propaganda minister's speech had embodied the very goals of the Rotary movement.[62] While some Rotarians were thrilled about their movement's affinities with Nazi ideals, they probably also understood that their clubs played a role in the Nazis' orchestrated spectacle. During the Olympics, when the regime was trying to hide its anti-Semitism (it removed anti-Jewish street signs in Berlin), Rotary presented Germany's bourgeois, cosmopolitan face to the rest of the world. Whether for cynical propagandistic purposes or out of a commitment to transnational friendship, Rotarians helped present a temporarily deracialized version of the Nazi marketplace to an international audience.

Even more than the Olympics, the Schaffendes Volk exhibition of 1937 spoke directly to Rotary's businessmen. As we saw in the preceding

---

[60] Alf Lüdtke, "The 'Honor of Labor': Industrial Workers and the Power of Symbols under National Socialism," in *Nazism and German Society, 1933–1945*, ed. David F. Crew (London: Routledge, 1994), 67–109.

[61] Conrad Matschoss, director of Verein deutscher Ingenieure, to president of Club Berlin, 31 October 1935, GStA PK, I. HA rep. 228, no. 72.

[62] RC Bielefeld, Wochenbericht, vol. 2, no. 7/59 (31 August 1936), GStA PK, I. HA rep. 228, no. 121.

chapter, the Düsseldorf exposition suggested that German creativity and productivity could lead to consumer satisfaction. Even at a time when the regime was restricting access to civilian products, the Nazis made sure to put the consuming power of the working individual front and center: the private spheres of the male laborer and the female homemaker were sites of economic virtue. Rotary Clubs had members representing large-scale producers of both industrial and consumer goods, and they avidly attended Schaffendes Volk. For example, members of Club Düsseldorf, including Henkel boss Hugo Henkel, invited all German and foreign Rotarians to attend the event, to come to club meetings during its duration, and to be in contact with the president of Düsseldorf's chamber of industry and commerce about business opportunities.[63] Schaffendes Volk served a key function for Rotarians. It brought together the marketing of German products, as well as the ideology of self-sufficiency embodied in the Four Year Plan, with the organization's cherished ideals of international camaraderie. Much like the Olympic games the year before, which Rotarians saw as an opportunity to showcase their country, Schaffendes Volk represented Germany's attempt to highlight its post-Depression economic prowess and to celebrate high-quality production, mass consumption, and business networking. But with fewer people watching around the world, the Nazis felt no need to remove racism from the festivities as they had during the Olympics. The Nazi commercial ideal was on full display in Düsseldorf.

As with the Nazi regime, there was a tension in Rotarians' attitudes toward consumption. For businessmen the rise of consumer capitalism challenged Germany's producerist ethic and threatened to unleash the dangerous force of the masses. But it also offered new opportunities for profit and economic influence. Rotarians came to terms with this tension by enlisting their own fraternal ethos of sacrifice and achievement and, at times, merging it with National Socialist precepts. They portrayed consumers fundamentally as "producers," whose individual achievements were expressions of the spirit of sacrifice. Like artists, athletes, and business leaders themselves, consumers – in their capacities as workers and housewives – engaged in the process of "creation," an honorable exercise in individual initiative that, in turn, fortified the nation. Rotarians, like the Nazis, hoped to school these masses in righteous forms of labor and leisure.

---

[63] In Monatsbrief des Governors, Middle of April 1937, GStA PK, I. HA rep. 228, no. 121.

CONFRONTING THE UNITED STATES

Thus far we have seen how Rotarians attempted to understand elite and mass culture in the distinct setting of Third Reich and how their thinking converged with the Nazis' own understanding of commercial relations. While they addressed international developments in mass marketing and consumption, their discourses reflected the hopes and fears that accompanied the onset of Nazi rule. But in the Third Reich, Rotary was not only in dialogue with its own political surroundings. As Rotarians looked for ways of understanding mass consumption, it was inevitable that they would turn to the spiritual home of their movement, the United States. Already in the Weimar years, Rotarians and other business elites' relationship to the United States was marked by an ambivalence. They derived inspiration from America as the paradigm of consumer capitalism and business sociability, but they questioned the ability of the American model to function in Germany. For intellectual and business leaders, the United States had the allure of democracy and the vibrancy of a modern, pulsating industrial society. But it also represented a cultural wasteland, pandering to the lowest common denominator through its mass media.[64] Regardless of these criticisms, America was the trend setter in most forms of production and commerce – Fordism, Taylorism, advertising, and public relations. The American economy was the site of much curiosity among Weimar elites, who often traveled to factories in the United States to witness firsthand the changes taking place in American industry.[65]

This obsession with the United States did not end upon the Nazi seizure of power.[66] Hitler may have diverted Germany from "American" models of political democracy and consumer capitalism, but the United States remained a point of orientation for German elites after 1933. During the Third Reich, Rotarians devoted some of their weekly lectures to discussions of American history, society, and culture. H. E. Steche, a factory owner and member of RC Leipzig, lectured in 1936 about the American Civil War, proclaiming that President Abraham Lincoln and General Robert E. Lee reminded him of Hitler in their decisiveness.

---

[64] See, e.g., Friedrich Schönemann, *Die Kunst der Massenbeeinflussung in den Vereinigten Staaten von Amerika* (Stuttgart: Deutsche Verlags-Anstalt, 1924), 102–41.

[65] Nolan, *Visions of Modernity*, 36–42.

[66] See Phillip Gassert, *Amerika im Dritten Reich: Ideologie, Propaganda und Volksmeinung, 1933–1945* (Stuttgart: Steiner, 1997); and Hans Dieter Schäfer, "Amerikanismus im Dritten Reich," in *Nationalsozialismus und Modernisierung*, ed. Michael Prinz and Rainer Zitelmann (Darmstadt: Wissenschaftliche Buchgesellschaft, 1991), 199–215.

But he also contrasted the Americans' altruistic desire to reconstruct the postbellum South with the shabby treatment Germany had received after World War I.[67] More common were lectures about Paul Harris, the father of the Rotary movement and its symbolic leader. Since his retirement as president of RI in 1912, Harris had remained active in the movement, lecturing about world peace and international brotherhood. He visited Germany in the summer of 1932, where he attended several club meetings and participated in a "friendship tree" planting in Berlin. Rotarians in Germany revered Harris as their patron saint, albeit not without an (unfounded) concern in the Nazi Party and among closely associated clubs that the Rotary founder had "Jewish ancestry."[68]

Because of the Nazi Party's complicated views of the United States – as economic inspiration and competitor – Rotarians toed a careful line in their lunchtime reflections about America. On the one hand, they praised Franklin Roosevelt for his activism and his capabilities as a "führer." On the other hand, they denounced him as a "social democratic president" who meddled in the economy (conveniently ignoring Hitler's own interventionism), pandered to the masses, and waged an attack on the propertied.[69] Despite mixed feelings about the United States, Rotarians still welcomed American and other foreign visitors in the spirit of Rotarian and German goodwill. These visitors came to the meetings of their sister clubs and took part in their festivities. Edwin Mims, an English professor at Vanderbildt University in Nashville, Tennessee, lectured to Club Bielefeld in 1936 about the need for better relations between Germany and the United States.[70] Other Americans came to the 1936 Olympics, where Rotary sponsored social and cultural events for their foreign visitors in the spirit of international camaraderie that accompanied the games.

Many German Rotarians also traveled to the United States in the 1930s to see firsthand the movement's spiritual homeland and the capital of the mass commercial culture about which they had been talking for so long. They have left behind a fascinating collection of travel reports,

---

[67] H. E. Steche, Lecture on Civil War, 28 April 1936, GStA PK, I. HA rep. 228, no. 652.

[68] Walter Woelz, RC Hanover, to 73. District Governor Otto Kroeger, 2 December 1933, and other letters in GStA PK, I. HA rep. 228, no. 751.

[69] Arthur Kaiser, Travel report in RC Chemnitz, Wochenbericht, #8/VII-276 (20 August 1935), and Rot. Freudenberg über seine Nordamerikareise, RC Mannheim, 30 March 1936, GStA PK, I. HA rep. 228, no. 612.

[70] RC Bielefeld, Wochenbericht, vol. 2, no. 5/57 (17 August 1936), GStA PK, I. HA rep. 228, no. 113.

often written in the spirit of Alexis de Tocqueville, who had made the trek overseas in the 1830s to reflect on American political, cultural, and social habits. In the 1920s and early 1930s, Rotarians mirrored the obsessions of the German press when they drew attention to Al Capone and the "gangsterism" that pervaded American society, as well as to the precarious state of Germandom in the United States. The kidnapping of Charles Lindbergh's baby also riveted Germans from all walks of life, who found something alluring in this frightening underside of America. These travel reports, delivered in speeches to colleagues upon return, had a ritualistic quality, as visitors offered rote reflections on their arrival in New York harbor, their first glimpses of skyscrapers in "the land of unlimited possibilities" or "the golden land of freedom," and their travels farther south and west. There were some overwhelmingly sympathetic reports, such as that of Breslau Rotarian Alfred Bielschowsky, who in 1934 reported to his club his favorable impressions of the United States after a two-month visit. A pioneer in opthalmological research, the Jewish Bielschowsky eventually left Germany for the country he so admired, settling in New Hampshire in 1937, where he founded the Dartmouth College Eye Institute.[71]

As in the Weimar years, business leaders in particular were drawn to the United States. Manufacturers visited Henry Ford's Rouge River plant in Michigan to witness and debate the feasibility of bringing together mass production and mass consumption. Rotarians from the business world traveled to Macy's department store in New York and Marshall Field's in Chicago to gather information on the merits and dangers of "Jewish" commerce and the threat mass retailing represented to independent owners.[72]

While RI's headquarters in Chicago generally welcomed all visiting Rotarians, the American media was more withholding. In 1936 Alfred Hugo Neuhaus, a cigarette manufacturer from Club Mannheim, along with forty-five other tobacco magnates, visited the factories of Lucky Strike, Chesterfield, and Philip Morris, where they were warmly greeted despite dispiriting headlines in the Richmond newspaper declaring, "German Nazi Tobacco Moguls Arrived in Virginia." The Rotarians were, however, turned away by the management of Camel, which refused to receive people from the "new Germany."[73] Rotarians

---

[71] Bielschowsky, "Eindrücke von einer Reise durch Nord-Amerika," 11 June 1934, GStA PK, I. HA rep. 228, no. 612.

[72] On the visit to Marshall Field's, see report by Rot. Kaiser.

[73] Dr. Alfred Hugo Neuhaus, "Bericht über meine Amerika–Studienreise von Mitte März bis Ende April 1936, RC Mannheim, 12 May 1936, GStA PK, I. HA rep. 228, no. 612.

responded with outrage to such affronts. As early as April 1933, Rotary Germany had issued a condemnation of the "horror stories" being disseminated in the foreign (notably American and British) press. In a letter to RI's European headquarters in Zurich, it protested the "rumors" that Jews were being harmed in Germany and expressed its disgust with such untruths. This disingenuous letter of protest was prepared on 1 April, the very day the well-publicized boycott of Jewish stores began.[74]

Rotarians visited the United States not only in their capacities as club members and private citizens. The Reich Group Industry (Reichsgruppe Industrie) and the Reich Association for Wholesale, Import and Export Trade (Reichsverband des Gross-, Ein- und Ausfuhrhandels) sent Rotarian Arthur Kaiser, the owner of an import/export business and member of RC Chemnitz, overseas to observe a number of economic institutions, including the offices of Marshall Field's, the Federal Reserve, and Swift and Company of Chicago, a beef slaughterhouse and shipping firm that was one of America's largest companies, with 55,000 employees in the late 1920s.[75] Kaiser was interested not only in how American business dealt with imports and exports, but also in the unique social setting that underpinned this commercial society. Like other visitors during the Third Reich, he reflected on racial tensions in the United States, arguing that the strained relationships between whites, Asians, and blacks should foster some sympathy for the racial situation in Germany. This sympathy could be elicited, declared Kaiser, "despite Samuel Untermeyer," a New York lawyer who in 1933 had declared a "holy war against Germany" by calling for a boycott of German goods. Given Germany's dependence on exports to the United States, Untermeyer had hoped to compel the German government to reinstate Jews in their positions within the civil service.[76]

Other Rotarians besides Kaiser expressed their disgust at American politics and culture. Mannheim Rotarian Otto Freudenberg, a leather manufacturer, was particularly disdainful of New York City, which greeted him with a snowstorm of massive proportions that made travel nearly impossible. He heaped scorn on the Polish and Russian Jews who were

[74] RC Halle, Wochenbericht, vol. 4, no. 38/139, 1 April 1933, GStA PK, I. HA rep. 228, no. 584.
[75] Report by Rot. Kaiser.
[76] On the boycott and Untermeyer see Werner E. Braatz, "German Commercial Interests in Palestine: Zionism and the Boycott of German Goods, 1933–1934," *European History Quarterly* 9, no. 4 (October 1979): 481–513.

on strike during his 1936 visit and who were no doubt inspired by an increasingly "communist" U.S. president. He bemoaned the anti-German sentiments in America, particularly among the "non-Aryan" crowd. The "Jewish press" was whipping people into a frenzy by portraying Hitler as some "wild tyrant." And while he took some comfort in the presence of anti-Semitism in the United States, he was frustrated by the "Jewish" department stores that were boycotting German products. The only relief from this punishing visit came on his return trip, when he learned on the ship that Hitler had remilitarized the Rhineland.[77] Through Freudenberg's words we see how inseparable reflections on the United States were from domestic discussions of Jews and commerce. Freudenberg adopted the tropes of anticommunism and anti-Semitism and employed them to assess the state of affairs across the Atlantic.

Hostility to the United States manifested itself not only in travel reports. In 1934 the Rotary Club of Rawlins, Wyoming, sent a questionnaire to 1,200 Rotary Clubs in seventy countries, asking them about their members' perceptions of American politics, European–American relations, the state of the world, and the six Rotary goals. This was an unusual and controversial undertaking by a club, which was forbidden to involve itself in the politics of other countries. Indeed, Paul Harris was not amused when he learned about the Rawlins questionnaire.[78] In Germany, a district governor, Otto Kroeger, directed clubs to send only answers that he had personally approved. One of those came from a lumber industrialist in Club Hanover, Baron Albrecht Knigge, who composed a dismissive letter. Knigge condemned the Treaty of Versailles and President Wilson's anti-German propaganda that he felt had led the United States to war with Germany in 1917. Without a hint of irony, he condemned Americans' vulnerability to propaganda, which could lead people to blindly follow their leaders into war. The United States, the letter continued on a different note, was marred by economic dysfunction, such as the artificial creation of needs and thus the overproduction of consumer goods. This false demand led, in Knigge's mind, to the establishment of new industries and the overwhelming "power of the machine." The trend toward automation in America was fundamentally dehumanizing. "The changes have come so suddenly that the masses find themselves in a mystical state of mental confusion with no apparent way out." Countering

---

[77] Freudenberg travel report, delivered 30 March 1936, GStA PK, I. HA Rep. 228, no. 612.
[78] On Harris's response see http://www.rotaryfirst100.org/presidents/1910harris/paulharris
/political (accessed 29 July 2009).

this tyranny of the machine, "which robs the people of living space," was the only way to overcome global unemployment.[79]

Next to his tirade against the machine, Knigge, like Freudenberg, did not hesitate to offer his views on race in America, declaring that "in no other land in the past fifty years has the race problem played such a horrible role as in the USA. To open the gates of immigration to all people would be suicide for the race that's still dominant in the USA." As the capstone to his tirade, Knigge condemned "Americanism" – a vague collection of negative traits (hyperindividualism, superficiality, an over-zealousness about money, and a vapid modernity) that he saw as America's worst export. He predicted that "modernism will eventually collapse in America and, with that, throughout the rest of the world."[80]

What is striking about these positive and negative assessments of the United States is the continuity in thinking throughout the interwar years, as German business leaders reflected on the challenges of importing American commercial culture into Germany. Despite the dramatic rise of Hitler, attitudes had changed little. Before and after 1933, Rotarians reported on the remarkable consumer opportunities in the United States. At the same time they emphasized the potential incompatibility of American market capitalism with Germany, where high-quality products and the ethos of the individual shopkeeper still reigned. In short, Rotarians served as representative interwar figures whose weekly discussions mirrored the familiar tensions inherent in German elites' (and Nazis') attitudes toward mass consumption and mass society more broadly – the attraction and the repulsion, the interest in expanding profits without compromising product quality, the desire to protect Germany from the excesses of America, and the anxious defense of one's social position. As they had done in the 1920s, Rotarians and other elites used the United States as a tool with which to understand themselves. The dialectic of fascination and disdain, and the cautious hope that America's race problem would legitimate Germany's own approach to the "Jewish question," kept many Rotarians attuned to developments across the Atlantic.

During the Third Reich, Rotary Germany faced the challenge of surviving as an organization and demonstrating that it occupied an organic place in

---

[79] Knigge, Beantwortung des Fragebogen des R. K. Rawlins, sent from Walter Woelz, District Secretary from 1935–36, to Bezirksführer Kroeger, 20 April 1934, GStA PK, I. HA rep. 228, no. 751.
[80] Ibid.

a Volksgemeinschaft. Yet there was more to this story than the struggle to stay relevant. From 1933 to 1937 Rotarians proceeded with a project they had begun with the first club founding in the Weimar years: confronting the rise of mass consumer society and maintaining their elitist vision of service in a rapidly changing social and political environment. Like the Nazi regime, these business leaders explored the relationship between people and the products they consumed, and they investigated the benefits and limits of the American capitalist model. Rotary's time in the Third Reich was short, but it is important to realize that, for Rotarians themselves, dissolution was not a foregone conclusion. For almost five years many Rotarians sincerely believed that they could merge bourgeois sociability with the racial and political demands of the new regime. Indeed, they felt that it was in the very context of a Leistungsgemeinschaft – an "achievement community" that valued individual performance in service of the common good – that a synthesis of social elitism, professional ethics, and National Socialist ideals would take hold.

Through this focus on Rotarians, one can gain broader insight into the National Socialist market ideal and its circulation among economic leaders. In their speeches and publications, the Nazis proclaimed a commitment to free enterprise, competition, productivity, and personal success – themes that spoke directly to the business world. In the early years of the Third Reich, therefore, company leaders and economists felt that the Nazi marketplace could sustain both conventional business practices and the social and professional institutions that supported them. The immediate survival of Rotary seemed to bear out this hope. Despite pressures from the regime, the organization maintained a certain freedom to pursue its mission, from international outreach and philanthropy to discussing the pressing issues of the day at luncheon meetings.[81] The Nazis did not cast aside the tradition of the men's association, but rather utilized this semiautonomous site of sociability to enlist support for the state. Other "secret" societies, like the Freemasons, felt the wrath of the Nazis from the start. But the regime understood that Rotarians were influential social, cultural, and business leaders, and it called on them to deliver the message to their international friends that Germany was a stable, peace-loving state that would not disrupt the flow of commerce

---

[81] In a similar vein, Eric Kurlander has traced the continuities in liberal thinking after 1933 and the ability of liberal democrats to sustain their political discussions. Eric Kurlander, *Living with Hitler: Liberal Democrats in the Third Reich* (New Haven, CT: Yale University Press, 2009), 9–10.

or the international networks that sustained it. Rotarians, for their part, felt a certain gratitude to the regime for allowing them to pursue their visions of gentlemanly association in a state that formally denounced any trappings of the "bourgeois era" and "America." From 1933 to 1937 Rotarians experienced a managed normality. At the behest of the regime, they were able to continue their club activities in a familiar manner, albeit in the absence of any racially undesirable members. For a time, it hardly seemed sensible for the regime to dismantle a popular expression of civil society and incur the wrath of the business and social elites on whom it depended to give economic force to the Nazi revolution.

This autonomy went only so far, however. The Nazis had people within Rotary who reported to the Gestapo the comings and goings of visitors and the weekly topics of discussion, and the organization can hardly be said to have represented a counterculture during these years. Yet the regime refrained from dictating the agenda of club meetings. Rotarians, like other Germans, did engage in a form of "voluntary obedience" to the regime, as they celebrated National Socialism with full force.[82] The magazine *Der Rotarier* (The Rotarian) presented nonpolitical articles or ads aimed at the professional man, such as the constant ads for decaffeinated coffee brand Kaffee HAG, which presumably took away nervous jitters and enhanced business performance.[83] Yet it also dutifully paid homage to Hitler, the Nazi party, and their various successes in foreign and domestic policy. Rotarians packaged themselves as socially engaged and patriotic professionals, both out of political expedience and due to the fact that some of the post-1933 members sincerely supported the regime and its radical notions. In 1937, however, this balancing act became impossible, as the regime, now on a war footing, stepped up its process of "spiritual Aryanization."[84] As the country emerged from the Great Depression, Hitler could afford to elevate his ideological goals above his practical ones. Rotary, as a "bourgeois" manifestation of the Nazi marketplace, became increasingly anachronistic

---

[82] The term comes from Neil Gregor, ed., *Nazism, War, and Genocide* (Exeter: University of Exeter Press, 2005), 21.

[83] "If you are overburdened with work," HAG ads told Rotarians, "then you need a stimulant during the day and deep, restful sleep at night." Decaffeinated Kaffee HAG was the answer. HAG ad, *Der Rotarier*, no. 9 (1935): 228.

[84] The term comes from Bernd Semrad, "Die geistigen 'Ariseure': Die 'Wiener Schule' der Werbeforschung im Dienste des Nationalsozialismus – Ein Werkstattbericht," in *Die Spirale des Schweigens: Zum Umgang mit der nationalsozialistischen Zeitungswissenschaft*, ed. Wolfgang Duchkowitsch, Fritz Hausjell, and Bernd Semrad (Münster: Lit, 2004), 249–71.

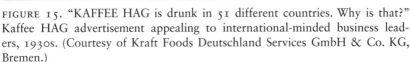

Jn 51 Ländern der Welt wird KAFFEE HAG getrunken. Warum wohl?

Kaffee Hag auch im Speisewagen

FIGURE 15. "KAFFEE HAG is drunk in 51 different countries. Why is that?" Kaffee HAG advertisement appealing to international-minded business leaders, 1930s. (Courtesy of Kraft Foods Deutschland Services GmbH & Co. KG, Bremen.)

and unnecessary to the regime, which was soon to embark on a new wave of anti-Semitic measures and step up its war preparations. With the dissolution of Rotary Germany, the regime shut down a potentially alternative form of social networking and silenced the rich discourses that accompanied it.

Rotarians' ability to maintain some organizational and ideological independence brings to light continuities with the Weimar years and before. When Rotarians dined at the same clubs in 1937 as they had ten years earlier, when they talked about arts, literature, social engineering, and mass consumption, they were engaging in decades-old conversations about the changing face of the modern world. Under the storm clouds of war and despite an international disdain for Hitler, foreign visitors still came to Germany as they had before 1933 (albeit in smaller numbers), engaging in Rotarian rituals, planning youth exchanges, or talking about life in small-town America and in the big cities of Latin America and Asia. International expressions of concern about Germany's domestic and foreign policy were answered with assurances that the country remained a welcoming place. This transnational civil discourse represents on the surface another challenge to the notion that after 1933 the Nazi revolution permeated all aspects of society in rapid order.

To be sure, Rotary Germany existed only during a period of Nazi ideological experimentation and consolidation, and thus it is not a perfect test case for measuring the regime's reach into everyday life. Moreover, we cannot underestimate the damage that the state wrought on this and other institutions through its policies of racial exclusion. Published speeches, articles, and minutes cannot convey the sense of disruption that members of associations felt as their colleagues were ostracized and persecuted. In addition, the fact that Nazis began to join Rotary Clubs in larger numbers could only serve to remind old members that the organization had fundamentally changed. Finally, by assuring the world that things were "normal" in Germany, Rotarians were essentially doing the regime's bidding – offering proof that all was well under Hitler when it really was not. Despite all this, until 1937, when the regime was fully in charge of social and intellectual institutions, certain trappings of civil society persisted. They were not about democratic freedoms, which had been rapidly abolished, but instead manifested themselves in the persistence of quasi-independent sites of social and intellectual interaction.

The obsession with the United States was perhaps the greatest continuity in the interwar years. For German elites, Rotarian or not, America represented both an alluring model for and a counterpoint to the German economy. From a philosophical perspective, many German Rotarians (and for that matter Rotarians worldwide) echoed Tocqueville's criticisms of American individualism and self-interestedness. They also engaged with the United States so actively because German professional life increasingly depended on the forms of exchange – mass cultural and mass market – found there. In the new setting of the Third Reich, business leaders posed the following questions: Could they emulate America's regime of mass production and consumption without losing Germany's unique artisanal traditions? Could social and cultural leaders combine social activism with an elitist outlook, as distinct from America's seemingly more democratic impulses, in the new Germany? Many Rotarians believed they could.

If Rotary Germany reflected both the continuities between the Weimar and Nazi periods and the relative autonomy of some organizations, it also displayed the possibilities of compatibility with National Socialism. Indeed, many Rotarians felt real affinities between their movement and the new regime. These went beyond mere linguistic coincidences, where vague and easily malleable concepts of achievement, sacrifice, and service could be shaped to conform to multiple worldviews. The Weimar Republic had been a crucible of modernity and experimentation, when Germans felt the rhythm of cultural change coupled with political instability. But the sudden emergence of a nationalist and racist ideological order compelled elites to examine whether a bourgeois age was coming to an end with the ascendancy of the politicized masses. Was there still a place for elites in the new society? In answering this question, some Rotarians felt that National Socialism put into greater relief concerns that had defined intellectual discourse before 1933. National unity, cultural pride, and philanthropy were hallmarks of Rotarianism before Hitler, and after 1933 they arguably had even greater import. Voluntarism, charity, loyalty, camaraderie, virtue, honor, goodwill, and customer service – these were elements of the Rotary ethos that found a home in the Third Reich. Rotarians thus discovered in the radical Nazi experiment the opportunity to pursue questions about the nature of mass society in a new, nationalist pitch. They could combine their hesitant attentiveness to the masses with their own ethos of individual achievement and merit.

This convergence of Rotary and Nazi ideals was centered predominantly on the economy. The marketplace was the key site of a new business morality, where abstract notions of performance and sacrifice came together with the practical work of producing for and selling to the masses. This intense focus on consumer society was not due simply to the fact that many "producers" (i.e., economic leaders) joined Rotary. Rather, as we have seen, the economy itself became the lynchpin of the German ideological reordering – as an embodiment of a national awakening, as a symbol of suppressed Jewish power, and as a site of material gratification. Ultimately, Rotarians' intellectual exchanges lent stability to the regime. The freedom to proceed with the project of understanding mass society gave them a false sense that they were welcome in the Third Reich in their multiple identities as international club men, would-be cultural figures, and nationalist professionals. Like many institutions in prewar Nazi Germany, Rotary lent a normality to the regime, allowing foreigners and Germans alike to see certain continuities in the public sphere, even as it was changing rapidly and violently.

This is not to suggest an inherent compatibility between Rotary and National Socialism. Rather, it is to show how the Nazi regime successfully cultivated the idea that mainstream economic and cultural ideals could successfully merge with Nazi ideals. Ironically, then, for Rotarians it was "bourgeois society" – however loosely defined – that paved the way for the Nazi revolution. It was not simply a dialectical relationship, in which the seeds of the next phase of history were contained within the earlier one. Nor did Rotarians make a Faustian pact with the regime – survival for a short while in exchange for blind loyalty. Rather, for some, the original ideals of Rotary laid the groundwork for active participation in the Volksgemeinschaft. This was especially the case for business leaders. Thinkers going back to Justus Möser and Hegel had pondered the implications of the market exchange, whether based on local traditions, guild privileges, or a strong and protective state.[85] The Nazis had found their own version of "the virtuous economy" (Möser), based on sacrifice, individual achievement, a mixture of state control and free enterprise, racial unity, and an organic relationship between civic-minded producers and gratified consumers. A clear expression of the Nazi marketplace came from Heinrich Burchard, a director with Deutsche Bank in Hamburg, who joined his local Rotary Club in early 1937. In conveying his enthusiasm for Rotary, he announced to his new friends, "If the economy once appeared to me as an end in itself, I know better today. It is *never* an end in itself; rather, a healthy economy is the most elemental life expression of a healthy Volk."[86]

[85] On Möser see Jerry Z. Muller, *The Mind and the Market: Capitalism in Modern European Thought* (New York: Knopf, 2002), 84–103.

[86] Burchard speech on 3 March 1937, Anlage zum Wochenbericht Nr. 469 X/35, GStA PK, I. HA rep. 228, no. 618.

4

Finding the "Voice of the Consumer"

The Society for Consumer Research in the 1930s

The preceding chapter took as its starting point elite perceptions of mass consumer society. Economic and cultural leaders maintained a keen interest in consumption, even as the state limited consumers' access to nonprivileged goods and services. For Rotarians, social engagement and intellectual curiosity motivated discussions about commerce and consumption. Rather than bringing these discussions to a halt, the onset of a new political regime heightened the interest in the masses' relationship to their material and cultural surroundings. Rotarians' engagement with larger social themes always had a practical element, as businessmen aimed to promote their companies' products and forge social connections that would benefit their firms. But it also had an idealistic component. These elite men put forth a vision of a perfected economic and political order, based on a combination of enlightened self-interest and the communal virtues of trust, sacrifice, and dedication to nation. They in turn helped give shape to the Nazis' market ideals and bolstered the regime's attempts to understand the spiritual and racist dimensions of the economy.

This chapter looks at another institutional setting where economic leaders explored the contours of mass society. This was the Society for Consumer Research (Gesellschaft für Konsumforschung – GfK), an organization that, upon its founding in 1934, devoted itself to understanding not just the abstract meanings of consumption, but also Germans' own perceptions of their lives and the goods they consumed. Today the GfK Group is the fourth-largest market research organization in the world, with 7,500 employees serving in sixty countries.[1] Over the seventy-five years of its existence, it has stood at the helm of the market research industry in Germany, spearheading efforts to integrate the latest scholarly findings about consumer psychology and behavior into the broader work of company self-promotion. This chapter focuses on the GfK and its intellectual milieu in order to continue our exploration of business leaders' ideas about consumer society. But it combines an examination of elite discourse with a look at the grass roots by considering what consumers were actually saying in 1930s and 1940s about their lives, their purchasing habits, and the state. As we will see, the GfK's oft-stated goal of discovering the "voice of the consumer" was not merely a rhetorical gesture. Rather, from 1936 to 1945, the GfK produced dozens of reports about men's and women's attitudes toward shopping and consuming. These reports offer a window onto the mind-set of Germans, who made decisions in the marketplace against the backdrop of scarcity, price controls, and the regime's attempts to engineer a racially pure economy.

The GfK was at its core a business enterprise, funded by consumer goods manufacturers who wanted information about the reception of their products. But for its founders and directors, consumer research was also an intellectual undertaking. At the center of this thinking about consumers and consumption stood the Mensch – the human being – who had desires and needs that could not be ignored by big business or the state. This chapter, by exploring both the activities of the GfK and the discourses that surrounded them, raises larger questions about the symbolic and actual force of consumption during the Third Reich. Much like Rotarians and their focus on the nexus between transatlantic business practices, consumption, and altruism, the GfK attempted to forge a synthesis between the practical work of business and humanist ideals. The fact that this endeavor took place in a racist, authoritarian society posed specific challenges to the GfK's directors. Could (and should) the organization engage in dispassionate scholarship in a country permeated by ideological passions? How could the GfK's practice of conducting "open conversations" with consumers function in a setting where people had to watch what they said for fear of reprisal by the state? What was the formal relationship of the GfK to the party and state authorities? How did the GfK's work reflect the priorities of the Nazi marketplace? How did

[1] See the GfK's corporate website at http://www.gfk.com/index.php?lang=en&content path=http%3A//www.gfk.com/english/unternehmen/missionneu.php%3Flang%3Den (accessed 25 July 2006).

the opinions expressed in GfK reports reflect a combination of consensus and coercion in the Third Reich? In answering these questions, this chapter offers a portrait of an organization that kept its prewar intellectual project free of National Socialist control but that spoke to some of the same themes about commerce and consumption that the Nazi regime was itself confronting.

There is an even larger historiographical issue at stake here. As we saw in the Introduction, Götz Aly has suggested that public support for National Socialism was bought through the material betterment of most Germans.[2] Among many of his contentions, Aly argues that through progressive social legislation and the distribution of goods pillaged from Jews, the German population enjoyed the policies of a socially engaged dictatorship. Scholars have excoriated both Aly's scholarship and many of his theses, among them the idea that widespread public support for Nazism resulted from social bribery. For our purposes, Aly's ideas beg the question of what Germans actually thought about their material existence. Did Germans in the 1930s and 1940s actually see themselves as the beneficiaries of national economic well-being? In their guise as consumers, did Germans feel that they were better off under National Socialism? And if so, did this engender support for the regime? The answers varied over time and are difficult to pin down. But the consumer research reports, at the very least, give us some insight into what German consumers were actually thinking about.

WILLIAM VERSHOFEN AND THE ORIGINS OF GERMAN CONSUMER RESEARCH

The Society for Consumer Research was founded during the early years of the Third Reich, but it was the product of German business leaders' and economists' longer commitment to understanding the possibilities opened up by mass consumption. Companies and graphic designers in the late nineteenth century were already deeply engaged in advertising. But "marketing," premised on a wider collection of strategies aimed at selling goods, garnered less attention. Although economists had long recognized the power of consumption (Adam Smith had pointed out that consumption is the sole end of production),[3] they had not given priority

---

[2] Götz Aly, *Hitler's Beneficiaries: Plunder, Racial War, and the Nazi Welfare State* (New York: Metropolitan, 2007).

[3] Wilhelm Vershofen, *Handbuch der Verbrauchsforschung*, vol. 1 (Berlin: Carl Heymanns, 1940), 16.

to understanding why consumers bought what they did and how companies could influence this purchasing behavior. There was a long-standing
assumption in Germany that a product, if well made, would effectively
sell itself. This idea was a reflection of the "quality" ethos that permeated
German business culture. Consumers would select a product seemingly
independently of aggressive promotion by the company. Once they discovered reliable merchandise, they would spread the word and would
themselves remain loyal to their favorite brands. In the cases where customers patronized primarily neighborhood "mom and pop" stores, this
assumption bore an element of truth. The shopkeeper still served as the
"expert," who communicated the advantages of a particular product to
customers without the help of flashy advertisements.[4] But with the rise
of mass markets and department stores, print and point-of-sale advertising became even more essential than human beings to the promotion of
goods.

As we saw in Chapter 2, after World War I business leaders and
politicians gave more thought to new forms of persuasion, whether in
the economy or in politics. The German defeat precipitated widespread
reflection about the supposed superiority of U.S. propaganda, which was
seen as having relied upon amoral, "scientific" approaches to publicity
in ways that ultimately benefited the American war effort.[5] Total war,
combined with rapid developments in mass culture, compelled elites to
think about new and more sophisticated forms of agitation. During the
Weimar years "economic propaganda," notably advertising, exploded in
popularity. What we might call "marketing," in turn, witnessed increased
attention. Already in the first two decades of the twentieth century,
universities had begun offering advanced degrees in business administration (*Betriebswirtschaftslehre*), which included the study of "sales theory" (*Absatztheorie*).[6] At these new business schools around Germany,

---

[4] See Uwe Spiekermann, "From Neighbour to Consumer: The Transformation of
Retailer–Consumer Relationships in Twentieth Century Germany, in *The Making of the
Consumer: Knowledge, Power and Identity in the Modern World*, ed. Frank Trentmann
(Oxford: Berg, 2006), 147–74.

[5] Corey Ross, "Mass Politics and the Techniques of Leadership: The Promise and Perils of
Propaganda in Weimar Germany," *German History* 24, no. 2 (April 2006): 184–211.

[6] See Peter Mantel, *Betriebswirtschaftslehre und Nationalsozialismus: Eine Institutionen-
und personengeschichtliche Studie* (Wiesbaden: Gabler, 2009), 15–34; Heike Franz,
*Zwischen Markt und Profession: Betriebswirte in Deutschland im Spannungsfeld
von Bildungs- und Wirtschaftsbürgertum (1900–1945)* (Göttingen: Vandenhoeck &
Ruprecht, 1998), 25–67; and David E. Lindenfeld, "The Professionalization of Applied
Economics: German Counterparts to Business Administration," in *German Professionals,*

economists also conducted research on how to understand consumer behavior. Known as "market" or "economic" "observation," this work was not yet devoted to the idiosyncratic behaviors of consumers. Instead it entailed examining broader economic trends: which products were being sold and in what volume, how certain sectors were performing, and what constituted the basis for regional and national productivity. Against this backdrop, the mastermind of the GfK, Wilhelm Vershofen, emerged as a pioneering figure.

It is important to focus on Vershofen at some length, as he was the main intellectual force behind German consumer research during a forty-year period that spanned the Weimar Republic, the Third Reich, and the early years of the West German "economic miracle" in the 1950s. In 1919 Vershofen, a prolific philosopher, novelist, and economist, became head of the interest group for the German porcelain industry, which engaged in some of the earliest forms of market observation in Germany. He also established an independent market research institute in Bamberg that would become the intellectual progenitor of the GfK. In 1921 Vershofen took a teaching assignment at the Nuremberg Business School, which had been founded two years earlier, and in 1923 he became a professor of economics at Nuremberg University. He subsequently moved his research organization to Nuremberg and formally named it the Institute for Economic Surveillance of German Products (Institut für Wirtschaftsbeobachtung der Deutschen Fertigware – IfW).[7]

During the 1920s the IfW focused on gathering statistics and doing cost comparisons relating to foreign markets, but this was clearly not Vershofen's chief interest. At the university he lectured regularly about the methodological and theoretical foundations of market observation, and in 1929 he founded a new journal, *Der Markt der Fertigware* (the finished-goods market), to reflect the new scholarly direction of his institute. In the journal's first issue, Vershofen explained the difference between the IfW and other organizations, such as the Institute for Business-Cycle Research (Institut für Konjunkturforschung), which had been established

1800–1950, ed. Geoffrey Cocks and Konrad H. Jarausch (Oxford: Oxford University Press, 1990), 213–31.

[7] It has also been translated as "Institute for Economic Observation of the German Finished Goods Industry." See Alfred C. Mierzejewski, *Ludwig Erhard: A Biography* (Chapel Hill: University of North Carolina Press, 2004), 10–11. On Vershofen's career see Björn Sven Ivens, *Wilhelm Vershofen: Professor der Absatzwirtschaft? Ein Rückblick zu seinem 125. Geburtstag*, Working paper no. 109 (August 2003), Chair for Marketing, Universität Erlangen–Nürnberg.

in Berlin in 1925 as a way of monitoring economic fluctuations and business cycles.[8] While the Berlin group's emphasis was on the German market broadly speaking, with connections to the major federal and regional economic institutions, Vershofen's think tank focused on the narrower sector of finished goods, which were the country's biggest exports. Included in this category were clothes, medicines, cigarettes, and numerous household and luxury items.[9]

Vershofen's interest in finished goods was based on more than its importance for the export economy. This focus also allowed him to pursue his interest in the everyday act of buying, something that attention to the capital goods industry would not allow. The typical store customer cared little about the raw materials that had formed the merchandise. Rather, he or she established a direct connection to the final product, and understanding how this connection took place would be significant from an intellectual and practical standpoint. Vershofen wrote often about this evolving interest not just in commodities but also in the people who bought and used them. His goal was to examine both the sociological conditions and fashion trends that surrounded these goods, and the factories that produced them. The idea, he wrote, was to bring "scholarship and praxis together."[10] All the data he collected would be pointless if it did not get back to the company. But market observation was conducted not only to provide information to firms so that they could sell their products more effectively. For Vershofen, the market was also the "embodiment of social relations," and by studying the things people bought and sold, one gained insight into economic and class realities.[11] In his or her power to elucidate larger trends and attitudes, the consumer, according to Vershofen, was the most important figure in the economy.

But who was this consumer? It was not entirely clear, Vershofen argued, because until the 1920s economists had unduly neglected this individual. "Everyone talks about 'his majesty, the customer,'" agreed the *Frankfurter Zeitung* in 1935, but economists had been oddly unwilling

---

[8] J. Adam Tooze, *Statistics and the German State, 1900–1945: The Making of Modern Economic Knowledge* (Cambridge: Cambridge University Press, 2001), 103–13.

[9] "Geleitwort," *Der Markt der Fertigware* 1 (1929): 1–2, GfKA. On market research during this period, see Claudia Regnery, *Die Deutsche Werbeforschung, 1900 bis 1945* (Münster: Monsenstein und Vannerdat, 2003), 263–70; Bergler, *Entwicklung der Verbrauchsforschung*, 76; and Kurt Kühn, "Die Bedeutung der industriellen Marktforschung," *Markt und Verbrauch* 13, nos. 1 and 2 (1941): 3–4, GfKA.

[10] "Geleitwort," 1–2.

[11] Ibid.

to look closer at him as a factor in production, distribution, and consumption.[12] Vershofen and his colleagues echoed this sentiment, but it was not simply "customers" they were talking about. "Every person is a consumer," wrote Johannes Martin Ditterich, a member of the editorial board of the IfW's chief publication *Die Deutsche Fertigware* (The German finished good).[13] Every person in the modern economy shopped to satisfy basic needs and wants, revealing an axiom that many economists overlooked: "The very purpose of production is consumption."[14]

This may seem an obvious point, but it was not during the Weimar years, when a producerist ethos of quality still reigned. In the 1920s economists began to wrestle more directly with the meaning of mass production and its effects on human beings. Like many of his contemporaries in Weimar Germany, Vershofen developed a fascination with business practices in the United States, particularly with Henry's Ford's attention, according to Mary Nolan, to "every element of production, distribution, financing, and labor policy at the Ford works."[15] Yet Vershofen found troubling consequences in Ford's assembly-line production, including the nervous exhaustion of workers and, more dangerously, the diminishing of product quality.[16] Vershofen and other industrial leaders were skeptical about the ability of American mass production methods to work in the German setting, and these doubts informed his views about consumption.

At the core of Vershofen's concerns were human beings, not only how they responded to the rationalization and speedup of the factory, but also how they functioned as consumers, and more important, as individuals embedded in a social environment. "The object of consumer research," he argued, "is the human being – how he behaves, not the goods he consumes."[17] The Mensch as economic actor was a theme that ran through all of Vershofen's teaching and writing. Human beings, he wrote, "economize in order to secure their existence – in order to let

[12] *Frankfurter Zeitung* (1 September 1935). Quoted from Georg Bergler, *Die Entwicklung der Verbrauchsforschung in Deutschland und die Gesellschaft für Konsumforschung bis zum Jahre 1945* (Kallmünz: Michael Laßleben, 1959), 104.

[13] From *Merkblatt der Gesellschaft für Konsumforschung, e.V.* (1937). Quoted from Bergler, *Entwicklung der Verbrauchsforschung*, 109.

[14] Bergler, *Entwicklung der Verbrauchsforschung*, 10.

[15] Mary Nolan, *Visions of Modernity: American Business and the Modernization of Germany* (Oxford: Oxford University Press, 1994), 31.

[16] Ibid., 70, 88, 91.

[17] "Bericht über die Ordentliche Mitgliederversammlung der GfK," *Vertrauliche Nachrichten für die Mitglieder der GfK*, no. 15 (July 1941): 19, GfKA.

their abilities ... unfold."[18] Vershofen's primary intellectual challenge was determining why human beings acted certain ways in a modern marketplace. And his chief means of meeting this challenge was consumer research.

THE FOUNDING OF THE SOCIETY FOR CONSUMER RESEARCH

By the time the Nazis came to power in 1933, there were a number of research institutes nominally devoted to the functioning of the market. Most of them predated the onset of the Great Depression, but with the devastating economic downturn, they had become involved in measuring the prospects for recovery and future market activity. The Depression prompted Vershofen and other economists to think even more deeply about the effects of the economy on human beings (psychologically and materially) and how one actually gained access to their motivations.[19] In an economy devastated by shortages and low purchasing power, what did people choose to buy? This question preoccupied not only intellectuals and policy makers but also company managers. At the time only a few firms, such as the artificial fabrics producer Vereinigte Glanzstoff and the Sunlicht detergent company, had in-house market research branches, and it became clear to Vershofen that a more formal organization serving the interests of business would be an important addition to the national economic landscape. One company leader who took a particular interest in this sort of organization was Wilhelm Mann, a director of IG Farben and future sales director of Bayer. Both Mann and Vershofen observed marketing and consumer research practices in the United States, where individual companies sent correspondents across the country to determine which products sold and why.[20] In proposing the idea of a German consumer research organization, both men hoped to model their work, in part, on American conventions, but also to improve upon them by centralizing work within one organization and building up a network of paid employees and well-trained correspondents who would conduct more in-depth interviews with consumers in diverse regional settings. It was not enough to look at buying habits through statistics – what Vershofen referred to as budget and purchasing power research. They would have to get closer to

[18] Bergler, *Entwicklung der Verbrauchsforschung*, 186.
[19] Ivens, *Wilhelm Vershofen*, 27.
[20] Vershofen, *Handbuch*, 115.

the consumer, through a body of well-prepared correspondents wielding questionnaires.

In their plans for a consumer research office, Mann and Vershofen turned to three economists who would help launch this undertaking and who came to represent, with Vershofen, the "Nuremberg circle" or "Nuremberg school" of market research. The first was Erich Schäfer, who had codirected the IfW. He had written his dissertation under Eugen Schmalenbach, professor at the University of Cologne and founder of German business management studies.[21] Schäfer was already respected as an expert in market observation and was a professor at the business college in Leipzig. The second was Georg Bergler, who joined the GfK shortly after its founding. Bergler had studied under Vershofen in Nuremberg and received his Ph.D. in 1928 under the direction of Wilhelm Rieger, a pioneer in the area of German business administration. He had recently authored a book on brand names in the chemical and pharmaceutical industries.[22] Finally, there was Ludwig Erhard, the future economics minister and chancellor of West Germany. Erhard had come to the IfW in 1925, having completed his Ph.D. in economics at the University of Frankfurt three years earlier with a dissertation about theories of money, and he soon presided over a series of IfW-sponsored courses on consumer economics and issues of quality production and consumer demand.[23]

Before this organization could move forward, members of the Nuremberg school needed the support of leading businessmen and politicians. In February 1935 Mann, Vershofen, Erhard, and Schäfer met with executives of a number of companies, including Henkel chemicals, Bayer pharmaceuticals (as part of the IG Farben combine), and Rosenthal porcelain, as well as with the directors of the various economic groups (*Wirtschaftsgruppen*) representing textiles, foodstuffs, and paper. They also consulted representatives from the central trademark protection organization, the Markenschutzverband, a body that would take a keen interest in future GfK studies dealing with the public perception of branded goods. Many of these companies and organizations, which approved of

[21] Lindenfeld, "Professionalization of Applied Economics," 222.

[22] Georg Bergler, *Das Schrifttum über den Markenartikel* (Berlin: Deutscher Betriebswirte-Verlag, 1934).

[23] Mierzejewski, *Ludwig Erhard*, 10, 16. For biographies of the IfW founders, see Oliver Hemmerle, *Tausend Jahre Absatz: Anmerkungen zum Marketing als Teil der Betriebswirtschaftslehre im '3. Reich'* (Mannheim: AK-Unigeschichte, 1999), iii–xv; and Wilfried Feldenkirchen and Daniela Fuchs, *Die Stimme des Verbrauchers zum Klingen Bringen: 75 Jahre Geschichte der GfK Gruppe* (Munich: Piper, 2009), 47–55.

FIGURE 16. The GfK directors from 1935; from left to right, Ludwig Erhard, Wilhelm Vershofen, and Georg Bergler. (Courtesy of the GfK Association, Nuremberg.)

Vershofen and Mann's ideas for a market research organization, would play an active role in the GfK. Finished-goods companies had a large financial stake in determining why their goods sold over another company's, and some of the leading firms became paying members of the GfK. Next to Bayer and Henkel, two firms that had long paid attention to sales and advertising, there was the Lingner Works of Dresden, which produced Odol mouthwash, toothpaste, and other oral hygiene products; Dr. Oetker, the foodstuffs manufacturer; AEG electronics; coffee giant Kaffee HAG; peppermint drops manufacturer Dr. Hillers; and a number of middle-sized companies representing the hygiene, consumer products, and precious metals and porcelain industries.[24] Notable too was the presence on the future GfK board of Ernst Reichard, the head of the Nazi Advertising Council. Finally, a key player was Vershofen's friend Hanns Brose, who was an expert on branding and advertising. Throughout the Nazi years other members of the business world, academia, and government would lend their support to the GfK through lectures, articles for the organization's publications, and financial support. Among these was Carl Goerdeler, mayor of Leipzig, honorary Rotarian, and national

---

[24] For these members see "Bericht über die Ordentliche Mitgliederversammlung der GfK," 16–17, GfKA; and Bergler, *Entwicklung der Verbrauchsforschung*, 88, 91.

price commissioner. Goerdeler maintained close contact with Erhard and Bergler, and during his denazification hearing in 1945, Bergler would cite his personal connections to Goerdeler, who had been executed in 1944 for his role in the failed assassination of Hitler.[25]

On 24 June 1935 the GfK was officially launched as a nonprofit organization registered in Berlin, headquartered in Nuremberg, and funded by the Deutsche Länderbank, which was the in-house bank of IG Farben.[26] Farben's Wilhelm Mann, head of the bank, became the president of the GfK, and Georg Bergler the managing director starting in 1936. Erhard and Schäfer were part of the organizational leadership, and there was also an administrative board made up of representatives of some of the leading consumer goods firms in Germany. The GfK also established a press office to educate the public about its aims. Over the following years, the directors established the goals and modus operandi for the association. The GfK made it clear from the start that while it provided quantitative and qualitative data to companies, it would not offer advertising or marketing advice.[27] This meant in practice that the GfK would conduct interviews with consumers, the IfW – as the intellectual arm of the GfK – would prepare a final report based on the data, and then the company that had commissioned the study would incorporate the findings into its broader sales and marketing strategies as it saw fit. This reluctance to give marketing advice was a practical issue (the GfK and IfW were not equipped to do so), but it also reflected a larger point embraced by the Nuremberg school: consumer research should serve private economic interests, but it was also part of a larger national project to understand the mass public.[28]

Determining who actually makes up the "public" is never an easy undertaking, and this was especially the case in the Third Reich, where the Nazi regime addressed people in various guises – as workers, mothers, fathers, consumers, and members of the Volk. For its part, the GfK did not embrace a völkisch understanding of the masses, but rather adopted an approach that acknowledged the diversity of the German consumer

[25] On Goerdeler see Bergler, *Entwicklung der Verbrauchsforschung*, 47 and File "Georg Bergler," F/1 no. 2199, University personnel files, Universitätsarchiv, Friedrich-Alexander-Universität Erlangen-Nürnberg [hereafter Erlangen]. In his hearing, Bergler was eventually declared free of guilt.
[26] Bergler, *Entwicklung der Verbrauchsforschung*, 102.
[27] Ibid., 175; and "Bericht über die Tätigkeit der Gesellschaft für Konsumforschung im Vereinsjahr 1937," *Vertrauliche Nachrichten*, no. 7 (May 1938): 2, GfKA.
[28] Bergler, *Entwicklung der Verbrauchsforschung*, 8.

base, indeed in ways that ran counter to the social and racial homogeneity promoted so vociferously by the Nazis. National Socialist ideologues saw a fundamental need to forge the very disparate regional, class, and occupational identities into a greater sense of Germanness, with individual geographic regions and cultural traditions forming a national whole. While, as we will see, the GfK's directors tried to combine individualism with a larger communal understanding, in practice the organization depended on a less ideological conception of the public. In order to provide the most objective data to a company, the GfK emphasized the vast differences in motivations and capacities behind the purchase of a product. Its studies were to reflect the diversity of dialects, professions, incomes, gender, and lifestyles.

To fulfill this goal of probing an amorphous public, the GfK divided the country into a network of regions, each the responsibility of one correspondent, except larger, urban areas, where there were two or more. Once the GfK contracted to do a study for a company, it prepared an introduction to the project and then put together a so-called report sheet (*Berichtbogen*), which was a series of questions for correspondents to pose and then provide answers to after completing interviews. Unlike a typical questionnaire, which relied on the interviewee's answering specific questions, the correspondent filled out the report, with the freedom to interpret answers from interviewees and to reflect on larger sociocultural issues and challenges that might be of use to the IfW when processing the material.[29] The GfK placed a lot of stock in these reports, which its directors felt opened a window onto consumer mentalities for the first time in Germany. The majority of the correspondents were women, whom the GfK vetted to make sure that they had a good interviewing style and did not come across as "know-it-alls."[30]

This sort of data gathering was not per se new in Germany, nor was consumer research new to the twentieth century. As Georg Bergler pointed out in a postwar history of the GfK, consumer research had existed since the very first entrepreneur sought information about his customer base.[31] Moreover, there were a number of tried and true methods companies and proprietors had used to access consumer opinions, such as in-shop questionnaires, price surveys, and mail-in customer feedback cards. In particular, many of the large German publishing houses relied on this last

[29] Vershofen, *Handbuch*, 121.
[30] Ibid., 120, 123; and Bergler, *Entwicklung der Verbrauchsforschung*, 126–35.
[31] Bergler, *Entwicklung der Verbrauchsforschung*, 6.

method.[32] More recently, the Sunlicht soap corporation had set up its own questionnaire organization, which carried out extensive interviews with housewives in the 1930s.[33] The Nazis engaged in consumer research as well. In 1934 NS-Hago, the Nazi trade and commerce organization, sent out "millions of questionnaires" to housewives to determine where they shopped and what they bought.[34] In the United States, the Gallup organization (the American Institute of Public Opinion), founded in 1935, served as the international model for public opinion research.[35]

Unlike Sunlicht and Gallup, however, the GfK rejected the method of posing "yes or no" questions. This approach, the Nuremberg school felt, did not bring one close enough to the motivations that lay behind choices in the marketplace; it simply provided statistical data of minimal use. The GfK's innovation lay in the fact that it did not engage merely in the gathering of statistics, but in the gathering of people's impressions, based on face-to-face discussions. Correspondents conducted conversations with shoppers, workers, and homemakers about a particular product. They encouraged them to "speak freely" in the hope of revealing "the voice of the consumer" that had lain dormant for so long. By presumably facilitating frank discussions, rather than gathering answers to rote questions, the GfK hoped not only to make consumers more comfortable and more inclined to express their opinions, but also to position them more squarely in the process of market exchange. This "rediscovery of the consumer"[36] had potentially great political implications. If the Nazis wanted primarily to position Germans within a regime of production, celebrating their individual labor as a sacrifice to the Volksgemeinschaft, the GfK hoped to reveal the humanity of shoppers and their dialectical relationship to producers. These "unknown consumers"[37] would thus reclaim their place in society as essential components of a well-functioning whole.

SHOPPING AND COMPLAINING IN THE RACIAL STATE: THE GFK REPORTS, 1936–1939

The Society for Consumer Research embarked on its first investigations at an inauspicious moment. Hitler was reshaping the economy along

---

[32] Ibid., 9.

[33] Ibid., 14.

[34] Ibid., 28–29.

[35] See Sarah E. Igo, *The Averaged American: Surveys, Citizens, and the Making of a Mass Public* (Cambridge, MA: Harvard University Press, 2007), 103–49.

[36] Ibid., 91.

[37] Ibid., 105.

militaristic lines, and with the Four Year Plan for war readiness proclaimed in 1936, the Nazi economy was marked by the regulation of consumer goods and the enactment of price controls. Nonetheless, in January 1936 the GfK issued its first report, commissioned by its president, Wilhelm Mann. It was titled "The Trademarked Image: An Investigation into the Degree of Recognition of the Bayer Cross Logo (with a simultaneous consideration of the advertising effectiveness of the trademarked image more generally)."[38] The Bayer cross, still recognizable today on the company's products, had been a valuable corporate logo since 1904 (for both Bayer and its parent conglomerate, IG Farben), and Farben manager and GfK cofounder Mann hoped to gain insight into how effective it actually was in selling products.

As would become typical with subsequent GfK reports, the eighty-two-page Bayer study began with a synopsis of the investigation's purposes, methods, and results. It issued a caveat that the GfK was still a work in progress, and thus the interviews could not be conducted throughout the entire Reich. Still, some 2,668 opinions were gathered in select areas of southern and southwestern Germany, Hamburg, Berlin, and East Prussia. Consumers expressed their opinions about Bayer products like aspirin and Pyramidon pain killer tablets, and they offered their perceptions of a number of companies with recognizable branded goods: Kupferberg sparkling wine, Zeiss Ikon cameras, Kaiser's coffee, Pfeilring beauty products, Reemstma cigarettes, and J. A. Henckels Zwillingswerke knives. "The consumer has a great urge to offer his own opinion," Vershofen told his colleagues at a membership meeting in 1941, and this first GfK report bore out that observation with quotations from people from all walks of life.[39] "Brand-name products are guaranteed to be better," declared a teacher.[40] "The trademark does not in and of itself indicate a mark of quality," countered the wife of a civil servant, "but only repeated use."[41] A housewife argued that she paid attention to the trademark image to determine whether the product was "of *German* origin" and thus of higher quality.[42] These were just a few of dozens of similar quotes – from widows, bookstore

[38] "Das Warenzeichen: Eine Untersuchung über den Bekanntheitsgrad des Warenzeichen 'Das Bayerkreuz,'" S 1900 001, GfKA. For Mann's own reflections on this report, see Wilhelm Rudolf Mann, "Das Bayer-Kreuz" (1976), 1.13.1, pp. 17–22, BAL.
[39] "Bericht über die Ordentliche Mitgliederversammlung der GfK," 20, GfKA.
[40] "Das Warenzeichen," 61.
[41] Ibid., 62.
[42] Ibid., 51.

owners, insurance representatives, medical students, painters, and engineers. They were interspersed with detailed tables that charted purchasing decisions according to specific demographic criteria, such as age. In a synopsis of its overall findings, the report emphasized a few basic points that might be of use to Bayer and other companies: the name of a manufacturer provided greater incentive to purchase an item than the specific product brand name; 75 percent of all those questioned considered a brand name a sign of quality; and more men than women recognized the Bayer cross.[43]

This first report by the GfK satisfied many of the initial goals of the organization. It combined quantitative and qualitative data, it served the needs of its contractor, and it spoke to larger economic and cultural themes like the increasing use of generic goods and the threats this entailed. Finally, it brought to light the consumer's voice, albeit in short snippets. Indeed, the reports that followed the trademark study expanded the opportunities for consumers to express their opinions. A 1939 study of Opel, the largest automaker in Europe, found that the majority of Germans interviewed made plans to purchase an Opel. The popularity of this car eclipsed that of the not yet manufactured Volkswagen, which came in second place (presumably not in first place because of the long wait to purchase one), as well as of Mercedes, Ford, and Chrysler, among others.[44] Consumers praised Opel's durability, fast performance, and modest use of oil and gasoline.[45]

Consumers' assessments were not always positive, and a striking feature of the GfK reports is how willing consumers were to complain about overexposure to product promotion. In certain respects the nature of this grumbling was in keeping with Nazi priorities, especially when it came to criticizing aggressive advertising.[46] But consumers went farther, often bemoaning the material conditions that were a result of state policies. A January 1939 GfK study found women bitterly unhappy about the seemingly diminished quality of Persil laundry detergent at a time when the fats used to manufacture it were in short supply. "What's wrong with Persil"? women asked, as they cited examples of their favorite detergent creating holes in their linens and leading to a "Persil sickness" that

---

[43] Ibid., v–vi.
[44] "Untersuchung über die Automarke 'Opel,'" June 1939, S 1939 013, p. 2, GfKA.
[45] Ibid., 3.
[46] See Hartmut Berghoff, "'Times Change and We Change with Them': The German Advertising Industry in the Third Reich – Between Professional Self-Interest and Political Repression," *Business History* 45, no. 1 (January 2003): 128–47.

caused a rash on their skin.[47] While manufacturer Henkel insisted that Persil's ingredients had not changed, housewives swore that something was amiss.[48]

Sometimes the issues at stake were bigger than the public reception of a product. A 1939 report commissioned by the major Karlsruhe beauty products manufacturer, P. Wolff & Sohn (whose chief product line was Kaloderma creams and soaps and whose director was a founding GfK member), used the GfK to help avert a potential trademark threat by a rival skin and hair care company that was also called Wolff. The GfK's task was to create scenarios that tested a salesperson's knowledge of the competing products. Correspondents went undercover into two hundred perfumeries, drugstores, and beauty salons in Germany and twenty additional shops in newly annexed Austria to look at how hair lotions, skin balms, and shaving creams were sold in face-to face transactions. What made this investigation particularly interesting was that the correspondents themselves were not told the purpose of their assignment. They simply had to enter a store and say, "I would like a bottle of hair lotion (or a tube of skin or shaving cream) from Wolff!"[49] They played only a "passive" role and then reported what had happened at the store counter.

In the final report, the correspondents described in detail their experiences: walking into the store, glancing at the product selection, requesting a tube of shaving cream, and then having the proprietor ask the key question, "Do you mean Wolff in Karlsruhe?" The correspondent would answer in the affirmative, and the goods would be packed up. No doubt to the relief of the report's sponsor, most proprietors knew considerably more about Wolff & Sohn products than about any competing merchandise with the same name.

The Wolff report indicates that the GfK, despite perceiving its work as contributing to the human and social sciences, could nonetheless be important for partisan business purposes. A core goal of the GfK was to provide "value-neutral" information to private companies, and in 1934 the organization probably could not have predicted that it would be drawn into the contentious world of competing trademark claims.

---

[47] "Hausfrau und Waschmittel," January 1939, S 1939 007, p. 74, GfKA.

[48] On women's broader reactions to the Four Year Plan austerity measures, see Nancy R. Reagin, *Sweeping the German Nation: Domesticity and National Identity in Germany, 1870–1945* (Cambridge: Cambridge University Press, 2007), 110–80.

[49] "Untersuchung über den Markennamen 'Wolff,'" June 1939, S 1939 012, p. 5., GfKA.

But there was no complaining on the part of Vershofen and his team. The Nuremberg school was not content to remain a small think tank straddling the business world and the world of letters and sciences. Rather, its members hoped to gain an ever greater influence in the intellectual and business life of Germany. The success of this endeavor is attested to by both the growth of the organization and the attention it garnered. By 1937, a year after its first report, the GfK employed four hundred correspondents covering five hundred "consumption districts" (*Konsumbezirke*), and on the eve of World War II, it had about seven hundred correspondents. One hundred research and staff members, drawn from pools of educated applicants, helped process the data it gathered.[50]

What did the public think of this new experiment in consumer research? As the organization issued more and more reports, it inevitably encountered criticism of its methods. The most basic complaint came from consumers who resented correspondents' attempts to interview them. Some saw the questioning as an "unjustified meddling into their most personal matters" or, in the case of doctors interviewed for a Bayer study, as a waste of their time.[51] Others considered such interviews nothing more than a "good advertising gimmick" for a specific product or company.[52] Such mistrust was often compounded by correspondents' difficulties in getting consumers to reveal themselves – to "unlock their 'secrets.'"[53] Moreover, the question remained as to how one could conduct such interviews in a setting that put severe limits on candid expression. This was a challenge that the GfK faced from the outset, when it embarked on its first investigations. The Gestapo became suspicious of correspondents wandering around asking people questions. Occasionally they would even be arrested.[54] Likewise, the government regularly challenged the work of the GfK, inquiring whether the Nuremberg school members were qualified to be leaders according to National Socialist principles.[55] The GfK

[50] "Bericht über die Tätigkeit der Gesellschaft für Konsumforschung im Vereinsjahr 1937," 1.
[51] "Die Zigarette im Urteil des Letzten Verbrauchers," August 1939, S 1939 006–1, p. 5, GfKA. The Bayer study is "Die 'Bayer'"-Vertrauenswerbung im Urteil der Ärzte," August 1939, S1939 010–1, GfKA.
[52] "Die Zigarette im Urteil des Letzten Verbrauchers," 6.
[53] Ibid.
[54] Bergler, *Entwicklung der Verbrauchsforschung*, 126.
[55] Erhard to Vershofen, 8 November 1937, GfKA, in Institut für Wirtschaftsbeobachtung der deutschen Fertigware papers, GfKA; courtesy of Volker Preuss. I thank Mr. Preuss for his assistance.

also encountered hostility from representatives of the DAF, which argued that the Nuremberg group represented only business interests and thus ignored the purchasing power of the broader population.[56]

Next to these reactions were the critical voices of advertising and business professionals. Upon hearing of the organization's establishment, some asserted that the GfK was naively taking on an impossible task: with so many differences among people – in incomes, expenses, and behaviors – it would be impossible to do more than generalize about shopping habits and motivations. A writer from the *Deutsche Zeitung* pointed out that people often made irrational purchasing decisions, for example, buying cars that they could not afford. Thus it would be impossible to draw any larger conclusions.[57] Other critics found some of the findings of the GfK too obvious: one already knew that women bought more panty hose in big cities than in the countryside![58] Still others argued that the GfK was working on a weak scientific basis.

The GfK responded to these criticisms and challenges by taking some of the more academic evaluations to heart, agreeing that consumers had different guises and that it was difficult to gauge motivation, but insisting that it could indeed study consumers in all of their complexities – as simultaneously irrational and rational beings. Vershofen, however, rejected politicized accusations that the GfK was alternatively a socialist enterprise and in the pockets of capitalists.[59] In reality, wrote Vershofen, we are engaged in *Gemeinwirtschaftspolitik*, whereby "private economic interests must be placed second to communal economic interests."[60] In making this statement, Vershofen was not simply making a concession to the regime's collectivist understanding of market relations. He truly believed that the GfK's work served the broader good. Despite this insistence, however, the question of whether the GfK could simultaneously attend to private enterprise and the public good continued to dog the organization. Two issues of fundamental importance to Nazi ideology exemplified this issue: health and gender.

---

[56] Ibid.
[57] "Organisierte Vebrauchsforschung," *Deutsche Allgemeine Zeitung* (3 September 1935). Quoted from Bergler, *Entwicklung der Verbrauchsforschung*, 103.
[58] Konrad Ebert, "Aufgaben und Verfahren der Marktanalyse," *Vierteljahresheften zur Wirtschaftsforschung* (April 1939). Quoted in Bergler, *Entwicklung der Verbrauchsforschung*, 113.
[59] Vershofen to Professor Sven Helander, 6 March 1937, GfKA; courtesy of Volker Preuss.
[60] Ibid.

SMOKING, FASHION, AND GENDER

Practically speaking, what did it mean to combine communal and private interests in the the Third Reich? In post–World War II recollections of businessmen, a common complaint was that the state's demands for cooperation and ideological assimilation had run counter to the commercial interests of their firms.[61] Recent research, however, has revealed how compatible private enterprise and Nazi aims could be.[62] Much depended on the company and the sector it represented. Certainly, arms manufacturers found a ready place in the Third Reich, as did the makers of ideologically privileged consumer goods like "people's radios."[63] But what about the thornier case of a company that sold products that were anathema to the regime's ideological aims? What were the fates of companies that made products deemed damaging to the racial body? This was a key question with which cigarette manufacturers and, in turn, the GfK grappled. On the one hand, policy makers demanded the creation of a healthy populace. On the other hand, the state and private companies had a stake in fulfilling consumers' desires for relaxation and small pleasures, among which smoking featured prominently.

Indicative of this tension was one of the most interesting studies to emerge from the GfK, one that reveals the tensions accompanying the quest to merge public and private aims. The nearly two-hundred-page report, titled "The Cigarette in the Judgment of Consumers," opens a window onto smoking behavior and the limits of ideological control in the Third Reich.[64] The report, issued a few weeks before the outbreak of World War II, came out at a time, according to historian Robert Proctor, when Germany was the only country to have had "a broad medical recognition of both the addictive nature of tobacco and the lung cancer hazard of smoking."[65] In their quest to engineer a hygienically pristine race,

---

[61] See S. Jonathan Wiesen, *West German Industry and the Challenge of the Nazi Past, 1945–1955* (Chapel Hill: University of North Carolina Press, 2001), 226–28.

[62] See, e.g., Jonas Scherner, *Die Logik der Industriepolitik im Dritten Reich: Die Investitionen in die Autarkie- und Rüstungsindustrie und ihre staatliche Förderung* (Stuttgart: Steiner, 2008).

[63] Wolfgang König, *Volkswagen, Volksempfänger, Volksgemeinschaft: "Volksprodukte" im Dritten Reich: Vom Scheitern einer nationalsozialistischen Konsumgesellschaft* (Paderborn: Schöningh, 2004).

[64] "Die Zigarette im Urteil des Letzten Verbrauchers."

[65] Robert N. Proctor, *The Nazi War on Cancer* (Princeton, NJ: Princeton University Press, 1999), 173.

the Nazis waged a frontal assault on smoking by, among other things, prohibiting it in waiting rooms and Nazi Party offices and launching anti-smoking educational campaigns that emphasized the dangers of tobacco to the male libido and to völkisch health in general.[66]

Reading the GfK report on smoking, one would never guess that it was written in such a restrictive environment. Ten thousand smokers across Germany (almost 90 percent of them men) were asked which brands they smoked, what these brands connoted, and which were more satisfying. The goal was to determine the popularity of a number of brands, notably Astra, which sponsored the study. The answers were broken down by gender, age, income, and region, among other categories.[67] The report began by pointing out that, like that for bread, demand for cigarettes was inelastic, neither rising nor falling with the fortunes of the consumer sector more generally. Yet the political context did have an effect on sales. "During so-called nervous times or times of political high tension," the market value of cigarettes peaked. Thus, argued the report, this link between politics and sales could be of interest to the general public, not just the smoker.[68] The political context, however, was important not only as an indicator of sales figures. It also had a sociopsychological component. Wrote one correspondent:

The cigarette is a symptom of our present age: concentrated enjoyment on account of a dearth of time. It is certainly not philosophical to assert that the wide-reaching transformations that have taken place since the war in our public and private lives, in our professional and in our intimate spheres of life, have brought with them a change in the feelings of and demands for enjoyment that the cigarette has and will continue to evoke.[69]

These comments, issued less than a month before the outbreak of World War II, can be read as a commentary on the political events that were taking place in Germany. While the correspondent was using familiar language about the speedup of modern life, he or she was also reflecting more directly on the psychological effects of contemporary politics. If the cigarette represented a quick retreat from the pressures of work and family life, it also was a respite from the anxiety-producing uncertainties that had accompanied public life since 1918: military defeat, inflation, the Depression, the Nazi political reordering, and the new fears of

[66] Ibid., 174–75, 189.
[67] "Die Zigarette im Urteil des Letzten Verbrauchers," 2.
[68] Ibid., 4.
[69] Ibid., 12.

war brought about by the Munich crisis and the Nazis' overrunning of Czechoslovakia. Almost 30 percent of respondents said that they had begun smoking more "in recent years," while only 12 percent had cut down on their smoking.[70] Indeed, between 1930 and 1937 per capita consumption of cigarettes went up by 21 percent.[71] In contrast, the cigar became a symbol for an earlier, seemingly more placid era in German history, when Old World leisure had not been interrupted by the traumas of war and economic instability.

What did the report conclude? Much of the information concerned statistics on regional and professional variations. Westphalia (presumably as the most industrialized part of the country) turned out to have had the most smokers (7.1 for every nonsmoker), and the Saar had the fewest (only 2 smokers for every nonsmoker).[72] Bavaria had the lowest ratio of cigarette to cigar smokers (only 1.9 cigarette smokers for every cigar smoker, compared with 9 cigarette smokers for every cigar smoker in Saxony), perhaps indicating that in more rural areas like Bavaria, people had the leisure to smoke cigars, whereas in highly industrialized cities, factory workers and urbanites turned to cigarettes.[73] A correspondent in rural Franconia confirmed this view that farmers, particularly women, as a rule spurned cigarettes. They were expensive and were considered to be the "nail in one's coffin."[74] Cigars were not seen as problematic in this regard, considered by most interviewees to be healthier than cigarettes and generally reserved for the upper classes and the bourgeoisie. It is not surprising that young people, still looking for the quick fix, preferred cigarettes. According to one correspondent, one had to be forty years old to realize that there was no more to expect from life. At that point, one sought "the intensification of the remaining enjoyments," such as cigars.[75]

As for the report's sponsor, Astra was preferred by professionals – doctors, dentists, salespeople, civil servants – whereas workers wanted a stronger cigarette. According to the GfK, "handworkers" had different needs than "brainworkers."[76] While some were attracted to Astra as a

---

[70] Ibid., 17.

[71] Jonathan Lewy, "A Sober Reich? Alcohol and Tobacco Use in Nazi Germany," *Substance Use & Misuse* 41, no. 8 (2006) 1179–95.

[72] "Die Zigarette im Urteil des Letzten Verbrauchers," 8.

[73] Ibid., 9.

[74] Ibid., 11.

[75] Ibid., 15.

[76] Ibid., 68.

cigarette of the upwardly mobile, others avoided it because of its trendiness and complained that the name sounded "un-German" or "oriental" and that it was for "beginners and women."[77] They preferred stronger cigarettes like Zuban, Bergmann, Salem, R6, and Maryland, the last a particularly strong cigarette.[78] As a lighter, "more fashionable" product with low nicotine, Astra was a chic "lady's cigarette."[79] The brand name reminded one Swabian salesman of a "lovely and vivacious woman."[80] Whatever the connotations, it was clear to the report's authors that a new age of anxious mass enjoyment had dawned. The era of the cigar had passed: "The cigar is a means of enjoyment for the satisfied, for the pensive, for the *vita contemplativa*; the cigarette is a symbol of haste, of urgency, of the money–time relationship – in short, of the nervousness of our time."[81]

The GfK cigarette study sheds light on the contradictions between Nazi ideological prescriptions and reality "on the ground." It was one thing to wage a campaign against smoking. It was quite another to ban it altogether, at the risk of creating an edgy, unsatisfied, and unproductive populace. In any modern state, what health professionals or government agencies advocate (for either scientific or ideological reasons) does not necessarily have immediate or long-range effects on the population. In fact, while Hitler and like-minded physicians spoke vociferously about the dangers of tobacco, there was no intention of banning smoking completely.[82] Thus, even with antismoking mandates in place, the Nazi regime could never claim to regulate every aspect of an individual's private behavior. Nor did it want to. The GfK report did not refer to the antismoking laws, but it nonetheless drew attention to the reality that smoking played an important social, cultural, psychological, and economic role in a society marked by political uncertainty. While there is no evidence that the Nazis took this specific report to heart, they undoubtedly understood that the morale of the population was dependent on simple pleasures like smoking. There were also business priorities that helped maintain smoking trends, with German tobacco farmers relying on the cigarette industry for profits, as well as on imports and exports of tobacco.[83] Only during the war, with

---

[77] Ibid., 83.
[78] See Vorbemerkungen in ibid. and graph in ibid., 177.
[79] Ibid., 82, 83.
[80] Ibid., 82.
[81] Ibid., 12.
[82] Lewy, "A Sober Reich?" 1187.
[83] Proctor, *The Nazi War on Cancer*, 242.

the rationing of cigarettes and limits on acreage devoted to tobacco, did consumption decline, starting in 1942.[84]

The smoking report also called into question the power of the regime to expunge class analysis from sociological research. Whether or not the regime approved, the GfK was committed to coming as "close to reality" as possible.[85] It therefore gathered statistics on household incomes, with special attention to whether a family lived in a rural or urban setting and to how tax burdens affected this.[86] Class was therefore indispensable to Nazi era consumer research. The term "class" itself never appeared in GfK reports (the less value-laden term *Schicht*, or "stratum," was preferred), but the organization nonetheless revealed through its statistics the social variation in smoking, with workers smoking in greater numbers and opting for stronger tobacco, and wealthier elites having the time for the luxury of a pipe or indulging in the status of a lighter cigarette. We are reminded that despite the regime's claims to be crafting a homogeneous racial community, the population remained differentiated in consumption habits and attitudes, and the regime widely accepted this fact in practice.

Finally, the cigarette study brought into stark relief a preoccupation with gender that had been a hallmark of advertising and company public relations since the prior century and that would remain so throughout the Third Reich. More than simply uncovering an incidental relationship between a specific brand and female smokers, the GfK gave prominence to gender in its investigations. This was not due merely to the fact that some brands were coded as female or that women made the majority of household purchasing decisions. Rather, the GfK hoped to understand modern consumers – their desires and modes of thinking – specifically as men and women. How did the two sexes behave differently in the marketplace? How did each react to the other's purchasing habits? Several GfK reports and discussions examined these questions.[87] In a study about beauty products, the GfK found that while women liked to apply especially fragrant creams and body sprays, men complained about being constantly immersed in an atmosphere of scents, the majority of which smelled "too cheap." Men should not have to be exposed

---

[84] Ibid.

[85] Bergler, *Entwicklung der Verbrauchsforschung*, 97.

[86] Vershofen, *Handbuch*, 92–109.

[87] On gender and the GfK see Christoph Conrad, "Observer les consommateurs: Études de marché et histoire de la consommation en Allemagne, des années 1930 aux années 1960." *Mouvement Social* no. 206 (January–March 2004): 17–39.

to overpowering perfumes, the correspondent concluded, and "the small secrets of women should remain just that – secrets."[88]

Other reports approached gender differences in a less whimsical manner – for instance, a 1937 study on the "differences in the consumer behaviors of both sexes."[89] One might assume that in the context of a gender-conservative society, the GfK would simply reproduce common stereotypes about women as shoppers – compulsive, overwhelmed by the bounty of products, and intellectually vulnerable in the face of aggressive sales pitches. But the report forthrightly challenged such assumptions. One might be tempted to assume, it argued, that women were "instinctive" while men were "rational" in their purchasing habits. "Quite the contrary!" declared the study. "Women think and behave more rationally … than men."[90] Men went to one store and, if they were unable to find what they were looking for right away, settled for something potentially inferior, just to be free of the torments of shopping. On the other hand, the GfK argued, women had no problem going from store to store to find a product that satisfied their desires and that represented a better value for the cost, even if in the end they had to pay more money. These habits rested, according to the GfK report, on deeper differences between how men and women conceived of a product's uses. Because women did most of the household shopping, determining the origins of certain preconceptions about a product's uses "in the feminine psyche" represented "one of the most important objects of consumer research."[91]

To get at this deeper sense of difference, the GfK looked at the gendered use of toiletries. In this area, it could not entirely distance itself from standard tropes about women. While for men, the utility of personal hygiene products was key (how well did a shaving cream, soap, or deodorant work?), for women, beauty products and cosmetics served "erotic" and "social" purposes – presumably to entice men and to make themselves seem attractive to their peers. It may have been tempting to cast the female relationship to cosmetics as irrational, but the GfK was quick to indicate that women's inclinations in these matters were, in fact,

[88] "Die verschiedene Gerüche von Schönheitsmitteln," *Vertrauliche Nachrichten*, no. 6 (February 1938), 21, GfKA. On marketing and the beauty products industry during this period, see Uta Poiger, "Beauty, Business, and International Relations," *WerkstattGeschichte* 16, no. 45 (2007): 53–71.

[89] "Verschiedenheiten in der Verbraucherhaltung der beiden Geschlechter," *Vertrauliche Nachrichten*, no. 4 (September 1937): 1–6, GfKA.

[90] Ibid., 1.

[91] Ibid., 2.

FIGURE 17. "Why do women like to shop?" the GfK asked. Buying flowers on Alexanderplatz, Berlin, 1936. (172 423; courtesy of Landesarchiv Berlin.)

the *rational* results of careful calculations about what could best serve "a deeply felt purpose." Women were at their core emotional, with deep-seated needs satisfied by consumption, whereas men thought primarily about utility and cost. Yet in a familiar twist, the GfK cast men, in this regard, as irrational and women as rational because men did not engage in a calculus of wants and needs so much as respond on a gut level to cost and convenience.[92]

Here we can see a tension that ran throughout the work of the GfK. On the one hand, the GfK economists rejected the idea that shoppers

[92] Ibid., 2–6

acted only on a conscious level when making purchasing decisions. Consumption, they found, was often an irrational act, albeit more so for men than women. "As much as he is supposed to think rationally in economic matters," wrote Vershofen, "the consumer in reality remains a human being, and therefore, like all things human, extremely interesting."[93] On the other hand, the GfK had access only to what people said in conversations, which by the Nuremberg school's own acknowledgment was more important than access to deeper motivations. The GfK thus faced two problems: How could it speak about the irrational without drawing on the intellectual apparatus, namely depth and behavioral psychology, used to understand it? And if it were trying to understand consumers' motivations, how would the impressionistic gathering of quotes achieve this end?

THE CONSUMER, THE HUMAN BEING, AND PSYCHOLOGICAL MOTIVATION

The GfK's interest in rational and irrational behavior was part of its larger dedication to understanding the human being. Over the course of the 1930s and 1940s, the Nuremberg school grappled with the meaning of consumer desires and the modes of accessing them. It studied publications from Europe and the United States, drew upon German sociology and psychology, and tried to find the balance between offering an intellectually rich inquiry into human motivation, providing useful data to companies, and avoiding controversial academic territory. This was not an easy task, for in the 1930s immersing oneself in consumer (or applied) psychology meant studying Freudian psychology and American behaviorism, two "foreign" intellectual forces. Inevitably, an interest in the irrational led GfK publications to occasionally employ concepts like the "unconscious" or "subconscious."[94] Yet the Nuremberg economists were careful not to invoke specifically the "Jewish science" of Freud. Nor did they enter into extended dialogue with the ideologically acceptable Jung. Indeed, despite their interest in the irrational, the Nuremberg economists ultimately shied away from a comprehensive look into the unconscious. While their interests overlapped with depth psychologists', the

[93] Vershofen to Mann, 22 May 1940, NL Vershofen, MS 2763, box 9, Mann file, Erlangen.
[94] H. F. J. Kropff, "Versuch einer Klärung der Problematik der deutschen Verbrauchsforschung," *Markt und Verbrauch* 14, nos. 1 and 2 (1942): 25–42, GfKA.

Nuremberg economists asserted their primary desire to locate the social rather than the emotional roots of the purchasing act.

This does not mean that the Nuremberg school invoked behavioral psychology either, which had come to the fore in the United States in the 1920s and 1930s. Behaviorism was predicated on the scientific predictability of human actions, as first promoted by J. B. Watson in the 1910s and 1920s.[95] It directly contrasted itself to Freud by focusing on, in the words of psychiatrist Adolf Meyer, "life itself … not the imagined cesspool of the unconscious."[96] Watson hoped to predict human activity and formulate laws of behavior that would ultimately enable experts to engineer a better society. Behaviorism was therefore anathema to the basic goal of the Nuremberg school, which was to understand underlying motivations, but to embed them in ever-contingent (and thus scientifically unpredictable) economic and social relations.[97] How this rejection of predictability, in particular, jibed with the GfK's fundamental purpose of providing useful information to companies was never quite explained. In practice, the GfK funneled data to companies, which hoped to devise marketing strategies based on some level of scientific rigor. But members of the Nuremberg school saw themselves as sociologists rather than scientists, and thus it is unclear how the companies for which the GfK did research could rely on such impressionistic information.

The GfK never resolved these tensions, but the intellectual impetus behind them becomes clearer when one traces the theories that the GfK and the Nuremberg school did explicitly draw upon. In lieu of Freud, Jung, and behaviorism, the Nuremberg school turned to the concept of *Verstehen*, or "understanding," made famous by Max Weber, Wilhelm Dilthey, Werner Sombart, and Friedrich Schleiermacher.[98] According to sociologist Frank Elwell, "Weber used the term [*Verstehen*] to refer to the social scientist's attempt to understand both the intention and the context of human action, whereby the sociologist becomes empathetic with the individual, developing an understanding of the meaning that individuals

[95] John B. Watson, *Psychology from the Standpoint of a Behaviorist* (Philadelphia: Lippincott, 1919).

[96] Quoted in Eli Zaretsky, *Secrets of the Soul: A Social and Cultural History of Psychoanalysis* (New York: Knopf, 2004), 83.

[97] Vershofen, *Handbuch*, 66.

[98] See Hans Proesler, "Problematik des Verstehens," *Markt und Verbrauch* 11, no. 4 (April 1939): 157–66, GfKA; and Proesler, "Über das Verstehen in der Verbrauchsforschung," *Markt und Verbrauch* 13, nos. 11 and 12 (1941): 279–84, GfKA. For an overview of this concept, see Michael Martin, *Verstehen: The Uses of Understanding in the Social Sciences* (New Brunswick, NJ: Transaction Publishers, 2000).

attach to various courses of action."[99] This search for the inner motivations conditioned by social reality was part of the Nuremberg school's, and especially Vershofen's, commitment to understanding the Mensch. What did people think about their lives? How were thoughts and behaviors mediated by the world of products? How were feelings and actions conditioned by communities, whether familial, occupational, or national? What were human beings' "spiritual needs?"[100] Rejecting a homo economicus model, the Nuremberg school disputed the "materialist" notion that "I am what I can achieve."[101] Even in the midst of a Nazi Leistungsgemeinschaft, there was more to existence than performance. To the GfK, consumer research held the promise of understanding the humanistic underpinnings of the market.

Here we begin to see the contours of the GfK's psychology and its resonance in a society that rejected bourgeois and Marxist understandings of the economy: the Nuremberg circle drew on a rich German sociological tradition and made it relevant in a setting where "American" and "Jewish" materialism was discarded.[102] Its interest in the nonmaterial contours of the economy echoed the Nazis' attempt to access the spiritual dimensions of commerce and labor. But such queries were not specific to consumer psychology, to the GfK, or to Nazi Germany. The GfK's engagement with the human psyche must be understood within the context of broader attempts among industrialists, labor leaders, government officials, and psychologists after World War I to create a "human economy" (*Menschökonomie*) that would increase industrial production and national might by matching a person with a job that drew on his or her innate skills.[103] This entailed the establishment of a central labor administration and the provision of vocational training, counseling, and psychology to workers. This practice of "psychotechnics" was most notably manifested in the work of the German Institute for Technical Labor Training, which, according to Mary Nolan, "strove to create a

[99] Frank W. Elwell, "Verstehen: Max Weber's Home Page," http://www.faculty.rsu/edu/ ~felwell/Theorists/Weber/Whome.htm#Printable (accessed 3 October 2006).
[100] Proesler, "Problematik des Verstehens," 157.
[101] Bergler, *Entwicklung der Verbrauchsforschung*, 91.
[102] On German sociology in the Third Reich see Carsten Klingemann, "Social-Scientific Experts – No Ideologues: Sociology and Social Research in the Third Reich," in *Sociology Responds to Fascism*, ed. Stephen P. Turner and Dirk Käsler (London: Routledge, 1992), 127–54.
[103] David Meskill, "Human Economies: Labor Administration, Vocational Training and Psychological Testing in Germany, 1914–1964" (Ph.D. Diss., Harvard University, 2003).

new, conservative worker and factory community (*Betriebsgemeinschaft*) through factory education programs and company social policy."[104] The recognition of workers as human beings was aimed, in part, at keeping employees conscientious and distracting them from thoughts of class struggle. But it also reflected a major shift in applied and theoretical psychology toward the study of personality traits and character.

Meeting the psychological needs of human beings meant looking at them as both producers and consumers. The earliest studies of consumers, both in Europe and in North America, had been premised on the idea that researchers could understand why people acted in certain ways and bought certain products. In the 1920s motivational and humanistic psychology was gaining influence on both continents, its breakthrough coming with the publication of Abraham Maslow's article "A Theory of Human Motivation" in 1943. After World War II Maslow perfected his so-called hierarchy of human needs, with primitive physiological demands being the most fundamental and safety, love, esteem, and self-actualization proceeding upward on the pyramid of needs.[105] Even before the devising of this schema, consumer researchers understood that many of these needs could be satisfied through the purchasing of goods.

The GfK was therefore part of a larger twentieth-century inquiry into motivations of and influences on modern humans, and the relationship of material goods to consumer needs. But while the organization drew its inspiration from broad intellectual trends, it did not hesitate to cultivate ties with organizations devoted to a revamped "German" psychology. For example, the Nuremberg school established contacts with the German Institute for Psychological Research and Psychotherapy through the efforts of Hans H. Meyer-Mark, an advertising consultant in Berlin and one of the key figures in the founding of the latter organization.[106] Otherwise known as the Göring Institute, it was headed by Matthias Heinrich Göring, a neuropathologist and psychotherapist who was the cousin of Reich Marshal Hermann Göring.[107] Along with its regular explorations into Jungian psychology and its training of

[104] Nolan, *Visions of Modernity*, 21, 187–205.
[105] A. H. Maslow, "A Theory of Human Motivation," *Psychological Review* 50, no. 4 (July 1943): 370–96; and Maslow, *Motivation and Personality* (New York: Harper, 1954).
[106] On Meyer-Mark and the Göring Institute's links to the GfK, see Geoffrey Cocks, *Psychotherapy in the Third Reich: The Göring Insitute* [2d ed.] (New Brunswick, NJ: Transaction Publishers, 1997), 146. Also Bergler, *Entwicklung der Verbrauchsforschung*, 68.
[107] Cocks, *Psychotherapy in the Third Reich*, 6, 110–14.

psychotherapists, the institute was active in trying to create a racially pure, psychologically healthy group of workers and soldiers. Göring invited Vershofen on a number of occasions to lecture about consumer psychology at the institute.[108] The Nuremberg school and the Göring Institute also maintained personnel ties. Felix Scherke, who helped found the Göring Institute in 1935–36 and would become comptroller of the renamed Reich Institute in 1944, had been previously associated with the Nuremberg school.[109] The author of a number of books on industrial management and psychology, Scherke became a professor at Nuremberg University after World War II. The institute's politically active and highly respected medical doctor and psychotherapist, I. H. Schultz,[110] worked closely with the GfK on Bayer's "goodwill advertising" study, offering a "medical-psychological" assessment of how doctors and laypeople perceived Bayer products.[111] Finally, throughout World War II the two institutes would be in regular contact about the methodology of "motivational research" (*Motivforschung*).[112]

Despite these overtures to the Göring Institute, the Nuremberg school situated itself more squarely among marketing and consumer experts than among clinical and theoretical psychologists, often conducting spirited debates about the nature of individual and group psychology within more specialized marketing journals, including the GfK's own publications. Such discussions went to the heart of the organization's project and indeed the entire enterprise of consumer research. Debates emerged in the 1930s over the GfK's hostility to scientific verifiability and repeatability. Whereas, as we have seen, Vershofen and his cohort saw their work as essentially non-experimental – and as such part of the human or social sciences – some consumer researchers outside the Nuremberg school saw their work as a more rigorous undertaking, with results that could become "rules," as in the natural sciences, and then applied consistently to marketing.

Much of this debate hinged on the issue of how successfully one could access and then generalize about inner motivations. One of the GfK's most spirited interlocutors was Hanns F. J. Kropff, a consumer

---

[108] Bergler, *Entwicklung der Verbrauchsforschung*, 68.
[109] Cocks, *Psychotherapy in the Third Reich*, 252.
[110] Ibid., 165.
[111] "Die 'Bayer'-Vertrauenswerbung im Urteil der Ärzte," and "Die 'Bayer'-Vertauenswerbung im Urteil des Laien," August 1939, S 1939 010–2, GfKA. See also Bergler, *Entwicklung der Verbrauchsforschung*, 68.
[112] Bergler, *Entwicklung der Verbrauchsforschung*, 178.

psychologist who, along with Ernest Dichter, represented the "Vienna school" of motivational research. Considered by some to be a father of modern advertising, Kropff was a marketing consultant very much influenced, like his colleague Dichter, by Freud.[113] He also learned much from another Viennese colleague, Paul Lazarsfeld, one of the leaders of empirical social science, who was more interested in the statistical analysis of behaviors – accessed through market surveys and focus groups – than in the unconscious.[114] In keeping with the mood of the 1930s, Kropff became impressed by the propagandistic possibilities of advertising. By the end of the decade, both Dichter and Lazarsfeld had emigrated to the United States, while Kropff stayed in Europe and became a member of the Nazi Party and a Hitler devotee.[115] During this period he professed the human "desire to follow a leader."[116] He maintained a healthy interest in the unconscious, but he also accepted the premises of behaviorism. In short, the human being, Kropff asserted, was a unity of body and soul.[117]

Kropff's interest in behaviorism led him to appreciate the work of his colleagues across the Atlantic. His 1941 book, *Die psychologische Seite der Verbrauchsforschung* (The psychological side of consumer research), merged his ideals about the Mensch with American psychological empiricism. This reverence for American practices rankled members of the Nuremberg school. In a scathing review of the book, Hans Proesler, who had written a companion volume to Vershofen's 1940 *Handbuch der Verbrauchsforschung*, offered harsh words about Kropff's approach.[118] While the United States, Proesler conceded, had indeed been pathbreaking in consumer psychology, one had to acknowledge that Germans had different traditions and habits and a different "spiritual constitution." As an avowed Nazi, Kropff would presumably have agreed with this idea of national uniqueness, but he was loath to use a belief in German superiority as an excuse to reject American methods. As befit both the Vienna circle and American behaviorism, Kropff argued in his book that

[113] Bernd Semrad, "Die 'Wiener Schule' der Werbung?" *Wiener Journal: Das Magazin der Wiener Zeitung* 20 (18 September 2004): 12–14.
[114] On Lazarsfeld see Daniel Horowitz, *Anxieties of Affluence: Critiques of American Consumer Culture, 1939–1979* (Amherst: University of Massachusetts Press, 2004), 52–54.
[115] Hemmerle, *Tausend Jahre Absatz*, viii.
[116] Bernd Semrad, "Die 'Wiener Schule' der Werbung," 14.
[117] Kropff, "Versuch einer Klärung der Problematik der deutschen Verbrauchsforschung," 28.
[118] Hans Proesler, *Handbuch der Vebrauchsforschung* [companion to Vershofen's first volume] (Berlin: Carl Heymanns, 1940), 117–21.

one could discover laws governing the motives of consumers vis-à-vis the objects around them. Proesler, in contrast, believed that one could, at best, develop "typical" characteristics or, drawing from Weber, "ideal types." While conceding that applied psychology did belong in consumer research, Proesler argued that consumer research could never be a natural science, but rather a human science or *Geisteswissenschaft*. For Proesler the material and technical characteristics of a product were of minor importance, and the same went for the intentions and expectations of the producer, advertiser, or seller. Rather, to the extent that products brought personal or social enjoyment, the GfK was interested only in the judgments of the consumer. The focus had to be on the human being buying the product: what need would it serve and what desire would it satisfy?[119]

These distinctions between both writers' positions seem rather esoteric, but they ultimately revolved around the role of external influences on the consumer. Whereas Kropff saw "outside influences" on the shopper as essentially coming from marketing and advertising, Proesler and the Nuremberg school emphasized income, family and career influences, and social prestige. In short, for the Vienna circle, deep emotional desires existed a priori, but political and market forces outside the individual exercised a powerful secondary effect. For the Nuremberg school, on the other hand, the individual was ipso facto inextricable from the group, and his or her desires as individuals could not be measured or quantified. People, argued Proesler, are always and necessarily "part of a living whole," and thus any consumer research must recognize one's situation within a group.[120]

One must avoid making too much of these differences between the Vienna and the Nuremberg schools. Both accepted the idea that consumers, by virtue of their position in a mass society, were amenable to outside influences that could tap into irrational wants and needs. And while the Vienna consumer researchers used the term "unconscious" more than the Nurembergers, they both took an interest in it. The broader point is that consumer research in the Third Reich cannot be reduced to easy labels – like Freudian, Jungian, or behaviorist. Rather, it was a hodgepodge of ideas and traditions, some of which resonated with, and some

[119] For these quotes see Proesler, "Ansatzpunkte für die psychologische Betrachtungsweise in der Verbrauchsforschung [review of Kropff, *Die psychologische Seite der Verbrauchsforschung* (Leipzig: Meiner, 1941)], *Markt und Verbrauch* 13, nos. 1 and 2 (1941): 226–34, GfKA
[120] Proesler, *Handbuch*, 117–21.

of which diverged from, official Nazi views on human psychology. This reveals the extent to which intellectuals' explorations into the human psyche and behaviors could draw rather freely on ideas that predated National Socialism. During the 1930s and 1940s German (and Austrian) consumer research was a mixture of ideas that bespoke an interest in individual and group psychology, traditional ideas about community, and Nazi organicism. In this respect it fit in well with the Nazis' market ideal, which made ample room for pre-1933 preoccupations and discussions that could be used to bolster the regime's racial aims.

THE GFK AND THE UNITED STATES

The Nazi regime, as we have seen, engaged in a running dialogue with "foreign" ideas. In exploring the meaning of commerce and consumption, it necessarily had to confront the influence of the United States – as an alternative model of capitalism and as a provider of high living standards that the Nazis strove to surpass. The regime thus encouraged elites – whether intellectuals, Rotarians, or company leaders – to engage with the United States. Accordingly, the GfK showed a greater fascination with U.S. practices than its sharp rejection of American empiricism suggests. While Hanns Kropff had more respect for the methods of American consumer research than the GfK did, both were intrigued by the largest consumer economy in the world. Vershofen always denied that the impetus for his endeavors came from the United States and that he was merely imitating his American counterparts with his organizations (indeed, Vershofen's IfW was set up before George Gallup's institute).[121] But Vershofen and his colleagues did not hesitate to study and dissect the practice of consumer research across the Atlantic.[122]

To better understand American methods, the Nuremberg economists courted Elisabeth Noelle, a keen follower of trends in public opinion research who spent a year in the United States in 1937–38 and would later become the most prominent conductor of opinion polling in West Germany through her Allensbach Institute for Public Opinion Research.[123]

---

[121] Bergler, *Entwicklung der Verbrauchsforschung*, 45, 71.
[122] See, e.g., Mann to Vershofen, 15 October 1941, NL Vershofen, MS 2763, box 9, Mann file, Erlangen.
[123] Brose to Vershofen, 7 December 1944, NL Vershofen, MS 2763, box 5, file "Schriftwechsel Brose, 1935–1944," Erlangen. Noelle's husband and postwar collaborator, Erich Peter Neumann, worked for Propaganda Minister Goebbels's magazine *Das Reich* in the early war years.

In the final years of the Third Reich, Noelle's studies of public opinion polls, commercial research, and market analysis in the United States provoked spirited discussions – and mostly doubts – in Nuremberg about whether American methods were applicable in Germany.[124] Noelle and the GfK economists returned repeatedly to Gallup's use of "yes or no" questions; such an easy dichotomy ran against the rigorous practices of German *Wissenschaft*. They dismissed the organization as "unscholarly" and looked askance at its encouragement of rushed surveys rather than intensive explorations into the consumer psyche. Despite its own misgivings, the Nuremberg group also found Gallup's outright rejection of motivational research troubling; Gallup, wrote Vershofen, "believes that most people do not know why they have developed a certain opinion," so they clearly did not want to bother asking about motivation.[125]

Vershofen and his colleagues criticized not only Gallup's American Institute of Public Opinion, but also the more politically oriented Fortune Survey and the Crossley Poll, the latter two having been launched in 1935 and 1936, respectively. The Nuremberg school rejected the "pseudo-scientific" practice of straws polls, the organizations' links to journalists, and the notion that the more people interviewed, the more accurate a report was.[126] They also criticized the Americans' depiction of their work as an expression of democracy: "democracy" was a disingenuous catchphrase whose advocates professed an interest in the public's opinions without respecting the individual's view. The fact that George Gallup had made his name by predicting the presidential victory of Franklin Roosevelt in 1936 based on polling was a source of suspicion. Noelle felt that American public opinion research was misused, essentially mutating into propaganda on behalf of the U.S. government and big companies under the guise of true public expression. She wrote of the "fiction of the sovereignty of the individual" in the United States.[127] Naturally, such political polling had no place in a dictatorship, and it behooved German observers like Noelle to belittle it. But Noelle and the Nuremberg economists truly believed that American methods promised more than they could deliver.

---

[124] E.g., Elisabeth Noelle, *Meinungs- und Massenforschung in U.S.A.: Umfragen über Politik und Presse* (Frankfurt am Main: Moritz Diesterweg, 1940).

[125] Vershofen, "Zur Praxis der Meinungsforschung in USA," *Markt und Verbrauch* 14, nos. 9 and 10 (1942): 201–5, GfKA. On Gallup see also Gerhard Goy, "Opinion Research," *Markt und Verbrauch* 11, no. 7 (July 1939): 299–307, GfKA.

[126] Bergler, *Entwicklung der Verbrauchsforschung*, 171; and Goy, "Opinion Research."

[127] This phrase is cited in Carl Hundhausen's review of her book in *Markt und Verbrauch* 14, nos. 5 and 6 (1942): 120–25, GfKA.

It was not just political democracy but also cultural democracy that aroused disdain. A writer in *Markt und Verbrauch*, one of the GfK's periodicals, exposed the empty use of the democracy ideal, incongruously citing German sociologist Ferdinand Tönnies, who was skeptical of propaganda and media-driven mass movements, and Adolf Hitler as worthwhile critics of opinion research.[128] Many Nazi thinkers portrayed democracy as a cover for an American selfishness that took the forms of a plutocracy and a cutthroat economy. In this vein the Nuremberg school declared that it was doing work that went beyond the "go-it-alone" spirit of America; it was instead contributing to the greater good by conducting studies that would find answers for the entire economy.[129] Understanding the consumer in his or her totality would help society in *its* totality. The irony of these observations is that the Nuremberg school was critiquing both the hyperindividualism of American business and society and the fact that Americans did not pay *enough* attention to individuals. To German thinkers in the 1930s, this was not necessarily a contradiction. Both the Nazi leadership and members of the Nuremberg school saw a new type of "individualism" emerging in Germany that moved beyond bourgeois selfishness and protected people from the conformity associated with American mass culture.[130] By integrating the total person into a total society, Nazi ideologues and consumer researchers in their own ways hoped to preserve a seemingly richer notion of the individual and a communal sprit that, they claimed, had eroded on the other side of the Atlantic.

The GfK's adherence to communitarian ideals and its critical stance toward the United States ultimately helped position it comfortably within the Nazi ideological landscape, even as it pursued intellectual dialogues that transcended Germany's borders. While the directors saw their work as part of transcontinental discourses about consumption, the GfK could proceed with its work throughout the Nazi years because its investigations into the nature of the Mensch – as individual and member of an organic whole – paralleled and nourished the Nazis' racialized inquiry into human motivations and susceptibilities. And they carefully culled their information from international trends in psychology without ever

---

[128] Goy, "Opinion Research," 301. Goy refers to *Mein Kampf* and Tönnies's 1922 work, *Kritik der öffentlichen Meinung* (Berlin: Julius Springer, 1922); translated as *A Theory of Public Opinion* (New York: Rowman and Littlefield, 2000).

[129] Bergler, *Entwicklung der Verbrauchsforschung*, 115.

[130] See Hundhausen's review in *Markt und Verbrauch* 14, nos. 5 and 6 (1942): 120–25, GfKA.

embracing the science of "the other," whether American or Jewish. Ultimately, even if they eschewed racist language, the Nuremberg school could not deny the nationalist import of its work. "The work of the Society for Consumer Research," wrote a member of the administrative board in 1937, "is service to the German economy and thereby service to the German *Volk* itself."[131]

When assessing the legacy of the GfK, one must determine how much to bind the organization's history to its founding years in Nazi Germany. Should we see this early period as the launch phase in a longer, storied history of consumer research that transcended any features specific to the Third Reich? Or did the ideology and politics of National Socialism contribute to the rapid genesis of the GfK? The answer is both. On the one hand, there was a basic continuity in the GfK's work; pre-1933 dialogues and marketing practices persisted into the Third Reich and informed international discussions about consumer behavior and psychology. On the other hand, the GfK's fascination with finished goods, merchandising, marketing, and consumer wishes took on a specific cast in the Third Reich. As we have seen, the Nazis held out the promise of a "German" consumer society that would bind together racial equals. Even if the reality was different – an attenuated consumer sector and a war economy – the GfK reports, grounded in an organicist sociology, gave the state a sense that it was creating a world of abundance. A nazified Germany was stocked with perfumes, automobiles, toiletries, cigarettes, fancy clothes, and the attending human desires for status, free time, and sex appeal. In addition, the state, which through Goebbels's propaganda ministry already boasted a keen understanding of the masses, recognized the powerful contribution the GfK could make to the study of mass psychology.[132]

There were thus many points of convergence in the GfK and Nazi projects: the celebration of community-oriented consumption, the totalizing view of society, and the rejection of materialism alongside the celebration of material goods. The Nuremberg school's urge to craft a distinctly German methodology with which to practice consumer research was also compatible with the aims of the Third Reich. Drawing on the "German"

---

[131] Johannes Martin Ditterich, in *Merkblatt der Gesellschaft für Konsumforschung e.V.* (1937), excerpted in Bergler, *Entwicklung der Verbrauchsforschung*, 111.
[132] On Goebbels, marketing, and mass influence, see Gerhard Voigt, "Goebbels als Markentechniker," in *Warenästhetik: Beiträge zur Diskussion, Weiterentwicklung und Vermittlung ihrer Kritik*, ed. Wolfgang Fritz Haug (Frankfurt am Main: Suhrkamp, 1975), 231–60.

notion of Verstehen, the Nuremberg school expected to use different means to understand its consumers and, more significantly, to truly *find* different consumers – and human beings – than those populating Britain and the United States. This German consumer was a modern shopper, with wants and needs not dissimilar to anyone's in an advanced industrialized country. But this was not a "mass man" – a slave to fashion and other conformist trends imposed by the hyperdemocracy of the Anglo-American world. In Germany consumers were individuals, who found existential meaning in their own accomplishments as producers, homemakers, and members of familial, local, and national-racial communities. Nor did they squander their household incomes on cheap, mass-produced goods; they bought well-crafted finished goods that exemplified the ethos of high-quality manufacturing, even if they were products of the assembly line.

Beyond this ideological resonance, the GfK also maintained formal links to the Nazi Party. Members of the Advertising Council sat on the GfK board, and the organization received annual contributions from the DAF (despite its criticisms of the GfK).[133] Likewise, many board members, who represented large companies, were also party members. Finally, as we will see in the next chapter, war tied the work of the Nuremberg school directly to Nazi aggression. The GfK thus never was – nor could be – an independent force in a political setting where all research organizations had been ideologically coordinated.

Despite these formal ties and ideological affinities, the GfK was neither an arm of the Nazi Party nor particularly nazified, and it was able to maintain a basic intellectual autonomy in the prewar Third Reich. The individuals who led the GfK had little use for the regime's biological racism. While adhering to organic views of society, Vershofen himself was no "blood and soil" theorist (he instead belonged to the so-called conservative revolution),[134] and he explicitly rejected the Nazis' ideal of the master race.[135] Ludwig Erhard, despite a close working relationship with the regime, was fundamentally an economic liberal who did not busy himself with racial theories. And all told, the GfK's publications were remarkably free of Nazi language.[136] In short, the work of the GfK complemented

---

[133] Mann to Vershofen, 24 October 1941, Box 9, Mann file, NL Vershofen, MS 2763, Erlangen.
[134] Hemmerle, *Tausend Jahre Absatz*, iv.
[135] Ibid.
[136] The GfK made ample use of the term "Gemeinschaft" and much less often "Volksgemeinschaft." For the use of the latter, however, see Hans Proesler, "Problematik des Verstehens," *Markt und Verbrauch* 11, no. 4 (April 1939): 157–66, GfKA.

Nazi aims, but the organization was not born of fascistic tendencies. It was fundamentally an expression of larger developments in mass market-ing and mass psychology.[137] In Britain, the mass-observation movement, which produced detailed descriptions of everyday people in the most mundane of situations, was a product of the late 1930s, and the GfK devoted attention to this artistic and intellectual development. Likewise, as we have seen, market researchers, pollsters, and opinion researchers found their footing in the United States around the same time the GfK was launched. The GfK was thus part of a larger transatlantic enterprise that accompanied the rise of the modern consumer: monitoring his or her influence on the economy and politics. The GfK's goal of locating the consuming Mensch within the community had its origins in the pre-Nazi years, but it found a particular resonance in the Third Reich. It reflected both conventional practices of marketing and the ideological imperatives of the Nazi marketplace.

[137] Goy, "Opinion Research," 299.

5

World War II and the Virtuous Marketplace

In the fall of 1939, Germany witnessed a wave of panic buying. With the Nazi invasion of Poland, consumers began hoarding brand-name products and clearing store racks in the hope that these goods would retain some value if the currency collapsed. This "shopping psychosis," as reported by the Society for Consumer Research, manifested itself in unexpected ways. Not only were there runs on stores in cities, but also farmers, who did not typically buy luxury goods, were purchasing one or even two grand pianos so that they could possess something of material value.[1]

This frenzy was not a sudden expression of anxiety with the onset of war. Rather, it was the culmination of years of economic insecurity that had accompanied the implementation of the Four Year Plan for military readiness in 1936. If Germans were already on a war footing, however, they recognized after the invasion of Poland that their lives as consumers would inexorably change. The same can be said of producers. While the prior years had seen the increased regulation of consumer goods and the advertising of them, market professionals understood that war demanded a rethinking of selling strategies, now based even less on private business aims and more on supporting the military effort. This chapter focuses on the tense interrelationship between war, state ideology, commerce, and consumption. It first looks at the regime's promotion and regulation of buying and selling during wartime. It then considers the challenges companies faced as they tried to adhere to the

---

[1] "Verbraucher und Markenartikel in den ersten Kriegsmonaten," December 1939, p. 12., S 1939 015, GfKA.

new demands that they no longer serve their own interests but those of the state. As we will see, despite a shrinking of the civilian economy, business elites continued the project of defining, understanding, and selling to the consumer, but they did so under the starker demands that they adhere to a wartime morality. A cluster of obligations – serving the state, serving the racial community, and serving the war – meant that companies had to curtail their own inclinations to address their private business needs first. Moreover, as World War II proceeded, shortages limited the range of marketing strategies, and the semiautonomy of economic elites was increasingly challenged, as they could not escape being drawn into the more violent aims of the regime. In short, after 1939 the contradictions inherent in the Nazi marketplace proved irreconcilable: the regime could not make war, engineer a new market sensibility, and provide rich consumer opportunities at the same time.

CONSUMPTION DURING THE WAR

Before addressing how consumers and producers responded to the war economy, let us consider how the Nazi leadership envisioned consumption during World War II. The Third Reich, as we know, was marked by the interplay between utopian visions and often harsh realities, and during the war, official messages about patriotic forms of consuming accompanied the daily rituals of scrimping and belt tightening. In certain respects, the Nazi leadership found war conducive to its economic and social ideals. National Socialism had always preached individual sacrifice and communal thinking, and war gave selflessness a new urgency. With limitations placed on the consumer economy, self-denial took on real meaning after 1939, as Germans pushed their dreams of economic abundance to an indefinite postwar future. Political leaders and economists promised a great payoff for wartime sacrifices. Wrote *DDV* in early 1941: "When the war is over and the great creations in Germany ... begin ... then those needs that are now unmet ... will be satisfied without serious difficulty."[2]

The many regulations issued since 1933 about competition, advertising, and virtuous economic behavior anticipated economic realities after 1939, when the state intervened even more in the market and the populace was asked to balance material desires with attention to the

---

[2] "Des Verbrauchers Anteil am Erfolg," *DDV* 10, nos. 1 and 2 (January 1941): 21–22.

commonweal. The declaration that "military strength comes before purchasing power" (*Wehrkraft geht vor Kaufkraft*) captured the idea that consumption would be subservient to war production. Goods were sold on the basis of their "importance to the war effort," and political leaders openly conceded that the economy was based on "guns instead of butter."[3] Customers were given food ration cards and clothes vouchers and asked to place their names on customer waiting lists to obtain finished goods.[4]

As we have seen, the Nazi leadership had laid the ideological groundwork for these sacrifices through the "consumer education" and household management campaigns accompanying the Four Year Plan. With the outbreak of war, it stepped up these efforts to instruct the public about proper consumer behavior. The Fight against Waste campaign continued, and a new scrap collection program encouraged households to turn over items, particularly metals, that could be of use in the war effort.[5] And as in the prewar years, correct laundering habits continued to draw great attention. Under the premise that "laundry is the valuable property of the Volk!"[6] the state and private industry went to great lengths to convince consumers to wear clothes that hid dirt, to not wipe their razors on towels (forcing them to be washed), to avoid cutting bread directly on a tablecloth (leading to holes), and to learn how to correctly remove food, blood, and urine stains from clothes.[7] For this *Waschaktion* they even created a mascot. This faux enemy, the so-called *Dreckspatz* (grubby kid or filthy beggar), was a mischievous little bird who appeared in numerous wartime ads as the culprit responsible for the wasteful dirtying of clothes. "We're on his trail" (*Wir sind ihm auf der Spur*), declared numerous ads, which depicted the Dreckspatz leaving muddy footprints on freshly laundered linens.[8]

Economists and political leaders offered new rationales for these limitations. They stressed how war allowed Germany to realize its long-standing desire to "align consumption with production."[9] The shrinking

[3] For these quotes see ibid.
[4] On these and other measures during the war, see Jill Stephenson, *Hitler's Home Front: Württemberg under the Nazis* (London: Hambledon Continuum, 2006), 153–92.
[5] Uwe Westphal, *Werbung im Dritten Reich* (Berlin: Transit, 1989), 145–47.
[6] Rundfunk-Text zum Thema "Wäschesparen!" ca. June 1943, R5002/21, BAB.
[7] "Das Waschfibel," ca. 1940–41, pp. 401–5, R5002/26, BAB.
[8] "Bericht über den Zusatzauftrag zur Anschlagaktion Z 32/43 der Zentralstelle für staatspolitisch wichtige Anschlagaktionen. 1. Plakat der Dreckspatzserie 'Wir sind ihm auf der Spur,'" 5 June 1944, R5002/4, BAB.
[9] Wolfgang Clauß, "Unabhängige Ernährung," *DDV* 8, no. 31 (November 1939): 1036–37.

FIGURE 18. *The War Laundry Primer of the German Housewife*: "Take care of your laundry ... and protect yourself against the *Dreckspatz*." (R 5004/4, p. 84; courtesy of the Bundesarchiv Berlin.)

demand that followed a contraction in supply was cast as a positive development; it eliminated an unhealthy materialism present in other advanced economies and fostered German economic independence. Of course, the regime knew that consumers did not altruistically refrain from demanding goods for the sake of the nation. Therefore, the public's excess purchasing power was brought to heel by war taxes, rising prices, and the increased costs of keeping some high-quality goods on the shelves. Consumers only grudgingly gave up their purchasing expectations, but the government nonetheless praised them for their selflessness. According to *DDV*, "The German economy's increased performance during the war is due to people not only as producers but also – as paradoxical as it might sound – as consumers," who made do with less in order to support the "great national task" of war.[10] The consumer – especially the housewife, who was most seriously affected by shortages on a daily basis – was as much a hero as the factory worker. Nazi publications continually cited the government's desire to avoid the home-front hardships of World War I, inviting consumers and producers to share the fruits of victory on the battlefield.

While acknowledging the disruptions to consumption, the regime ultimately depicted them as temporary inconveniences in service of a bright post-victory future, when Germans could enjoy unprecedented material comforts. This "new order" would witness a "cultural and economic blossoming," offering racially fit people throughout Nazi-dominated Europe the experience of personal security and the joys of buying cars, consumer durables, and a bounty of food items.[11] The combination of military victories, the real privations of war, and the hope of their immanent end created a powerful tool for social control. The economy was at once embodied in a present marked by shortages and a future that would be defined by abundance. This dialectic between deprivation and wealth, between reality and promises, arguably, helped maintain the loyalty of the population during the war years. It both valorized immediate behavior and made anticipated gains dependent on patience and compliance.

The Nazis' sanguine reflections on scarcity, sacrifice, and leisure must be placed in their proper context. They were issued from 1939 through 1941, when Germany looked forward to victory. But even during a period of wartime optimism, this language was powerful precisely because it did not reflect daily realities. To be sure, shortages on the home front were not as severe as during World War I, and as Götz Aly points out, the average consumer maintained a higher standard of living during World War II by means of price controls and income redistribution plans.[12] However, when we look closer at the consumer marketplace, we see widespread

---

[10] "Des Verbrauchers Anteil am Erfolg," 22.
[11] "Um die neue Ordnung Europas," *DDV* 8, no. 29 (October 1939): 993–94; Jakob Werlin, "Motorisierung in Europa," *DDV* 9, no. 30 (October 1940): 970–72.
[12] Götz Aly, *Hitler's Beneficiaries: Plunder, Racial War, and the Nazi Welfare State* (New York: Metropolitan Books, 2007), 70.

dislocation. After one year of war, per capita civilian consumption had fallen by 11 percent, and it would continue to decline.[13] Specialty shops shut down when the well of luxury goods dried up, and long lines snaked around remaining stores, while wealthy customers made deals with shopkeepers to snap up scarce goods. Consumers, in the meantime, were discouraged from engaging in private transactions. Hoarding, profiteering, and participation in the black market were illegal and eventually punishable by death, and the government banned the unofficial barter of used goods.[14] The latter was considered an unhealthy form of economic exchange because there was no mechanism for ensuring that both parties were satisfied with a transaction. In order to stifle the public's "exchange psychosis," Germans were forbidden to advertise used goods, and cities instead set up public distribution centers to process the cookware and furniture that passed from hand to hand.[15]

One of the ironies of these regulations is that they ultimately benefited large-scale manufacturers and retailers at the expense of small businesses.[16] After twenty years of denouncing department stores and single-price shops as threatening to the independent owner, the Nazis in 1940 lifted the so-called department store tax. As we have seen, whatever dangers this "Jewish" form of competition had represented, department stores were seen as better equipped than smaller retailers to provide commodities to the public.[17] Indeed, in 1943 the economics ministry ordered the closing of small shops that were not absolutely necessary for the war economy or the provisioning of the population. At the same time, regional governors and city leaders pushed through anti–department store measures against the wishes of Berlin, shutting down or forcing the mergers of hundreds of department stores, discount chains, and branch stores. The sometimes "confused, improvisational nature of the 'Third Reich,'" according to Heinrich Uhlig, was put on full display with this approach to department stores.[18]

---

[13] Adam Tooze, *Wages of Destruction: The Making and Breaking of the Nazi Economy* (New York: Viking, 2006), 353.

[14] Robert Gellately, *Backing Hitler: Consent and Coercion in Nazi Germany* (Oxford: Oxford University Press, 2001), 81; Stephenson, *Hitler's Home Front*, 167.

[15] "Gebrauchtwarentauschstellen," *DDV* 12, no. 22 (August 1943): 668.

[16] Ludolf Herbst, *Der Totale Krieg und die Ordnung der Wirtschaft: Die Kriegswirtschaft im Spannungsfeld von Politik, Ideologie und Propaganda, 1939–1945* (Stuttgart: Deutsche Verlags-Anstalt, 1982), 13.

[17] Heinrich Uhlig, *Die Warenhäuser im Dritten Reich* (Cologne: Westdeutscher, 1956), 183–88.

[18] Ibid., 186.

Whether it concerned manufacturing or point-of-sale transactions, the Nazis tried to reach into every corner of the market during the war. Take the seemingly inconsequential example of the vending machine. For years vending machines had been a source of controversy, representing to some the thrilling technification of selling, but to others (like the Nazi leadership) the depersonalization of the market, unhealthy competition with the independent shop owner, and the erosion of face-to-face exchange.[19] By 1940 these "mute sellers" now stood empty, unable to accept coupons or food ration cards or to process extra taxes on items like cigarettes. In principle, this development benefited the small businessman, who felt threatened by new technologies of selling that did not involve personal contact. But in an economy of scarcity, the ideological importance of empty vending machines was lost on all participants in the marketplace. It was a pyrrhic victory for neighborhood proprietors, who were doing poorly, and consumers, who had less to purchase, and now with less convenience.

Here we see an absurd culmination of the Nazis' conflicted economic policies. On the one hand, the regime hoped to eliminate dangerous expressions of consumer culture; vending machines threatened the livelihood of restaurateurs and food vendors, and it facilitated hurried and spiritually depleting forms of consumption. On the other hand, the Nazis prioritized war production over civilian consumption and thus disadvantaged the very individuals who stood to gain from the end of mechanized selling, namely food proprietors. Throughout the 1930s the regime had not faced in such stark terms the contradictory nature of the Nazi marketplace; until war broke out, building a flourishing consumer society, protecting big and small business, monitoring commercial activity, and preparing for war did not necessarily seem contradictory. Indeed, as the German economy recovered, the regime could claim to have created a workable market model based on a combination of bourgeois and National Socialist norms. But under conditions of wartime scarcity, regulating and purifying a collapsing marketplace seemed utterly useless, and the empty vending machine brought this point home.

COMPETITION AND MARKETING IN WARTIME GERMANY

The consumer marketplace was a troubled institution during World War II. How, then, did producers and marketers conduct business during this

---

[19] "Ende des Warenautomaten?" *DDV* 8, no. 32 (November 1939): 1051.

period? In order to address this question, we must first determine the extent to which the Nazis really sought to limit commercial activity in the name of völkisch morality. As we have seen, on a theoretical level, the regime welcomed the dearth of goods during wartime. A concentration of industries producing fewer products could mean less competition, and thus a departure from the supposedly corrosive expressions of "Jewish" hypercapitalism. As a practical matter, however, the regime never suspended economic competition – neither during the 1930s nor during the war. If this seems an obvious point by now, it is nonetheless one that the Nazis themselves felt pressed to repeat to the business community. According to a 1941 editorial in the business journal *Wirtschaftsdienst*, critics made the mistake of confusing the Nazis' state-directed economy (*staatlich gelenkte Wirtschaft*) with a command economy (*staatswirtschaft*). In the former, there was still plenty of room for competition and for the "personal initiative of the salesman and entrepreneur."[20] Indeed, such business virtues fit comfortably into Nazi doctrine based on the struggle for survival – between species, races, nations, and companies. "We cannot," asserted a 1940 article in *DDV*, "imagine the German economy without competition; indeed, it is the basis of progress."[21] "War does not nullify the ground rules of competition," the newspaper continued in a later article; in fact, the dearth of goods meant that companies bid more intensely for customers.[22] Given the potential for rampant abuses in the marketplace, however, the regime continued to advocate a "healthy competition" under the watchful eye of the state.[23]

What did this phrase mean, given the increasing control the regime wielded over the economy? Nazi economic theorists never explained coherently what forms of wartime competition were "healthy," but in their many references to it, two business imperatives emerged. First, the regime redoubled its efforts to promote performance and achievement.[24] During the 1930s, as we have seen, Leistung embodied at once

---

[20] "Die Front der Kaufleute und Unternehmer," *Wirtschaftsdienst* 26, no. 8 (21 February 1941): 137–38. On the role of the wartime entrepreneur, see also "Dem deutschen Unternehmer eine Gelegenheit!" *Wirtschaftspolitische Parole* 6, no. 8 (April 1941): 233–37.
[21] "Werbung mit volkswirtschaftlichen Gesichtspunkten," *DDV* 9, no. 3 (January 1940): 99–100.
[22] Alfred Maelicke, "Leistungssteigerung und Wirtschaftswerbung," *DDV* 9, no. 3 (1940): 103–5.
[23] "Werbung mit volkswirtschaftlichen Gesichtspunkten," 99.
[24] See, e.g., "Leistungsbuch," *Nationalsozialistische Wirtschaftspolitik* 1943, no. 10 (November 1943): 383–84.

profitability, competitiveness, and the idea of individual and *völkisch* accomplishment. After war broke out, companies were still expected to prove their value to the state and to customers by exercising personal initiative, maintaining a healthy output, and demonstrating performance.[25] "Productivity (*Leistungfähigkeit*) and dependability mark the ... German economy especially well," declared a Dresden lignite company in a 1941 advertisement, before reminding readers that "mighty are the tasks that our homeland must fulfill during this war that was forced upon us."[26] The second imperative was for companies to continue advertising. Advertising was one of the clearest manifestations of the competitive urge, pitting products against each other in the public space and in the private imagination. Given their own focus on propaganda and visual agitation, the Nazis defended wartime advertising. Advertising was not simply a necessary evil, however. It was an edifying exercise. It taught the public which goods to buy by appealing to "convictions and character" – of producers, consumers, and all members of the Volk.[27] Wrote Henkel's advertising director Paul Mundhenke, "The task of the advertiser is to absorb the essence and advantages of the goods entrusted to him and with the creative power of his personality to interpret them accurately and convincingly for the consumer. I did that with arguments appropriate to peacetime, and I am doing that today with arguments suited to wartime."[28] Whether reflecting individual creativity or serving pragmatic business aims, advertising was imbued with a characteristic Nazi vitality: "Whoever advertises testifies that he lives," declared *DDV*.[29]

These nationalist messages about Leistung and advertising were aimed not only at Germans but also at foreigners. As we have seen, companies and the state considered brands "cultural goods" that ultimately bolstered the country's reputation abroad. During the height of German wartime optimism, companies looked forward to expanding markets in Africa, Asia, the Americas, and a German-dominated Europe.[30] German

---

[25] See "Privatinitiative und Improvisation," *Vierjahresplan* 7, no. 12 (December 1943): 416; and "Unternehmer müssen sein!" *Vierjahresplan* 7, no. 9 (September 1943): 324–25.

[26] Advertisement for Aktiengesellschaft Sächsische Werke in *DDV* 10, nos. 1 and 2 (January 1941): 59.

[27] "Werbung mit volkswirtschaftlichen Gesichtspunkten," 99.

[28] Paul Mundhenke, "Gedanken über unsere Werbung," H2o 1941, pp. 16–18, HA. For the last quote see p.15.

[29] Maelicke, "Leistungssteigerung und Wirtschaftswerbung,"103.

[30] On the accompanying need to advertise abroad during the war, see Heinrich Hunke, "Auslandspropaganda" (speech given in Berlin in 1941), NS18/655, BAB. On marketing abroad see also Wilfried Feldenkirchen and Susanne Hilger, *Menschen und Marken: 125 Jahre Henkel, 1876–2001* (Düsseldorf: Henkel, 2001), 89.

business and political leaders hoped that pharmaceutical goods, watches, fine mechanics, and optical goods, when marked with the phrase "made in Germany," would continue to serve as bearers of quality and as ambassadors for the German economy. "The German product with an exact indication of its origin," wrote the GfK's Georg Bergler in 1940, "becomes a silent advertiser and messenger for Germany in the home of the foreign buyer. The more messages we can send around the world, the better." Branded goods embodied the goodwill of a company, built trust abroad, served as a marker of superior quality (as opposed to, according to Bergler, the "kitsch and trash" produced elsewhere), and advertised not just German production but also, more generally, "German ideas."[31]

Such market diplomacy was hardly new, but it had a greater urgency during the war, when Germany's reputation and its network of financial relations were being battered. The foreign household, argued Bergler, was the ultimate site of advertising, as the primary place where non-Germans recognized the greatness of Germany in the act of consumption. As German troops marched through Europe, the Wehrmacht's propaganda magazine *Signal* made this view clear by punctuating celebratory images of fighter planes and smiling soldiers with ads for fine German products of "the highest reputation": Olympia typewriters, Zeiss Ikon cameras, and Khasana perfumes.[32]

Other important sites of Leistung were trade fairs and international exhibitions, where visitors could observe German products as part of a public spectacle. Just as advertising persisted during the war, so did this site of marketing. The Nazis had already limited the number of trade fairs and shows before 1939, and the war only accelerated the clampdown. In typically vague fashion, new regulations in 1940 banned all exhibitions except those that were economically essential and had the permission of the Advertising Council. In 1939 there had been 117 *Messen*, a steady drop from the 634 in 1934. But the famous fairs in Vienna, Cologne, and Leipzig were kept alive, and the regime used those in Königsberg and Breslau to supersede Polish fairs that were considered competitive.[33] "Educational shows," exhibitions of

---

[31] For these quotes see Georg Bergler, "Der deutsche Verbrauchsgüterexport," *DDV* 9, no. 30 (October 1940): 981–83.

[32] These three ads accompany the article "Geschichte wiederholt sich nicht: Ein Schlußwort zu dem Vergleich Hitler – Napoleon," reprinted in *Signal 1941/1942* (Hamburg: Jahr, 1977), 87–89. The phrase about the highest reputation comes from the Khasana ad.

[33] Hans Ruban, "Das deutsche Messe- und Ausstellungswesen," *DDV* 9, no. 8 (March 1940): 210–12.

technological innovations, and RVA demonstrations were encouraged, and as it had done during peacetime, Henkel continued to open "Persil institutes" abroad (e.g., Zurich in 1940), where housewives could watch company specialists demonstrate German superiority in the science of laundering.[34] All of these measures helped serve the regime's imperial mission, which entailed not just the spread of German military power, but also the promotion of German economic might as a uniting force in a Nazi-dominated Europe.

Given these examples of foreign merchandising and display, it may appear that wartime marketing was "business as usual." According to Harry Damrow, the advertising director for the hotel and restaurant business Aschinger during the Third Reich, "The war began, and advertising went on."[35] But this was not without its challenges. Official attitudes about competition, Leistung, and advertising were strikingly imprecise, and nobody realized this more than company leaders, who faced a series of impediments to implementing their selling strategies. Part of this had to do with the dearth of goods to actually sell. But the Nazis also limited the range of marketing options by monitoring practices that crossed the line of völkisch acceptability. As before the war, companies were forbidden to give the impression in their ads that they were sponsored by state institutions or had a special relationship to National Socialism. Nor could a firm exploit the economic misfortunes of a competitor for its own profit. Moreover, companies had to keep "economic advertising" and political propaganda distinct: "Advertising," declared Advertising Council president Heinrich Hunke, "must never lose its economic character and become propaganda."[36] In other words, during wartime, ads still had to reflect the fundamental business aim of selling products rather than serving as a conduit for state propaganda. Basic market norms needed to persist in the midst of a war economy.

This last injunction was particularly difficult to observe, because the regime actually never wanted to depoliticize marketing. During the war, companies were regularly encouraged to use "economic arguments" about thriftiness or loyalty within their ads. Indeed, it was through regular exposure to ads that people were supposed to learn about correct

[34] Feldenkirchen and Hilger, *Menschen und Marken*, app. 35.

[35] Harry Damrow, *Ich war kein geheimer Verführer: Aus dem Leben eines Werbeleiters* (Rheinzabern: Dieter Gitzel, 1981), 57. In the German, the phrase is in the present tense: "Der Krieg beginnt. Der Werbung geht weiter."

[36] Heinrich Hunke, "Hinweise zur Kriegsdienenden Werbung," reprinted in Westphal, *Werbung im Dritten Reich*, 175.

market behavior.[37] In 1943 Hunke issued a dozen guidelines for "war-
serving advertising." Companies had to counsel consumers to collect
scrap materials and used packaging, avoid damaging household goods,
save their pennies, and even demonstrate a "politeness and willingness to
help."[38] The Reich price commissioner forced companies to make large
contributions to a fund that would produce such "neutral advertising."
In these noncompetitive ads, a business was allowed to mention its own
name, but could not, wrote Paul Mundhenke, "lyrically sing the praises
of ... products or promote their sale."[39] It is clear with these mandates
that the regime was caught in a bind. On the one hand, it wanted to make
a gesture toward "normal" market activity by strictly delineating politics and business. It also wanted to protect Nazi ideology from negative
expressions of commercialism. On the other hand, it knew that company
advertisers, as creators of effective product imagery, were in the perfect
position to promote the state's goals. This tension was already evident in
the 1930s, but it became more pronounced during the war, as the regime
grew more intent on regulating private behavior.

Despite its vigorous defense of wartime advertising, the regime was
clearly ambivalent about this commercial medium, which could both
serve and undermine Nazi ideology. Such concerns were amplified by
critics who, more than ever, saw ads as a wasteful use of resources that
drove up prices. In response, proponents asserted that advertising actually lowered prices by increasing the mass demand (and therefore production of) books, cars, bicycles, and refrigerators, leading to increases
in the overall performance of the economy. This theoretical point was
a risky one to make during the war, when such goods were not readily
available. But advertisers were anticipating a post-victory marketplace
that would depend upon long-standing ad campaigns. It would be economically destructive to get rid of ads, argued Nazi economist Alfred
Maelicke, as it would take years and tremendous financial resources for a
company to restart an ad campaign that had been shut down. Bringing the
two components of "healthy competition" together, the regime reminded
the business world that advertising ultimately increased performance by
improving product quality.[40]

Perhaps the greatest challenge to advertising during World War II was
the disappearance of brand-name goods from shelves. While pro-Nazi

[37] "Werbung mit volkswirtschaftlichen Gesichtspunkten."
[38] Hunke, "Hinweise zur Kriegsdienenden Werbung."
[39] Mundhenke, "Gedanken über unsere Werbung."
[40] Maelicke, "Leistungssteigerung und Wirtschaftswerbung."

economists asserted that quality and confidence in products could be sustained during the war, in reality this was highly unlikely after the onset of hostilities, when Germans witnessed an onslaught of ersatz products and generic goods. This concern over generic products was not new; the years of recovery in the 1930s also saw "community products" (*Gemeinschaftserzeugnisse*) like the "people's radio" supplant traditional brands.[41] During World War II, however, business leaders worried with more urgency about the consequences of turning away from famous names, which were carriers of goodwill, integrity, and quality. In 1940 Hans Ruban, managing director of the Advertising Council and editor in chief of *DDV*, asked: "Are branded goods in danger?"[42] He had in mind famous names like Persil, which had been pulled from the market a few days after the outbreak of World War II. The Reich Office for Chemistry had replaced Persil and competitive brands with a so-called standard laundry detergent, whose ingredients and packaging were determined by the authorities.[43] Kaffee HAG, another company we have looked at in detail, ceased producing coffee in the fall of 1939. The company had already been forbidden to advertise its staple product the year before in anticipation of the regime's rationing of coffee.[44] The public was now asked to make do with an ersatz malt drink.

How did Germans respond to the dearth of goods? According to a GfK correspondent, the "rule" of hording changed from "goods at any price" to "high-quality goods at any price."[45] Name-brand products, in the minds of the public, were simply better and thus that much more desirable during war. In the Pomeranian town of Schlawe, the most popular shoe brands (Salamander, Mercedes, and Trommler, a company that had been bought by the SA), women's handbags (especially Goldpfeil), and more practical items like camping stoves were sold out in the local stores by mid-November 1939. In other towns and cities, the most expensive beauty creams such as Wolff & Sohn's were entirely gone, as were cheaper Nivea and Palmolive products.[46] Consumers went on a rampage, running from

---

[41] Wolfgang König, Volkswagen, Volksempfänger, Volksgemeinschaft: *"Volksprodukte" im Dritten Reich – Vom Scheitern einer nationalsozialistischen Konsumgesellschaft* (Paderborn: Schöningh: 2004), 232–42.

[42] Hans Ruban, "Markenartikel im Kriege," *DDV* 9, no. 6 (February 1940): 162–64.

[43] Feldenkirchen and Hilger, *Menschen und Marken*, 88 and app. 35.

[44] Svenja Kunze, "'Kaffee HAG schont Ihr Herz': Zur Entstehung und Entwicklung eines klassischen Markenartikels in der deutschen Kaffeebranche, 1906–1939," *Hamburger Wirtschafts-Chronik* 4 (2004): 85–120.

[45] "Verbraucher und Markenartikel in den ersten Kriegsmonaten," 12.

[46] For this list of the most "missed" products, see the appendix in ibid.

store to store looking for familiar toiletries, soaps, and clothes. A store owner from Bad-Kreuznach reported on the reaction of women when he provided them the brands they had been seeking: "You should see how the eyes of the women sparkle. You would think that they had just received a present."[47] Consumers also longed for their favorite food brands, such as Maggi, Knorr, Kornfrank, and Dr. Oetker products. "The interest in brand names," the GfK reported, "has spread to the lowest social stratum. In other words, today the circle of consumers [who desire] branded goods encompasses almost every sector of the population."[48]

Not all branded products disappeared. Wartime advertisements made it clear that a variety of popular goods were still available. They ran the gamut from lightbulbs to pens to cigarettes. With regard to the latter, whatever ideological qualms the regime had about products harmful to the Volk body gave way in the name of public need. For the first two years of the war, cigarette ads abounded. Astra promised "more joy" for its smokers, Kur Mark boasted about its pristine manufacturing process, and Reemstma conjured romantic images of rural life in the Balkans. Its series of "Macedonian sketches" in support of its R6 brand showed peasants in traditional garb chatting or producing goods. This evoked the völkisch allure of foreign lands that would soon fall under the control of the Wehrmacht.[49] At the end of 1941, the regime prohibited the advertising of tobacco in public spaces and prohibited the use of women, athletes, and cars in cigarette ads.[50] But in journals and magazines, tobacco advertising persisted, even as cigarettes in bombed-out cities became harder to obtain.

Even when a popular product was no longer on the shelf, companies kept its memory alive, hoping that when it returned to the market after the war, consumers would instantly flock to it. Advertising with the phrase "Persil-Werke Düsseldorf" (Persil Works Düsseldorf), for example, allowed Henkel to exploit its long-standing association with its most popular product without claiming that it was in fact available.[51] This strategy ran some risk, according to Paul Mundhenke, of unnecessarily stoking the dreams of housewives and turning them against ersatz products.[52] But he predicted in 1941 that when Persil reappeared, "a storm of jubilation

[47] Ibid., 18.
[48] Ibid.
[49] For these ads see *DDV* 9, no. 12 (April 1940), unpaginated.
[50] Erik Lindner, *Die Reemstmas: Geschichte einer deutschen Unternehmerfamilie* (Hamburg: Hoffmann & Campe, 2007), 240.
[51] Feldenkirchen and Hilger, *Menschen und Marken*, app. 35.
[52] Mundhenke, "Gedanken über unsere Werbung," 18.

FIGURE 19. Window-shopping in wartime Cologne. Stein's photography store and Palm cigar shop, ca. 1943–45. (RWB 19328/39. Photographer: Erich Behnke, Cologne; courtesy of Landesarchiv Nordrhein–Westfalen.)

would move through the hearts of German housewives."[53] Henkel also continued to conduct "internal advertising" through its employee magazine, often linking the war effort to its own products. The company sent regular care packages to its "Persil fighters," who entered battle for "Führer, firm, and fatherland,"[54] and Henkel employees in uniform supposedly declared during military review, "I am a Persil representative" (*Ich bin Persil-Vertreter*).[55] If, according to the GfK, "the pain over lost brand-name goods is considerable,"[56] such "memory advertising" (*Erinnerungswerbung* or *Erinnerungsreklame*) probably did not relieve this anguish. But it did hold out the promise of the public's future reunion with its favorite goods.

The mandated discontinuation of famous products was a major problem facing manufacturers. Another had to do with proscriptions against selfish economic behavior. For companies, the regime's wish to reconcile competition and altruism was simply too difficult to realize, especially as

[53] Ibid., 17.

[54] See, e.g., *Blätter vom Hause* 20, no. 9 (1940): 224, HA.

[55] Letter from 11 April 1940, excerpted in ibid. It is unclear whether soldiers really wrote these letters. They may have been composed by the magazine's staff in Düsseldorf.

[56] "Verbraucher und Markenartikel in den ersten Kriegsmonaten," 14.

the war continued. It was one thing to call for a restrained competition in the name of community. It was another to forswear the self-interestedness that drove marketing in the first place. Although companies continued to produce ads for their own products, the Nazi regime directed their efforts increasingly toward public service propaganda. Henkel was forced to change the name of its advertising department to "consumer education" department, reflecting the fact that almost all of the company's marketing was on behalf of public campaigns.[57] With the assistance of the RVA, Henkel's market competitors Sunlicht and Böhme Fettchemie, along with the DF, which represented the interests of housewives, produced a mountain of materials – films, print ads, radio spots, and lectures – directing people toward correct laundering practices.[58] For Henkel and its competitors, this educational work provoked conflicts with the party and state over whether a firm was sufficiently self-abnegating. As "lecture ladies" (*Vortragsdamen*) traveled the country to speak about washing habits, they faced criticism from officials that their talks did not serve the war effort but rather the company's interests.[59] Despite their agreement not to mention specific Henkel products, the lecturers were seen as still representing corporate priorities over the public good, leading Henkel to constantly reiterate its sense of sacrifice.[60] The main detergent producers also butted heads with the party about how best to reach consumers as shortages grew worse. In the fall of 1942, the DF argued that offering washing tips at a time when laundry supplies were running short only angered women. In contrast, the private companies, desperate to maintain some form of access to the public, felt that in an economy of scarcity, businesses needed more "educational" contact with consumers.[61] This difference of opinion was in part a turf war, with the DF wanting to take over the training and employment of the lecture ladies from private companies. The DF eventually pulled out of the two-and-a-half-year-old lecture series "Proper Washing" (*Sachgemässes Waschen*) in November 1942, citing unnamed misdeeds by one of Henkel's lecturers, and the desire to replace speeches with written brochures.[62] The

---

[57] Mundhenke, "Gedanken über unsere Werbung," 15.
[58] See the letters, film scripts, and ads in R5002/4, BAB.
[59] Mundhenke to RVA, 9 April 1943, R5002/21, BAB.
[60] Mundhenke to RVA, 5 December 1942, R5002/21, BAB.
[61] Sitzungsbericht des RVA stattgefundene Werbe- und Fachbeirat-Sitzung der Waschmittelindustrie, 30 October 1942, R5002/43, BAB.
[62] Mundhenke to RVA, 17 November 1942, R5002/21, BAB.

private companies and the RVA proceeded without the support of the main housewives organization.[63]

The shift in priority from promoting private company needs to meeting the demands of the state provoked conflict not only between the government and firms, but also among companies. We have already seen how businesses had difficulty meeting regulations about unfair competitive practices before 1939. This challenge became even greater during the war, when firms worried about existing regulations and makeshift rules concerning proper behavior, and often fought over the limited opportunities available for advertising. For example, in the initial weeks of the war, there was an agreement among laundry detergent and soap companies (chiefly, Henkel, Böhme Fettchemie, and Sunlicht) not to advertise on behalf of themselves. But when Böhme began "memory advertising" for its gentle wash Fewa product, Henkel protested, wondering why it had agreed to give up such ads when it would have the largest market share in Germany after the war. It was only then, according to Paul Mundhenke, that the company went on to produce its own memory ads. Henkel was not about to take things passively when it felt aggrieved. The firm also complained that its competitor Sunlicht was unfairly using its public education brochures to promote one of its products. "Henkel must be given the same right," Mundhenke asserted.[64]

These conflicts between companies could take a litigious turn. In 1940 Allgäuer, a producer of condensed milk, sued the J. M. Gabler-Saliter Company for using the term "alpine milk" (*Alpenmilch*). The former firm had been employing the phrase, along with a picture of a mountainous landscape, to market its canned milk, and it demanded that the defendant stop using the same phrase. The Berlin supreme court asked the GfK to investigate whether consumers associated "alpine milk" only with the plaintiff's firm, or whether they felt it referred generally to milk produced in the Bavarian Alps, thus open to use by any company that drew milk from cows in the region. The GfK, which conducted a survey for the court, revealed that both were the case: 75 percent of housewives felt "alpine milk" could refer to any condensed milk from the Alps, but these women also identified such a product with the Allgäuer company by a 9 to 1 margin over the competing products made by Gabler-Saliter, Nestle, and Libby.[65] The

[63] Mundhenke to RVA, 15 January 1943, R5002/21, BAB.
[64] Aktennotiz betr. Aufklärungsaktion "Sachgemäßes Waschen," 12 July 1940, R5002/17, BAB.
[65] "Auskunft in Sachen Allgäuer Alpenmilch-Gesellschaft gegen Gabler-Saliter für den 31. Zivilsenat des Kammergerichts (Berlin)," S 1940 21, GfKA.

court decided in favor of the defendant, arguing that the plaintiff could not stake claim to as broad a term as "alpine milk." The decision, however, was overturned on appeal the next year, again indicating the lack of consensus about the rules of marketing during war.[66]

In another case in the fall of 1942, the Friedrich Siemens Works, a producer of gas appliances, gauged the public response to its name. The company was engaged in a legal struggle with the larger and more renowned electrotechnical firm in Berlin over who owned the brand name "Siemens."[67] Given the similarity of the company names, their origins within one family, and the existence of a third Siemens company (a producer of glass canning jars in Dresden), this was not an easy determination. With the help of the GfK, the company found that regardless of age, region, or marital status, the majority of those surveyed associated Siemens with electrical products, many not having heard of the gas appliances company that sponsored the survey (its products were marketed mostly in Eastern Europe). It is not clear what the Friedrich Siemens Works did with this report or how the legal action played out, but both this and the Allgäuer case show that, during the war, combative rules of play were still in effect when it came to trademark protection.

Clearly some companies were flummoxed by the rules of dignified competition. Others were confused by the state's seemingly ad hoc determinations that they had violated a party rule or public decency. As a large finished-goods retailer in Wesermünde, the Schlüter furniture and rug company provides one example of this. In October 1939 it produced two advertisements for its carpets. The first bore the claim: "Still today we offer the same volume to choose from, meticulous service, carpets at a good value, and free delivery." The second stated that "choice and a good value for the price are still today so considerable that a purchase will bring you joy." These seemingly harmless assertions struck the regime as dangerous references to wartime conditions. According to the Advertising Council, the phrase "still today," with its pointed adverb, only drew attention to the fact that people were in fact experiencing wartime privations. Moreover, by reminding its clients that it still had merchandise that the public knew was unavailable at other stores, Schlüter was using its own good fortune to harm its competitors.[68] Schlüter's owner

[66] Appeals court judgment, 23 June 1941, S 1940 20–2, GfKA.
[67] "Die Bedeutung des Wortes 'Siemens' als Warenkenzeichnung," November 1942, S 1942 009 GfKA.
[68] President of Werberat to Möbelfabrik Louis Schlüter Möbel- und Teppichhaus, 15 November 1939, R55/344, BAB.

was astounded by these reprimands. He protested to the Advertising Council that his claims were truthful and actually served the public good during war by countering the constant refrain that everywhere "goods are scare." Moreover, he argued, it was ultimately in the service of newlyweds (and presumably in keeping with the Nazis' pro-natalist policies) to reveal that couples could still furnish their apartments during the war.[69] The Reich economics ministry was sympathetic to Schlüter's position, arguing that references to a large inventory and good prices "are always an especially effective means of advertising and reflect the foundation of competitive advertising."[70] The propaganda ministry ultimately mandated that the words "still today" be removed from all ads but that references to good prices and wide selection could remain.[71]

There was a contradiction at the heart of the Advertising Council's Schlüter ruling. On the one hand, the regime took great pains to convince consumers that during war life went on, albeit with sacrifices; Schlüter's ability to provide "normal" furnishings would presumably bolster this aim. On the other hand, the Nazis also felt that any reminder of a specific company's economic good fortune came at the expense of competing firms. We see here that finding a balance between profit, clean competition, and the public good remained a major challenge during World War II.

The Schlüter case reminds us that during the war companies did not merely surrender to a halfhearted marketing guided only by the needs of the state. There was a push and pull relationship between the regime and private companies. Despite the Nazis' lofty rhetoric about sacrifice and community, more prosaic business concerns about competition were still omnipresent during the war. In an economy defined by price regulations and rationing, the most basic capitalist concerns about markets and proprietorship persisted; a trademark, a company name, and an even playing field were deemed sacred. The Nazi regime would not necessarily have disagreed with this. But its goal of both protecting basic marketing norms and using businesses to promote selfless economic behavior became increasingly unmanageable during World War II. As the mechanisms of supply and demand broke down, the desire among civilian producers to protect one's market territory grew more pronounced and the tensions within the Nazi marketplace grew more insurmountable.

[69] Unnamed owner of Schlüter (Louis Schlüter?) to the president of the Werberat, 18 November 1939, R55/344, BAB.
[70] Dr. E. Koehler, Economics Ministry, to RMVP, 30 November 1939, R55/344, BAB.
[71] RMVP to Schlüter, January 1940, R55/344, BAB.

MARKET RESEARCH DURING THE WAR

Given the dearth of goods, state demands for selfless advertising, and the Advertising Council's unpredictable interventions, companies proceeded cautiously in their marketing. As we have seen, the pressure on firms to function primarily as corporate citizens, however, did not mean that they abandoned their business aims. The perpetuation of self-interested economic activity is evidenced not only by the earlier examples of protests and litigation, but also by the thriving practice of market research throughout World War II. As the main organization involved in consumer reporting, the Society for Consumer Research continued to receive the financial support of companies to investigate shoppers' mind-sets. While the GfK was increasingly pushed to take up war-related projects, the partly profit-driven, partly intellectual enterprise of consumer research remained active until the end of World War II. This section will pick up from the discussion in the preceding chapter by following the GfK projects in the 1940s. The ongoing work of the GfK reveals the delicate balance the regime maintained between private corporate aims, consumer desires, and popular control during wartime.

By the time World War II broke out, the GfK had attained a prominent position in the world of consumer research, advertising, and marketing. Its network of correspondents was widening, the number of corporate board members was increasing, and reports were flowing out of the offices in Nuremberg, often gaining the positive attention of party and government organs. The GfK published a newsletter for its associates, next to *Markt und Verbrauch*, which was circulated widely among advertising professionals and economists. By September 1939 the GfK had produced elaborate reports on consumers' views about a number of well-known companies: Bayer, Schering, and Merck in the pharmaceuticals industry, Henkel in the chemicals field, and Ford, Opel, and Volkswagen in the auto sector, as well as studies of the food, porcelain, and metalware industries. For the correspondents themselves, the *Menschensuche* – the "search for people" to interview – was like an adventure. Armed with a protective identification card, a cheat sheet of questions, and reminders not to put words into people's mouths, "in contrast to the American practice,"[72] these employees traveled to villages and into homes, where

---

[72] Georg Bergler, *Die Entwicklung der Verbrauchsforschung in Deutschland und die Gesellschaft für Konsumforschung bis zum Jahre 1945* (Kallmünz: Michael Laßleben, 1959), 135.

they sometimes conducted hourlong interviews with an entire family present. They usually earned one pfennig per questionnaire, which they returned to the main office.[73]

It is ironic that the GfK initiated its cutting-edge research at a time when tightening regulations limited the volume of consumer goods. The run-up to the war and the war itself presented a quandary for the GfK. Rationing, price setting, and a managed economy would presumably have deprived the organization of its raison d'être. Without normal market exchange, how would companies benefit from studying consumers' supposed "choices"? If, after September 1939, they had such a concern, Wilhelm Vershofen and his colleagues did not air them. They asserted publicly their continuing, even increased, relevance in this new economic setting. In the fall of 1939, GfK associate Ludwig Erhard expressed his confidence that the war would give his organization new opportunities for work, and in the optimistic summer of 1940, when the Nazis' long-term dominance of Europe seemed ensured, he and Vershofen exchanged reflections on the coming post-victory peace.[74] In an appendix to the first volume of his and Proesler's handbook for consumer research (*Handbuch der Vebrauchsforschung*), Wilhelm Vershofen also declared his desire to keep the GfK germane at a time when the economy was being centralized. The steering of the market and the rationing of goods, he argued, made understanding the demands of the consumer even more vital.[75] He had long embraced the rule that "man cannot live by bread alone," implying his rejection of an overly materialist understanding of consumption, and during the war Vershofen found the rationalist model even more deficient. It was that much more important to understand the effects of economic controls on the population when Germans had less choice in what they consumed. The government and companies had to understand how a constrained consumer economy worked or did not work in conjunction with war.

The GfK proved its relevance by working for both private companies and the state. Over the course of the war, it produced studies for Siemens, Bayer, and J. Weck & Co., a manufacturer of mason jars, as well as for party organizations like the Central Office for Public Health (Hauptamt

[73] Ibid., 131.
[74] Erhard to Verhofen, 7 September 1939, and Erhard to Vershofen, 4 July 1940, in Institut für Wirtschaftsbeobachtung der deutschen Fertigware papers, GfKA, courtesy of Volker Preuss.
[75] Wilhelm Vershofen, *Handbuch der Verbrauchsforschung* vol. 1 (Berlin: Carl Heymanns, 1940), 174–75.

für Volksgesundheit der NSDAP), which, together with the Dr. Hillers peppermint company, commissioned a massive study on the intake of vitamin C drops among coal miners. (It found miners convinced that vitamin C was designed to make them work harder and that it had sexual side effects.)[76] The Nuremberg economists also found that their interviewing techniques could be put use to build more extended profiles of a country at war. The December 1939 study cited in the opening paragraph of this chapter stands out as a revealing snapshot of consumer psychology at the onset of hostilities. The GfK discovered Germans in a panic mode, buying and hording numerous goods that they could not afford.[77] Gold and silver jewelry, watches, and expensive porcelain were flying off the shelves. Consumers were snapping up cameras, radios, record players, entire furniture sets, fur coats, electric ovens, and refrigerators. In the fear that money would become worthless, rural consumers went to extremes, buying typewriters and other goods that "normally would be totally unnecessary on a farm" but that were now seen as valuable objects. As a rule this "senseless buying frenzy" transcended class and income divisions, leading to the almost complete emptying of shelves. Some products remained limited to the upper classes, however, as wealthy women, haunted by the shortages of luxury items during World War I, spent hundreds of marks on expensive perfumes and creams in the days following the outbreak of war.

GfK correspondents reported with clear fascination this "flight into material assets," born of the horrible memories of the Great Inflation of 1923. Time and again they cited fears of inflation as the main reason for the "insecurity and mistrust" sweeping the nation. Rumors about wild price hikes helped provoke a "nervous, worked-up atmosphere" that had by the end of 1939 settled into a sort of "illness" that infected the mass of consumers.[78]

The initially panicked public response would develop into a more resigned making-do, and the GfK documented the mixture of optimism and dissatisfaction that Germans invested in the economy and the

---

[76] On the "Vitamin C-Aktion im deutschen Bergbau 1941" and its initiation by Hundhausen see Bergler, *Entwicklung der Verbrauchsforschung*, 172; Peer Heinelt, *PR-Päpste: Die kontinuierlichen Karrieren von Carl Hundhausen, Albert Oeckl und Franz Ronnenberger* (Berlin: Karl Dietz, 2003), 51, 52; and Christoph Conrad, "Observer les consommateurs: Études de marché et histoire de la consommation en Allemagne, des années 1930 aux années 1960." *Mouvement Social*, no. 206 (January–March 2004): 17–39.
[77] "Verbraucher und Markenartikel in den ersten Kriegsmonaten," 2.
[78] Ibid.

practice of marketing in wartime. In a GfK study about the reception of Bayer ads, consumers looked forward to the use of the company's tropical medicine "in our future colonies" but also berated Bayer for producing unnecessary ads in a setting where free enterprise was limited. The quality of Bayer was already well known, argued several interviewees, and the company bought ad space only to financially support newspapers and magazines.[79] During a time of shortages, some consumers did not readily countenance the seemingly cozy relationship between the media and corporations.

Consumers were critical not only of advertisements and other forms of economic "propaganda." As the war dragged on, some were also put off by the regime's constant directives about frugal household consumption. This was revealed in a GfK study commissioned by the RVA in the fall of 1942, which is worth considering in detail to indicate the public's attitude toward propaganda and the challenges the Nuremberg economists faced in fulfilling government contracts. With this report, the GfK's specific task was to evaluate the effectiveness of the regime's "enlightenment work" (*Auflklärungsarbeit*) on the consumer and thereby determine where the RVA might amplify its efforts in the "national economic, home economic, and cultural spheres."[80] After interviewing five thousand people, the GfK concluded that the public on the whole supported the RVA's efforts to school consumers, and statistics within the report seemed to bear out this assessment. But the many negative quotes within the report belied such a sweeping conclusion. Consumer after consumer complained about the RVA's work, or claimed to have "never thought about it," leading one correspondent to remark with frustration that people appeared to "move blind and deaf through the world." It's like "running against a wall," complained another, in reference to many people's indifference to or even outright dismissal of the RVA's work. "People are so distrustful," complained another correspondent. Housewives, in particular older women, felt insulted by the propaganda, asserting that they already knew how to wash, cook, and clean in a thrifty manner without being preached to by the government.[81] Other people complained that they had never even received RVA propaganda, indicating that there were distribution problems, especially on

---

[79] "'Die Bayer-Wertwerbung 1941' in Urteil des Lesers," Summer 1941, S 1941 007, pp. 33 and 41, respectively, GfKA.

[80] "Die Arbeit des Reichsausschusses für Volkswirtschaftliche Aufklärung im Urteil des Verbrauchers," Spring 1943, S 1943 008, p. 1, GfKA.

[81] For these quotes see ibid., 15.

farms and in villages.[82] Consumers' expressions were often harsh, to the
surprise of the GfK interviewers: "A waste of paper!" "Enough Already!"
"Yet another piece of trash."[83] The paper devoted to producing these materials, argued a Nuremberg housewife, would find better use in the printing of children's schoolbooks.[84] Consumers also expressed their desires for
higher-quality goods, rather than constant reminders about how to make
do with so little.

More than the reports for private companies, this study spotlighted
the population's discontent during a time of wartime scarcity. But they
are notable not only for highlighting consumers' frustrations, but also
for revealing a widespread suspicion of the government and its "education" efforts. Despite the GfK's finding that the German public felt
positive about the RVA, in the report interviewees regularly expressed a
view that government propaganda was nothing more than *Reklame*, or
a form of hucksterism practiced by advertisers and state officials in trying to sway the public. Many people, according to one correspondent,
expressed "a strong distrust of anything that has to do with the words
Aktion or *Propaganda*."[85] One correspondent discovered that in the
"newly incorporated regions" of the Reich, such as western Poland and
Lorraine, consumers had an almost entirely dismissive attitude toward
any measure coming from the Reich government. It is not clear why the
new areas of the Reich were so unresponsive to propaganda, though one
correspondent attributed it to these populations' not having had "ten
years of National Socialist schooling" like the Reich Germans.[86] With
respect to the claim that RVA literature had not reached everyone, the
GfK asserted that the war simply distracted people and made them less
willing to pay attention to propaganda materials. Indeed, the efforts to
feed families and the constant worry about loved ones on the front left
people apathetic or angry, and many interviewees simply wanted to talk
about the length of the war and the possibility of its ending soon.[87]

Such dismissive responses, it appears, left the GfK in a quandary about
how to present such discouraging data to the RVA. Even though it could
cite evidence of pervasive support, the Nuremberg economists did not find
appealing the prospect of having to present any disapproving opinions

[82] Ibid., 12.
[83] Ibid., 13.
[84] Ibid.
[85] Ibid., 10.
[86] Ibid., 11.
[87] Ibid., 169.

to a state and party agency. The document, therefore, issued a series of caveats to dampen its negativity. In effect, the GfK downplayed the significance of its own findings, pointing to the difficulty of determining the effects of household propaganda based solely on the reactions of interviewees. Rather, it conceded, the true measure would have to be in the data about, say, whether the demand for coal or the use of laundry detergent had actually receded. But what about the fact that so many consumers were unhappy with their economic situations? Here the GfK implored the RVA to put its results in perspective and not to take the grumbling as a sign that the campaigns were not working. As a rule, asserted the report, people had an easier time explaining why they disliked something than why they liked it:

It is solely the human joy of criticizing that is at work here and that could give the impression that the consumer has rejected the educational campaigns entirely. Furthermore, one must not forget that the educational work of the RVA, like every advertisement by definition, works on the level of the subconscious, even when it is rejected on the conscious level. It would therefore be totally wrong if the consumer's inability to respond positively, or even his or her dismissive attitude, were equated with failure.[88]

With these assessments, the RVA had evidence that sections of the population were unhappy not only about the economy, but also about the government itself. As with most GfK studies, it is not clear what the commissioning organization actually did with the findings, or whether the RVA took any comfort in the insistence that its propaganda was slowly working on the subconscious level. It is doubtful, however, that the RVA was surprised by these results. The report came out in April 1943, shortly after the German war effort had taken a terrible turn in Stalingrad. With dispiriting news emerging from the eastern front and Allied bombs falling on German cities, the population in the winter and spring of 1943 was on edge. That month the Social Democrats in exile wrote of "middle-class bitterness, growing unrest in the army, ... and a 'hope for the end.'"[89] This public desperation surely had an effect on the responses to the GfK's questions, which were collected as the Battle of Stalingrad ground down.

While the RVA was already aware of widespread dissatisfaction, it was no doubt unsettling to hear people complain so openly. How can

---

[88] Ibid., 7.
[89] *Sozialistische Mitteilungen* 48 (April 1943), http://library.fes.de/fulltext/sozmit/som-von-aussen.htm (accessed 25 April 2010).

we explain consumers' willingness to protest their conditions? It might
be due to the fact that the report protected interviewees' anonymity, thus
giving them license to grumble. But it is striking how willing Germans
were to criticize the government to strangers, who might, for all they
knew, have direct ties to the Gestapo. If there was a fear of speaking dis-
missively about state programs during the height of the war, it did not
manifest itself in this study. The results therefore challenge any lingering
assumptions that the population was paralyzed by fear of the state; rather,
anxiety was combined with both anger and a cautious optimism that the
war would be over soon. They also present a very different picture than
Götz Aly's portrayal of a populace bribed into lending its support by the
infusion of war booty and by progressive social policies.

Given the GfK's work for the RVA and its desire to massage its data,
one might surmise that the organization was fully under the thumb of
the regime. But when it came to its intellectual project of understanding
mass consumption, the Nuremberg school's wartime work only gradually
came to reflect Nazi priorities. Indeed, it showed a remarkable continuity with prewar, transnational discussions about marketing, advertising,
branding, and consumer psychology. In particular, the GfK remained
focused on the United States as a point of orientation; understanding the
consumer and, more broadly, Germany's relationship to modernity meant
comprehending the nature of American society, business, and culture. It is
well known that the war with the United States was accompanied by sustained anti-American propaganda, which depicted Franklin Roosevelt as
a war criminal, American society as a "Jewified" cultural wasteland, and
Americans – especially women – as superficial, spoiled, and unsatisfied.[90]
But in the scholarly and business worlds one can detect a greater mix of
envy, admiration, and disdain for the United States.

This is borne out by a wartime GfK report on household and kitchen
appliances in the United States, based on a study of American advertising. It was prepared in January 1943 by Carl Hundhausen, who, as we
saw, was a devoted Nazi, German nationalist, and avid America watcher.
Hundhausen was asked to survey the latest technological advances in
the United States to determine whether they might spark innovation in
similar branches of German industry, subsequently "eas[ing] the burdens

[90] G. Niegisch, "Verjudete USA-Wirtschaft!" *Wirtschaftspolitische Parole* 4, no. 2 (January
1939): 47–51; and D. Hammer, "Die Frau in den USA" (speech in Berlin, ca. 1942–43),
NS18/1075, BAB. See also Phillip Gassert, *Amerika im Dritten Reich: Ideologie,
Propaganda und Volksmeinung, 1933–1945* (Stuttgart: Steiner, 1997), 323.

on the housewife."[91] Because of a lack of access to American periodicals during the war, Hundhausen had to rely on advertisements from the 1930s. In the winter of 1942–43, he paged through old Sears Roebuck and Montgomery Ward catalogues, as well as *Life* magazine, *Printers' Ink*, and *Advertising Age*, to gather visual samples of cutting-edge appliances in the United States. The final report was a testament to the panoply of gadgets available to Americans: almost a hundred photocopied images of coffee machines, vegetable juicers, food mixers, irons, vacuum cleaners, gas ranges, automatic-timer thermostats, washing machines, and refrigerators were accompanied by detailed descriptions of their uses and advantages. With a note of envy, Hundhausen marveled at the time-saving devices and the penchant for automatic controls in household goods in the United States (though he worried that the rationalization of the home might diminish the "quality" of a housewife's work).[92] He concluded that, in "rich America" there was little concern for appliances that prevented the waste of food and raw materials.[93] Rather, Americans cared most about hygiene and saving time. Hundhausen did not explicitly contrast this to Germany, but it was clear that he was both in awe of and appalled by Americans' profligacy, which was hardly an option in Germany in early 1943, when cities were being attacked from the air and citizens were coaxing the last bits of nutrition out of rationed food supplies.

The GfK conducted other studies on the United States during the war, including a 1944 report on nutrition.[94] Vershofen and his colleagues also read with interest American books that acknowledged the importance of communal interests over individual gain, such as radical intellectual Alfred M. Bingham's *Insurgent America*, which called for a middle-class uprising against capitalism.[95] This wartime fascination with the United States reveals how consistent the intellectual mission of the GfK remained, even

---

[91] "Technischer Stand der Haushaltmaschinen, Apparate u. Geräte in U.S.A. Untersuchung auf Grund der amerikanischen Wirtschaftswerbung," end of January 1943, S 1943 002, p. 6, GfKA.

[92] Hundhausen expressed this concern at a GfK meeting on home economics a few months later. See report on the GfK meeting concerning the theme "Wandlungen in der Hauswirtschaft?" 7 July 1943, R63/180, BAB.

[93] "Technischer Stand der Haushaltmaschinen," 12.

[94] "Entwicklung neuartiger Nahrungsmittel in Amerika während des Krieges" (1944). See Bergler, *Entwicklung der Verbrauchsforschung*, 152.

[95] Alfred M. Bingham, *Insurgent America: The Revolt of the Middle-Class* (New York: Harper and Brothers, 1935). Cited in Hundhausen/Vershofen exchange: "Verbraucherforschung – Ein Meinungsaustausch," *Markt und Verbrauch* 12, nos. 11 and 12 (Fall 1940): 258–73.

FIGURE 20. In 1943 the GfK studied this and other advertisements to prepare a wartime report on American household conveniences. *Montgomery Ward Catalogue*, no. 122 (Spring 1935): 311.

with the contraction of the civilian economy upon which the enterprise of consumer research was based. Because the Nuremberg school saw its work as a meeting of theory and praxis, it could fall back on the former when the conditions for the latter were inhospitable. But in fact, the GfK did not have to retreat into the world of ideas. Even amid the regulated economy of wartime Germany, both aspects of the GfK enterprise remained alive. The organization continued to interview increasingly disgruntled consumers, and it measured the consumption of restricted goods. In short, the GfK explored the question that drove a specific study in 1941: "What would the consumer buy if tomorrow he could shop freely again?"[96] Fueling this dual enterprise were the driving intellectual concerns of the time: the meaning of mass society, individualism, community, and capitalism, and their relationship to the everyday act of shopping. Even a devastating war did not stop Vershofen and his colleagues from pursuing their exploratory mission into mass consumer society.

THE GFK AND NAZI IMPERIALISM

The GfK's interest in the United States reveals an autonomy with respect to its primary intellectual agenda. Despite its own anti-American propaganda, the state had little inclination to temper ongoing discussions about the enemy if they could lead to a more efficient and prosperous postbellum Germany. This is not to say that the GfK was left to its own devices. Quite the contrary. As World War II proceeded, the Nazi regime found ways of exploiting a consumer research organization well versed in observational techniques. The GfK became involved in policies that were explicitly part of the effort to establish a German-dominated economic region in Europe. This major link to the regime's wartime policies came through the Southeastern Europe Society (Südosteuropa Gesellschaft – SOEG), a Vienna-based organization that played a key role in the expropriation of resources and the planning of economic policy in the occupied and unoccupied areas of Southeastern Europe.[97] The SOEG would turn to the GfK for help.

---

[96] This was the driving question behind a GfK investigation titled "Die Bedarfslage im Frühjahr 1941." See Bergler, *Entwicklung der Verbrauchsforschung*, 178.

[97] On the SOEG, see Dietrich Orlow, *The Nazis in the Balkans: A Case Study in Totalitarian Politics* (Pittsburgh: University of Pittsburgh Press, 1968), 16–66. On the importance of Southeastern European markets to the Nazis, see Werner Suhr, "Die Wirtschaftsdurchleuchtung des südosteuropäischen Raumes," *Der Markenartikel* 11, no. 2 (March–April 1944): 17–20.

The GfK's work with the SOEG had its origins in the Anschluss of 1938. After the annexation of Austria, the GfK established a consumer research branch in Vienna, headed by Hanns Kropff.[98] It is unclear what data this Austrian counterpart produced in its first two years, but in 1941 the Vienna organization took a new form and a new name: the Vienna Institute for Economic Research (Wiener Institut für Wirtschaftsforschung – Vienna Institute). The German economics minister, Walther Funk, placed it under the direct control of the SOEG,[99] which along with the GfK and president Wilhelm Mann's company, IG Farben, funded the institute. The IfW in Nuremberg provided personnel to Vienna and was in charge of carrying out the scholarly work based on the data it gathered. The institute was, according to Vershofen, "effectively a branch of the GfK."[100] Next to Vershofen, familiar figures from the GfK sat on the advisory board – Georg Bergler, Wilhelm Mann, Ludwig Erhard, Johannes Martin Ditterich – as did local Viennese economic leaders, a representative from the Advertising Council, and members of the SOEG.[101] With Kropff eventually taking on an advisory role, day-to-day operations were handled by Vershofen's former doctoral student, Rolf Grünwald, who had graduated from the Hindenberg-Hochschule (the new name of Business School of Nuremberg) in 1938 and who worked at the IfW. Grünwald was eager to bring the Nuremberg school's ideas and methods to the Vienna Institute.

The Vienna Institute was officially launched in June 1941, the same month that the Nazis invaded the Soviet Union. In preparation for Operation Barbarossa, the Nazis had overrun Yugoslavia and Greece in April and May, initiating a brutal occupation that would result in massive causalities on Balkan soil and in the death camps of Poland. Later in 1941 Hungary, Romania, Bulgaria, and Croatia joined a military pact with the Axis powers with the aim of expanding their own territories. The Wehrmacht rapidly established hegemony in Southeastern Europe, and pro-Nazi economists set to work planning for the cultivation of future markets in the postwar "new order." The hope was that an increase in the purchasing power and standard of living in this region

[98] Heinelt, *PR-Päpste*, 51.
[99] Orlow, *Nazis in the Balkans*, 43.
[100] "Bericht über die Ordentliche Mitgliederversammlung der GfK, 24 June 1941," *Vertrauliche Nachrichten* 15 (July 1941): 17, GfKA.
[101] For correspondence among these individuals concerning the business of the Vienna Institute, see R63/73 and 180, BAB. On consultations between the Advertising Council and the Institute, see Heinrichsbauer to Erhard, 17 September 1941, R63/180, BAB.

would result in greater demand for German manufactured goods and would position these traditionally poorer parts of the continent in a prosperous, economically integrated Europe. Wilhelm Mann's colleague Anton Reithinger, an economist within the Reich Statistical Office and the director of IG Farben's economics department, helped promote this vision that outward-looking firms like Farben shared – that of an economically vibrant Southeastern European realm under German tutelage.[102]

At this moment of supreme confidence, when Germans predicted victory on all fronts, the SOEG, according to Dietrich Orlow, "began its activities as an agency which was to play an important part in establishing and administering the New Europe."[103] It drew into its leadership active Nazis. Economics Minister Walther Funk was the official patron of the organization, and Baldur von Schirach served as the SOEG's president. Schirach had been replaced as head of the Hitler Youth in 1940 and was now *Gauleiter* of Vienna, where he was responsible, among other things, for the movement of Viennese Jews to concentration camps. In charge of daily operations was the organization's secretary, August Heinrichsbauer, a former business lobbyist and supporter of "left-wing" Nazi Gregor Strasser before the latter's falling out with Hitler in 1932. While not a party member himself, Heinrichsbauer had close connections to Funk and other Nazis in Berlin, and he represented the SOEG's most direct contact to the GfK, presiding over studies in conjunction with Vershofen.[104] Finally, Reinhard Heydrich, deputy Reich protector of Bohemia and Moravia, cosponsored an SOEG convention in December 1941 in Prague, where he lectured about the economy in occupied Czechoslovakia.[105]

---

[102] Anthon Reithinger, "Die Kaufkraftsteigerung als wichtiges Problem der europäischen Neuordnung," *DDV* 10, nos. 1 and 2 (January 1941): 72–74. On Reithinger's work with IG Farben, see Peter Hayes, *Industry and Ideology: IG Farben in the Nazi Era* (Cambridge: Cambridge University Press, 1987), 272–73.

[103] Orlow, *Nazis in the Balkans*, 15.

[104] On Heinrichsbauer's career see S. Jonathan Wiesen, *West German Industry and the Challenge of the Nazi Past, 1945–1955* (Chapel Hill: University of North Carolina Press, 2001), 74.

[105] Reinhard Heydrich, "Die Wirtschaft als maßgeblicher Faktor der staatlichen und politischen Neuordnung Böhmen und Mährens im Reich," in program for the *Tagung der SOEG und der Deutschen Gesellschaft der Wirtschaft in Böhmen und Mähren*, Prague, 17 and 18 December 1941, NL Vershofen, MS 2763, box 9, files: "Südosteuropa-Gesellschaft/April 1941–November 1941" and "Wiener Institut für Verbrauchs- u. Absatzforschung, November 1941–November 1943" [hereafter "SOEG files"], Erlangen.

For Vershofen and other Nuremberg economists, a major concern was to control the staffing and the methodologies employed in Vienna, as well as to prove that consumer research was still relevant in a total war. The challenges were immediate, as the Vienna Institute instantly felt pressured to conduct studies that would benefit policy makers interested in economic production but that risked diverging from the GfK's primary interest in finished goods and mass consumption.[106] In the fall of 1941 Heinrichsbauer had the Vienna Institute conduct a study on the beer industry in greater Vienna. By exploring what cold beverages people consumed, the Nazis hoped both to cut unneeded production capacity and to impose new anti-alcohol measures.[107] Despite pressure not to disappoint party members, Vershofen was furious when he learned about this push to investigate the production side of the economic equation. Moreover, he reminded Heinrichsbauer that the GfK was interested in *finished goods*. Yet Vershofen ultimately agreed to the project, and Ludwig Erhard was placed in charge of the "business economics" angle of the beer study.[108]

Here we see the beginning of the GfK's wartime shift from a "consumer research" organization to a state-sponsored "market research" institution. Despite Vershofen's desire in the early 1930s to establish a niche in *consumer* studies, the exigencies of war forced him to reconsider this. The work of the IfW and the GfK came to resemble that of the Advertising Council's marketing division, which after being established in 1940 conducted studies about Scandinavia, the Baltic States, Bulgaria, Turkey, and other countries.[109] Even this pragmatic shift did not guarantee the success of the new institute in Austria. After economists in Nuremberg and Vienna established working relations with the Nazi authorities, research was continually interrupted by the government's threats to shut down both institutes.[110] With much pleading on the part of Vershofen, however, the GfK and the Vienna Institute persisted, with the latter investigating markets for textiles, bicycles, motorcycles,

[106] Vershofen to Grünwald, 5 November 1941, NL Vershofen, box 9, SOEG files, Erlangen.
[107] On this report, "Der Getränkverbrauch in Wien," see Grünwald to Bergler, 7 August 1942, NL Vershofen, box 9, SOEG files, Erlangen, and Heinrichsbauer to GfK, 16 November 1942, R63/180, BAB.
[108] See Erhard to Heinrichsbauer, 24 January 1942, R63/180, BAB.
[109] Westphal, *Werbung im Dritten Reich*, 140. See also Pamela E. Swett, "Preparing for Victory: Heinrich Hunke, the Nazi Werberat, and West German Prosperity," *Central European History* 42, no. 4 (December 2009): 675–707.
[110] Vershofen to Heinrichsbauer, 1 March 1943, and Grünwald to Vershofen, 21 March 1943, NL Vershofen, box 9, SOEG files, Erlangen.

automobiles, pens, typewriters, pocket watches, alarm clocks, and mason jars.[111] The Viennese work culminated in October 1943 with the release of a hundred-page study of the economy of "the new German eastern realm."[112] The report, which was heralded by Hermann Göring in his capacity as Four Year Plan plenipotentiary, focused on Hungary, Romania, Bulgaria, Yugoslavia, Greece, and Turkey, and its themes included the ethnic makeup and climactic conditions of the region, as well as living standards, social divisions, marital status, building plans, and the outlook for the export of German finished goods (most prominently pharmaceuticals, household appliances, books, and office supplies) to this area.[113] For Rolf Grünwald, the report's author, this investigation contributed to a larger goal of understanding Germany's economic opportunities in all of occupied Eastern Europe.[114] Reading the report, one could almost forget that across the territories under examination – with the temporary exception of Hungary – Jews and "partisans" had been murdered as part of this broader economic-ethnic engineering.

During the last two years of the war, both the GfK in Nuremberg and the Vienna Institute enjoyed the support of the authorities, but they searched widely for projects to make up for their increasing cash shortfalls. Vershofen and Wilhelm Mann began calling on old contacts to give projects to the Vienna Institute in order to keep it from closing. In 1944, at the cost of 1,500 reichsmarks per month, IG Farben commissioned regular studies from the financially strapped Vienna Institute on purchasing habits in Southeastern European and potential markets for the company's products. In September 1944 leading producers of glass, ceramics, and wood arranged for a study from the GfK on the specific needs for finished goods (there was, for example, a dearth of bedroom dressers

[111] Grünwald to Bergler, 19 January 1943, NL Vershofen, Box 9, SOEG files, and Grünwald to Vershofen 12 April 1944, Box 5, File: "Wiener Institut, 1. December 1943 bis 23. December 1959" (continuation of two files in box 9) [hereafter box 5, SOEG file], and Grünwald to Vershofen, 29 April 1944, NL Vershofen, box 5, SOEG file, Erlangen. On textiles specifically, see "Marktuntersuchung über Textilerzeugung und Textilverbrauch in den Südostländern," questionnaire prepared by Vershofen, July 1941, R63/155, BAB.

[112] Heinelt, *PR-Päpste*, 51.

[113] "Der Südosteuropäische Wirtschaftsraum und seine Bedeutung als Absatzmarkt für Konsumfertigwaren," prepared by Rolf Grünwald, October 1943, in NL Vershofen, box 9, SOEG files, Erlangen. See also the revised version of this from the following year, "Südosteuropa als Absatzmarkt für Konsumfertigwaren" (1944), R63/275 and 276, BAB.

[114] Rolf Grünwald, "Neues Werden im deutschen Osten," *Südost-Echo* (4 December 1942), in NL Vershofen, box 9, SOEG files, Erlangen.

but not of beds) in bombed-out cities.[115] At one point, Grünwald and Vershofen also considered soliciting work from the armaments ministry, though it is unclear what came of this idea.[116]

As late as March 1944, Otto Ohlendorf, deputy secretary of state in the economics ministry, expressed his support for the continued work of the institute, perhaps under the influence of Erhard, who was working with the SS *Standartenführer* on matters relating to postwar planning.[117] In October of that year, the Vienna Institute was destroyed in an Allied bombing attack, forcing employees to relocate to a temporary building until the end of the war. Amid the heavy bombing of Vienna, Grünwald conducted research on war damage in the Austrian cities of Klagenfurt, Salzburg, and Innsbruck.[118] He and his associates spent much of the day in bomb shelters, and at night they would work by candlelight and flashlight.[119] Meanwhile, in Nuremberg in the last years of the war, the GfK increasingly conducted studies in conjunction with party and government organizations, such as an investigation into the consumption of crispbread (*Knäckebrot*), carried out by the Main Office of Public Health,[120] and an examination of how wartime regulations affected the use of laundry bleach and other stain removers.[121] Wilhelm Mann, who was a member of the Reich Committee for Combating Cancer, also considered a national public poll on views about cancer.[122] With more and more of its correspondents being called off to war, the GfK's work became sporadic, with the final study having to do with the building industry. The last meeting of the board took place in April 1945, but the GfK's headquarters had been destroyed the prior autumn.[123]

---

[115] Vershofen to Grünwald, 19 September 1944, NL Vershofen, box 5, SOEG file, Erlangen.

[116] Vershofen to Grünwald, 20 September 1944, NL Vershofen, box 9, SOEG files, Erlangen.

[117] Alfred C. Mierzejewski, *Ludwig Erhard: A Biography* (Chapel Hill: University of North Carolina Press, 2004), 21–22.

[118] Leiter der Reichsstelle für Raumordnung (im Auftrag Puttkammer) to Wiener Institut, 19 September 1944, NL Vershofen, box 5, SOEG file, Erlangen.

[119] On Ohlendorf see Vershofen to Grünwald, 5 March 1945, NL Vershofen, box 5, SOEG file, Erlangen.

[120] Vershofen to Mann, 28 February 1942, NL Vershofen, MS 2763, box 9, Mann file, Erlangen.

[121] "Wandlungen in den Einkaufsgewohnheiten für Zusatzwaschmittel," January 1944, S 1944 006, GfKA.

[122] Mann to Vershofen, 17 November 1942, NL Vershofen, MS 2763, box 9, Mann file, Erlangen.

[123] Bergler, *Entwicklung der Verbrauchsforschung*, 102.

The wartime work of the GfK, and that of the Vienna Institute in particular, raises a question about how deeply the Nuremberg school became enmeshed in the policies of military occupation and genocide. Clearly, the GfK, like many institutions, saw working for the war effort and ingratiating itself with the regime as survival mechanisms. To keep alive its project of understanding consumers, the Nuremberg economists felt they had to accommodate themselves to Nazi wartime demands; without commissions from the state, there would be no funds to pursue its intellectual aims. But Vershofen and his colleagues surely knew that planning the new economy in Southeastern Europe had a political and racial dimension. It was a major component of the Nazis' imperialist and autarkic plans, and by conducting research for the very organization responsible for this economic reordering, the SOEG, the Nuremberg school contributed to the oppressive policies in the East. It was not directly responsible for the crimes in the Balkans, but by being drawn into the Nazis' occupation policies, the GfK cannot claim to have stood on the sidelines, merely beating out a marginal existence while the war raged.

The connections between consumer research, marketing, and crimes against humanity are indirect. But the important point is that the "normal" work of selling goods and promoting brands always took place alongside, and often overlapped with, the Nazis' violent racial aims. To the Nazi leadership, links between a German *Grossraumwirtschaft* – filled with new markets and new consumers – and a racially "cleansed" population in the East was self-evident.[124] To be sure, in contrast to Aryanization and the exploitation of slave labor in ghettos and camps, the daily work of marketing seems like a banal footnote to Hitler's brutal policies. But on the pages of Nazi economic journals, this could reveal itself to be a gruesome banality. For example, an article on the economic "dejewification of Europe" appeared in *DDV* in 1941.[125] It was filled with country-by-country statistical breakdowns of the Jewish presence in business – from Bulgaria to Hungary to Romania to Western Europe – and it promised great economic advances with the removal of Jews. As *DDV* readers contemplated how the absence of Jews would "strengthen the productivity of the European economy," they could also consider

[124] On *Grossraum* and race see Mark Mazower, *Hitler's Empire: How the Nazis Ruled Europe* (New York: Penguin, 2008), 237. See also the articles published by the Gesellschaft für Europäische Wirtschaftsplanung und Grossraumwirtschaft, in *Nationale Wirtschaftsordnung und Grossraumwirtschaft*, 1941 and 1942 volumes.

[125] Alfred Maelicke, "Die Entjudung in Europa," *DDV* 10, nos. 1 and 2 (January 1941): 74–80.

the five advertisements that accompanied the article: one for Deutsche
Bank, another for NSU "Quick" motorcycles, another for Kathreiner
malt coffee, another for a commemorative plaque bearing the image of
a cathedral, and a final one for a Berlin ad agency, offering its skills in
advertising within a firm, across Germany, and abroad. The text of the
article and the accompanying ads together offered the varied motifs of
the Nazi economy: the power of the banking industry; the celebration
of motorized speed; the necessity of wartime ersatz products and coffee substitutes; the embrace of nationalism and tradition; the supposed
normality of business life, with the persistence of domestic and overseas
marketing; and the removal of Jewry from the "entire organism of the
national state." Here was the Third Reich in microcosm – a fascist state
friendly to industry, demanding sacrifice and loyalty, holding out the
promise of mass mobility, and totally devoted to racial purity. The work
of the GfK and the Vienna Institute during the war bespoke the pas-
tiche of ideals that constituted the Nazi marketplace, at once representing
the voice of business, the desires of the consumer, the intellectual work
of understanding the masses, and the necessity of toeing the regime's
imperialist and racist line.

The story of the GfK during World War II is, therefore, not a one-
sided portrait of complicity. Rather, as with many institutions in Nazi
Germany, it is one of opportunity, exploitation, conformity, and survival.
Throughout the war the GfK, like its Vienna branch, struggled to remain
relevant. Between July 1941 and the end of 1943, it undertook twenty-
six investigations. But in the summer of 1943, the GfK stopped taking
on new assignments from private companies and henceforth worked for
the state. Ironically, even as the organization tried to prove its utility
to the regime, more and more companies were becoming members of
the GfK.[126] These members would serve as the foundation of a renewed
organization, which continued its efforts to discover the voice of the consumer in the rubble of a destroyed Germany.

By the end of World War II, private advertising and marketing had all but
disappeared from Germany. There was little left for companies to work
with. Severe shortages of paper and packaging – products that were in
any case being diverted to military use – meant limited opportunities for
ad campaigns. Already starting in April 1941, newspapers with a circulation of more than fifty thousand could no longer offer ads larger than

---

[126] Bergler, *Entwicklung der Verbrauchsforschung*, 181.

one-quarter of a page; for newspapers with lower print runs, a half-page was allowed.[127] The sizes were shrunk even further as the war proceeded, such that by January 1945 a typical edition of *DDV* contained only a few pages of advertising at the end. There were still ads for the products of daily life – pencils, tools, wine, stoves, and watches – and typical advertising motifs: trust, family, home, and security. But gone was any visual appeal.[128] At most there were the basics: a company logo, a watch, a roll of toilet paper, the silhouette of a doctor listening to a patient's heart.[129] In May 1941 travel guides, maps, and brochures could no longer contain ads from "outside" companies, and two years later, all ads were banished from reference works, address books, and most other publications other than newspapers and magazines.[130] Nor could one distribute ads without permission. By September 1944 little profit-driven advertising remained; all ads that were not directly approved or that did not have specific war- or state-related aims were prohibited.[131] The regime's attempts to balance private needs, competition, quality, and public good foundered in the midst of total war.

Such limitations did not stop business leaders from imagining a happier, consumer-friendlier postwar Germany. In 1940, when victory looked immanent, they had shared visions of a new order that would increase Germans' standard of living. In this consumerist utopia, the connections between supply and demand would be reestablished and a vibrant German economy, driven by consumption, would dominate Europe. After the tides of war had turned in 1943, economic leaders still clung to this image, with some blindly adhering to the Nazi vision until the end and others illegally mapping a post-Nazi order. After leaving the GfK (following a bitter falling-out with Wilhelm Vershofen), Ludwig Erhard began drawing together his postbellum ideas, arguing in 1944 that "the best method for satisfying public needs remains a competitive market," based on a massive increase of consumer goods.[132] While

[127] Matthias Rücker, *Wirtschaftswerbung unter Nationalsozialismus: Rechtliche Ausgestaltung der Werbung und Tätigkeit des Werberats der deutschen Wirtschaft* (Frankfurt am Main: Peter Lang, 2000), 216.
[128] See, e.g., ads in *DDV* 14, no. 1 (January 1945) and *DDV* 14, no. 2 (January 1945) respectively; ads placed at the end of the issues.
[129] See ads in *DDV* 13, no. 5 (February 1944); ads placed at the end of the issue.
[130] Rücker, *Wirtschaftswerbung unter Nationalsozialismus*, 218.
[131] Ibid., 219; and Sitzungsbericht des RVA stattgefundene Werbe- und Fachbeirat-Sitzung der Waschmittelindustrie, 17 May 1944, R5002/43, BAB.
[132] Quote taken from Mierzejewski, *Ludwig Erhard*, 20.

not everyone agreed with him about free markets, economic leaders nonetheless understood shopping and consuming as key components of any future economy. As for companies themselves, until the war was over they would have to eke out an existence that was essentially severed from the consumer. Through propaganda films or state-sponsored drives, they did their best to assure consumers that their products would be back soon.

Here we are reminded that, even during war, companies tried to offer the appearance of business normality. The Nazis asked them to reconcile their interest in profit with service to the state, but also to offer a semblance of business as usual. For large companies that produced war material, this was quite practical. But firms that sold mostly civilian goods found this request difficult to fulfill. Companies noted worriedly, for example, that many of their advertisers and salesmen had gone off to the front, forcing them to curtail traditional practices such as visiting customers in their homes.[133] For larger marketers like Henkel, it did not help that its "consumer education" department was destroyed by Allied bombs in May 1943.[134] Until the final stages of the war, however, companies displayed their remaining wares, put money into consumer research, and created ever smaller advertisements. And their intellectual work proceeded apace, as businessmen, economists, and market professionals debated the nature of American consumption, the practice of consumer psychology, and the methods of mass persuasion. They discussed the meaning of liberalism, command economics, and the relationship between supply and demand until the last days of World War II.[135] For them, understanding the German consumer of the present and future meant engaging in economic debates that transcended the time and space of the Third Reich and the war. Why did the regime allow these dialogues to continue? In part, it simply could not control them. The power of the Nazi state was not such that it could eviscerate all discussions that did not prima facie contribute to völkisch thought. But it did not necessarily want to put an end to these deliberations. The government reckoned that to dispense with all conventional marketing practices would unnecessarily exacerbate the already severe ruptures experienced by the business world and hamper

[133] Besprechung mit Herrn Mundhenke der Firma Henkel, 3 May 1940, R5002/43, BAB.
[134] Mundhenke to RVA, 3 June 1943, R5002/21 BAB.
[135] See articles throughout *DDV* in 1944 and 1945, e.g., Wilhelm Hietmüller, "Völkische Wirtschaftsfreiheit oder liberale Reform? *DDV* 14, no. 1 (January 1945): 19–22.

FIGURE 21. "Business as usual" amid wartime ruins. Bombed-out department store in Charlottenburg neighborhood of Berlin, with a sign proclaiming, "Hertie, Open!" ca. 1944. (C7824; courtesy of Landesarchiv Berlin.)

the revival of a postwar consumer marketplace. It also wanted to learn from them and take advantage of them.

If the regime maintained a modicum of economic normality during the war, it was of dubious value. With the stifling of profit-based activities, the superficial remnants of the market did little to reassure companies that were not directly involved in war production. Nor were consumers under any illusions about the health of the economy. They had high purchasing power, but fewer goods to buy, and those that were available, they snapped up. Given the dearth of clothing, household goods, and luxury items, consumers lost much significance, but not all of it. Companies still tried to reach them – through advertising, films, product demonstrations at department stores, public lectures, and goodwill campaigns. And despite increasingly harsh punishments for grumbling toward the end of the war, Germans still maintained the ability to complain. Housewives bemoaned ersatz goods, bristled at inept ad campaigns, and cursed the government's attempts to school them in domestic habits that they had already learned from their mothers. In the meantime, Germans took advantage of the limited consumer opportunities that still existed. KdF vacations offered the real opportunity for escape, movies transported Germans to foreign lands, and with their diminished numbers, trade fairs and industrial exhibits offered an alternative experience of consumer bounty and the exotic. These were more than simply ersatz forms of consumption; they demonstrate that mass culture and leisure persisted throughout the war. But they did not live up to the regime's lofty predictions. In 1942, as German cities were already smoldering, Joseph Goebbels argued that the war would "secure the preconditions for a national prosperity which will give our people the amount of earthly happiness they deserve."[136] By 1945, however, the promise that Germans could have it all – a racially purified society and a modern consumer economy that provided material and spiritual pleasures – had long been shattered.

[136] Lead article for *Das Reich* (31 May 1942), reprinted in J. Noakes and G. Pridham, eds., *Nazism – 1919–1945: A Documentary Reader* [vol. 4] (Exeter: University of Exeter Press, 2000), 486–87.

Conclusion

Sixty-five years after the end of the Third Reich, historians are still trying to understand the appeal of National Socialism. Recent scholarship has detected in Nazism a set of values that many Germans came to accept in the 1930s and 1940s.[1] Rather than simply offering a negative story of a homeland beset by political and racial enemies, Nazism offered an affirmative – if corrupted – ethos, based on racial superiority, economic and military might, and the promise of affluence. Many Germans were open to the principles of National Socialism and "thought themselves into" the Volksgemeinschaft because it offered them both ideological clarity and material comfort.[2] Whatever appeals Germans found in the Nazis' vision, however, it was still, to use Geoff Eley's words, a "morally coercive" one, and understanding the relationship between free will and duress under National Socialism remains one of the tasks of the historian.[3]

In this book I have attempted to study a site of both autonomy and coercion in the Third Reich, namely the marketplace. From 1933 to 1945 the regime forcibly steered the economy along ideological lines. Most obviously, it geared the country's resources toward war and expelled Jews from German commercial life. But in more mundane areas – in the selling and consuming of everyday necessities and luxuries – the Nazis sought a balance between persuasion and force, between pragmatism

[1] Peter Fritzsche, *Life and Death in the Third Reich* (Cambridge, MA: Belknap Press, 2008); Claudia Koonz, *The Nazi Conscience* (Cambridge, MA: Belknap Press, 2003).
[2] This phrase is taken from Geoff Eley's blurb for Fritzsche, *Life and Death*, back cover.
[3] Geoff Eley, Review of Stefan Berger, *Inventing the Nation: Germany* (London: Arnold, 2004), in *English Historical Review* 121, no. 490 (February 2006): 243–46; and Eley, blurb for Fritzsche, *Life and Death*.

and ideology. They tried to promote the positive features of consumer society, such as healthy competition and the wide provision of goods and services, and expel what they perceived to be its decadent features, such as overindulgence and ethnic heterogeneity. For business leaders and everyday Germans, the regime's promotion of a racially and morally sanitized consumer capitalism translated into a certain freedom to pursue their own interests in the market. The Nazis' regulations about advertising, merchandising, and retailing did not stop manufacturers from gauging public demand or consumers from responding to advertising campaigns.

It is important to note that reenvisioning the marketplace was a goal shared by many interwar thinkers; it was not just a Nazi project. The emergence of mass markets and politicized consumers, the misery on the home fronts of World War I, the booms and busts of the 1920s, and the Great Depression – all of these developments provoked European and American elites to consider the relationship between material contentment and national prosperity. But the Nazis' linking of market relations to biology violently demarcated their efforts from those of other countries. The consumer society Hitler sought to create was centered on racial purity rather than on regulating capitalism in ways that protected business interests while fostering the expansion of a middle class.

The Nazis' commercial vocabulary and companies' practice of marketing were conventional in many respects. The language of achievement and trust that pervaded speeches, essays, and advertisements in the Third Reich was not, in and of itself, National Socialist. But the regime enlisted stock concepts from the world of commerce in its political crusade. It tied familiar features of business ethics (attentiveness to customers, truth in advertising, corporate integrity) and consumer privileges (the right to honest salespeople and high-quality products) to a larger project of racial cleansing. Jews were portrayed as the enemies of these values, and the Nazis removed them from the economy in the name of völkisch morality. In the meantime, the institutions that had a large stake in the market, whether individual companies or male civic associations like Rotary, adhered to "bourgeois" business mores while also serving a perverted Nazi ethic. To various degrees, Germany's economic elite accepted the brutal duality of Nazi commercial morality: humanizing the market while denying some people their humanity entirely.

One must avoid generalizing about the business community during this period. How private industry responded to the Nazis' commercial vision depended on a number of factors, including what sector a company belonged to, how large it was, and what the current state of the civilian economy was. Generally, small firms had more trouble obeying an injunction they saw as threatening their ability to compete. But in the first years of the Third Reich, many nonmilitary producers with large marketing apparatuses believed they could navigate the mix of pragmatism and ideology that marked Nazi commercial policies; as the economy recovered, they found that the regime's approach to commerce could be in keeping with their own business goals. By the end of the 1930s, however, the contradictions inherent in the Nazi marketplace were too deep for even the larger manufacturers to ignore. By the time World War II broke out, price freezes, limitations on consumer goods, and Germany's retreat from world markets had translated into unfavorable conditions for civilian producers. Ideology, whether manifested in racial persecution or the bellicose search for "living space," gained the upper hand over pragmatism, and the measured autonomy that businessmen and consumers enjoyed was replaced by belt-tightening measures and limited commercial opportunities under a war economy.

For marketers, the Nazi years presented a host of challenges. Advertising was essentially used by the regime to supervise consumption, and over time, the state turned the ad industry into a tool to ready the public for war. The regime favored producer goods over consumer products, and demands that the public temper its purchasing habits and that advertisers Germanize their repertoire resulted, according to Hartmut Berghoff, in a "bureaucratic nightmare with meager economic results" for the ad industry.[4] Market professionals gained some respect but little of the material rewards they were seeking, in part because the output of commercial advertising did not increase as it might have under a free-market system.

This bleak picture should not obscure the opportunities that the Nazi marketplace presented to business leaders. A closer look at commerce from the perspective of individual companies indicates that firms could profit from selling goods to a racially homogeneous customer base, even when consumers were feeling the absence of some of the goods they had come to expect in a recovering economy. The 1930s witnessed companies building

---

[4] Hartmut Berghoff, "'Times Change and We Change with Them': The German Advertising Industry in the Third Reich – Between Professional Self-Interest and Political Repression," *Business History* 45, no. 1 (January 2003): 128–47.

FIGURE 22. Salesman in front of HAG and Persil window display, 1930s. (Courtesy of Kraft Foods Deutschland Services GmbH & Co. KG, Bremen.)

their in-house advertising branches, which produced arresting representations of products and messages about the firm that resonated with a public hungry for visual spectacles.[5] In their advertising and sales divisions, companies hired apprentices who studied the latest selling techniques around the world and wrote scholarly reports on their experiences.[6] And consumer researchers found rich opportunities to apply their understanding

---

[5] On advertising branches and their increased importance, see Dirk Reinhardt, *Von der Reklame zum Marketing: Geschichte der Wirtschaftswerbung in Deutschland* (Berlin: Akademie, 1993), 447; and Alexander Schug, "Vom Newspaper Space Salesman zur integrierten Kommunikationsagentur: Die 120-jährige Entwicklungsgeschichte der Werbeagentur Dorland," *Zeitschrift für Unternehmensgeschichte* 49, no. 1 (2004): 5–25.

[6] See, e.g., Rundschreiben an die kaufm. Lehrlinge (Abiturienten), 20 December 1933, 074-001-003, BAL; and Wilhelm Mann, "Der Ideelle Wert der 'Bayer'-Lehrlings-Ausbildung," *Die Brücke* 1 (1936): 50–58, in 74/001-003, BAL.

of mass psychology to the marketing of goods. To be sure, companies still battled consumers' fears that product promotion was extraneous and made goods more expensive.[7] Some businessmen themselves remained wary of pouring resources into a medium more suited to the mass consumerism of the United States. But the overall picture of marketing in the Third Reich is one of experimentation and a halting modernization. A compatibility with the regime's aims, continuities with pre-1933 practices, and a narrow autonomy when it came to the devising of selling strategies meant that marketers did not have to start from scratch in 1945.

When the Nazi regime did come to an end, market professionals were poised to resume work almost immediately. The Society for Consumer Research saw essentially no break in its activities. The organization began its first postwar report, a study of Nuremberg's building and construction industry during the "peaceful years of 1935 to 1939," in the spring of 1945 and released it in three installments over the course of July, August, and September of that year.[8] In the fall of 1945, Wilhelm Vershofen met with industrial psychologist Hans Meyer-Mark, formerly of the Göring Institute, to discuss the GfK's future work.[9] And over the next decades, the GfK would produce studies very similar to those under National Socialism, whether in assessing the effectiveness of Persil ads or studying American advertising practices.[10] Finally, the GfK leadership would continue to weigh in on questions of advertising, marketing, and consumption. Most notably, GfK alumnus Ludwig Erhard helped mastermind West Germany's "economic miracle" as economics minister and then chancellor. Consumers represented for Erhard "the driving force" of the market economy, and he invested advertising with the power to fulfill their desires.[11]

---

[7] "Verteuert Werbung die Ware?" *HAG-Post*, no. 2 (20 January 1938), box R2 94/7, file 0096 4891, KFA.

[8] "Bericht über die Struktur der Nürnberger Bauwirtschaft in den Friedenjahren 1935/1939 und über die derzeitige Baukapazität Nürnbergs und seines nordbayerischen Einzugsgebietes," Summer 1945, S 1945 001–1 and S 1945 001–2, GfKA.

[9] Wilhelm Vershofen to Hanns Brose, 22 November 1945, NL Vershofen, MS 2763, file "Schriftwechsel Brose, 1935–1944," Erlangen.

[10] E.g., "Vergleich zweier Anzeigen für 'Persil' in Nürnberg," May 1955, S 1955 020, GfKA; and "Inventur der amerikanischen Werbeforschung," February–March 1954, S 1954 004, GfKA. On the postwar years, see Wilfried Feldenkirchen and Daniela Fuchs, *Die Stimme des Verbrauchers zum Klingen Bringen: 75 Jahre Geschichte der GfK Gruppe* (Munich: Piper, 2009), 83–129.

[11] See, e.g., Ludwig Erhard, "Marktwirtschaft und Werbung gehören entrennbar zusammen," *Wirtschaft und Werbung* 6, no. 12 (December 1952): 327–28. More generally see Alexander Nützenadel, "Consumerism, Material Culture, and Economic Reconstruction in Cold War Germany," *Journal of Contemporary History* 42, no. 2 (April 2007): 387–96.

The field of marketing more broadly witnessed continuities in both personnel and theoretical interests. Some of the most prominent names in interwar and Nazi era marketing had flourishing careers after 1945. In the 1950s Hanns Kropff remained active as a theorist and professor of advertising at the University of Frankfurt.[12] Hans Domizlaff's 1939 book, *Gewinnung des öffentlichen Vertrauens* (Winning the public trust), has been reissued a number of times since 1945, most recently in 2005, and his insights into branding, advertising, and market technology are still studied.[13] Moreover, the fathers of West German public relations, like Carl Hundhausen, could attribute their beginnings to their work for private industry and the state during the Third Reich.[14] Finally, the key social organizations for businessmen, such as Rotary, reestablished themselves in West Germany, and their members continued to pursue an interest in mass culture, consumption, and America.[15]

It is not surprising, then, that the innovations of the postwar years had their origins in the interwar years. One such area was motivational research (MR), usually associated with Austrian émigré Ernest Dichter's acclaimed and controversial practice in the United States. According to MR, researchers could gain access to the true sentiments behind the decision to purchase a product or vote for a particular political candidate. Through the use of psychoanalytic theories, motivational researchers lent their skills to companies to determine what emotional wants and needs – such as the desire for status or security – lay behind the purchasing act. Manufacturers could, in turn, produce, package, and market merchandise in shapes and with colors and language that would appeal to the deepest needs and wishes, which were often unknown to consumers themselves.[16] MR was a quintessential product of the cold war

---

[12] Bernd Semrad, "Die 'Wiener Schule' der Werbung?" *Wiener Journal: Das Magazin der Wiener Zeitung* 20 (18 September 2004): 12–14.

[13] Hans Domizlaff, *Die Gewinnung des öffentlichen Vertrauens* [7th ed.] (Hamburg: Gesellschaft für angewandtes Marketing, 2005).

[14] Peer Heinelt, *PR-Päpste: Die kontinuierlichen Karrieren von Carl Hundhausen, Albert Oeckl und Franz Ronneberger* (Berlin: Karl Dietz, 2003).

[15] See S. Jonathan Wiesen, "The Modern Guild: Rotary Clubs and Bourgeois Renewal in the Aftermath of National Socialism," in *Conflict, Catastrophe, and Continuity: Essays on Modern German History*, ed. Frank Biess, Mark Roseman, and Hanna Schissler (New York: Berghahn Books, 2007), 297–317.

[16] Ernest Dichter, *The Strategy of Desire* (Garden City, NY: Doubleday, 1960); see also Daniel Horowitz, *Anxieties of Affluence: Critiques of American Consumer Culture, 1939–1979* (Amherst: University of Massachusetts Press, 2004), 48–78.

West, when the consumerism of the United States and Western Europe prompted new and more aggressive forms of advertising and selling. But it was born of an earlier decade, when the mass production of goods prompted marketers to access shoppers' inner motivations. The GfK, despite its ambivalent relationship to the unconscious, was a product of this quest.

In postwar West Germany, admen still faced the challenge of selling not only products but also the benefits of their work. The Nazi years had seen a push to "advertise on behalf of ads," and so too did the 1950s, when Wilhelm Vershofen marveled at the urge, even among company leaders, to both rely on and dismiss advertising.[17] The Federal Republic, despite the flood of consumer goods that accompanied its economic revival, still embraced a producerist ethos, and lingering suspicions about "American" modes of mass selling persisted. While West Germany saw the arrival of U.S.-style, full- service ad agencies in the 1950s, it was not until the late 1960s that "marketing" emerged as a discrete practice and a field of study.[18] It was only in 1979 that a German journal devoted itself exclusively to marketing.[19]

Against this backdrop, the West German Frankfurt school theorists and leftist activists railed against the excesses of consumer society.[20] In the meantime, the East German government initiated extreme measures – like the banning of commercial advertising altogether in 1975 – to remove distracting and "capitalist" forms of commerce from the German Democratic Republic (GDR).[21] Today's attempts to curtail abuses in the marketplace stem less from these sorts of anticapitalist impulses than from the consumer rights and environmental movements, which hope to reign in, but not dismantle, market economics. Indeed, they represent system-friendly attempts to regulate the marketplace and determine the

---

[17] Wilhelm Vershofen, "Für und gegen Werbung," *Wirtschaft und Werbung* 13, no. 3 (December 1959): 899–900.
[18] Harm Schröter, "Die Amerikanisierung der Werbung in der Bundesrepublik Deutschland," *Jahrbuch für Wirtschaftsgeschichte* 1997, no. 1 (1997): 94–115; Hartmut Berghoff, ed., *Marketing-Geschichte: Die Genese einer modernen Sozialtechnik* (Frankfurt: Campus, 2007), 38–39.
[19] Berghoff, *Marketing-Geschichte*, 38–39.
[20] See Andreas Wirsching, "Konsum statt Arbeit? Zum Wandel von Individualität in der modernen Massengesellschaft," *Vierteljahrshefte für Zeitgeschichte* 57, no. 2 (April 2009): 171–201.
[21] Pamela Swett, S. Jonathan Wiesen, and Jonathan R. Zatlin, eds., *Selling Modernity: Advertising in Twentieth Century Germany* (Durham, NC: Duke University Press, 2007), 17.

rules of engagement. In this vein, the Law against Unfair Competition, which the Nazis exploited for their own ends, is still in effect in Germany, with its most recent revision in 2008. This reminds us again how National Socialism appropriated existing legal and business norms and augmented them with its own racist conceptions.

One final continuity in German marketing is worth noting, namely attempts both before and after 1945 to invest commerce with ideological meaning. Whereas the market in the 1930s was to be the handmaiden of racial revival, in the 1950s and 1960s it was (in West Germany) the embodiment of freedom against all forms of totalitarianism. Free enterprise, the freedom to advertise, the freedom to accumulate goods, buy property, and get rich – all were seen as virtuous exercises that set "the West" apart from Soviet communism. And brand names still had a special resonance. As in the 1920s and 1930s, branding in the postwar years was seen as ushering in comfort and solidifying national reputations. In West Germany, the return of one's favorite goods in the late 1940s was met with especially deep emotions; these products represented a normality that had been interrupted by World War II.[22] This sentimental relationship to brands is not lost on some Germans today, whose nostalgia for the GDR manifests itself in a longing for favorite brands from before 1989.[23]

The significance of these continuities is debatable. The presence of Nazi era marketers and businessmen in the Federal Republic does not mean that West Germany inherited a "fascist" understanding of mass persuasion. The continuity of elites, some of them former Nazis, was a reality in all areas of West German public life – politics, academia, business, and culture.[24] But marketing practitioners' hands-on experiences during the Third Reich invariably informed their later work. Hans Domizlaff remained a marketing adviser to Siemens and Reemstma through the 1960s. And Hanns Brose put his experience with Nazi era "communal advertising" to work in the 1950s on behalf of *Die Waage*, a state- and industry-sponsored initiative to sell the merits of the market economy to West Germans.[25] Where Brose once tried to convince consumers to

---

[22] See "Die Währungsreform im Spiegel der Vebrauchermeinungen," Fall 1948, S 1948 001, GfKA.

[23] This sentimentality is sympathetically spoofed in the film *Goodbye Lenin* (2003).

[24] See, e.g., Norbert Frei, *Karrieren im Zwielicht: Hitlers Eliten nach 1945* (Frankfurt am Main: Campus, 2001).

[25] Mark E. Spicka, *Selling the Economic Miracle: Economic Reconstruction and Politics in West Germany, 1949–1957* (New York: Berghahn Books, 2007), 114.

sacrifice on behalf of the Volksgemeinschaft, he now asked them to revel in the material promise of free enterprise.[26]

Brose's career trajectory might suggest a fundamental opportunism among market professionals and an apolitical desire to serve one's master. Certainly, there are examples of businessmen declaring their fealty to National Socialism and only a few years later asserting a commitment to economic and political liberalism.[27] But more significantly, these continuities point to the universality of marketing and its indispensability in different political contexts. Whether fascist, democratic, or communist, states have placed experts in mass persuasion at their disposal. Sustaining the public and securing its loyalty means enlisting marketers to sell visions of the good life. In very different contexts, the purveyors of products, lifestyles, and ideologies draw on similar tools, from posters and merchandise displays, to applied psychology, to radio dramas selling the benefits of an economic vision. In turn, governments have tried to protect the public from abuses of these important media.

In recognizing such continuities, we must not underestimate the uniquely violent setting of Nazi Germany. From the regime's perspective, buying and selling in the Third Reich was always part of the drive toward military expansion and racial engineering, and we must therefore ask whether marketing helped tie the German population to the Nazis' ideological aims. Did marketing effect a positive orientation toward the Nazi regime and thus allow it to carry out its crimes? The answer is yes. While the Nazi regime failed to bring about its vision of an Aryan consumer society, and its consumption policies were often confused, the state and marketers together helped Germans feel part of a grand mission to overtake other countries in quality of life. Mass consumption and leisure programs like Strength through Joy were part of this process. So were advertisements, billboards, and trade fairs, which offered a semblance of normality. The visual spectacles of economic recovery – displayed in a company profile shown before a feature film, in a store window, or in a national exhibition frequented by millions of visitors – reassured Germans that their identities as consumers would be respected in ways they had not been during World War I and the economic crises that followed. In

[26] Dirk Schindelbeck, "'Asbach Uralt' und 'Soziale Marktwirtschaft': Zur Kulturgeschichte der Werbeagentur am Beispiel von Hanns W. Brose (1899–1971)," *Zeitschrift für Unternehmensgeschichte* 40, no. 4 (1995): 235–52.
[27] See, e.g., the career of economic theorist Josef Winschuh discussed by S. Jonathan Wiesen in *West German Industry and the Challenge of the Nazi Past, 1945–1955* (Chapel Hill: University of North Carolina Press, 2001), 119–20.

turn, many Germans acknowledged their support for a regime that had bettered their lives and promised to do even more.

These visions of commercial plenty were always juxtaposed with highly visible forms of racism, and consumers could not miss this infusion of Nazi ideals into the marketplace. Advertisements could not have swastikas in them, but on the street and in periodicals, they were surrounded by the imagery of racial awakening: uniforms, flags, anti-Semitic ordinances, and kiosks displaying Nazi newspapers that explored the Jews' "bloodlust" or the uselessness of mentally and physically disabled people. Marketers were prohibited from using protected Nazi concepts in their campaigns, but they drew readily on the exclusionary tropes of nationalism, militarism, and aggressive chauvinism that filled the party's speeches and publications. This merging of commerce and race does not mean that every consumer shared the regime's genocidal aims. But it does mean that Germans could link their economic good fortune and their inclusion in the Volksgemeinschaft to the Nazis' larger struggle against enemies of all kind.

Despite the connections between economic recovery and support for the regime, we must not overstate the level of consumer satisfaction and its relationship to politics. As the GfK research demonstrated, Germans were not blindly and uniformly content in the 1930s and early 1940. While Götz Aly sees a population whose loyalty was bought through access to material goods, the consumer research of the 1930s and 1940s belies this conclusion. The universal desire for creature comforts was met in the Third Reich on the one hand by gratification, in the form of necessities and – for some – luxuries, and on the other hand by a sense of loss and nostalgia. During the war in particular, Germans of basic means pined for their favorite products that were off the market, complained about shortages, bemoaned the quality of generic goods, and dismissed Nazi propaganda as wasted paper.

Such complaining is a reminder that consent in the Third Reich was not all-encompassing; support for National Socialism could be combined with anger at the regime. And loyalty to the Nazi cause and the war effort was based not only on a sense of material well-being. Nationalism, belief in the Führer, racism, concern for loved ones on the battlefield – a constellation of emotions and commitments explains more about the origins of consent than any ill-begotten riches. Ultimately, grumbling in the Third Reich was a function of both entitlement and anxiety. By the time World War II broke out, Germans had come to enjoy a heightened standard of living that they hoped could be maintained in wartime and after the cessation of hostilities. They gave Hitler credit for rescuing the economy, expanding the borders of the Reich, and initiating a racial "awakening," and they experienced deprivations on the home front with a mix of frustration and optimism that the Führer would again make good on his bountiful promises.

This dialectic of comfort and denial was a defining feature of Nazi society, and both the state and market professionals exploited it whenever they could. They promised material abundance while Germans still experienced Depression era shortages; they offered exotic colonial imagery to a public still mourning the loss of Germany's overseas empire; and they reminded wartime consumers that their favorite household products would return to their lives after the war was won. Moreover, to extent that Germans did feel good about their material conditions, marketers assured them that more and even better consumer opportunities lay ahead under National Socialism. In short, German market professionals were keenly aware that they were functioning in an exceptional ideological setting. Even when they did not overtly traffic in the regime's hatreds, they proclaimed the uniqueness of the German Volk, and boasted about a more "organic" relationship with the public than their counterparts enjoyed in Britain or the United States. Thus when organizations like the GfK embarked on a mission of "understanding the soul," they hoped to come in contact not with consumers per se but with Germans.[28] More than simply producing data about cars and toiletries, they felt they were mapping the inner life of the Volk, which combined dreams of fulfillment in the marketplace with a communalist thinking absent in other cultures.[29]

These grandiose goals notwithstanding, marketing in the Third Reich had powerful implications precisely because Germans did *not* conform to National Socialism's reductive norms. Even in a dictatorship, people's private yearnings and habits could not entirely be colonized by the state. The working woman who smoked and drank survived in a society that advocated traditional gender divisions. The consumer publicly asserted her devotion to sacrifice, but privately (and in the case of the GfK reports, not so privately) demanded better products. And the company adman

[28] The GfK borrowed the phrase "understanding the soul" from Werner Sombart; see Hans Proesler, "Über das Verstehen in der Verbrauchsforschung," *Markt und Verbrauch* 13, nos. 11 and 12 (1941): 279–84.

[29] See Georg Bergler, *Die Entwicklung der Verbrauchsforschung in Deutschland und die Gesellschaft für Konsumforschung bis zum Jahre 1945* (Kallmünz: Michael Laßleben, 1959), 174, 185.

both celebrated National Socialism and objected to its irrational advertising regulations. To be sure, such complexities do not indicate the flourishing of a compensatory personal liberty in the absence of political freedom. But they do reveal the sometimes improvisational nature of Nazi rule, the contradictory dynamics of German society, and the blurry nature of consent.

While marketing affords a look at everyday life and the limits of Nazi power, its practitioners can hardly be called transgressive figures. Market professionals in the Third Reich did not take a defiant stance toward the state, and they did not consider all the regime's intrusions to be unique to the Nazi dictatorship. In many respects the commercial regulations they faced were similar to what their colleagues encountered in other countries. Comparative advertising, the use of product rebates, and retail price maintenance were subjects of legislation abroad in the 1930s.[30] And many of the attitudes about consumption in the Third Reich bespoke a widely shared understanding of shopping's psychological and gendered dimensions. The statement "While the man's job is to earn money, the women's job is to spend it correctly" emanated from a National Socialist primer on correct laundering during World War II.[31] But it might as easily have come from an American advertising executive or a British domestic scientist.

Nazi era commerce, then, is not the story of apolitical professionals doing their work in a uniquely inauspicious setting. Nor is it about ideological businessmen promoting an overtly National Socialistic ethic. Rather, it is about how conventional business norms and practices became tied to horrible crimes. The well-documented forms of corporate complicity under Nazism, such as plunder, the Aryanization of Jewish businesses, and the use of forced labor not only served the Nazis' racial and political aims. They also served an individual company's raison d'être, namely the selling of goods and services for profit. When automobile firms like Daimler-Benz or pharmaceutical companies like Bayer aided Nazi criminality, they did so not per se in the name of racial engineering, but in the name of selling cars and aspirin.

The misdeeds of market professionals in the Third Reich are more indirect than the crimes of greed and opportunism that landed industrialists in the dock in Nuremberg. But as Wilhelm Mann of the IG Farben board

---

[30] On the latter policy in the United States, for example, see Jonathan Bean, *Beyond the Broker State: Federal Policies toward Small Business, 1936–1961* (Chapel Hill: University of North Carolina Press, 1996), 67–88.
[31] *Waschfibel*, ca. 1940, p. 41, R5002/26, BAB.

lent support and resources to consumer research, his company was presiding over the murderous employment of slave laborers in Auschwitz. As coffee producer Kaffee HAG discussed the merits of product placements, it also provided libations to the Nazis' militarized youth. Conducting market research in Southeastern Europe in 1942 meant acknowledging the potential of the Wehrmacht to maintain its brutal hold on occupied countries. In short, as they pursued their work, market professionals in the Third Reich may not have engaged in anything but a rational calculus of sales and profits. But they accepted the persecutory thrust of National Socialism and the opportunities it created for business.

In the end, the Nazi marketplace could not sustain itself. It crumbled in the midst of war, which sidelined the consumer and put most business decisions fully in line with the regime's military priorities. And it collapsed under the weight of its own contradictions. Celebrating the producer, providing for the consumer, striving for autarky, and preparing for an imperialist war proved irreconcilable, even in the booming economy of the Third Reich. More important, the Nazi commercial vision was always an amalgam of ideas that were never articulated as a coherent doctrine and thus could never be realized as such. Multiple market imaginaries existed in the Third Reich, and the Nazis created an unworkable composite of them: the "bourgeois market" offered the values of competitive performance; consumer capitalism supplied the tools for the mass provisioning of the population; socialist traditions provided a vision of commerce that addressed the needs of the working majority; and völkish ideologies supplied the language of organic nationalism. The interplay of sometimes competing traditions was not specific to the Third Reich, nor was the failure to rid the market of corrupting influences. But the centrality of biology in the Nazi commercial vision *was* distinct. The success of the Nazi marketplace depended on winning a racial war of expansion, and when the Nazi military disintegrated in 1945, so did the millenarian vision of joyful Aryans working, buying, and selling in a German-controlled Europe.

Archival Sources and Bibliography

Archiv der Gesellschaft für Konsumforschung, Nürnberg

Institutional publications
  Markt und Verbrauch
  Merkblatt der Gesellschaft für Konsumforschung
  Mitteilungsblatt der Gesellschaft für Konsumforschung
  Vertrauliche Nachrichten für die Mitglieder der GfK
Reports and studies, 1936–1955

Bayer AG, Corporate History and Archives, Leverkusen

Company newspapers and magazines
  Die Erholung
  Von Werk zu Werk
  ZP: Zentral-Nachrichtenblatt für die "Bayer"-Werbung
Files on education, exhibitions, sales, culture, pharmaceuticals, patents, politics,
  radio, sport, film, and advertising
Miscellaneous books, pamphlets, films, exhibition materials, and speeches

Böttcherstrasse Archiv, Bremen

Binder "Böttcherstrasse und 3. Reich"
Files on Ludwig Roselius
Newspaper clipping binders

Bundesarchiv Berlin

Partei-Kanzlei der NSDAP (NS 6)
Rechnungshof des Deutschen Reichs (R 2301)
Reichsausschuss für Volkswirtschaftliche Aufklärung Gmbh (R 5002)
Reichsführer SS (NS 19)

Reichsministerium für Volksaufklärung und Propaganda (R 55)
Reichsorganisationsleiter der NSDAP (NS 22)
Reichspressechef der NSDAP (NS 42)
Reichspropagandaleiter (NS 18)
Reichswirtschaftsministerium (R 3101)
Südosteuropa Gesellschaft (R 63)

Bundesarchiv-Filmarchiv, Berlin

Henkel – ein deutsches Werk in seiner Arbeit (1938)

Company Archives, Kraft Foods Deutschland GmbH, Bremen

Company newspapers and magazines, and HAG Press publications
  Die Güldenkammer
  HAG-Post
  Internationale Zeitschrift "Die Böttcherstrasse"
Kaffee HAG Archive
Miscellaneous materials on Ludwig Roselius

Geheimes Staatsarchiv Preußischer Kulturbesitz, Berlin

Rotary International files (Hauptabteilung I, rep. 228)
  Club files
  Der Rotarier magazine

Historisches Archiv, Krupp, Essen

Company newspapers and magazines
  Krupp: Zeitschrift der krupp'schen Werksgemeinschaft
  Krupp'sche Mitteilungen
Miscellaneous files on public relations

John W. Hartman Center for Sales, Advertising & Marketing History, Duke University

J. Walter Thompson Company Archives

Konzernarchiv der Henkel KGaA, Düsseldorf

Advertising files (H20)
Company newspapers and magazines
  Blätter vom Hause
  Henkel-Bote
Films, 1927–1939 (H430)
Press Office files (Zug-No. 438)

Landesarchiv-Berlin

Photo archive

Nordrhein–Westfälisches Hauptstaatsarchiv, Düsseldorf

Miscellaneous files on Reichsausstellung Schaffendes Volk
Photo archive

United States Holocaust Memorial Museum, Washington D.C.

Photo Archive

**Universitätsarchiv, Friedrich-Alexander-Universität
Erlangen-Nürnberg, Erlangen**

NL Wilhelm Vershofen (unsorted)
University personnel files

Nazi-Era National Magazines, Newspapers, Newsletters, and Journals

Die Deutsche Handelswarte
Der Deutsche Unternehmer
Der Deutsche Volkswirt
Die Deutsche Volkswirtschaft
Deutsche Zukunft
Der Gauwirtschaftsberater
Der Markenartikel
Nationalsozialistische Wirtschaftspolitik
Schriftenreihe: Absatzwirtschaft
Seidels Reklame
Vierjahresplan
Westdeutscher Beobachter
Wirtschaftsdienst
Die Wirtschaftspolitische Parole (formerly *Mitteilungen der Kommision für Wirtschaftspolitik der NSDAP*)
Wirtschaftswerbung
Zeitschrift für Betriebswirtschaft
Zeitschrift für Handelswissenschaftliche Forschung

Published Books and Scholarly Articles

Abelshauser, Werner. "Guns, Butter and Economic Miracles." In *The Economics of World War II*. Edited by Mark Harrison, 122–76. Cambridge: Cambridge University Press, 1998.

Aly, Götz. *Hitler's Beneficiaries: Plunder, Racial War, and the Nazi Welfare State*. New York: Metropolitan, 2007.

Ambrosius, Gerold. *Staat und Wirtschaft im 20. Jahrhundert*. Munich: Oldenbourg, 1990.

Aycoberry, Pierre. *The Social History of the Third Reich, 1933–1945*. New York: New Press, 1999.

Baerwald, Friedrich. "How Germany Reduced Unemployment." *American Economic Review* 24, no. 4 (December 1934): 617–30.

Bähr, Johannes, Axel Drecoll, Bernhard Gott, Kim C. Priemel, and Harald Wixforth, eds. *Der Flick-Konzern im Dritten Reich*. Munich: Oldenbourg, 2008.

Bajohr, Frank. *"Aryanization" in Hamburg: The Economic Exclusion of Jews and the Confiscation of Their Property in Nazi Germany*. New York: Berghahn, 2002.

Baranowski, Shelley. *Strength through Joy: Consumerism and Mass Tourism in the Third Reich*. Cambridge: Cambridge University Press, 2004.

Barkai, Avraham. *From Boycott to Annihilation: The Economic Struggle of German Jews, 1933–1943*. Hanover, NH: University Press of New England, 1989.

Nazi Economics: Ideology, Theory, and Policy. New Haven, CN: Yale University Press, 1990.

Bavaj, Riccardo. *Die Ambivalenz der Moderne im Nationalsozialismus: Eine Bilanz der Forschung*. Munich: Oldenbourg, 2003.

Baynes, Norman H., ed. *The Speeches of Adolf Hitler* [vol. 2: April 1922–August 1939]. Oxford: Oxford University Press, 1942.

Bean, Jonathan. *Beyond the Broker State: Federal Policies toward Small Business, 1936–1961*. Chapel Hill: University of North Carolina Press, 1996.

Beck, Hermann. *The Fateful Alliance: German Conservatives and Nazis in 1933 – The Machtergreifung in a New Light*. New York: Berghahn Books, 2008.

Berghahn, Volker R. "Das 'Deutsche Kapitalismus-Modell' in Geschichte und Geschichtswissenschaft." In *Gibt es einen deutschen Kapitalismus? Tradition und globale Perspektiven der sozialen Marktwirtschaft*. Edited by Volker R. Berghahn and Sigurt Vitols, 24–42. Frankfurt am Main: Campus, 2006.

Berghoff, Hartmut. "Enticement and Deprivation: The Regulation of Consumption in Pre-War Nazi Germany." In *The Politics of Consumption: Material Culture and Citizenship in Europe and America*. Edited by Martin Daunton and Matthew Hilton, 165–84. Oxford: Berg, 2001.

"Methoden der Verbrauchslenkung im Nationalsozialismus: Konsumpolitische Normensetzung zwischen totalitärem Anspruch und widerspenstiger Praxis." In *Wirtschaftskontrolle und Recht in der nationalsozialisten Dikatur*. Edited by Dieter Gosewinkel, 281–316. Frankfurt am Main: Vittorio Kostermann, 2005.

"'Times Change and We Change with Them': The German Advertising Industry in the Third Reich – Between Professional Self-Interest and Political Repression." *Business History* 45, no. 1 (January 2003): 128–47.

ed. *Konsumpolitik: Die Regulierung des privaten Verbrauchs im 20. Jahrhundert*. Göttingen: Vandenhoeck & Ruprecht, 1999.

ed. *Marketing-Geschichte: Die Genese einer modernen Sozialtechnik*. Frankfurt am Main: Campus, 2007.

Bergler, Georg. *Die Entwicklung der Verbrauchsforschung in Deutschland und die Gesellschaft für Konsumforschung bis zum Jahre 1945.* Kallmünz: Michael Laßleben, 1959.

Das Schrifttum über den Markenartikel. Berlin: Deutscher Betriebswirte-Verlag, 1934.

Bernays, Edward. *Propaganda.* New York: Liveright, 1928.

Betts, Paul. "The New Fascination with Fascism: The Case of Nazi Modernism." *Journal of Contemporary History* 37, no. 4 (October 2002): 541–58.

Binder, Elisabeth. *Die Entstehung unternehmerischer Public Relations in der Bundesrepublik Deutschland.* Münster: Lit, 1983.

Bingham, Alfred M. *Insurgent America: The Revolt of the Middle-Class.* New York: Harper and Brothers, 1935.

Blaich, Fritz. "Wirtschaft und Rüstung in Deutschland, 1933–1939." In *Nationalsozialistische Diktatur, 1933–1945: Eine Bilanz.* Edited by Karl Dietrich Bracher, Manfrerd Funke, and Hans Adolf Jacobsen, 285–316. Düsseldorf: Droste, 1983.

Wirtschaft und Rüstung im "Dritten Reich." Düsseldorf: Schwann, 1987.

Borscheid, Peter, and Clemens Wischermann, eds. *Bilderwelt des Alltags: Werbung in der Konsumgesellschaft des 19. und 20. Jahrhunderts.* Stuttgart: Steiner, 1995.

Braatz, Werner E. "German Commercial Interests in Palestine: Zionism and the Boycott of German Goods, 1933–1934." *European History Quarterly* 9, no. 4 (October 1979): 481–513.

Brady, Robert A. *The Spirit and Structure of German Fascism.* London: Victor Gollancz, 1937.

Breckman, Warren G. "Disciplining Consumption: The Debate about Luxury in Wilhelmine Germany, 1890–1914." *Journal of Social History* 24, no. 3 (Spring 1991): 485–505.

Briesen, Detlef. *Warenhaus, Massenkonsum, und Sozialmoral: Zur Geschichte der Konsumkritik im 20. Jahrhundert.* Frankfurt am Main: Campus, 2001.

Brose, Hanns W. *Die Entdeckung des Verbrauchers: Ein Leben für die Werbung.* Düsseldorf: Econ, 1958.

Götterdämmerung des Markenartikels? Neue Wege zu neuen Käufern. Gärtner: Schwarzenberg, 1934.

Buchheim, Christoph. "Das NS-Regime und die Überwindung der Weltwirtschaftskrise in Deutschland." *Vierteljahrshefte für Zeitgeschichte* 56, no. 3 (July 2008): 381–414.

Buchheim, Christoph, and Jonas Scherner. "The Role of Private Property in the Nazi Economy: The Case of Industry." *Journal of Economic History* 66, no. 2 (June 2006): 390–416.

Callmann, Rudolf. *Der Unlautere Wettbewerb: Kommentar zum Gesetz gegen den unlauteren Wettbewerb mit Notverordnung vom 9. März 1932 und zu dem materiellerechtlichen Vorschriften des Gesetzes zum Schutze der Warenbezeichnungen.* Mannheim: J. Bensheimer, 1932.

Casson, Herbert N. *Tips for the Traveling Salesman.* New York: B. C. Forbes, 1927.

Twelve Tips on Window Display. London: Efficiency Magazine, 1931.

Charles, Jeffrey A. *Service Clubs in American Society: Rotary, Kiwanis, and Lions.* Urbana: University of Illinois Press, 1993.

Ciarlo, David. *Advertising Empire: Race and Visual Culture in Imperial Germany.* Cambridge, MA: Harvard University Press, 2010.

Cohen, Lizabeth. *A Consumers' Republic: The Politics of Mass Consumption in Postwar America.* New York: Knopf, 2003.

"The New Deal State and the Making of Citizen Consumers." In *Getting and Spending: European and American Consumer Societies in the Twentieth Century.* Edited by Susan Strasser, Charles McGovern, and Matthias Judt, 111–26. Washington, DC: German Historical Institute/Cambridge University Press, 1998.

Cocks, Geoffrey. *Psychotherapy in the Third Reich: The Göring Insitute* [2d ed.]. New Brunswick, NJ: Transaction Publishers, 1997.

Confino, Alon. "Introduction to 'Histories and Memories of Twentieth Century Germany.'" *History and Memory* 17, nos. 1–2 (Autumn 2005): 4–11.

Confino, Alon, and Rudy Koshar. "Régimes of Consumer Culture: New Narratives in Twentieth-Century German History." *German History* 19, no. 2 (May 2001): 135–61.

Conrad, Christoph. "Observer les consommateurs: Études de marché et histoire de la consommation en Allemagne, des années 1930 aux années 1960." *Mouvement Social*, no. 206 (January–March 2004): 17–39.

Crossick, Geoffrey, and Heinz-Gerhard Haupt, eds., *The Petit Bourgeoisie in Europe, 1780–1914.* London: Routledge, 1997.

Damrow, Harry. *Ich war kein geheimer Verführer: Aus dem Leben eines Werbeleiters.* Rheinzabern: Dieter Gitzel, 1981.

Daunton, Martin, and Matthew Hilton, eds. *The Politics of Consumption: Material Culture and Citizenship in Europe and America.* Oxford: Berg, 2001.

Davis, Belinda J. *Home Fires Burning: Food, Politics, and Everyday Life in World War I Berlin.* Chapel Hill: University of North Carolina Press, 2000.

Dean, Martin. *Robbing the Jews: The Confiscation of Jewish Property in the Holocaust, 1933–1945.* Cambridge: Cambridge University Press, 2008.

De Grazia, Victoria. *The Culture of Consent: Mass Organization of Leisure in Fascist Italy.* Cambridge: Cambridge University Press, 1981.

Irresistible Empire: America's Advance through Twentieth Century Europe. Cambridge. MA: Harvard University Press, 2005.

Preface to *Selling Modernity: Advertising in Twentieth-Century Germany.* Edited by Pamela E. Swett, S. Jonathan Wiesen, and Jonathan R. Zatlin, xiii–xviii. Durham, NC: Duke University Press, 2007.

Dichter, Ernest. *The Strategy of Desire.* Garden City, NY: Doubleday, 1960.

Dietrich, Donald J. "Catholic Theology and the Challenge of Nazism." In *Antisemitism, Christian Ambivalence, and the Holocaust.* Edited by Kevin P. Spicer, 76–101. Bloomington: Indiana University Press, 2007.

Ditt, Karl. "Die Konsumgenossenschaften im Dritten Reich." *Internationale wissenschaftliche Korrespondenz zur Geschichte der deutschen Arbeiterbewegung* 23, no. 1 (1987): 82–111.

Döbbelin, O. F., ed. *Tausend und ein Slogan.* Berlin: Kurt Elsner, 1937.

Domizlaff, Hans, *Die Gewinnung des öffentlichen Vertrauens* [1939] [7th ed.]. Hamburg: Gesellschaft für angewandtes Marketing, 2005.

Eley, Geoff. *Reshaping the German Right: Radical Nationalism and Political Change after Bismarck*. New Haven, CN: Yale University Press, 1980.

Erker, Paul. *Industrie-Eliten in der NS Zeit: Anpassungsbereitschaft und Eigeninteresse von Unternehemern in der Rüstung- und Kriegswirtschaft, 1936–1945*. Passau: Rothe, 1994.

Erker, Paul, and Toni Pierenkemper, eds. *Deutsche Unternehmer zwischen Kriegswirtschaft und Wiederaufbau: Studien zur Erfahrungsbildung von Industrie-Eliten*. Munich: Oldenbourg, 1999.

Evans, Richard J. *The Third Reich in Power*. New York: Penguin, 2006.

Ewen, Stuart. *PR! A Social History of Spin*. New York: Basic Books, 1996.

Farias, Victor. *Heidegger and Nazism*. Philadelphia: Temple University Press, 1987.

Faye, Emmanuel. *Heidegger: The Introduction of Nazism into Philosophy in Light of the Unpublished Seminars of 1933–1935*. New Haven, CN: Yale University Press, 2009.

Feldenkirchen, Wilfried, and Daniela Fuchs. *Die Stimme des Verbrauchers zum Klingen Bringen: 75 Jahre Geschichte der GfK Gruppe*. Munich: Piper, 2009.

Feldenkirchen, Wilfried, and Susanne Hilger. *Menschen und Marken: 125 Jahre Henkel, 1876–2001*. Düsseldorf: Henkel, 2001.

Feldman, Gerald. *Allianz and the German Insurance Business, 1933–1945*. Cambridge: Cambridge University Press, 2001.

The Great Disorder: Politics, Economics, and Society in the German Inflation, 1914–1924. Oxford: Oxford University Press, 1997.

Ferguson, Michael. *The Rise of Management Consulting in Britain*. Burlington, VT: Ashgate, 2002.

Fischer, Heinz D., and Ulrike G. Wahl, eds. *Public Relations / Öffentlichkeitsarbeit: Geschichte–Grundlagen–Grenzziehungen*. Frankfurt am Main: Peter Lang, 1993.

Franz, Heike. *Zwischen Markt und Profession: Betriebswirte in Deutschland im Spannungsfeld von Bildungs- und Wirtschaftsbürgertum (1900–1945)*. Göttingen: Vandenhoeck & Ruprecht, 1998.

Frei, Norbert. *Karrieren im Zwielicht: Hitlers Eliten nach 1945*. Frankfurt am Main: Campus, 2001.

"Wie modern war der Nationalsozialismus?" *Geschichte und Gesellschaft* 19, no. 3 (July–September 1993): 367–87.

Frei, Norbert, Ralf Ahrens, Jörg Osterloh, and Tim Schanetzky, eds. *Flick: Der Konzern, die Familie, die Macht*. Munich: Karl Blessing, 2009.

Frese, Matthias. *Betriebspolitik im "Dritten Reich": Deutsche Arbeitsfront, Unternehmer und Saatsbürokratie in der westdeutschen Grossindustrie, 1933–1939*. Paderborn: Schöningh, 1991.

"Vom 'NS-Musterbetrieb' zum 'Kriegsmusterbetrieb': Zum Verhältnis von Deutscher Arbeitsfront und Grossindustrie, 1936–1944." In *Der Zweite Weltkrieg: Analysen, Grundzüge, Forschungsbilanz*. Edited by Wolfgang Michalka, 382–401. Munich: Piper, 1989.

Frevert, Ute. "Vertrauen: Historische Annäherungen an eine Gefühlshaltung." In *Emotionalität: Zur Geschichte der Gefühle*. Edited by Claudia Benthien, Anne Fleig, and Ingrid Kasten, 179–97. Cologne: Böhlau, 2000.

Friebe, Holm. "Branding Germany: Hans Domizlaff's *Markentechnik* and Its Ideological Impact." In *Selling Modernity: Advertising in Twentieth Century Germany*. Edited by Pamela Swett, S. Jonathan Wiesen, and Jonathan R. Zatlin, 78–99. Durham, NC: Duke University Press, 2007.

Fritzsche, Peter. *Life and Death in the Third Reich*. Cambridge, MA: Belknap Press, 2008.

Fulda, Bernhard. *Press and Politics in the Weimar Republic*. Oxford: Oxford University Press, 2009.

Gassert, Phillip. *Amerika im Dritten Reich: Ideologie, Propaganda und Volksmeinung, 1933–1945*. Stuttgart: Steiner, 1997.

Gellately, Robert. *Backing Hitler: Consent and Coercion in Nazi Germany*. Oxford: Oxford University Press, 2001.

Gewirtz, Sharon. "Anglo-Jewish Responses to Nazi Germany, 1933–1939: The Anti-Nazi Boycott and the Board of Deputies of British Jews." *Journal of Contemporary History* 26, no. 2 (April 1991): 255–76.

Geyer, Michael. "The Stigma of Violence, Nationalism, and War in Twentieth-Century Germany." *German Studies Review* 15, special issue (Winter 1992): 75–110.

Gillingham, John. *Industry and Politics in the Third Reich*. London: Methuen, 1985.

Goergen, Jeanpaul. *Walter Ruttmann: Eine Dokumentation*. Berlin: Freunde der Deutschen Kinemathek: 1988.

Goldman, Marshall I. "Product Differentiation and Advertising: Some Lessons from the Soviet Experience." *Journal of Political Economy* 68, no. 4 (August 1960): 346–57.

Gregor, Neil. *Daimler-Benz in the Third Reich*. New Haven, CN: Yale University Press, 1998.

——— ed. *Nazism, War, and Genocide*. Exeter: University of Exeter Press, 2005.

Gries, Rainer, Volker Ilgen, and Dirk Schindelbeck, eds. *"Ins Gehirn der Masse kriechen!" Werbung und Mentalitätsgeschichte*. Darmstadt: Wissenschaftliche Buchgesellschaft, 1995.

Guenther, Irene. *Nazi Chic? Fashioning Women in the Third Reich*. Oxford: Berg, 2004.

Hachtmann, Rüdiger. "Eine Erfolgsgeschichte? Schlaglichter auf die Geschichte der Generalverwaltung der Kaiser-Wilhelm-Gesellschaft im 'Dritten Reich.'" http://www.mpiwg-berlin.mpg.de/KWG/Ergebnisse/Ergebnisse19.pdf (accessed 27 July 2009).

Hake, Sabine. "Mapping the Native Body: On Africa and the Colonial Film in the Third Reich." In *The Imperialist Imagination: German Colonialism and Its Legacy*. Edited by Sara Friedrichsmayer, Sara Lennox, and Susanne Zantop, 163–88. Ann Arbor: University of Michigan Press, 1998.

Hartog, Arie. "Eine bloße Fortsetzung der Politik mit anderen Mitteln? Zur Ideengeschichte der Böttcherstrasse bis 1945." In *Projekt Böttcherstrasse*. Edited by Hans Tallasch, 341–60. Delmenhorst: Aschenbeck & Holstein, 2002.

Hasse, Jürgen. *Übersehene Räume: Zur Kulturgeschichte und Heteropologie des Parkhauses.* Bielefeld: Transcript, 2007.

Haupt, Heinz-Gerhard, and Claudius Torp, eds., *Die Konsumgesellschaft in Deutschland, 1890–1990: Ein Handbuch.* Frankfurt am Main: Campus, 2009.

Hayes, Peter. *From Cooperation to Complicity: Degussa in the Third Reich.* Cambridge: Cambridge University Press, 2004.

Industry and Ideology: IG Farben in the Nazi Era. Cambridge: Cambridge University Press, 1987.

"Industry under the Swastika." In *Enterprise in the Period of Fascism.* Edited by Harold James and Jakob Tanner, 26–36. Aldershot: Ashgate, 2002.

Head, David. *"Made in Germany": The Corporate Identity of a Nation.* London: Hodder & Stoughton, 1992.

Heinelt, Peer. *PR-Päpste: Die kontinuierlichen Karrieren von Carl Hundhausen, Albert Oeckl und Franz Ronneberger.* Berlin: Karl Dietz, 2003.

Hemmerle, Oliver. *Tausend Jahre Absatz: Anmerkungen zum Marketing als Teil der Betriebswirtschaftslehre im "3. Reich."* Mannheim: AK-Unigeschichte, 1999.

Henderson, Susan. "Böttcherstrasse: The Corporatist Vision of Ludwig Roselius and Bernhard Hoetger." *Journal of Decorative and Propaganda Arts* 20 (1994): 164–81.

Herbert, Ulrich. "Good Times, Bad Times: Memories of the Third Reich." In *Life in the Third Reich* [2d ed.]. Edited by Richard Bessel, 97–111. Oxford: Oxford University Press, 2001.

Hitler's Foreign Workers: Enforced Foreign Labor in Germany under the Third Reich. Cambridge: Cambridge University Press, 1997.

Herbrand, Nicolai Oliver, and Stefan Röhrig, eds. *Die Bedeutung der Tradition für die Markenkommunikation: Konzepte und Instrumente zur ganzheitlichen Ausschöpfung des Erfolgspotenzials Markenhistorie.* Stuttgart. Neues Fachwissen: 2006.

Herbst, Ludolf. "Die nationalsozialistische Wirtschaftspolitik im internationalen Vergleich." In *Der Nationalsozialismus: Studien zur Ideologie und Herrschaft.* Edited by Wolfgang Benz, Hans Buchheim, and Hans Mommsen, 153–76. Frankfurt am Main: Fischer, 1993.

Der Totale Krieg und die Ordnung der Wirtschaft: Die Kriegswirtschaft im Spannungsfeld von Politik, Ideologie und Propaganda, 1939–1945. Stuttgart: Deutsche Verlags-Anstalt, 1982.

Herzog, Dagmar. *Sex after Fascism: Memory and Morality in Twentieth-Century Germany.* Princeton, NJ: Princeton University Press, 2005.

Hesse, Jan-Otmar. "Zur Semantik von Wirtschaftsordnung und Wettbewerb in nationalökonomischen Lehrbüchern der Zeit des Nationalsozialismus." In *Wirtschaftssteuerung durch Recht im Nationalsozialismus: Studien zur Entwicklung des Wirtschaftsrechts im Interventionsstaat des "Dritten Reichs."* Edited by Johannes Bähr and Ralf Banken, 473–508. Frankfurt am Main: Vittorio Klostermann, 2006.

Horowitz, Daniel. *Anxieties of Affluence: Critiques of American Consumer Culture, 1939–1979.* Amherst: University of Massachusetts Press, 2004.

Hundhausen, Carl. *Werbung um öffentliches Vertrauen: "Public Relations."* Essen: W. Girardet, 1951.

Hucker, Bernd Ulrich. "'Die Kaffeebohne und die Kunst' – Ludwig Roselius (1874–1943): Ein Unternehmer, die geistigen Wurzeln seiner Welt und die Bremer 'Böttcherstrassenkultur.'" In *Persönlichkeit und Zeitgeschehen: Beiträge zur Geschichte des 17. bis 20. Jahrhunderts.* Edited by Alwin Hanschmidt and Bernd Ulrich Hucker, 161–81. Vechta: Eiswasser, 2001.

Hunter, Meredith Rucker. "Gambling." In *A Comparative Perspective on Major Social Problems.* Edited by Rita J. Simon, 131–52. Lanham, MD: Lexington Books, 2001.

Igo, Sarah E. *The Averaged American: Surveys, Citizens, and the Making of a Mass Public.* Cambridge, MA: Harvard University Press, 2007.

Imort, Michael. "'Planting a Forest Tall and Straight like the German Volk': Visualizing the *Volksgemeinschaft* through Advertising in German Forestry Journals, 1933–1945." In *Selling Modernity: Advertising in Twentieth Century Germany.* Edited by Pamela Swett, S. Jonathan Wiesen, and Jonathan R. Zatlin, 102–26. Durham, NC: Duke University Press, 2007.

Ivens, Björn Sven. *Wilhelm Vershofen: Professor der Absatzwirtschaft? Ein Rückblick zu seinem 125. Geburtstag,* Working paper no. 109 (August 2003). Chair for Marketing, Universität Erlangen-Nürnberg.

James, Harold. *The Deutsche Bank and the Nazi Economic War Against the Jews.* Cambridge: Cambridge University Press, 2001.

———. "Innovation and Conservatism in Economic Recovery: The Alleged 'Nazi Recovery' of the 1930s." In *Reevaluating the Third Reich: New Controversies, New Interpretations.* Edited by Thomas Childers and Jane Caplan, 114–38. New York: Holmes & Meier, 1993.

Janssen, Hauke. *Nationalökonomie und Nationalsozialismus: Die deutsche Volkswirtschaftslehre in den dreißiger Jahren.* Marburg: Metropolis, 1998.

Jenkins, Jennifer. *Provincial Modernity: Local Culture and Liberal Politics in Fin-de-Siècle Hamburg.* Ithaca, NY: Cornell University Press, 2003.

Jungbluth, Rüdiger. *Die Oetkers: Geschäfte und Geheimnisse der bekanntesten Wirtschaftsdynastie Deutschlands.* Frankfurt am Main: Campus, 2004.

Kaes, Anton, Martin Jay, and Edward Dimendberg, eds. *The Weimar Republic Sourcebook.* Berkeley: University of California Press, 1994.

Kershaw, Ian. *The "Hitler Myth": Image and Reality in the Third Reich.* Oxford: Oxford University Press, 1987.

———. *The Nazi Dictatorship: Problems & Perspectives of Interpretation* [4th ed.]. London: Arnold, 2000.

Kirk, Tim. *The Longman Companion to Nazi Germany.* New York: Longman, 1995.

———. *Nazi Germany.* Houndsmill: Palgrave, 2007.

Kleinschmidt, Christian. *Konsumgesellschaft.* Göttingen: Vandenhoeck & Ruprecht, 2008.

———. *Der Produktive Blick: Wahrnehmung amerikanischer und japanischer Management- und Produktionsmethoden durch deutsche Unternehmer, 1950–1985.* Berlin: Akademie, 2002.

Klingemann, Carsten. "Social-Scientific Experts – No Ideologues: Sociology and Social Research in the Third Reich." In *Sociology Responds to Fascism*. Edited by Stephen P. Turner and Dirk Käsler, 127–54. London: Routledge, 1992.

Kocka, Jürgen, ed. *Bürger und Bürgerlichkeit im 19. Jahrhundert*. Göttingen: Vandenhoeck & Ruprecht, 1987.

König, Gudrun M. *Konsumkultur: Inszenierte Warenwelt um 1900*. Cologne: Böhlau, 2009.

König, Wolfgang. *Geschichte der Konsumgesellschaft*. Stuttgart: Steiner, 2000.

Volkswagen, Volksempfänger, Volksgemeinschaft: "Volksprodukte" im Dritten Reich: Vom Scheitern einer nationalsozialistischen Konsumgesellschaft. Paderborn: Schöningh: 2004.

Koonz, Claudia. *The Nazi Conscience*. Cambridge, MA: Belknap Press, 2003.

Kraft, Alfons. *Interessenabwägung und gute Sitten im Wettbewerbsrecht*. Munich: Beck, 1963.

Kreimeier, Klaus. *The Ufa Story: A History of Germany's Greatest Film Company, 1918–1945*. New York: Hill and Wang, 1996.

Kunczik, Michael. *Geschichte der Öffentlichkeitsarbeit in Deutschland*. Cologne: Böhlau, 1997.

Kunze, Svenja. "'Kaffee HAG schont Ihr Herz': Zur Entstehung und Entwicklung eines klassischen Markenartikels in der deutschen Kaffeebranche, 1906–1939." *Hamburger Wirtschafts-Chronik* 4 (2004): 85–120.

Kurlander, Eric. *Living with Hitler: Liberal Democrats in the Third Reich*. New Haven, CT: Yale University Press, 2009.

Laak, Dirk van. "'Arisierung' und Judenpolitik im 'Dritten Reich.' Zur wirtschaftlichen Ausschaltung der jüdischen Bevölkerung in der rheinisch–westfälischen Industrieregion." http://www.geschichtskultur-ruhr.de/links/dvlaak.pdf (accessed 21 January 2010).

Lamberty, Christiane. *Reklame in Deutschland, 1890–1914: Wahrnehmung, Professionalisierung und Kritik der Wirtschaftswerbung*. Berlin: Duncker & Humblot, 2000.

Lange, Marius. *Zwischen Demokratie und Diktatur: Unternehmerische Öffentlichkeitsarbeit in Deutschland, 1929–1936*. Frankfurt am Main: Peter Lang, 2010.

Le Bon, Gustave. *The Crowd: A Study of the Popular Mind* [1895]. Atlanta: Cherokee Publishing, 1982.

Lehming, Eva-Maria. *Carl Hundhausen: Sein Leben, sein Werk, sein Lebenswerk – Public Relations in Deutschland*. Wiesbaden: Deutscher Universitäts-Verlag, 1997.

Lerner, Paul. "Consuming Pathologies: Kleptomania, Magazinitis, and the Problem of Female Consumption in Wilhelmine and Weimar Germany." *WerkstattGeschichte* 42 (Summer 2006): 46–56.

Lewy, Jonathan. "A Sober Reich? Alcohol and Tobacco Use in Nazi Germany." *Substance Use & Misuse* 41, no. 8 (2006) 1179–95.

Lindenfeld, David E. "The Professionalization of Applied Economics: German Counterparts to Business Administration." In *German Professionals, 1800–1950*. Edited by Geoffrey Cocks and Konrad H. Jarausch, 213–31. Oxford: Oxford University Press, 1990.

Lindner, Erik. *Die Reemstmas: Geschichte einer deutschen Unternehmerfamilie.* Hamburg: Hoffmann & Campe, 2007.

Loberg, Molly J. "Berlin Streets: Politics, Commerce and Crowds, 1918–1938." Ph.D. diss., Princeton University, 2006.

Lüdtke, Alf. "The 'Honor of Labor': Industrial Workers and the Power of Symbols under National Socialism." In *Nazism and German Society, 1933–1945.* Edited by David F. Crew, 67–109. London: Routledge, 1994.

Maiwald, E. W. *Reichsausstellung Schaffendes Volk–Düsseldorf 1937: Ein Bericht.* Düsseldorf: A. Bagel, 1939.

Mantel, Peter. *Betriebswirtschaftslehre und Nationalsozialismus: Eine Institutionen- und personengeschichtliche Studie.* Wiesbaden: Gabler, 2009.

Marchand, Roland. *Creating the Corporate Soul: The Rise of Public Relations and Corporate Imagery in American Big Business.* Berkeley: University of California Press, 2001.

Martin, Michael. *Verstehen: The Uses of Understanding in the Social Sciences.* New Brunswick, NJ: Transaction Publishers, 2000.

Maslow, A. H. *Motivation and Personality.* New York: Harper, 1954.

"A Theory of Human Motivation." *Psychological Review* 50, no. 4 (July 1943): 370–96.

Mason, Timothy. "Der Primat der Politik: Politik und Wirtschaft in Nationalsozialismus." *Das Argument* 41, no. 8 (December 1966): 473–94.

Mazower, Mark. *Hitler's Empire: How the Nazis Ruled Europe.* New York: Penguin, 2008.

McClintock, Anne. *Imperial Leather: Race, Gender and Sexuality in the Colonial Contest.* New York: Routledge, 1995.

McPhail, Clark. *The Myth of the Madding Crowd.* New York: Aldine de Gruyter, 1991.

Menne, Bernhard. *Krupp: Deutschlands Kanonenkönige.* Zurich: Europa, 1937.

Merritt, Richard L. *Democracy Imposed: U.S. Occupation Policy and the German Public, 1945–1949.* New Haven, CN: Yale University Press, 1995.

Meskill, David. "Human Economies: Labor Administration, Vocational Training and Psychological Testing in Germany, 1914–1964." Ph.D. dissertation, Harvard University, 2003.

Mierzejewski, Alfred C. *Ludwig Erhard: A Biography.* Chapel Hill: University of North Carolina Press, 2004.

Milward, Alan S. *War, Economy, and Society, 1939–1945.* Berkeley: University of California Press, 1977.

Mommsen, Hans, and Manfred Grieger. *Das Volkswagenwerk und seine Arbeiter im Dritten Reich.* Düsseldorf: Econ, 1996.

Muller, Jerry Z. *The Mind and the Market: Capitalism in Modern European Thought.* New York: Knopf, 2002.

Neebe, Reinhard. *Grossindustrie, Staat, und NSDAP, 1930–1933: Paul Silverberg und der Reichsverband der Deutschen Industrie.* Göttingen: Vandenhoeck & Ruprecht, 1981.

Neumann, Franz. *Behemoth: The Structure and Practice of National Socialism, 1933–1944* [1942]. Chicago: Ivan R. Dee, 2009.

Noakes, J. and G. Pridham, eds. *Nazism – 1919–1945: A Documentary Reader.* Exeter: University of Exeter Press, 2000.

Noelle, Elisabeth. *Meinungs- und Massenforschung in U.S.A.: Umfragen über Politik und Presse.* Frankfurt am Main: Moritz Diesterweg, 1940.

Nolan, Mary. *Visions of Modernity: American Business and the Modernization of Germany.* Oxford: Oxford University Press, 1994.

Nützenadel, Alexander. "Consumerism, Material Culture, and Economic Reconstruction in Cold War Germany." *Journal of Contemporary History* 42, no. 2 (April 2007): 387–96.

Orlow, Dietrich. *The Nazis in the Balkans: A Case Study in Totalitarian Politics.* Pittsburgh: University of Pittsburgh Press, 1968.

Overy, R. J. "Cars, Roads and Economic Recovery, 1932–1938." *Economic History Review* 28, no. 3 (August 1975): 466–83.

The Nazi Economic Recovery: 1932–1938. London: Macmillan, 1982.

"Unemployment in the Third Reich," *Business History* 29, no. 3 (July 1987): 253–81.

Perry, Joe. "Nazifying Christmas: Political and Popular Celebration in the Third Reich." *Central European History* 38, no. 4 (December 2005): 572–605.

Peters, Nicolaus, ed. *Der neue deutsche Walfang: Ein praktisches Handbuch seiner geschichtlichen, rechtlichen, naturwissenschaftlichen und technischen Grundlagen.* Hamburg: "Hansa" Deutsche Nautische Zeitschrift Carl Schroedter, 1938.

Petropoulos, Jonathan. *The Faustian Bargain: The Art World in Nazi Germany.* Oxford: Oxford University Press, 2000.

Plumpe, Werner. "Die Unternehmen im Nationalsozialismus – Eine Zwischenbilanz." In *Wirtschaftsordnung, Staat und Unternehmen. Neuere Forschungen zur Wirtschaftsgeschichte des Nationalsozialismus: Festschrift für Dietmar Petzina zu seinem 65. Geburtstag.* Edited by Werner Abelshauser, Jan-Otmar Hesse, and Werner Plumpe, 243–66. Essen: Klartext, 2003.

Poiger, Uta. "Beauty, Business, and International Relations." *WerkstattGeschichte* 16, no. 45 (2007): 53–71.

Priester, Hans E. *Das deutsche Wirtschaftswunder.* Amsterdam: Querido, 1936.

Prinz, Michael, and Rainer Zitelmann. *Nationalsozialismus und Modernisierung.* Darmstadt: Wissenschaftliche Buchgesellschaft, 1991.

Proctor, Robert N. *The Nazi War on Cancer.* Princeton, NJ: Princeton University Press, 1999.

Proesler, Hans. *Handbuch der Vebrauchsforschung.* [Vol. II] Berlin: Carl Heymanns, 1940.

Rasch, Manfred, Karl-Peter Ellerbrock, Renate Köhne-Lindenlaub, and Horst A. Wessel, eds. *Industriefilm – Medium und Quelle: Beispiele aus der Eisen- und Stahlindustrie.* Essen: Klartext, 1997.

Reagin, Nancy. "*Marktordnung* and Autarkic Housekeeping: Housewives and Private Consumption under the Four Year Plan, 1936–1939." 19, no. 2 (June 2001): 162–83.

Sweeping the German Nation: Domesticity and National Identity in Germany, 1870–1945. Cambridge: Cambridge University Press, 2007.

Regnery, Claudia. *Die Deutsche Werbeforschung, 1900 bis 1945.* Münster: Monsenstein und Vannerdat, 2003.

Reinhardt, Dirk. *Von der Reklame zum Marketing: Geschichte der Wirtschaftswerbung in Deutschland.* Berlin: Akademie, 1993.

Roselius, Ludwig. *Briefe und Schriften zu Deutschlands Erneuerung.* Oldenburg: Gerhard Stalling, 1933.

Roseman, Mark. "National Socialism and Modernisation." In *Fascist Italy and Nazi Germany: Comparisons and Contrasts.* Edited by Richard Bessel, 197–229. Cambridge: Cambridge University Press, 1996.

Ross, Corey. "Mass Politics and the Techniques of Leadership: The Promise and Perils of Propaganda in Weimar Germany." *German History* 24, no. 2 (April 2006): 184–211.

Media and the Making of Modern Germany: Mass Communications, Society, and Politics from the Empire to the Third Reich. Oxford: Oxford University Press, 2008.

"Visions of Prosperity: The Americanization of Advertising in Inter-war Germany." In *Selling Modernity: Advertising in Twentieth Century Germany.* Edited by Pamela Swett, S. Jonathan Wiesen, and Jonathan R. Zatlin, 52–77. Durham, NC: Duke University Press, 2007.

Rücker, Matthias. *Wirtschaftswerbung unter Nationalsozialismus: Rechtliche Ausgestaltung der Werbung und Tätigkeit des Werberats der deutschen Wirtschaft.* Frankfurt am Main: Peter Lang, 2000.

Saldern, Adelheid von. *Mittelstand im "Dritten Reich": Handwerker - Einzelhändler - Bauern.* Frankfurt am Main: Campus, 1979.

Schäfer, Hans Dieter. "Amerikanismus im Dritten Reich." In *Nationalsozialismus und Modernisierung.* Edited by Michael Prinz and Rainer Zitelmann, 199–215. Darmstadt: Wissenschaftliche Buchgesellschaft, 1991.

Das Gespaltene Bewußtsein: Über deutsche Kultur und Lebenswirklichkeit, 1933–1945. Berlin: Ullstein, 1984.

Schäfers, Stefanie. *Vom Werkbund zum Vierjahresplan: Die Ausstellung "Schaffendes Volk," Düsseldorf 1937.* Düsseldorf: Droste, 2001.

Scherner, Jonas. *Die Logik der Industriepolitik im Dritten Reich: Die Investitionen in die Autarkie- und Rüstungsindustrie und ihre staatliche Förderung.* Stuttgart: Steiner, 2008.

Schildt, Axel. "Das Jahrhundert des Massenmedien: Ansichten zu einer künftigen Geschichte der Öffentlichkeit." *Geschichte und Gesellschaft* 27, no. 2 (April–June 2001): 177–206.

"Ein Konservativer Prophet moderner nationaler Integration: Biographische Skizze der streitbaren Soziologen Johann Plenge, 1874–1963." *Vierteljahrshefte für Zeitgeschichte* 35, no. 4 (October 1987): 523–70.

Schindelbeck, Dirk. "'Asbach Uralt' und 'Soziale Marktwirtschaft': Zur Kulturgeschichte der Werbeagentur am Beispiel von Hanns W. Brose, 1899–1971." *Zeitschrift für Unternehmensgeschichte* 40, no. 4 (1995): 235–52.

Schoenbaum, David. *Hitler's Social Revolution: Class and Status in Nazi Germany, 1933–1939.* Garden City, NY: Doubleday, 1966.

Schönemann, Friedrich. *Die Kunst der Massenbeeinflussung in den Vereinigten Staaten von Amerika.* Stuttgart: Deutsche Verlags-Anstalt, 1924.

Schmidt, Elisabeth. *Musterbetriebe Deutscher Wirtschaft: Henkel & Cie A.G. Chemische Produkte Düsseldorf.* Leipzig: Übersee-Post, 1934.

Schrage, Dominik. "Integration durch Attraktion: Konsumismus als massenkulturelles Weltverhältnis." *Mittelweg 36* 12, no. 6 (2003): 57–86.

Schröter, Harm. "Die Amerikanisierung der Werbung in der Bundesrepublik Deutschland." *Jahrbuch für Wirtschaftsgeschichte* 1997, no. 1 (1997): 94–115.

Schug, Alexander. "Vom Newspaper Space Salesman zur integrierten Kommunikationsagentur: Die 120-jährige Entwicklungsgeschichte der Werbeagentur Dorland." *Zeitschrift für Unternehmensgeschichte* 49, no. 1 (2004): 5–25.

———. "Wegbereiter der modernen Absatzwerbung in Deutschland: Advertising Agencies und die Amerikanisierung der deutschen Werbebranche in der Zwischenkriegszeit." *WerkstattGeschichte* 34, no. 2 (2003): 29–52.

Schutts, Jeff. "'Die erfrischende Pause': Marketing Coca-Cola in Hitler's Germany." In *Selling Modernity: Advertising in Twentieth Century Germany.* Edited by Pamela Swett, S. Jonathan Wiesen, and Jonathan R. Zatlin, 151–81. Durham, NC: Duke University Press, 2007.

Schwarzkopf, Stefan. "Kontrolle statt Rausch? Marktforschung, Produktwerbung und Verbraucherlenkung im Nationalsozialismus zwischen Phantasien von Masse, Angst und Macht." In *Rausch und Diktatur: Inszenierung, Mobilisierung und Kontrolle in totalitären Systemen.* Edited by Árpad von Klimó and Malte Rolf, 193–209. Frankfurt am Main: Campus, 2007.

Schwarzwälder, Herbert. "Ludwig Roselius (1874–1943): Ein Mann ohne Schatten?" In *Berühmte Bremer.* Edited by Herbert Schwarzwälder, 118–51. Munich: Paul List, 1972.

Semmens, Kristin. *Seeing Hitler's Germany: Tourism in the Third Reich.* Houndmills: Palgrave, 2005.

Semrad, Bernd. "Die geistigen 'Ariseure': Die 'Wiener Schule' der Werbeforschung im Dienste des Nationalsozialismus. Ein Werkstattbericht." In *Die Spirale des Schweigens: Zum Umgang mit der nationalsozialistischen Zeitungswissenschaft.* Edited by Wolfgang Duchkowitsch, Fritz Hausjell, and Bernd Semrad, 249–71. Münster: Lit, 2004.

———. "Die 'Wiener Schule' der Werbung?" *Wiener Journal: Das Magazin der Wiener Zeitung* 20 (18 September 2004): 12–14.

Sheehan, James J. *German Liberalism in the Nineteenth Century.* Chicago: University of Chicago Press, 1978.

Siegrist, Hannes, Hartmut Kaelble, and Jürgen Kocka, eds. *Europäische Konsumgeschichte: Zur Gesellschafts- und Kulturgeschichte des Konsums, 18. bis 20. Jahrhundert.* Frankfurt am Main: Campus, 1997.

Silverman, Dan P. *Hitler's Economy: Nazi Work Creation Programs, 1933–1936.* Cambridge, MA: Harvard University Press, 1998.

Simon, Paul. *Meine Erinnerungen: Das Leben des jüdischen Deutschen Paul Simon, Rechtsanwalt in Mainz.* Mainz: Verein für Sozialgeschichte Mainz, 2003.

Smitis, Konstantin. *Gute Sitten und Ordre Public: Ein kritischer Beitrag zur Anwendung des par. 138 Abs. BGB.* Marburg: Elwert, 1960.

Sneeringer, Julia. "The Shopper as Voter: Women, Politics and Advertising in Post-Inflation Germany." *German Studies Review* 27, no. 3 (October 2004): 476–501.

Sombart, Werner. *Deutscher Sozialismus*. Charlottenburg: Buchholz & Weisswange: 1934.

Der moderne Kapitalismus: Historisch-systematische Darstellung des gesamteuropäischen Wirtschaftslebens von seinen Anfängen bis zur Gegenwart [1916]. Munich: DTV, 1987.

Spenceley, G. F. R. "R. J. Overy and the Motorisierung: A Comment." *Economic History Review* 32, no. 1 (February 1979): 100–13.

Spicka, Mark E. *Selling the Economic Miracle: Economic Reconstruction and Politics in West Germany, 1949–1957*. New York: Berghahn Books, 2007.

Spiekermann, Uwe. *Basis der Konsumgesellschaft: Geschichte des modernen Kleinhandels in Deutschland, 1850–1914*. Munich: C.H. Beck, 1999.

"From Neighbor to Consumer: Retailer–Consumer Relations in Twentieth Century Germany." In *The Making of the Consumer: Knowledge, Power and Identity in the Modern World*. Edited by Frank Trentmann, 147–74. Oxford: Berg, 2006.

"Vollkorn für die Führer: Zur Geschichte der Vollkornbrotpolitik im Dritten Reich." *1999* 16, no. 1 (March 2001): 91–128.

"Window–Display Advertising in German Cities during the 19th Century: A Story of an Enduring Success." In *Advertising in the European City: Historical Perspectives*. Edited by Clemens Wischermann and Elliott Shore, 139–71. London: Ashgate, 2000.

Spoerer, Mark. "Demontage eines Mythos? Zu der Kontroverse über das nationalsozialistische 'Wirtschaftswunder.'" *Geschichte und Gesellschaft* 31, no. 3 (July–September 2005): 415–38.

"Profitierten Unternehmen von KZ–Arbeit? Eine Kritische Analyse der Literatur." *Historische Zeitschrift* 268, no. 1 (February 1999): 61–95.

Von Scheingewinnen zum Rüstungsboom: Die Eigenkapitalrentabilität der deutschen Industrieaktiengesellschaften, 1925–1941. Stuttgart: Steiner, 1996.

Stachura, Peter D. *Gregor Strasser and the Rise of Hitler*. London: Allen & Unwin, 1983.

Stearns, Peter N. *Consumerism in World History: The Global Transformation of Desire*. London: Routledge, 2001.

Steigmann-Gall, Richard. *The Holy Reich: Nazi Conceptions of Christianity, 1919–1945*. Cambridge: Cambridge University Press, 2003.

Steiner, André. "Umrisse einer Geschichte der Vebraucherpolitik unter dem Nationalsozialismus der Vorkriegszeit." In *Wirtschaftsordnung, Staat und Unternehmen. Neuere Forschungen zur Wirtschaftsgeschichte des Nationalsozialismus: Festschrift für Dietmar Petzina zu seinem 65. Geburtstag*. Edited by Werner Abelshauser, Jan-Otmar Hesse, and Werner Plumpe, 279–303. Essen: Klartext, 2003.

"Zur Neuschätzung des Lebenshaltungskostindex für die Vorkriegszeit des Nationalsozialismus." *Jahrbuch für Wirtschaftsgeschichte* 2005, no. 2 (2005): 129–52.

Stephenson, Jill. *Hitler's Home Front: Württemberg under the Nazis.* London: Hambledon Continuum, 2006.

Stern, Kurt. *Masse-Persönlichkeit und Gemeinschaft: Ein Beitrag zur Frage der Auflösung der Masse.* Stuttgart: Verlag für Wirtschaft und Verkehr, 1938.

Strasser, Susan. "Customer to Consumer: The New Consumption in the Progressive Era." *OAH Magazine of History* 13, no. 3 (Spring 1999): 10–14.

Strasser, Susan, Charles McGovern, and Matthias Judt, eds. *Getting and Spending: European and American Consumer Societies in the Twentieth Century.* Washington, DC: German Historical Institute/Cambridge University Press, 1998.

Swett, Pamela E. "Preparing for Victory: Heinrich Hunke, the Nazi Werberat, and West German Prosperity." *Central European History* 42, no. 4 (December 2009): 675–707.

Swett, Pamela, S. Jonathan Wiesen, and Jonathan R. Zatlin, eds. *Selling Modernity: Advertising in Twentieth Century Germany.* Durham, NC: Duke University Press, 2007.

Szyszka, Peter, ed. *Öffentlichkeit: Diskurs zu einem Schlüsselbegriff der Organisationskommunikation.* Opladen: Westdeutscher, 1999.

Tallasch, Hans, ed. *Projekt Böttcherstrasse.* Delmenhorst: Aschenbeck & Holstein, 2002.

Tarde, Gabriel. *On Communication and Social Influence: Selected Papers.* Edited by Terry N. Clark, 277–96. Chicago: University of Chicago Press, 1969.

Tiersten, Lisa. *Marianne in the Market: Envisioning Consumer Society in Fin-de-Siècle France.* Berkeley: University of California Press, 2001.

Tönnies, Ferdinand. *Gemeinschaft und Gesellschaft* (1887) [8th ed.]. Leipzig: Buske, 1935.

A Theory of Public Opinion [1922]. New York: Rowman and Littlefield, 2000.

Tooze, J. Adam. *Statistics and the German State, 1900–1945: The Making of Modern Economic Knowledge.* Cambridge: Cambridge University Press, 2001.

The Wages of Destruction: The Making and Breaking of the Nazi Economy. New York: Viking, 2006.

Torp, Claudius. "Das Janusgesicht der Weimarer Konsumpolitik." In *Die Konsumgesellschaft in Deutschland, 1890–1990: Ein Handbuch.* Edited by Heinz-Gerhard Haupt and Claudius Torp, 250–67. Frankfurt am Main: Campus, 2009.

Townsend, Mary E. "The German Colonies and the Third Reich." *Political Science Quarterly* 53, no. 2 (June 1938): 186–206.

Trentmann, Frank. "Beyond Consumerism: New Historical Perspectives on Consumption." *Journal of Contemporary History* 39, no. 3 (July 2004): 373–401.

"Bread, Milk and Democracy: Consumption and Citizenship in Twentieth-Century Britain." In *The Politics of Consumption: Material Culture and Citizenship in Europe and America.* Edited by Martin Daunton and Matthew Hilton, 129–63. Oxford: Berg, 2001.

"Knowing Consumers – Histories, Identities, Practices: An Introduction." In *The Making of the Consumer: Knowledge, Power and Identity in the Modern World*. Edited by Frank Trentmann, 1–27. Oxford: Berg, 2006.

Turner, Henry A. *German Big Business and the Rise of Hitler*. Oxford: Oxford University Press, 1985.

Uhlig, Heinrich. *Die Warenhäuser im Dritten Reich*. Cologne: Westdeutscher, 1956.

Veblen, Thorstein. *The Theory of the Leisure Class*. New York: Macmillan, 1912.

Ver Eecke, Wilfried. *Ethical Dimensions of the Economy: Making Use of Hegel and the Concepts of Public and Merit Goods*. Berlin: Springer, 2008.

Vershofen, Wilhelm. *Handbuch der Verbrauchsforschung* [vol. 1]. Berlin: Carl Heymanns, 1940.

Voigt, Gerhard. "Goebbels als Markentechniker." In *Warenästhetik: Beiträge zur Diskussion, Weiterentwicklung und Vermittlung ihrer Kritik*. Edited by Wolfgang Fritz Haug, 231–60. Frankfurt am Main: Suhrkamp, 1975.

Von Prollius, Michael. *Das Wirtschaftssystem der Nationalsozialisten, 1933–1939: Steuerung durch emergent Organisation und politische Prozesse*. Paderborn: Schöningh, 2003.

Watson, John B. *Psychology from the Standpoint of a Behaviorist*. Philadelphia: Lippincott, 1919.

Wedemeyer, Manfred. *Den Menschen verpflichtet: 75 Jahre Rotary in Deutschland, 1927–2002*. Hamburg: Der Rotarier Verlags–GmbH, 2002.

Welsch, Marion, and Ariane Knackmuss, eds. *Willkommen in Club? Die Geschichte des Clubs von Berlin und das Schicksal seiner jüdischen Mitglieder im Nationalsozialismus*. Berlin: Edition Andreae, 2007.

Wessel, Horst A. *Filmschätzen auf der Spur: Verzeichnis historischer Filmbestände in Nordrhein–Westfalen*. Düsseldorf: Staatliche Archive des Landes Nordrhein–Westfalen, 1994.

   Kontinuität im Wandel: 100 Jahre Mannesmann, 1890–1990. Gütersloh: Mohndruck, 1990.

Westphal, Uwe. *Werbung im Dritten Reich*. Berlin: Transit, 1989.

Wiesen, S. Jonathan. "Miracles for Sale: Consumer Displays and Advertising in Postwar West Germany." In *Consuming Germany in the Cold War: Consumption and National Identity in East and West Germany, 1949–1989*. Edited by David F. Crew, 151–78. Oxford: Berg, 2003.

   "The Modern Guild: Rotary Clubs and Bourgeois Renewal in the Aftermath of National Socialism." In *Conflict, Catastrophe, and Continuity: Essays on Modern German History*. Edited by Frank Biess, Mark Roseman, and Hanna Schissler, 297–317. New York: Berghahn Books, 2007.

   West German Industry and the Challenge of the Nazi Past, 1945–1955. Chapel Hill: University of North Carolina Press, 2001.

Williams, Rosalind H. *Dreamworlds: Mass Consumption in Late-Nineteenth-Century France*. Berkeley: University of California Press, 1982.

Wilpert, Friedrich. *Rotary in Deutschland: Ein Ausschnitt aus Deutschem Schicksal*. Bonn: Buchhandlung H. Behrendt, 1991.

Wirsching, Andreas. "Konsum statt Arbeit? Zum Wandel von Individualität in der modernen Massengesellschaft." *Vierteljahrshefte für Zeitgeschichte* 57, no. 2 (April 2009): 171–201.

Wischermann, Clemens, Peter Borscheid, and Karl-Peter Ellerbrock, eds. *Unternehmenskommunikation im 19. und 20. Jahrhundert: Neue Wege der Unternehmensgeschichte.* Dortmund: Gesellschaft für Westfälische Wirtschaftsgeschichte, 2000.

Wolbring, Barbara. *Krupp und die Öffentlichkeit im 19. Jahrhundert: Selbstdarstellung, öffentliche Wahrnehmung und gesellschaftliche Kommunikation.* Munich: Beck, 2000.

Zaretsky, Eli. *Secrets of the Soul: A Social and Cultural History of Psychoanalysis.* New York: Knopf, 2004.

Zipfel, Astrid. *Public Relations in der Elektroindustrie: Die Firmen Siemens und AEG, 1847 bis 1939.* Cologne: Böhlau, 1997.

Zunz, Olivier. *Why the American Century?* Chicago: University of Chicago Press, 1998.

Index

consumer research, 156–9; in influence of U.S. practices, 141–2; in modernity and experimentation, 150–1; in PR practices, 80; in Rotary Clubs, 121–3

Werbeabeiltung (advertising department), 76

Wertheim (department store), 45

Westdeutscher Beobachter (WB), 21, 62

West Germany (Federal Republic of Germany): advertising and marketing in, 237; consumption in, 21; Nazi marketers and businessmen in, 236, 238; "economic miracle" of, 157, 235; Rotary clubs in, 236; Third Reich economy as basis for, 8–9

Wilson, Woodrow, 145

window displays, 35; for Bayer, 86–7; for Kaffee HAG, 114; for Persil, 235

Wirtschaftsdienst (journal), 198

Wirtschaftsgruppen (Reich Economic Groups), 161

Wirtschaftspolitische Parole (journal), 31–3

Wirtschaftswerbung (Advertising Council journal), 69

Wolff & Sohn (cosmetics), 167, 203

Wolfskehl, Karl, 125

women: and Astra cigarettes, 174; contribution as "housewife-consumers," 96–7; and gendered advertising, 175–8; household appliances for, 217; housewife "heroism," 195; in workforce, 13–14

Wonder of Life, The (exhibition), 94

World Advertising Congress (Welt-Reklame-Kongress, Berlin,1929), 65

World's Fair (1937, Paris), 84, 94

World War I: German defeat and losses, 88–9, 109–10, 142, 145; role of propaganda in, 109–10, 156; shortages during, 7, 37, 195

World War II, 20–1, 191–230; consumption patterns during, 192–7; Nazi death camps, 62, 125, 220, 243; Operation Barbarossa, 220; Stalingrad, Battle of, 215

Yugoslavia, 220, 223

Zeiss Ikon cameras, 166, 200

Zeller, Wolfgang, 77

Zweig, Arnold, 110